Yankee Yarns

Edinburgh Critical Studies in Atlantic Literatures and Cultures
Series Editors: Laura Doyle, Colleen Glenney Boggs and
Maria Cristina Fumagalli

Available titles
Sensational Internationalism: The Paris Commune and the Remapping of American Memory in the Long Nineteenth Century
J. Michelle Coghlan

American Travel Literature, Gendered Aesthetics, and the Italian Tour, 1824–1862
Brigitte Bailey

American Snobs: Transatlantic Novelists and Liberal Education, 1880–1920
Emily Coit

Scottish Colonial Literature: Writing the Atlantic, 1603–1707
Kirsten Sandrock

Yankee Yarns: Storytelling and the Invention of the National Body in Nineteenth-Century American Culture
Stefanie Schäfer

Forthcoming titles
Emily Dickinson and Her British Contemporaries: Victorian Poetry in Nineteenth-Century America
Páraic Finnerty

Following the Middle Passage: Currents in Literature Since 1945
Carl Plasa

Reverberations of Revolution: Transnational Perspectives, 1750–1850
Elizabeth Amann and Michael Boyden

The Atlantic Dilemma: Reform or Revolution Across the Long Nineteenth Century
Kelvin Black

www.edinburghuniversitypress.com/series/ECSALC

Yankee Yarns

Storytelling and the Invention of the
National Body in Nineteenth-Century
American Culture

Stefanie Schäfer

EDINBURGH
University Press

Edinburgh University Press is one of the leading university presses in the UK. We publish academic books and journals in our selected subject areas across the humanities and social sciences, combining cutting-edge scholarship with high editorial and production values to produce academic works of lasting importance. For more information visit our website: edinburghuniversitypress.com

© Stefanie Schäfer, 2021, 2023

Edinburgh University Press Ltd
The Tun – Holyrood Road
12(2f) Jackson's Entry
Edinburgh EH8 8PJ

First published in hardback by Edinburgh University Press 2021

Typeset in 11/13 Adobe Sabon by
IDSUK (DataConnection) Ltd

A CIP record for this book is available from the British Library

ISBN 978 1 4744 7744 4 (hardback)
ISBN 978 1 4744 7745 1 (paperback)
ISBN 978 1 4744 7746 8 (webready PDF)
ISBN 978 1 4744 7747 5 (epub)

The right of Stefanie Schäfer to be identified as the author of this work has been asserted in accordance with the Copyright, Designs and Patents Act 1988, and the Copyright and Related Rights Regulations 2003 (SI No. 2498).

Contents

Series Editors' Preface	vii
Acknowledgments	viii

Introduction	1
An Ambiguous National Character	2
The Yankee and Transatlantic Nationalism: Aims and Scope of this Study	4
Whiteness, Manhood, and the Body Politic	8
Literary Fraudulence, Activist Readership, and the Economy of Storytelling	10
Chapters and Coda	14
1. John Bull and Brother Jonathan: A Transatlantic Affair	22
From Allegory to Character: John Bull in Early British National Iconography	24
Transatlantic Kinship in Nineteenth-Century U.S. Print Culture: Between National Literature and Imperial Fantasy	32
The National Body as Image and Text: Thomas Nast's Uncle Sam and Humor Magazines	59
2. Theater of/for the Nation: The Stage Yankee as Metatheatric Sign	77
Yankee Theater and Drama Scholarship	77
Tales of Country and City: From Jonathan to Uncle Nat	90
The Stage Yankee at Large: International Projections and Yankee Ambiguity	118
3. The Yankee Peddler Conjures an American Marketplace	136
Monster, Wizard, Founding Father: The Yankee Peddler in Cultural and Economic Historiography	140

    The Secrets of the Yankee Peddler in Nineteenth-Century
       Literature   151
    Yankee Clocks and Wooden Nutmegs: "Yankee Notions"
       and the Making of a National Marketplace   175

4. **New England's "Homespun Yankee" in the Cultural and Literary Imagination**   197
    Fantasies of New England in Regional Historiography   199
    The Yankee Schoolmaster as American Educator   204
    "The Season of Youth for Nations and Individuals":
       New England Villages and Yankee Character   219
    John Neal's Down-Easters: Whittling, Storytelling Yankees   230
    Yankee Homespun   242

5. **Yankee Politics: A Coda**   270

Appendices   273
Bibliography   277
Index   301

Series Editors' Preface

Modern global culture makes it clear that literary study can no longer operate on nation-based or exceptionalist models. In practice, American literatures have always been understood and defined in relation to the literatures of Europe and Asia. The books in this series work within a broad comparative framework to question place-based identities and monocular visions, in historical contexts from the earliest European settlements to contemporary affairs, and across all literary genres. They explore the multiple ways in which ideas, texts, objects, and bodies travel across spatial and temporal borders, generating powerful forms of contrast and affinity. The Edinburgh Critical Studies in Atlantic Literatures and Cultures series fosters new paradigms of exchange, circulation, and transformation for Atlantic literary studies, expanding the critical and theoretical work of this rapidly developing field.

Laura Doyle, Colleen Glenney Boggs and
Maria Cristina Fumagalli

Acknowledgments

Yankee Yarns builds on the institutional support from the Friedrich Schiller Universität Jena's Pro Chance Program and the Institut für Anglistik und Amerikanistik, who funded my research at the Harvard Theater Collection in Cambridge, MA. A post-doc fellowship from Deutscher Akademischer Austauschdienst (DAAD) and the Library of Congress's Kluge Center German Scholar Fellowship in 2012/2013 enabled me to gather the materials for *Yankee Yarns*.

Many colleagues have helped me zoom in and out of the project. I am immensely grateful to Caroline Rosenthal for feedback, institutional support, and cheer. Many conversations with Alexandra Ganser, Katharina Gerund, and Heike Paul have enabled me to refine key points. Christoph Bode, Claudia Hammerschmidt, Kevin Hutchings, Sandy Petrulionis, Erik Redling, and Christine Schwanecke offered commentary that percolates through this book's structure and scope, and Edinburgh University Press's Ersev Ersoy and James Dale helped see it through publication.

I am indebted to Thomas Nast Verein Landau e. V. and to its late president Hubert Lehmann for access to Thomas Nast's oeuvre.

My gratitude goes to Jim and Jane Bellieu for Virginia dinners and to Kathleen O'Reilly for hosting me; to my fellow Kluge fellows Ilaria Andreoli and Oksana Marafioti for advice and excursions; to Lindsay Tuggle for poetic vistas, even from the other side of the world; to Andrew Sola for academic knack and clear-eyed commentary; and to Saskia Hilpisch for two decades of shared transatlantic experience.

My family's trust and support, the laughter and sorrows we shared, have encouraged me always. I dedicate this book to them.

Introduction

> Yankee Doodle came to town,
> A-Riding on a pony
> He stuck a feather in his hat
> and called it Macaroni.
> Yankee Doodle, keep it up!
> Yankee Doodle Dandy
> Mind the music and the step
> and with the girls be handy. (American folk song)

Like so many cultural traditions in the U.S., the folk song "Yankee Doodle" is a foreign import. It was adapted from an English folk tune in the French and Indian Wars (1754–63), when the English troops invented the new text to mock their colonial opponents. A little later, in the Revolutionary War, the colonists found this image endearing; they simply sang it back to the British in a cheeky affirmation of their own provincialism.

Today, most Americans know several stanzas of "Yankee Doodle" by heart, but many wonder about the meaning of the famed "macaroni" in the first stanza (neither the name of the pony nor a reference to Italian pasta). The "Macaronis" were a fashionable group of young men in London at the time of the Revolutionary War who dressed extravagantly and questioned sexual norms (McNeil 1999). "Yankee Doodle" therefore tells two stories: the story of the provincial ignoramus awkwardly imitating London fashions, and the story of the smart colonial who mocks the effeminate urban dandies, invents his own rugged masculinity, and simply goes ahead. The clash between the backwoods colonialist and the self-reliant settler circumscribes the Yankee's ambiguity in the U.S. cultural imaginary.

The Yankee is the oldest rendition of American individualism, pragmatism, and desire for independence, the first embodiment of national fantasy in the white settler nation. Yet, this vernacular and streetsmart character is hardly hero material. He causes discomfort in the popular imagination and has long been overlooked in cultural and literary history and in American Studies. *Yankee Yarns* examines the Yankee's ambiguities in U.S. literature, drama, and visual culture in the nineteenth century. It reads the Yankee as a transnational and provincial figure to examine the cultural practice of storytelling and fraudulence at the heart of U.S. regional and national character.

An Ambiguous National Character

The Yankee is ubiquitous in American cultural history, but he appears in so many different texts, political discourses, and spatial configurations that he is hard to grasp. At the very origin, the figure is a European creation and a transnational fantasy. The etymology of "Yankee" is debated, but in its widely accepted meaning, it belittles a commoner: "Yankee" allegedly originated in the Dutch North American colony, as a diminutive of the name "Jan"; adding the suffix "-ke" transformed the man into a manikin or boyish figure, and the spelling was changed to avoid a shift in pronunciation.[1] The Yankee's first appearance in "Yankee Doodle" coincides with his first appearance on the stage and is also a product of a transatlantic imagination. Royall Tyler's play *The Contrast* (1787) includes an American character among a cast from the comedy of manners. Tyler's Brother Jonathan was the only addition to a plot adapted from the English playwright John Sheridan's *The School for Scandal* (1777), and he was first created by English actor James Hackett.

Tyler's *Contrast* marked the beginning of the Yankee's trajectory from the revolutionary stage and the realm of provincial literature (Rezek 2015) into a striking number of other texts, genres, and media. The Yankee appears in different personas: as "Brother Jonathan," he allegorizes a transatlantic family quarrel with his English father John Bull; as "Uncle Sam," he impersonates a virile and expansionist government; as Yankee peddler or schoolmaster, he acts as a harbinger of New England capitalism to the South; as a "New Englander," he accommodates a regional and national myth. The Yankee also crosses genre and media boundaries. He is sketched, staged, and sung, always alive and kicking.

The Yankee's typical feature is his idiosyncratic way of speaking. The poem "Yankee Phrases" iconizes his dialect and (mis)pronunciations, sayings and aphorisms so successfully it was reprinted in U.S.

magazines at least five times between 1803 and 1822 (see Appendix I).[2] In "Yankee Phrases," the story of the Yankee's unsuccessful wooing of the Yankee girl Jemima is dwarfed by the Yankee's telling manner. His only stylistic element, comparison, ranges from plausible to grotesque, and may well tip from poetic to non sequitur in a single phrase: "pleasures are brittle as glass // though as a fiddle they're fine." The fun of this poem lies in the Yankee's concoction of ever-new similes and fabulation rather than the ill-fated wooing.

The Yankee also stands for various U.S. spaces and ideologies. "Yankee" designates the U.S. as nation; the section of the Northern states; the region of New England, and within this regional space its remotest rural communities. "Yankeedom" is often linked to U.S. national ideologies, such as the exceptionalist narrative of the "city upon a hill," expansionist politics in soft and hard power scenarios, and the advent of globalization and the U.S. business empire under the guise of "likeability" (Bramen 2017).

In sectional conflict, the Northern Yankee was juxtaposed to the Southern Slaveholder/Cavalier as early as 1785, when Thomas Jefferson distinguished their temperaments. In response to a French travelogue about Virginia, Jefferson made out a chart:

In the North they are	In the South they are
Cool	fiery
Sober	voluptuary
Laborious	indolent
Persevering	unsteady
Independant [sic]	independant [sic]
Jealous of their own liberties, and just to those of others	zealous for their own liberties, but trampling on those of others
Interested	generous
chicaning	candid
superstitious and hypocritical in their religion.	without attachment or pretensions to any religion but that of the heart.
(Jefferson 1975: 387)	

Jefferson adapts Eurocentric climate determinism: the warm South "unnerves and unmans both body and mind"; the Southerners become "careless about their expences [sic] and in all their transactions of business" (ibid.). Apart from a shared all-American "independence," the Northerners are the mannish opposites of the money-squandering Southerners. In 1785, Jefferson's letter portrays a U.S.-American cultural ideal of masculinity ("cool, sober, laborious, persevering") that fosters business in a (Northern) climate of liberty.

Today, Yankee expresses "nothing favorable," as Roger Martin concludes in his French "Iconoclastic Dictionary of the United States" (Martin 2005). While its title asks whether the U.S. is an empire of evil (*'Empire Du Mal?'*), the dictionary judges that "Yankees" are "cowards, damned men" ("lâches, damnés," 310). By the 1940s, even to Americans, Yankee has become an "awful word," as a Midwesterner complains:

> That Awful Word "Yankee"
> Willy-nilly, whether we are Northerners or Southerners, we are all "Yankees" now. None of us ever liked the word, not even the Yankees themselves. As a Hoosier [from Indiana], the writer has always been called a Yankee in spite of his protest that Yankees are Easterners, preferably New Yorkers and New Englanders—more or less culpable persons whom an Indiana Yankee calls "Yankees." And now, to add insult to injury, we must inform you that Yankee is a German word. The German name Johann (John) has two diminutive forms: "Hans" and "Yan." Like most nicknames that become very popular, each of these diminutives received an additional diminutive ending, resulting in "Hanschen" and "Yanke": These names were very prevalent in our pre-Revolutionary German-American settlements, notably among the Pennsylvania Germans. True to the German tradition, the Pennsylvania Germans were musical, so that when the recruiting for the Continental and Revolutionary armies required many fife players, the Pennsylvania "Yankees" were in great demand. "Yanke Dudelpfeifer" ("Johnny Doodlepiper") became a figure in the War of Independence, emerging with the spelling "Yankee." So we see that in the War Between the States, the "Johnnies" (Southerners) and the "Yankees" (Northerners) were really calling each other by the same name (Yankee=Johnny). And now world usage has dubbed us all Yankees. How strangely some things work out! (Roehm 1943)[3]

This polemic falls in line with WWII's Germanophobia: it bemoans that calling Americans "Yankees" means calling them by a German name. The Midwestern author hopes to distinguish himself from both the rural New Englander and the urban New Yorker; all in vain: Yankeedom is yoked to a negative image of Americans.

The Yankee and Transatlantic Nationalism: Aims and Scope of this Study

Not only is the Yankee hard to pin down, he also provokes mostly negative affective reactions. In the nineteenth century, the Yankee is enlisted in the project of nation-building, an anti-sentimental figure that interlinks a nostalgic past with an American imperial future. In contemporary culture, Yankee ways are often linked to criticisms of U.S. imperialism and military dominance. The New York Yankees' mission statement is set in Yankee manner, every new season, to win the World Series; anything less is a failure. The Yankee's self-assertion and cunning are sometimes applauded, but more often critiqued. He puts into practice the populist motto "America First" and may well be a foil for the politics of affect that characterized the Trump presidency.

Yankee Yarns seeks to map the Yankee's affective cultural work, his celebration of the nation state despite himself. By looking at the Yankee, warts and all, *Yankee Yarns* positions itself on one end of a range of U.S. (self-)stereotypes, positing the "Ugly American" as opposite to the desirable self-image of American niceness so compellingly examined by Carrie Tirado Bramen (2017). Bramen's study sketches a cultural history that begins with the invention of Yankee character and ends with the "likeable empire" (38), arguing that "American niceness is the mechanism through which memory and forgetting play out in the everyday exchanges and social practices that sustain a nation ideologically at home and abroad" (9).

Yankee Yarns takes a more condensed, figural focus, placing the Yankee as node and cipher of affective theatrics and transatlantic nationalism. In the U.S. cultural archive, the Yankee is the nation's contested face, voice, and body, impersonating hegemonic whiteness, masculinity, and the cultural imperative of "going ahead." *Yankee Yarns* seeks to recalibrate and contextualize this image: first, by reading the Yankee as a transnational figure and projection of what I call a transatlantic nationalism;[4] second, by linking his ambiguity to a culture of literary fraudulence, performance, and storytelling; and third, by mapping an affective history of Yankeedom. As provincial figure, the Yankee functions as a hyperbole for American literary production, linking the transatlantic literary space to the fantasy of an American body politic. His part as national character or hero is tarnished by his morally ambiguous character. Instead of impersonating the U.S., he haunts its cultural imaginary and questions its foundational concepts such as citizenship, community, and political economy: the figure upends regionalist essentialism and white settler indigenization, and interrupts positivist, nationalist, and exceptionalist narratives of the U.S. In the U.S., the demos and its subjects are entangled by a culturally specific transatlantic nationalism that grows, over the course of the nineteenth century, into an imperialist project not so much vested in territory, but "strictly business-driven" (Pease 1998).

Yankee Yarns traces Yankee types through the transatlantic literary sphere and cultural production. By mapping transatlantic nationalism, it closes an astonishing gap in U.S. cultural and literary history. I argue that the Yankee is ambiguous in three interrelated ways: first, semiotically, with regard to the content he carries; second, morally, with regard to his aesthetic or fabula, as hero figure or hypocrite; and third, intrinsically, as a character, with an innate obliqueness that leaves commentators wondering about his "true" or real intentions. As embodiment of progress or as the contorted mask of capitalism unleashed, the Yankee flies in the face of the European question about this new "American man." He unites U.S. audiences in variations of patriotic self-ridicule and offers a spectrum of Americanness to his readers that ranges from unruly adolescent to hypermasculine character unable and unwilling to conform to European manners and literary traditions.

The corpus selected for this study illustrates the versatility and dissemination of the Yankee figure throughout various media in the nineteenth century. It explores the symbolic economy of storytelling about the nation in historiographic representations of the Yankee and in canonized texts, including works by James Fenimore Cooper, Sarah Hale, Washington Irving, and John Neal. I read their Yankee figures alongside dramas, popular texts, magazine publications, and cartoons in a transnational and critical regionalist framework that critiques the narrative of U.S. "greatness."[5] The Yankee's transatlantic nationalism also reveals that the transatlantic literary space (Manning and Taylor 2007) is intricately bound to storytelling and to visual culture.[6]

Despite the Yankee's ubiquity in American popular culture, scholarship has paid next to no attention to the figure. The figure appears to cater poorly to research trends at different times, since he is too low-brow for the Myth and Symbol School and appears in literary genres less interesting to early Americanists. From the 1960s onwards, amidst the canon war, feminist literary critics understandably found little appeal in studying the Yankee as another rendition of the white man. At the same time, historians of U.S. drama turned to the figure with a dismissive overtone (Hodge 1964; Meserve 1986; see also Schäfer 2012). Since the 1990s, drama scholarship interest in the nineteenth century has unearthed the rampant racism in stage types featured in melodrama and in the minstrelsy show, yet anthologies and literary histories often repeat the problematic gesture of looking for national distinctions and describe nineteenth-century American drama as imitation of European traditions (see e.g. Grimsted 1987; Martin 2014; Nathans 2014; Richards 2014; Wilmer 2002).

Looking beyond American studies, the Yankee looms large in early collections of American humor (see e.g. Haliburton 1852) and, by the 1890s, was installed as an "American" character to create a vernacular whiteness that preserved Anglo-Saxon ties and excluded white European Others (Epp 2010). In the 1930s and 1940s, anthropologists and humor scholars turned to the Yankee: Richard Dorson (1940, 1941, 1943) and Walter Blair (1937 and 1987 [1944]) studied the figure's transatlantic English and continental European provenance, while B. A. Botkin anthologized him in his *Treasury of New England Folklore* (1989 [1947]). Economic and regional histories take the Yankee from folklore and literature to reiterate narratives of U.S. progress (Wright 1965 [1927]; Dolan 1964; Mussey 1937).

Two cultural histories make more than passing mention of the Yankee; Winifred Morgan's *An American Icon: Brother Jonathan and American Identity* (1989) locates him among "analogues and direct competition" (27) and tells the story of the "eighty-five years of his active life" (18) between the American Revolution and the end of the Civil War. Yet Morgan's narrative glosses over sectional differences and normalizes the Yankee's whiteness. For *Yankee Yarns*, I take a clue from Constance Rourke's 1931 *American Humor: A Study of the National Character*, which discusses American cultural types from a more inclusive cultural historical perspective (Rourke 2004). Rourke notes the Yankee's looks, his disposition for swapping, joking, and odd clothing, and negotiates his rumored origins from Scottish, Anglo-Saxon, and Southern English country bumpkins. She acknowledges his global presence in the Yankee theater and emphasizes that the Yankee is drawn by many hands and imagined by many authors, "from the South from the West, even from New England" (17). The Yankee, Rourke holds, is "a myth, a fantasy," and he uses "masquerade [. . .] appear[ing] a dozen things that he was not" (18). Rourke was an anti-elitist scholar whose focus on vernacular forms was viewed critically by her contemporaries; the first Americanists overlooked her writings, and humor scholar Walter Blair actively attacked her (Schlueter 2008). My reading of the Yankee takes its point of departure from Rourke's definition of the Yankee as cultural myth, shapeshifter, and performance artist.[7]

I understand national identity as projection and the nation as "both practice and theory" (Traister 2010: 23), in keeping with the New Americanists (see e.g. Berlant 1991 and Wald 1998). The Yankee answers both the desire for and the fear of an American body politic, and he projects images of manhood, politics, and citizenship.

Whiteness, Manhood, and the Body Politic

As postcolonial culture, the Early Republic was transfixed by British literature and nationhood. As Joseph Rezek has argued, the creation of a provincial literature and aesthetic references both the national and the literary ideal (2015: 15). Inventing an independent identity therefore entailed navigating colonial mimicry, performing an "American" character, and going local by consuming American goods. Contributions to transatlantic studies have explored such phenomena as the gendered gaze of the travelogue (Bailey 2019), literary neoclassicism (Buell 1987), Anglophilia (Tamarkin 2008; Yokota 2011; Hanlon 2013), and the making of the U.S. patriot consumer (Cohen 2017).

Next to the eastern pull, the struggle for a national character was also complicated by regional rivalries, federalism, and sectional nationalisms (Kramer 2011: 130). Historian Carroll Smith-Rosenberg has powerfully shown that the invention of the white settler-citizen comes at the cost of endemic violence and of disappearing racial, cultural, and political Others:

> American patriots faced in two directions. Looking east, they called themselves Sons of Liberty, true heirs of Augustan republicanism and the Scottish Enlightenment. Facing west, they become lords and proprietors of a vast continent. In a relation presumed by Washington but left unspoken, they faced south as well, where they lived masters in a land of slavery. The Manichean economy of colonial and postcolonial discourses doubly enriched them, simultaneously, constituting the citizen of the United States as white subject to savage/black brute and pure republican subject to degenerate British tyrant. Refusing the simple European dichotomies of colonizer and colonized, civilized and savage, the cultivated white American inhabited a privileged middle ground between metropolitan and wild, feudal and free worlds—a middle ground illuminated by the "whiteness" of his skin. Colors, red and black, framed and set off this whiteness. (Smith-Rosenberg 1992: 848)

From the 1780s onwards, white manhood was rendered "socially attractive, legally desirable, aesthetically ideal, a national imperative" (Nelson 1998: 11, 28). In a rhetoric that continued the Enlightenment tradition and remained operative in the nineteenth century (ibid. 6, 248), writing about the new republic was routinely done by white men whose "objectivity" soon effaced the pedigree of whiteness and masculinity. Much in the sense of Smith-Rosenberg's "middle ground [. . .] illuminated by [. . .] 'whiteness'" the intellectual, cultural, and political positioning of the new nation created what Lauren Berlant (1997) has called the iconic citizen, a hegemonic American oblivious to his own premises, claiming a "blinding whiteness" that left no space for Others.[8]

In the Early Republic, citizenship is cast as fraternal performance, when white men compete commercially in the public sphere,[9] engendering the concept of what Dana Nelson has called national manhood: "The new nation [. . .] will operate by and through analogies to a masculine social body whose interactions will be governed by scientific, rationally managed market relations" (Nelson 1998: 46). The republic was maintained and enacted by white men in economic competition, becoming, in Raewyn Connell's words, a "masculine institution" (1996: 73).

Nelson's exploration of national manhood pinpoints both a behavioral ideal of masculinity and the troping of the nation state as figural body politic. In the nineteenth century, the conservative Republican and expansionist Democratic parties promoted conflicting models of "restrained and martial" manhood (Greenberg 2005: 9, 11; see also Ditz 2011 and Kippola 2012), heralding feelings and taste opposite the martial ideal of the adventurous outsider, also replayed in the Yankee figure. In the Northern states, masculinity ideals shifted towards the artisan and the entrepreneurial, which sustained by the 1850s a newly rising middle class (see Leverenz 1989: 73).[10] These masculinity ideals found their correspondence in the fantasy of the corporeal nation state. The rise of the businessman is tethered to the prodigal son narrative that reconciled the volatile conflict of independence (Fliegelman 1982) and served as apologetic discourse for a perceived cultural immaturity, in domestic and in international matters (cf. e.g. Fluck 2000). Starting with colonial Puritan rhetoric, the American body politic is cast as material, affective, corporeal, as Bernd Herzogenrath (2010) has shown. The making of the citizen in the Early Republic thus requires the embodiment of the state. Dating from the English body politic in medieval and early modern Europe, the king's body was "a political reality" (Foucault qtd. in Herzogenrath 2010: 55) that over time depended on visual representation, as Nicholas Mirzoeff has argued. A body was required to "maintain the central illusion of modern state fetishism, that the state is a really existing and palpable body" (Mirzoeff 1995: 60, 61). The Yankee incorporates the state and projects American manhood in a self-reflective storytelling scenario, through performance and fraudulence. An ambiguous embodiment of the transatlantic nationalist project, the Yankee frames the very idea of a national literature and culture as a "speculation," a tall tale told by himself.

Literary Fraudulence, Activist Readership, and the Economy of Storytelling

The Yankee's ambiguity reverberates with the fraudulent character of antebellum literary production, in literary texts, and in the formation of implicit author and storyteller personas. Antebellum readers understood the very project of an "American" literature, as Lara Langer Cohen (2012) has shown, as fabrication in a double sense, as "in progress" and as "false." Like contemporary phenomena of inflated currency, land bubbles, or quack medicine, American literature was part and parcel of a culture of fraudulence and make-believe. Americans were neither assured about a national literature, nor a national character.[11] The development of an entire industry of literary criticism and of literary puffery bears witness to the need for a "memory of literature" in transatlantic print culture, as Julia Straub (2017) has argued. "Puffing" designates the inflation of the cultural or aesthetic value of texts by literary critics[12] and gestures towards Americanness. In Sarah Hale's *Northwood*, the protagonist compares American puffing to English gentlemanry:

> I do think the real English gentleman has more of dignity, and less of arrogance, than our purse-proud citizens. The Englishman is [. . .] free from *that puffing consequence* which is the most offensive part of the folly in our own countrymen. This may arise from the superiority of the former being established and acknowledged, whereas our own gentlemen are continually striving to maintain their precarious honors, and seem determined, by making the most of what they happen to possess, to indemnify themselves for the transientness of its continuance. (Hale 1852: 245, emphasis added)

Hale's Americans are empty bladders who inflate themselves to gain material "establishment" and social "acknowledgment" to grotesque self-display. The Yankee impersonates a puffed version of an American character in existence, but beyond reach. The audience has to conjure up an impersonation of the nation and venerate the Yankee's performance as its necessarily truncated version. Conversely, fraudulence puts the question of literary nationalism onto shaky ground. To an audience that has reason to doubt the sincerity of an American cultural experience, the Yankee as embodiment of the state must necessarily appear as a hoax.

The hiatus of fraudulence and storytelling in antebellum cultural production reaches back to the eighteenth century (see e.g. Schweighauser 2016a and Scheiding 2003). By employing various narrators, authors highlighted narrative mediation and challenged readers to form their own response (Schweighauser 2016b: 219–20), to respond to political controversies, and to deal with the "fiction of authorship" (Watts 1998: 21).[13] The literature of the new republic was characterized by its incitement of an "activist readership" (ibid. 22).

Next to literary texts, other media also spurred reader self-reflection and activism. In the first half of the nineteenth century, print and entertainment cultures defied such latter-day distinctions as high brow/low brow, oral/print cultures, or text/image (see Cohen 2012; Lehuu 2000; Levine 1988; Rose 1995). Magazines offered literary criticism alongside travelogues, and pictorial journalism fused textual and visual imageries. American readers of Yankee texts and images therefore coupled "activist readership" with media literacy. The mass proliferation of images created a distinctly American visual culture and, at the same time, engendered a cultural vision (Schneck 2003: 15).[14] The Yankee, on stage, in literary texts, and in pictures and cartoons, is deeply embroiled in an economy of national embodiment and self-reflective storytelling. He resonates with two contemporary cultural types: the con man and the tall tale storyteller or frontier screamer. Like the con man, the Yankee pursues a business interest by talking, luring his victims into giving up their property to him. Where the con man insists on personal sympathies and trust in an urban community, however, the Yankee acts as trader and engages his patrons in a focus on his wares (Rosenthal and Schäfer 2014). The Yankee and the frontier screamer are both ambiguous hero figures, since their vernacular humor plays out in their telling manner.[15] Both function as "comic demigod" variations of epic heroes such as Ulysses, as Richard Dorson (1941: 389) suggests. Dorson describes this as Brother Jonathan "drawing the self-styled 'long bow'" (1943: 245),[16] tethering the Yankee's English heritage to a muscular and white settler masculinity. Brother Jonathan's storytelling aims his weapon at his audience.

The tall tale's setting catered to the fascination of Eastern urban readers with the struggle for white settler civilization. The hero as fighter in the wilderness is a fantastic creature, "half horse, half alligator," as Davy Crockett famously quipped. For nineteenth-century audiences, listening to his tribulations became an exercise in imagined community formation, a "comic ritual capable of affirming their collective experience, often at the expense of cultural outsiders" (Wonham 1993: 22). The tall tale's historical and fictional protagonists were janus-faced, overwhelmingly white and male,[17] typically anti-intellectual: Davy Crockett and the Yankee share the motto "Go Ahead!".[18]

The tall tale hero and the Yankee enact American manhood in a national arena built from theatrics. As David Waldstreicher has shown, in the Early Republic festive culture created a "cultural obsession with [. . .] the self-representation of persons" (1997: 61). Foreign observers often commented on the American urge to perform. The Irish actor Tyrone Power, for instance, applauded their "mimetic gift [. . .] The Americans had in fact emerged as a theatrical race" (qtd. in Rourke 2004: 92). Constance Rourke observes that Americans, embracing their provinciality, turn to performance and make-believe:

> Characters in this period [the 1830s] often seemed larger than life. [. . .] Characters in public life were indeed one of the great creations of the time; and they often seemed to gain their emphasis less from a closely packed individuality than from bold and conscious self-picturization. [. . .] The new country made a strangely painted backdrop before which the American seemed constrained to perform; and every powerful force in pioneer life led toward outward expression. Self-consciousness had perhaps been induced early in the American by the critical scrutiny abundantly accorded him by the older races; and theatrical tendencies in the American character were heightened by a long intimacy with the stage. (Rourke 2004: 91–2)

The frontier, the transatlantic observing gaze by "older races," and the popularity of the theater required a performance of "Americanness." Humorous tales and anecdotes told by white American men therefore represent "a narrative skill and a philosophical stance" (Schmitz 1977: 471) published and republished over and over in magazines and almanacs.[19] Rourke describes Yankee storytelling as follows:

> Listless and simple, [the Yankee] might be drawn into a conversation with a stranger, and would tell a ridiculous story without apparent knowledge of its point. With no change of tone, out would leap an odd figure. "He walked away as slick as a snake out of a blackskin." "There we was amongst an ocean of folks and cutting up capers as high as a cat's back." (Rourke 2004: 18)

This setting features all the markers of the tall tale described as early as 1835 by John Neal in "Story-Telling." Neal typically performs his argument, asking his readers rhetorical questions and demanding their judgment ("altogether it was a story worth telling, reader, I'll leave it to you if it was not!"; 1835: 12). Neal calls storytelling "the great business of life" for historiography, mythmaking, and the remembrance of famous men (1, 3). However, the process is governed by a paradox, as Neal exclaims at the very beginning of his essay:

> What a difference between story-telling and story-tellers! Story-tellers are avoided—story-telling cultivated; the one as a nuisance—the other as an accomplishment; the former looked upon by the wise and thoughtful as no better than they should be, and all companionship with them as rather disreputable at the best. (Neal 1835: 1)

Neal's storyteller echoes the tall tale narrator, whose sincerity is undermined by the very fact that he tells stories. Neal argues that contents are less important than the performance of the teller: "if the *manner* is good, though not altogether new we are apt to be satisfied with our pennyworth, for the sake of the *matter*" (ibid. 5). The value of the story ("pennyworth") gestures at once to the minor importance of such fleeting entertainment, and to the successful invention of the American penny-press that published single sheets daily. The audience has to determine the truth value: "fifty to one you are a fool if you cannot see at a glance how much to believe" (ibid.).[20] Neal thus urges his readers to be quick and smart about the revenue they might gain from storytelling, and to cut the tellers some slack since the contents are unimportant anyways.

In this short piece, Neal puts this strategy into practice and, as Yankee author, impersonates a literary activist version of Yankeedom. His storytelling strategy was defined *post festum* in Mark Twain's famous essay "How to Tell a Story" (Twain 1962a [1897]). Like Neal, Twain distinguishes the "*manner* of the telling" from the "*matter*," arguing that the American telling manner's artistry is unrivalled: "The humorous story is strictly a work of art—high and delicate art—and only an artist can tell it [. . .] The art of telling a humorous story—understand, I mean by word of mouth, not print—was created in America, and has remained at home" (ibid. 239). Twain ennobles a cultural practice previously linked to regional and popular phenomena and viewed as an abomination by foreigners. By nationalizing the American humor story, Twain claims that the U.S.'s own cultural character is superior to European models.[21] The deadpan humor of American storytelling entangles the reader in suspense but conventionally refuses closure; it "divert[s] attention from [the story's] nub [...] string[ing] incongruities and absurdities together in a wandering and sometimes purposeless way [...], slurring the point" (Twain 1962a: 241).[22]

Magazines published tall tales extensively, conventionally with an embellishment that added to the cultural work of the stories. As Henry B. Wonham has shown, magazine samples usually foreground the idiosyncrasies of the teller and enhance the performance by parodying the yarnspinner's digressions from literary styles of the day (1993: 28; on magazine culture in the nineteenth century, see e.g. Chielens 1986 and Lanzendörfer 2016). In print culture, the tall tale was used to gesture at a national literary tradition. For instance, the *Spirit of the Times* (est. 1831) routinely framed tall tales with the travelogue or the dramatic farce, thus boxing the tale inside the tale. This left the task of discerning this narrative ball of wool to the reader. Like the activist readership in the novels of the Early Republic, the written tall tale therefore challenges readers: with the text in hand, they negotiate audience personas, as listeners to a yarnspinner, travelers to foreign lands, or viewers of a pastime sketch.

American humor stories garner a cultural awareness of storytelling and suspicion of the teller's intentions. Expectations of closure, meaningful detail, and maybe an innate moral as outcome are strategically subverted. Readers will know better than to look for content, but instead indulge in the teller's performance. In the Yankee's case, this way of storytelling may be described as a symbolic economy: the teller is imbued with the authority of the citizen, white and male, and with the typical Yankee sense of competition. He bargains for the audience's recognition and hopes to win their confidence in the same way as the con man will have his way with unsuspecting strangers and the businessman will go about his schemes. If his performance is successful, the teller gains recognition, maybe a business opportunity for trade; in return, the listener receives an education in deception and is entertained by the spectacle of self-immolation and make-believe. The Yankee impersonates a fantastic vision of the nation that is conjured by storyteller and audience.

Chapters and Coda

This study's title, *Yankee Yarns: Storytelling and the Invention of the National Body in Nineteenth-Century American Culture*, expresses the entanglement of two abstract entities that incorporate each other: the national body and the imagined community. It analyzes the dynamic of stories unfolding under the direction of the teller for the audience. As national embodiment, the Yankee impersonates fantasies of U.S. manhood and citizenship. As storyteller, his performance subverts such national(ist) thinking from the very beginning.

Yankee Yarns examines the Yankee's allegorical and theatrical bodies, the peddler and the homespun Yankee. The first part reads the Yankee as a transnational product of literary nationalist fantasies: Chapter 1 discusses his transatlantic kinship and coming-of-age narratives, while Chapter 2 maps the stage Yankee as theatrical invention of national character and nostalgic projection of a bucolic past. The second part considers the Yankee's conflicted cultural work as superhuman architect of a national marketplace, in Chapter 3 as contested Yankee peddler, and in Chapter 4 as palatable homespun Yankee who melts the material experience of being in America into Yankee yarn-spinning. In tracing how the Yankee is incorporated, despite himself, with the tools of the coming-of-age narrative and the homespun, I show how region, nation, and ultimately American identity are established in an economy of performed storytelling.[23]

The chapters examine different embodiments and Yankee types, in a roughly diachronic trajectory from the late Colonial to the Progressive Eras. Besides contrasting the literary texts to an exceptionalist cultural historiography of the Yankee as American, I read canonized works and popular texts by professionals together to do justice to the far-and-wide presence of the Yankee as a vehicle for negotiating national(ist) fantasies. The texts grapple with the Yankee's ambiguity and bear witness to the difficulty of fabricating this white male American body between transatlantic nationalism and the imperial masculinist narrative of the U.S.

Chapter 1, "John Bull and Brother Jonathan: A Transatlantic Affair," traces the Yankee as allegorical figure embroiled in a transatlantic family quarrel in writings by the Knickerbockers James Kirke Paulding and Washington Irving alongside popular fables and epic poems, such as *St. Jonathan: The Lay of a Scald* (Coxe 1838) and *Brother Jonathan's Epistle* (N.N. 1852a). The latter debate the aesthetic form and function of a national hero or saint and a national epic; for lack of both, the authors resort to comic inversion and the grotesque by imitating the English Augustan mock epic and verse satire. The second part of this chapter traces the emergence of Uncle Sam as national allegory in visual culture and the construction of a textual storytelling body in antebellum magazines.

Chapter 2, "Theater of/for the Nation: The Stage Yankee as Metatheatric Sign," links the stage Yankee and Yankee theater to transnational and nationalist reception. I examine how the stage Yankee evokes imaginary national spaces and carries a metatheatric commentary into the plot and, by extension, into the public sphere. He helps perform a fantasy of the nation, complete with bucolic pastoral ideal and urban cesspool. As the most embodied version of Yankeedom examined in this study, the stage Yankee also holds the most comic potential. From Tyler's *Contrast* (1787) and Thomas Fessenden's pamphlet *The Country Lovers/Jonathan's Courtship* (1795) onwards, sketches and farcical one-act plays complicate the stage Yankee's provinciality and the construction of national territories. Next to the rustic Yankee of Samuel Woodworth's *Forest Rose* (1825), an aged Yankee Uncle surfaces in James A. Herne's realist play *Shore Acres* (1892). In Tom Taylor's *Our American Cousin* (1858) and Silas Steele's *The Brazen Drum* (1846), the Yankee travels abroad looking for social, political, and economic gain.

Chapter 3, "The Yankee Peddler Conjures an American Marketplace," focuses on the Yankee peddler as business agent and hyperbole for U.S. capitalism. The itinerant vendor of the 1780s develops into the modern New England businessman whose circuit transforms a yet-to-be-fathomed national territory into an economic marketplace. The peddler's masks range from nostalgic representative of pre-industrial life to uncanny predator/magician in a threatening capitalist narrative, for instance in James Fenimore Cooper's *The Spy* (1821), and *Satanstoe* (1845) in Thomas Chandler Haliburton's *Sam Slick, the Clockmaker* stories, first published in 1835 (Haliburton 1995), or in temperance narratives. Among the Yankee figures, the peddler as professional is the most negative and mysterious one; the texts emblazon his wares and mitigate the itinerant vendor's story. His trickery with Yankee clocks and wooden nutmegs fuels sectional conflict.

The final chapter, "New England's Homespun Yankee in the Cultural and Literary Imagination," proposes a critical regionalist reading of New England as national homestead across a range of literary texts, capitalizing on Sarah Hale's New England novel *Northwood* (1827), the mock epic *A Yankee Among the Nullifiers* (Greene 1833), John Neal's Yankee gallery in his historical novels *Brother Jonathan, or The New Englanders* (1825) and *The Down-Easters* (1833), and John Greenleaf Whittier's long poem "Snow-Bound" (1866). I first read the proselytizing figure of the Yankee schoolmaster and his New England village origins as echoes of the coming-of-age allegory to then show how literary and visual cultures deal with the Yankee's ambiguity. In the sense of Eric Hobsbawm's concept of invented traditions, the figure of the New England Yankee is incorporated into an imagined shared history, a national body installed in a symbolic national landscape and cultural practice evoked in storytelling. The homespun Yankee melts material culture and an American business industry into Yankee yarns-pinning. He embodies, masculinizes, and commodifies the nation state.

The Coda meditates on "Yankee Politics" beyond the nineteenth century by tapping into Mark Twain's literary palimpsest *Connecticut Yankee in King Arthur's Court* (1889). Hank P. Morgan, from Hartford, Connecticut, has been read as self-enamored new Prometheus and prototype of a fascist dictator (Twain 1982: x). He describes himself as a "Yankee of the Yankees—and practical, yes, and nearly barren of sentiment, I suppose—or poetry, in other words" (ibid. 9). Morgan's Yankee politics promise liberation, but as President of the new republic, he lays to wreck the age of chivalry with weapons of mass destruction. Twain's time-traveling con man negotiates transatlantic anxieties and American vanity. He reminds us of the Yankee's affective and histrionic cultural work and the dark side to tall talk, fraudulence, and storytelling.

Notes

1. Hodge 1964: 42, n. 5. On the history of "Yankee Doodle" in the nineteenth century, see Gibbons 2008. In 1917, the etymologist Henry Harrison bemoaned the lack of systematic explanation of the word; he observed that the word was extinct in modern Dutch and Friesian, to conclude: "What evidently happened in America, then, was that the early Dutch colonists were in the habit of more or less contemptuously calling an English settler a *Janke* (pronounced nearly *Yanky*), that is a 'Johnnie'; and the name has ever since stuck to the resident of New England" (Harrison 1917, n.p.). Hodge stresses that the word has been used as noun, adjective, and verb and lists some other possible etymologies: the Massasoit word designated the pilgrims as invaders; a Cambridge farmer used the term to express "excellence"; the ridicule of Cromwell's Roundheads (1964: 193). Hodge lists another source: Oscar Sonneck, "Report on the 'Star-Spangled Banner', 'Hail Columbia', 'America', 'Yankee Doodle'," Washington: Government Printing Office, 1909.
2. "Yankee Phrases" was first published in the 1803 *Portfolio* and then republished verbatim at least five times until 1822 in a range of magazines and almanacs, including *The Village Magazine* (April 15, 1803: 4), *The Maryland and Virginia Almanac* (Baltimore, 1806),

G. Bourne's collection *The Spirit of Public Journals, or Beauties of the American Newspapers for 1805* (1806: 114–15), *The Lady's Miscellany* (February 16, 1811: 270–1), and *The Boston Castigator* (October 23, 1822: 4).

3. In this study, I reproduce graphic emphases in original and indicate when the emphasis is mine.
4. I use the term "transatlantic nationalism" to designate the specific American transatlantic fixation on British nationalism and the acknowledgment of American literary and cultural provinciality (Rezek 2015). British nationalism serves as a prototype of "both a nation and a nation state," marking the beginning of nationalism as a concept (Hastings 1997: 5). Nationalism, according to Eric Hobsbawm and Terence Granger, employs the invention of tradition to disguise the nation's novelty (1983: 13, 14). Modern nationalist characteristics were formed in "late eighteenth-century America and Europe" and included "repeated descriptions of national cultural difference, national geographical spaces, and the history of famous national events" (Kramer 2011: 1).
5. The recent turn to a Transnational American Studies is one expression of a post-exceptionalist understanding of the U.S., spearheaded by the New Americanists Donald Pease, John Carlos Rowe, and Winfried Fluck (see e.g. Pease 1994; Fluck and Pease 2014). The transnational origin of the American "national ideologies, identities, and ideas of state" has been established by W. M. Verhoeven (2002: 3) and by Philipp Schweighauser (2016a).
6. Manning and Taylor position Transatlantic Literary Studies amidst national and area studies, arguing that "[t]he transatlantic literary space [. . .] represents the textual collision of the 'integral' nation and those forces—material, ideological or aesthetic—that resist or distort the authority of the national imaginary" (2007: 6).
7. A different take on a folklore type percolates in Anthony Harkins's *Hillbilly: A Cultural History of an American Icon* (2004), which examines "the cultural and ideological construct" of the hillbilly (4) from its nineteenth-century antecedents (among which ranks Yankee Doodle) through twentieth-century popular culture. Harkins's take on the hillbilly capitalizes on the mythological construction of a regional type and links the figure's "continuous popularity and ubiquity" to the "dualistic nature" of his meaning (6).
8. Critical whiteness studies has put a finger on this discursive void; see e.g. Wiegman 1999, Painter 2010, or, for literary studies, Morrison 1992.
9. The domestic sphere, Dana Nelson argues, is commissioned to the newly enforced power of republican motherhood; see also Kaplan's "Manifest Domesticity" (Kaplan 1998). Nelson shows how the Federalist papers construe sensibility, as cultural concept of the late eighteenth century, as female and effeminate property and pin it onto the nation imagined as passionate and unruly woman in need of male disciplinary power.

10. This ideal formed the opposite to the agrarian concepts of the Southern states. On the role of professionals from the 1830s to the 1860s, see also Rose 1995; on the self-made man and American masculinity, see Kimmel 2012: 11–31. As a much-debated rule, white masculinity has been perceived as a concept "in crisis"; activism to reinforce white supremacy and patriarchy has embraced this crisis narrative and come to the defense of the system but taken different stances toward capitalism and democracy, as Michael Kimmel and Abby L. Ferber (2006) have argued.
11. The very campaign of magazines such as the *North American Review*, after the war of 1812, for a national literature bears witness to this development: generally, commentators were constricted by an argument that acknowledged the absence of a literary culture but that had to foreshadow great days of American literature to come in a positivist vein. McCloskey (1935) shows the campaign as well as involuntarily underpinning the feeling of transatlantic inferiority. Verheul (2012) gives an overview of the transatlantic ties despite calls for independence after the war of 1812.
12. Like the entire literary system, puffing was imported from Britain, where publishers routinely published criticism favorable to their author's novels and other works. See Cohen 2012, esp. 32–6, or for instance Laurel Brake's account of *Blackwood's* (2006, esp. 185).
13. See also Schweighauser 2016b: 223. Cynthia S. Jordan makes a similar argument about the interest American authors of the Early Republic developed in subdued or alternative voices and the multifaceted narratives that resulted from this; she addresses the consecutive "generations" of revolutionary and romantic writers who share a "concern with the language of 'fathers'": "In the romantic period [. . .], Cooper, Poe, Hawthorne, and Melville repeatedly criticized the patriarchal linguistic politics that tried to silence other views—'otherness' itself—in American culture, and their own experiments with narrative form reflect their attempts to unmask the fraud perpetrated by their cultural fathers and to recover the lost second story" (Jordan 1989: x).
14. Schneck also stresses that the belief in authentic representation engenders the awareness of fakery and ambiguity in visual culture (2003: 20–1). In the wake of the visual turn, Astrid Böger and Christof Decker (2007) map a transatlantic visual culture but also caution against abandoning the authoritative premise of a specific national culture at work in the visual. While the present study points to some of these issues, its main interest remains on the logic of storytelling.
15. Rose 1995: 39; see also Dorson 1941, 1943. On the history of the tall tale, see Wonham 1993 and also Brown 1989, which focuses on its survival as a cultural practice today; Schmitz 1977 links a close reading of Jacksonian tall tales to the panic of 1837 and the ensuing money crisis, focusing on the cultivation of the lie.

16. Dorson traced the connection between the Southwesterner and the Yankee in his dissertation, examining how Jonathan adventure stories in New England magazines reverberate with tall tale motifs. To the best of my knowledge, his remains the earliest of very few contributions that read together the two cultural types; Harkins 2004 cites the frontier hero as well as Yankee Doodle among the origins of the figure of the hillbilly.
17. Daniel Boone (1734–1820), Mike Fink (1770/80–1823) and Davy Crockett (1786–1836) were immortalized in folklore tales; their frontier bravado founded the pioneer myth serialized in popular magazines, such as the corrupt Mississippi lawyer Ovid Bolus (Baldwin 1987 [1853]), the clever trader Simon Suggs (Hooper 1993 [1845]), or the trickster storyteller Sut Lovingood (Harris 1966 [1867]). Their most widely known literary adaptation is probably Cooper's Natty Bumppo in the *Leatherstocking* novels. For an illustration of the overwhelmingly white and male identity of the tall tale hero, see e.g. Blair's illustrated narrative anthology (1987 [1944]); Harkins (2004) and Leeming and Page (1999) feature Native American, European American, African American, and Asian American myths. The few female frontier heroes like Sally Stormalong resemble their male models, but tend to fight frontier beasts with household tools. Their bodies are often depicted as abject or sexually unattractive in grotesque exaggeration, as exemplified in the title of Lofaro's *Riproarious Shemales and Sentimental Sisters* (2001).
18. The motto "Go Ahead!" serves as masthead of the Crockett almanacs (see e.g. the facsimile reproductions of the title pages in Lofaro 1978); the Yankee uses this motto most prominently in Thomas Chandler Haliburton's Sam Slick stories (see Chapter 3).
19. The dissemination of the Davy Crockett stories serves as a case in point. Stories about his adventures were featured in almanacs and published in the "Davy Crockett almanacs" between 1835 and 1850 (Lofaro 1978). He was fictionalized in Paulding's play *The Lion of the West* (1832) and published his autobiography with a ghost-writer after the publication of an unauthorized version. Crockett welcomed the cult around his persona and had little interest in stopping the exploitation of this persona. In the twentieth century he became a fixture in U.S. popular culture, with a TV series, songs, and iconic imagery.
20. On Neal's telling style, see e.g. Meyerlob 2012, or Schäfer 2016 and 2017.
21. Twain's comparatist view is selective, of course, and ignores the storytelling traditions of unreliable narrators such as Tristram Shandy. Note that he leaves out the German tradition, which contributes its share with the folklore fantasy stories of the lying braggart Baron Münchhausen (Hieronymus Carl Friedrich Freiherr von Münchhausen by full name, 1720–97).

22. Wonham has linked this process to more recent approaches to reader response theory; the tall tale constitutes reader communities and by extension imagined national communities: "the tall tale becomes a literary game in which contemporary theoretical notions of 'competence,' 'cooperation,' and 'community' come to life as parts of an actual drama of interpretation" (Wonham 1993: 10).
23. The economy of Yankee storytelling found its twentieth-century rendition in Alton H. Blackington's signature NBC radio program "Yankee Yarns" (1943–51), with stories collected by Blackington, a self-professed "dyed-in-the-wool Yankee", who also published them (see Blackington 1954).

Chapter 1

John Bull and Brother Jonathan: A Transatlantic Affair

In 2013, for the centennial of the suffragettes' march on Washington, *The Atlantic* ran a piece entitled "When America Was Female" (Franke-Ruta 2013). Recalling the suffragettes' disguise as Columbia in 1913, Garance Franke-Ruta bemoans that female national icons "fell out of vogue" after women got the vote. Their choice of Columbia claimed the nation and its founding for their struggle for equal rights. In light of renewed feminist activism, *The Atlantic* proposes to "revive [Columbia's] spirit, and return her to the pantheon of American characters for the years to come" (ibid.).

Franke-Ruta's call for a feminist revision critiques national iconography. Calling Columbia "Uncle Sam's older, classier sister," the article points to the different meanings of Columbia's "classical" image, linking her Greek and Roman origins to a socially elevated and more mature (because older) station in comparison to Uncle Sam. Yet, Columbia's alleged "classiness" is also related to her sexual value and attractiveness to the male gaze. To topple the all-male "pantheon" of American characters, it seems, Columbia is chosen because she exudes elitism and plays hard to get.

"When America Was Female" reiterates a persisting clash along the lines of gender and class in the American cultural imaginary. In the revolutionary period, Columbia and Miss Liberty represented the U.S. in visual and literary materials (Winterer 2005), but, as Carroll Smith-Rosenberg (1992, 2014) has argued, the female image stood no chance because "the virtuous republican political body [...] had to be male. The United States' self-fashioning as an independent and united nation rested on its celebration of manliness, virility, and *virtus*" (Smith-Rosenberg 2014: 44). This process entangles white virility with the disappeared Others (black, indigenous, female), making

"America without her black sister unimaginable" (Smith-Rosenberg 1992: 848).

This chapter explores the troping of the U.S. as male and the class-age divide between the classical allegory Columbia and the folksy Uncle Sam throughout the nineteenth century, when the quest for a national body, cultural independence from Britain, and inner turmoil in the U.S. brought about a sense of historical crisis and hermeneutic skepticism (Madsen 1996). This chapter examines, first, how canonized and non-professional authors employ Jonathan for political commentary on domestic and transatlantic issues, from the Revolution through the 1851 and 1878 World Exhibitions and the Civil War. I then proceed to Thomas Nast's contribution to the iconic Uncle Sam in *Harper's Weekly* in the 1870s and to the use of the Yankee body in humor magazines from the 1830s onwards.

My argument builds on Smith-Rosenberg's analysis of American national iconography and on recent transatlanticist scholarship, taking its cue from Paul Giles's suggestion that the "emergence of autonomous and separate political identities [. . .] can be seen as intertwined with a play of opposites, a series of reciprocal attractions and repulsions between opposing national situations" (2001: 1).[1] With Adrian Hastings (1997), I read England as a prototype for nationhood and nationalism and a culturally specific origin for American nationalism that is often overlooked in scholarly debates. The success of the Uncle Sam figure is therefore a transnational phenomenon intricately linked to the rise of modern national cultures at the turn of the nineteenth century. To substantiate this, I trace the English origins and transatlantic kinship of Uncle Sam/Brother Jonathan, from its beginnings in an English allegorical pamphlet in the 1700s to the nineteenth-century graphic satire embodiment of the government institutions and the nation as a whole. I discuss the history of national allegories and the shift to the male version as rendition of the national body in time.

As my analysis shows, Brother Jonathan marks the transition from allegory to national character, from static figure to living and breathing national type at home in both the cultural and the political realms. In literary debates, he is used to discuss colonial mimicry and the workings of what Elisa Tamarkin (2008) has called American "Anglophilia." In economy and politics, he forges a link between consumers of print culture and the government. As embodiment of the U.S.'s kinship with England, Brother Jonathan represents both the prodigal son embroiled in a family affair and the upstart self-made American man. Last but not least, the transition from female allegory to male character shifts the meaning from "America" to

"Americans": where the female allegory represented the nation as a cultural and geopolitical entity, the national character embodies traits, behaviors, and beliefs of the people. It democratizes the nation, at the cost of excluding its Others.

From Allegory to Character: John Bull in Early British National Iconography

From the beginning of the eighteenth century, the allegorical figure of John Bull socially evolves upward and outward, from country rube to Victorian squire and from English clothier to embodiment of Britain at large. He makes his first appearance in Scottish physician John Arbuthnot's pamphlet *Law is a Bottomless Pit*. An attack on Whig foreign policy, *Law* was integrated in Arbuthnot's *History of John Bull* (1712). *History* comments on the War of the Spanish Succession, spanning the years 1700, with Charles II of Spain's death, to 1712, when the English occupied Dunkirk. Arbuthnot renders this conflict in an allegorical-satirical narrative about the quarrels between the Englishman John Bull, the Spanish Lord Strutt, the French Lewis Baboon (Louis Bourbon), and the Dutch Nicholas Frog. To present the war, Arbuthnot chose the tropes of the lawsuit John Bull engages in with Strutt, and of the cudgel play among friends. War among nations thus becomes a mix between institutional exchange and physical ruse, both domains of manly power play.

In a nutshell, John Bull, a lowly but successful "clothier," loses his fortunes because of the lawsuit (that is, a war) with Lewis Baboon. Together with his friend Nicholas Frog (Holland), Bull works as a draper for Lord Strutt (Spain). Strutt fires the two and they sue him for compensation; in the end, Bull vows to avoid any more lawsuits and to stick to trading. Bull's mother is the Church of England, and together with his wife, Parliament, he has three unruly daughters: Polemia, Discordia, and Usuria, the three great sins of government. Arbuthnot thus employs traditional female allegorical figures to flesh out John Bull's character. They are his offspring and his weaknesses. This usage of classical allegory installed as a network around Bull allows him to be a character, a paterfamilias and henpecked husband at home who tries to prove himself to his male peers in his trade. Arbuthnot provides a detailed characterization:

> [John Bull] was [. . .] an honest plain-dealing fellow, cholerick, bold and of a very inconstant temper [. . .] very apt to quarrel with his best

friends, especially if they pretended to govern him. If you flattered him, you might lead him like a child. John's temper depended very much upon the air; his spirits rose and fell with the weather-glass. John was quick, and understood his business very well, but no man alive was more careless, in looking into his accounts, or more cheated by partners, apprentices, and servants. This was occasioned by his being a boon-companion, loving his bottle and his diversion; for to say truth, no man kept a better house than John, nor spent his money more generously. (Arbuthnot 1766: 12)[2]

Arbuthnot employs satiric nationalism (Knight 1989: 489) to attack England through the image of other nations. John Bull's surname carries a double reference, first to his bovine (choleric) character, and second to his love of beef (see also the French nickname for the English, "rosbifs"). The figure's design reverberates with literary fashions of its day; Arbuthnot was a friend and ally of Jonathan Swift and Alexander Pope, who turned to allegorical narratives, satires, and mock epics to escape censure, such as in Swift's *Tale of a Tub* (1704) or Pope's *Dunciad* (1728–43). Arbuthnot's animal symbolism echoes the allegorical writings of Bernard de Mandeville's *The Fable of the Bees* (1714), and Jean de La Fontaine, who revived Aesop's classical fables between 1668 and 1694. In Arbuthnot's text, animal traits exaggerate, ridicule, and typify John Bull, sketching the British people as dumb and voiceless chattel (Hunt 2003: 144).

John Bull's birth dates to a time when simplification (as in representing a country in a literary persona) and ambiguation (to escape political prosecution) were employed in political criticism. As allegorical character, John Bull expresses the struggle or redefinition of dominant ideology (cf. Hunt 2003: 2). In the spirit of the age, Britannia, the idealized allegory of the nation in classical garb, was met by a distinct member of contemporary English society: Arbuthnot's John Bull is a clothier, a trader and businessman, with flaws and an impulse for cudgel play. He is a man of some standing, has a choleric temper and is susceptible to flattery, and ultimately falls prey to his own whims.

John Bull emerges at the threshold of modernity, when the "dawning sense of national purpose and unity" (Matthews 2007: 810) turned towards modern nationalism. The concept of national character caters to the new ideas of nationhood and national identity and interlinks identity and ethics or responsibility (see Augst 2003; Epp 2010). The particulars of "character" are an invention of the eighteenth century, when a shift from "characters that typify to those that specify" (McGirr 2007: 1) expressed a new discomfort with the relation between appearance and reality. In the characters of John Bull and Brother Jonathan, this relation functions as a premise for decoding the meaning of the texts and images in which they are featured. The personas of John Bull and Brother Jonathan have to be read as constantly entwined in this mechanism of representational crisis which requires *allegoresis*, that is, reading allegorically. The willingness, on the reader's part, to read them as allegories for the nation requires acknowledging not only the existence of such a thing as national character, but also the correspondence between outward appearance and inward character: the bodies are a visual rendition of the character; they "operate as 'icons' that need no explanation" (ibid. 4).[3]

John Bull's character also carries the imprint of another development that influenced the conception of characters in literature: the invention, in the eighteenth century, of sexual difference. With the conviction that men and women were essentially different arose persisting anxieties about masculinity in crisis. Thus, "fribbling and foppery are represented not as harmless forms of male vanity, [. . .] but as the external signs of a deviant and potentially dangerous homosexual identity" (McGirr 2007: 15). The concept of an "Englishman" shifted towards the bourgeoisie, and the noble fop and rake became antagonists to the country gentleman, who impersonated the image of British masculinity by 1815. The British man is defined against two cultural Others used in Arbuthnot's "John Bull," the "Dutch trader and the [French] Continental slave to fashion and autocracy" (McGirr 2007: 23).

Arbuthnot's Bull is taken up in cartoons and emerges as a positive figure whose shortcomings make him all the more endearing. By the end of the eighteenth century, John Bull represented "no longer the English nation state, but the British national character" (Matthews 2007: 814). John Bull's success must be credited to caricatures, mainly in the humor magazine *Punch*. True to Arbuthnot's characterization, the cartoons first showed Bull as anti-hero, an unkempt country rube.[4] His appearance was tied more to fiscal politics than to imperialism (Taylor 1992). As Tamara Hunt has argued, he amalgamates the meaning of the national with the people (2003: 169). From 1840 onwards, he impersonated what Thomas Carlyle called, in *Past and Present* (1843), "the born conservative":

> the stupidest in speech, the wisest in action [. . .] slow to believe in novelties; patient of much error in actualities; deeply and forever certain of the greatness that is in Law, in Custom once solemnly established, and now long recognized as just and final. (Carlyle 2010: 160)

Carlyle finds both positive and negative traits and avoids condemning John Bull altogether. Bull's particular usage for a Whiggish argument, his provenance from the midst of English society, and his embodiment of "the bustling and programmatic English merchant" (Matthews 2007: 809) clashed with Britannia's more idealized image. Britannia's function as allegory provides an inroad for exploring the function of the American Brother Jonathan.

As the older impersonation of the nation, Britannia descends from classical goddesses and was revived as a hybrid between warrior and goddess of plenty in the English Renaissance. She combined the ideal of sovereignty (also transported, for instance, in allegorical representations of Queen Elizabeth I as Gloriana in Edmund Spenser's allegorical tale *The Faerie Queene*) with the principle of nourishment, in which Nature creates prosperity. In the eighteenth century, Britannia's provenance from classical sources and her association with learnedness and the ruling classes jarred with the social upheavals. As Emma Major (2012) has shown, she embodies the Protestant nation, and at turns the Church of England.

The transition from female national allegory to male national allegorical character shifts the reading process of the allegorical figure. Strikingly, this shift has been overlooked in scholarly discussions (see Delogu 2015: 12), which tend to normalize the female gender ascription of allegories: they simply have to be female (ibid.). As Marina Warner argues, in allegory, the female body is a depersonalized vessel which, deliberately, does *not* represent its gender identity:

> Liberty can hardly be said to represent the typical American woman, or Britannia the Englishwoman of collective consciousness. Men are individual, they appear to be in command of their own characters and their own identity, to live inside their own skins, and they do not include women in their symbolic embrace: John Bull, however comic, can never be a cow. [. . .] Uncle Sam and John Bull are popular figures; they can be grim, sly, feisty, pathetic, absurd, for they have personality. Liberty, like many abstract concepts expressed in the feminine, is in deadly earnest and one-dimensional. Above all, if John Bull appears angry, it is his anger he expresses; Liberty is not representing her own freedom. (Warner 2000: 12)

While Britannia's female form symbolizes the male subjects of Britain, it is used for demanding female care work such as mothering and nourishment (Major 2012: 18).[5] In Arbuthnot's *History*, Britannia as the Church of England is praised for her housekeeping and civility adapted from the period's conduct books. In cartoons, Britannia reappeared as fecund woman and mother with a horn of plenty and full breasts (see Matthews 2007). In a mixed-media strategy, images of Britannia also carried a written title indicating her identity, thus mingling allegory with emblems and creating "miniature allegory" (Daly 2003: 388) that communicated through words and symbolic pictures.

As stated above, the advent of a male character as allegory of the nation changes the reading task. Arbuthnot's original John Bull can be understood as national signifier only because he interacts with other figures who impersonate his "neighbors," France, Spain, and the Netherlands. From the beginning, John Bull appears in an international competition. Arbuthnot's narrative draws from the fable or parable, which represents one story but asks the reader to translate from what is said to what is meant.

The Bull allegory therefore speaks differently.[6] Described by Friedrich Schlegel as "an endless series of mirrors" (qtd. in Seyhan 2003: 444), allegory, in the case of Britannia and John Bull, foregrounds temporality and literary function in times perceived as historical threshold. The act of reading allegorically thus requires that readers attribute John Bull with the meaning "Great Britain." They accept the premise that the nation as entity exists and that it can be mediated through a body or story.

As a literary and rhetoric device, allegory has been employed for mythography and historiography. Critics agree that allegory adds a superhistorical and superterritorial perspective to a distinct time and place ("überzeitliche und überregionale Perspektiven," Freytag 1992: 332; see also Whitman 2003: 280–99). More specifically, following Walter Benjamin's argument in *Der Ursprung des Deutschen Trauerspiels* (1928), allegory itself represents the turn of history into modernity, as thoughts evaporate into images ("so verdunsten die Gedanken vielfach in Bildern," qtd. in Whitman 2003: 298). The success of the John Bull figure represents a modern invention of the nation which, from the very beginning, is embroiled in conflicts with other nations. The War of the Spanish Succession called for the figuration of England as John Bull. Bull's subsequent dissemination, in magazine and print culture, though, detached him from the historical event. He embodies the nation through time, as if it had always existed, as a "voice for ordinary citizens" who are morally superior because of their love for the nation (Hunt 2003: 49, 165).

John Bull's success proves wrong the literary avant-gardes of the day. Both the English Neoclassicists and the German Romantics dismissed allegory. Johann Wolfgang von Goethe famously preferred the symbol over the allegory because in the latter, the image is separable from the idea, whereas in the symbol they are mutually constitutive. In England, despite the fierce rejection of allegory by the literati, allegorical figures as well as allegorical narratives were successful and slightly altered, as Theresa M. Kelley argues, by using "popular instead of learned allegorical or iconographic materials" and placing a new interest on "narrative as the figured ground of allegory." The transition from allegory to allegorical character hinges on breaking with "the claim that allegorical figures should not or cannot act" (Kelley 1997: 72).[7] Like the classical allegories of Discord or Eloquence of the late eighteenth century, John Bull does indeed "walk and talk" (ibid. 76). Kelley does not include Arbuthnot's Bull in her assessment, but it seems that he pre-dated the reinvention of allegory in eighteenth-century England. In particular, John Bull counteracts the criticism by Joseph Addison, editor of *The Spectator*, who contended that allegories

> are very beautiful in poetry, when they are just shown, without being engaged in a series of actions [. . .] when such persons are introduced as principal actors and engaged in a series of adventures, they take too much upon them, and are by no means proper for a heroic poem which ought to appear credible in its principle parts. (Addison 1712: 435)

Published in the same year as Arbuthnot's pamphlet, Joseph Addison's criticism of the allegorical figures in Milton's *Paradise Lost* (1667) claims that epic poetry is no fitting framework for allegorical characters, since they are not credible as "actors" in "adventures." However, the epic often functions as allegorical history for empires, from Greece to Rome (Freytag 1992: 331), but also for the U.S.-American national epic, which features Brother Jonathan as national character, as I show below.

In early modern Europe, nations were routinely inscribed in visual or narrative allegories, specifically in the aftermath of the French Revolution.[8] In the Romantic tradition, the tropes of allegory, irony, and fragment relate the present to the past, "with redemptive potential" (Seyhan 2003: 437). The replacement of female figures in Roman garb by a male, vernacular character coincided with the rise of the modern nation state and pointed to social performance.[9] The practice of reading bodies and characters as nations becomes necessary at a particular moment of international relations and cultural exchange.[10]

The allegorical troping at work in the transition from Britannia to John Bull also applies to the American figure of Brother Jonathan/ Uncle Sam. As the previous argument has shown, first, imagining the national body as male and vernacular catered to the new nationalist demand. Furthermore, the Bull allegory was anchored in history and then used to embody the essence of a national character that was a new cultural phenomenon, but cast as longstanding typical behavior of an emboldened bourgeois English masculinity opposite other European identities. Satiric nationalism and political critique, the original functions of the Bull figure, were softened in an allegorical embodiment of conservatism, whose weaknesses are winked at.

Compared to John Bull, the American allegorical character Brother Jonathan performs an even more foundational role in national iconography. In U.S. literature, allegorical narratives are employed in times of crisis to highlight the "difficulties inherent in the activity of interpretation" and to "critique [...] hermeneutic methods" (Madsen 1996: 1, 4). In breaking away from the newly nationalist English kingdom, the colonists forged a national character who descended from the English. In casting the nation as one body and character, this figure comes to life where no uniform embodiment had been imagined. He calls into being a much-desired unity in national, spatial, and, ultimately, social dimensions. This unity is created, as the remainder of this chapter will show, with the tropes of the kinship and family narrative.

In American revolutionary discourse, childrearing and parentage loomed large. Jay Fliegelman has shown that the Revolution was framed by a "call for filial autonomy and the unimpeded emergence from nonage" (1982: 3). American writers adapted a new parental ideal that promoted "a more affectionate and equalitarian relationship with children" and that claimed their "right and obligation [...] to become fully autonomous and self-reasoning adults" (ibid. 1, 3). As vignette for this argument, commentators on both sides of the Atlantic enlisted the progress of the prodigal son, whose tyrannic parents condemn their children to live in a convent, barring them from marriage and procreation.[11] Conversely, in the Early Republic, American texts would elevate the moral status of the family and replace the English father-tyrant with the ideal, friendly American father figure of Washington, also a new model for Christ (ibid. 121, 122, 208).

As the revolutionary texts use the story of the prodigal son for justifying rebellion, the family ties of Brother Jonathan claim kinship and a new, paternal, affective, and egalitarian masculinity. This brings us back to the gender politics of national allegory. In the cultural imaginary of the U.S. in the nineteenth century, the prodigal son narrative draws a national allegorical character who is male and who develops over time, through his fatherhood. Whereas the female allegories of Columbia or Lady Liberty embodied static and eternal entities, Brother Jonathan has a personal history and an aging body. His narrative is framed by whiteness and masculinity, properties that venerate rebellion. The son's "right and obligation" to grow up and out implies that one day he will overshadow his father, as is illustrated prominently in Plate 1, "John Bull and Uncle Sam."

The sheet music cover of this patriotic song, with lyrics by an English member of parliament and music by an American composer, captures the history of transatlantic relations with the two national characters from the title, John Bull and Uncle Sam. In 1776, they fought an unequal fight, with a boyish, bare-knuckled Uncle Sam facing the Englishman's sword. In 1898, their reconciliation is shown with a civil handshake and a different size ratio; while John Bull was larger and taller than Uncle Sam before, he now looks up to the taller and matured man whose economic success is obvious in his neat dress. The position of the figures left and right of an orb reiterates the transatlantic map and implies their physical growth from a remote past to the viewer's present. The song tells the history of young Sam following the promise of freedom and John Bull's offer at companionship after their estrangement: "Dear Sam, of me you are a part, we must be, shall be friends." The refrain runs, "the Stars and Stripes and the Union Jack shall rule o'er Land and Sea."

The sheet music cover also shows an alteration in John Bull's dress that becomes necessary in the transatlantic constellation. In other images, Bull wears blue tails to indicate his Whig leanings, and a Union Jack waistcoat. Yet when he meets Brother Jonathan, John Bull's red coat recalls the English uniforms in the Revolutionary War, while the American dons the (republican) blue. The literary descriptions of John Bull by Washington Irving and James Kirke Paulding both feature the red waistcoat (see Hastings 1929: 68).

In the transatlantic setting, the character of John Bull as well as the allegorical narrative he appears in became the pedestal upon which an American national self-understanding was installed. It ensured biological kinship, masculinity and paternalism, and Anglo-Saxon whiteness while also supporting the need to break away. Bull, originally conceived by a Scotsman to critique the establishment, and designed as a businessman who had got ahead of himself, grew into an authoritarian father figure who unfairly hindered the growth and independence of his son Brother Jonathan.

The following section reads American adaptations of the Bull narrative to examine how they negotiate the desire for an American national allegorical character with transatlantic kinship and the literary nationalist debates of the antebellum era in the U.S.

Transatlantic Kinship in Nineteenth-Century U.S. Print Culture: Between National Literature and Imperial Fantasy

The complicated relationship between John Bull and his offspring Brother Jonathan overshadows the figures of Britannia and Columbia or Lady Liberty. The narrative of a transatlantic family quarrel vitalizes the allegorical bodies, foregrounds white masculinity, and anticipates the settler nation state. Brother Jonathan may have his faults and throw his tantrums, but he claims the future against a John Bull who is aging more or less gracefully.

Arbuthnot's text has been foundational for U.S. authors commenting on the transatlantic relationship and literary nationalism. Its adaptation in the U.S. demonstrates that, at the very core, the American Yankee is a gesture of cultural and literary mimicry (Clark 2013: 60, 78). In 1766, the *Newport Mercury* published a short satire, "The History of John Bull's Children," as a reaction to the Stamp Act on August 4. In this text, the thirteen colonies are John's three daughters from an extramarital relation with his maid. Cast out by his wife Parliament, they are nourished by a wild bear on the American shores (Fliegelman 1982: 116–17). In the Early Republic, John Hopkinson's *A Pretty Story* (1774) chronicles the history of U.S. settlement; England is shown as a farm with a large shop opposite the remote wilderness of America. Hopkinson's farm is run by "the Nobleman"; the Americans out in the wild are his descendants by blood. Jeremy Belknap's *The Foresters, an American Tale; [. . .] a Sequel to The History of John Bull, the Clothier* (1792/1796) renders the history of U.S. settlement, the Revolution, and the adoption of the Constitution in an allegorical narrative presented in epistolary form. Belknap's chief character is closer to Arbuthnot's irksome original, and the Americans are his domestics, apprentices, and tenants. The texts describe the relation as kinship row with a milder rendition of John Bull (Hopkinson) or as business relationship (Belknap), respectively.

In these texts, countries are represented as estates or, in the case of the U.S., settlements in the forest, where farmers cultivate new lands and found their own economies. The institutions of government are entangled in a family structure. The titular male character and founding "father" is a henpecked husband whose unruly wife commands the purse strings. This wife, in the English original, is Parliament; in the American texts, she is Congress. The legislative bodies in these allegories are modeled on a pestering mother-in-law and foolish luxury girl (Hastings 1929: 63), objects of male criticism in a typically chauvinist power play.

At the beginning of the nineteenth century, the kinship narrative was tethered to literary nationalist anxieties by non-professional authors and by the East Coast literati alike. Among the American adaptations of the John Bull allegory, the Knickerbocker School writers Washington Irving and James Kirke Paulding, the first post-revolutionary generation of authors, drew from the allegory's versatility in political and literary debates.

Irving's short sketch "John Bull" is included in *The Sketch Book of Geoffrey Crayon, Gent.* (1819–20; see Irving 1983b). Crayon, an older gentleman, shows a general reverence for England and English literature, describing literary inheritance through metaphors such as the fountainhead, the mine, and the ghost (McLamore 2000: 50), and like these emblems of times past, his reading is anachronistic: he draws from Elizabethan and Renaissance writings and prefers libraries over contemporary writers. Through Crayon's old-man confusions, Irving subjects the quest for an American literature to ridicule and burlesque, as Paul Giles (2001) has argued. Irving's nationalist agenda differed from a contemporary neocolonial framework on the one hand, and from his American brother-in-law Paulding's more radical nativist approach. Crayon's sketch of "John Bull" reverberates with the American literary scene and its transatlantic anxiety of influence.

Crayon's "Account of Himself" (Irving 1983a: 743–5) reminds the reader of "the youthful promise" of the U.S. while acknowledging also that "Europe was rich in the accumulated ties of ancient and local custom" (ibid. 744). Despite this admiration for Europe, Crayon expresses a harsh, irreverent viewpoint in "John Bull," with two stanzas from an "Old Song" that form a prologue to the sketch. These two stanzas ironically reduce Crayon's reverence for the Old World to a single defining quality, its old age. In the excerpt from the "Old Song," the title word "old" is repeated thirteen times in a comical overemphasis of the protagonist's ancientness. The song lists the topics of the subsequent sketch and sets its tone. Even before encountering Irving's "John Bull," we already know about his geriatric universe. It is little surprising, then, that Crayon finds John Bull unfit as national icon:

> One would think that in personifying itself, a nation would be apt to picture something grand, heroic, and imposing; but it is characteristic of the peculiar humor of the English, and of their love for what is blunt, comic, and familiar, that they have embodied their national oddities in the figure of a sturdy, corpulent old fellow, with a three cornered hat, red waistcoat, leather breeches, and stout oaken cudgel. (Irving 1983b: 1029)

In Crayon's view, English humor determines the shape and quality of the nation. John Bull becomes an ideal the British "endeavor to act up to, [a] broad caricature that is perpetually before their eyes" (1029–30). All faults, like swearing, impatience, anger, and "a coarseness of taste," Crayon claims, are embraced by the English. They explain their behavior by maintaining that they are "a real John Bull" (1030). Strangers inquiring into the character of the English are therefore best served if they look at "the innumerable portraits of John Bull, as exhibited in the windows of the caricature shops" (ibid.). Crayon's own description, much in the manner of his portrayal of characters in the *Sketch Book*, becomes a literary discussion: John Bull has "much less poetry about him than rich prose [. . .] little romance [. . .] but a vast deal of strong natural feeling" (1030–1). His old mansion is terribly run down, but also "extremely poetical and picturesque" (1039).

The sketch of John Bull shows him as irate victim of his own impulses. Notably, his compulsion to meddle wreaks chaos when Bull begins "incontinently to fumble with the head of his cudgel, and consider whether his interest or honor does not require that he meddle in the broil" (1031). Crayon concludes by wishing the old geezer well, hoping that he will "remain quietly at home [. . .] renew the jovial scenes of ancient prosperity, and long enjoy, on his paternal lands, an honorable, and a merry old age" (1039). Crayon is conflicted about the "choleric, bottle bellied old spider" and "sterling hearted old blade" (1031, 1038), but his message is clear: John Bull deserves respect, but he best keep to himself. Crayon saturates his sketch with images of old age and materials withered by the passing of time. Despite the admiration for Europe's "shadowy grandeurs of the past" he uttered in his "Account of Himself" (Irving 1983a: 744), he argues it is time for England to retire from the business of the world.

John Bull as vernacular epitome of modern English nationalism is neither to the taste of Geoffrey Crayon, nor to that of Irving himself.

Crayon's wish that John Bull keep quiet also links to his critique of the mass dissemination of Bull caricatures and the communal navel-gazing in the streets and public spaces. Crayon also discards the modern city; he prefers the "paternal lands" of Bull's mansion. However, in this estate setting, Bull does not serve as a figure of literary or cultural inheritance, as do the ghosts of Hessian soldiers or the fountainheads in other stories of the *Sketch Book*. In Crayon's view, he is best stored away, cut off, as his ancientness requires. Bull is useless for the present and future of the U.S.

Irving's brother-in-law, James Kirke Paulding, was a radical literary nativist, but like Irving, he also sketched a negative image of Bull. A prominent Knickerbocker and New York politician, Paulding was considered an equal to his now canonized contemporary literati James Fenimore Cooper, William Cullen Bryant, and Edgar Allen Poe (see Aderman and Kime 2003: 11). Even though his oeuvre lacks originality and imitates eighteenth-century English literary styles, his works were pirated and published without his consent in London almost immediately after their American publication (Rezek 2015: 200–5). Paulding wrote across genres, including novels and drama and shorter pieces. His allegories and fables played with imitation, parody, and national fantasy. His *New Mirror for the Traveller, and Guide to the Springs* (1828), a parody of guidebooks to the Niagara Falls, for instance, was taken seriously by some readers, and dubbed by the critics "the new *Pilgrim's Progress*," after John Bunyan's allegorical narrative about the trip to the city upon a hill.

For political commentary throughout his career, Paulding turned to Brother Jonathan and the fable of transatlantic kinship and mutual navel-gazing. His *Diverting History of John Bull and Brother Jonathan* called for a war in 1812; *A Sketch of Old England, by a New England Man* (1822) mimicked Irving's Geoffrey Crayon; *John Bull in America, or The New Munchhausen* (1825) invented a genteel British traveler enthusiastic about his experience of the U.S. In 1867, Paulding's son William edited these texts as *The Bulls and the Jonathans*. Paulding's son turns the tables on the British by showing how Americans exploited British tastes; the preface explains that, when meeting English travelers, Americans would put up a masquerade of American roughness to cater to the English taste for disgust:

> It remains then to inquire into the causes of this persistent slander [about American roughness]. There was an [English] national jealousy, for one thing, and a desire to prevent emigration for another. [...] I believe that our own countrymen may thank themselves daily for the

> many strange stories told of us by the genuine British traveler. There are, and always have been, many of them to whom "it is meat and drink to see a clown." They early began to stimulate that appetite for being disgusted or shocked which is so odd a concomitant of the Bull on his peregrination. Finding his maw so capacious, they have supplied him with ample and varied sustenance. (Paulding 1867: 166)

A century after the publication of Arbuthnot's *History of John Bull*, Paulding wrote *The Diverting History* on the fly in 1812 in support of President Madison's plea for war with Britain. *The Diverting History* was an immediate success, and was republished in 1813, 1819, and 1827; in 1835, Paulding included a slightly revised version in his collected works. Like Arbuthnot's allegory, Paulding represented the relations between different countries as family narrative. The bone of contention—that is, the English interventions in American trade with France—contests Jonathan's power inside his own new home, with American Congress as a "dithering old lady" (Aderman and Kime 2003: 53), and other American allies as "overseers of his farms" (Paulding 1812: 116) who have a duty to stand by him.

Both Irving and Paulding portrayed John Bull more harshly than their American predecessors, finding him "subdued" by his imprudence (Hastings 1929: 67) and outdated opposite Brother Jonathan's new claim to independence. In the 1835 edition of the *Diverting History*, Paulding emphasized this by adding the fable of the benevolent porcupine, which describes British benevolence as loving their dependents to death.

> The porcupine was once seized with an unaccountable bout of universal benevolence, so that he could never see any of the weaker sort of animals but he must pity them, and either carry them on his back or cover them with his body, for fear the sky might fall on them, as he said. The consequence was the poor little devils got so pricked and worried by the quills of their troublesome protector that in a short time they had scarcely a drop of blood left in their bodies, and were reduced to skin and bone. Upon this the wretched survivors came to him in a body, and with great humility requested, that in future when his majesty saw them in difficulty, he would graciously suffer them to get out of it as well as they could, without his "non-intervention." (Qtd. in Clark 2013: 74)

Jennifer Clark argues that the family relationship sketched by Paulding is fraught because of John Bull's blindness for his son's needs. The fable of the porcupine, I would add, undermines imperial power and cultural authority: the porcupine is merely bigger than the other animals he protects against their will. His concern that "the sky might fall on them" is as arbitrary as his sudden protective urge. The "little animals'" plea for independence preserves their bodies and physical integrity. Like Irving, who remarked on Bull's "incontinence," Paulding capitalizes on Bull's failure of reason, portraying him as an old man who, while he means well, has to be "brought to reason." Bull's crisis is a crisis of masculinity performance subjected to ridicule, as the marriage banter in the *Diverting History* shows:

> "Why you look like an old, battered, worn-out glutton---Your dancing days are over, John." "Are they, by jingo?" cried the squire. "I'll show you, my dear." And he tried to cut a great caper, but was seized with such a twinge that he roared out lustily, while Mrs. Bull laughed ready to split her sides. "Well, my dear," quoth the squire, whom the twinge had brought to reason, "I believe I am growing a little old." (Qtd. in Clark 2013: 73)

In the 1850s, Paulding became a commentator on sectional dissent and the rights of the American South, publishing anonymously three narrative vignettes in the vitriolic *Democratic Review*, a promoter of Jacksonian democracy and literary nationalism: the story of Uncle Sam's farm which is parceled out to his sons ("Uncle Sam and his B'Hoys," 1851); the story of the prodigal son whose adolescent tantrums should be corrected ("Brother Jonathan," 1853); and the story of the quest for and construction of a national saint who is typically tainted by his idiosyncrasies ("Saint Jonathan," 1855). Published amid sectional conflict and an increased sense of national crisis, the articles employ Brother Jonathan to rally nationalist sentiment and develop civil religion.

In "Uncle Sam and his B'Hoys" (Paulding 1851: 299), Paulding locates Sam's farm out West. It is growing fast since Sam's wife "breeds like a rabbit," and Uncle Sam has trouble keeping his children (i.e. the states) in order. The "b'hoys" of the title reminded readers of the Bowery B'hoy, the rowdy New York working-class icon that came to fame on the stage and in the 1849 Astor Place Riot. The family conflict erupts over Sam's business with his sons and the "necessary and proper clause" of the Constitution. In Paulding's story, Uncle Sam is an impatient and tyrannic father who accuses his children of "disunion, disaffection, and rebellion." The conflict can only be resolved by employing a "down East" lawyer who appeases both sides with endless unintelligible monologues. His interpretation of the conflict between Uncle

Sam and his children draws from the "great case of Bull vs. Brother Jonathan" of the Revolutionary War. The paternal family narrative is then applied to Uncle Sam, and the lawyer argues in favor of the states' right to rebellion, "provided they don't do it in a peaceable manner"; if Uncle Sam shows no resistance to their efforts, "the b'hoys will be a set of rebellious rascals." Breaking the union thus requires "a sufficient quantity of broken heads, and bloody noses" to make the rebels "heroes and patriots." Upon hearing this verdict, Uncle Sam braces himself for a fight, but his sons chicken out. Paulding's version satirizes the transatlantic family narrative and argues for federal power opposite state dissent; at the end of the parable, Uncle Sam becomes "a staunch advocate of club law," a rule based on power, not on debate.

Paulding's "Brother Jonathan" offers a sketch of national character that layers its rhetoric of the body politic into the national allegory (Brother Jonathan), the American people ("we"), and a masculine body symbolism. In two parts, "Brother Jonathan" applauds American strengths and outlines three vices in need of correction. The first phrase reiterates settler colonial ideology by positioning Brother Jonathan as new offspring from the transatlantic family: "Brother Jonathan—though a chip off the old block—has had his habits and character modified by being placed in a different position, and subjected to a new system of discipline from that of the races from whence he sprung" (Paulding 1853: 433). Paulding acknowledges Jonathan's biological heritage with organic metaphors (carved out of English wood, a sprig off their tree), but argues that life in the New World has formed him. In the remainder of the essay, Paulding proclaims the unity of the American "people" and applauds their pioneering spirit:

> The United States [. . .] are emphatically one great people, acting in concert in all their foreign relations. Though of an infinite diversity of sects, they are all Christians [. . .] Though descended from the most illustrious nations of the world, and having many fathers, [. . .] the entire mass becomes cemented together by the indissoluble tie of Liberty and Equality. [. . .] The title American Citizen supersedes all others, and the foreigner, like the lamb in the Fable, chooses for his mother, not the land of his birth, but that of his adoption. (Paulding 1853: 433)

Paulding celebrates a pluralist Christian citizenry while dispersing and silencing indigenous cultures and non-white epistemologies; his settlers do not fall victim to the "two extremes of effeminacy and barbarism" (436). He combines the trope of manifest destiny (coined by editor O'Sullivan in the *Democratic Review* in 1845) with flood imagery ("the deluge of North Americans which will overflow the country," 433; "emigrants slide into the great current," 434). Opposite this water metaphor in which individual parts dissolve in the great river of "Liberty and Equality" and drown out the entire land mass, he resorts to family narrative when talking about dissent. Sectional differences are "bickerings" in "our family circles, occasioning temporary interruptions of harmony" but always ending in reconciliation: "they may threaten separation, but will never apply for a divorce" (434).

Paulding projects the transatlantic family image he quotes at the beginning (the chip off the old block) onto an American white Christian national family. In the parts about the uniformity of the American people and their pioneering spirit, his rhetoric passes from "the people" to an individualized "citizen" who is "master of his mind and his body; accustomed from his early youth to a sphere of action and contemplation almost without limit" (436). The male white citizen is young ("To him, the present is almost nothing, the future all," ibid.) and develops like a "whirlwind," compared to the "snail" speed of his Northern neighbors in the British colonies "Canada, Nova Scotia, and New Brunswick" (437). The argument about the American achievements closes with this comparison, emblazoning the magic superlatives of the U.S.'s "irresistible progress [. . .] and incomprehensible ascent to the summit of power" (ibid.).

The article's turn to the nation's faults is indicated by the use of the "Brother Jonathan" allegory: "That our dearly beloved Jonathan has his faults, cannot be denied" (ibid.). In this part, the allegorical figure creates a familial scenario of biological kinship and cultural practice and switches from celebratory bombast to educational patronizing. The young man's faults are pointed out and explained; he has the "propensity to imitation" and "in opinion he is a slave" (ibid.). This is due to his rearing "under a king" and to his being "tied to the apron-string of his mother." Like John Bull, Brother Jonathan falls victim to female plotting, impersonated here by "the old lady" England, whose cultural and intellectual influence spans the ocean. Jonathan's temper also echoes Bull. Paulding describes Jonathan in "a state of spontaneous combustion," "bad as a mad bull in a crockery shop" (438). His "greatest fault" is a "horrible craving for money" (ibid.) that borders on religious worship ("Mercury and Plutus are his gods," ibid.). This devotion jars with the civil religion of the U.S: "You cannot worship God and mammon, nor kneel at the shrine of liberty while groveling at the hoof of the golden calf" (439). Pointing back to the opening phrase about Jonathan's change of character in the New World, this part calls for a change of perspective and of priorities ("He must think of something else"; "have some other standard," ibid.). Paulding finally explains Jonathan's shortcomings with his dependence on his "old mother, who despises an empty purse and worships millionaires" (ibid.). Real independence thus requires Jonathan to stop imitating England, bridle his temper, and make money for "the benefit of his fellow creatures, not forgetting himself" (ibid.).

Paulding thus blends an exceptionalist view of American citizenry as chosen people with an educational tract. For the former, he draws the image of a people united in pioneering spirit; for the latter, he resorts to an apologetic criticism of young Brother Jonathan's faults. Both concepts of America as community and as allegorical figure share a futurist orientation ingrained in pioneering and in growing up. Paulding's "Brother Jonathan" thus illustrates the political uses of the Brother Jonathan allegory: with his boyish character, Jonathan owns the future; his nonage allows commentators to excuse his present shortcomings as youthful follies, to correct him and to predict a grand future in which he will grow into his own and supersede his ancestor, the British Empire. While "Uncle Sam and his B'hoys" cautioned against the rule of a tyrannic federal government, the family narrative in "Brother Jonathan" mitigates sectional difference. Published less than a decade before the Civil War, "Brother Jonathan" transports the image of the transatlantic family into the unified national body of the U.S., normalizing internal conflict as family struggle and blanking out the details. The article addresses neither slavery nor tariffs and economic conflicts, but lays the family quarrel at the door of "ambitious pettifogging politicians" (434).[12]

Paulding's essay "Saint Jonathan," published in 1855 in the *United States Review*, the *Democratic Review*'s follow-up, posits the allegorical figure as national saint to install it in U.S. civil religion. It represents a mock-hagiographic proclamation of the U.S.'s new national patron, Saint Jonathan, in an ironic mode: this new national saint differs from other national figures in so many ways that readers may wonder about his qualifications. Saint Jonathan's "character is peculiar, his person is peculiar, his mode of life is peculiar, his country is peculiar, the age in which he lives is peculiar, and in a word he is *peculiarly peculiarized*" (Paulding 1855: 101). With this absurd repetition, Paulding hands over the "peculiarity" of this specimen to his readers, asking them to ponder "mankind's desire to deify their heroes and teachers" (99).

He paints Saint Jonathan before the reader's eyes in a detailed character sketch replete with contradictions:

> Fancy before you a young giant in the bloom of youth, graceful yet stalwart, dressed in all the peculiarities of rustic and fashionable costume. He wears his hat on one side, in true "wide-awake" style; his coat is one of the "true blues" each button bearing the star and eagle. His unmentionables [underwear] seem reluctantly taking leave of his boot-tops, and ineffectually endeavoring to make the acquaintance of his gay-colored vest. In a pair of huge hands, placed at a most respectful distance from his coatcuffs, are the ever accompanying jackknife and piece of pine, which, with untiring industry, he manufactures into articles of every fashion and use, from a fancy tooth-pick to the model of a steamship, which Uncle John Bull strives in vain to imitate or equal. His whole apparel is more striking than elegant, presenting a most strange combination of foreign gew-gaws and substantial homespun. [. . .] Every thing about him has the appearance of wealth, and the scantiness of his garments results from the extraordinary fact that his tailor cannot keep pace with his growth. (Paulding 1855: 100–1)

Paulding's Saint Jonathan illustrates most prominently the allegorization and animation of the national body in the guise of the Yankee. His reading of the Yankee's physique and appearance is bent on irony and ridicule. Saint Jonathan's dress is ragged; he has outgrown his clothes and combines foreign fashions with homespun garments in a hodgepodge. The clothes don't fit his body, but this is described as a social interaction, with cuffs maintaining a "respectful distance" from the hands and his pantaloon "taking leave" of the boots to "make the acquaintance" of his vest. The body is doubly grotesque, both in its ever-growing form and in its personified clothing. Similarly, the adjectives point to the body's fantastic quality, when "striking" meets "strange" or "wealth" meets "scantiness." His posture is uncommon, with cocked hat and a compulsion to whittling that suggests U.S. manufacturing and industrial production, notably the American steamboat that impressed the British at the 1851 Crystal Palace World Exhibition discussed further below. All these components render him "peculiar," or unfit to pose as national saint, since he is neither heroic nor elegant, as the "heavenly bodies" of the famous men deified in other cultures. Whereas the latter "appear enlarged [. . .] to the stature of gods" (100), Jonathan's body is constantly inflated out of proportion by "extraordinary growth." Paulding's national Saint Jonathan as a body politic carries a threefold, contradictory meaning:

he is ridiculous, but his youthful faults are excusable, and he foreshadows an imperial future.

Paulding breathes life into the national allegory by linking physical growth to character. He talks about Jonathan's most prominent character trait: his haste. It may cause him "a thousand dangers" and deprive him of reaping the benefits ("No pleasure charms him unless it be brief," 104). Jonathan's body is a machine, "constructed wholly on the high-pressure principle [...] whirled forward, like a congreve rocket"; he goes "a-puffing through the world, like one of his own locomotives" (103, 104). Despite this cyborg identity, however, Jonathan is also prone to catch organic sicknesses due to his insatiability. He "swallows his victuals whole, bolting down whole ship-loads of not the choicest viands of Europe"; he takes on too quickly European fashions and ideas. Yet Jonathan also ails from a disease inherited from his mother, England, the "black measles," a racist trope for slavery:

> When young they covered his whole body; but careful treatment has removed them from his upper extremities, and unfortunately no further [...] Some advise him to take a strong emancipatory purgative which, at the risk of his life, would remove them at once. While others insist that owing to certain constitutional defects, such a course would inevitably cause immediate and violent death; [...] but itchings and burnings return and some [...] timorous souls live in constant dread lest these convulsions will break up the Union of his members and send them off tangent-like to form a fragmentary cluster of saintly asteroids in the canonical system. (Paulding 1855: 104–5)

Paulding's anti-abolitionist stance sketches a white supremacist view of slavery as infestation of the body politic, disavowing the economic exploitation and gratuitous violence the enslaved are subjected to and reiterating the dehumanizing rhetoric of white nationalists. Warning that the "emancipatory purgatives" would kill the national body by tearing it apart through "constitutional defects" (referring to the Nullification Crisis of the 1830s), Paulding argues that physical integrity preserves the national body's power (opposite a hapless cluster of "saintly asteroids"). To calm the hysterics over national disintegration, Paulding praises Jonathan's youth and strength as well as his "soundness of constitution," a polysemy which conjures trust in the nation's institutions and in its prowess.

Paulding's national saint is framed by parody and performance, an ominous figure out of bounds that reverberates with the period's crude humor. Yet Paulding also postulates the "irresistible fascination" (101) that comes with the problem of "reading" the national body. He interrupts and complicates the allegoresis, the reading of this figure, shifting the task from the allegorical visual sign to the allegorical narrative, which hinges on the notion of character; the body of Brother Jonathan develops into a deeply ambiguous type:

> Yet, there is a fascination about him that is almost irresistible; and upon an intimate acquaintance his incongruities seem to harmonize, his rough ways to soften, and new attractions to unfold. He appears so frank and open-hearted that one would think his character might be read at a glance; yet, after years of observation, we are in doubt. What at first seemed simplicity assumes the appearance of calculation, and that artless verdancy ripens into deep design, though all appears honest, straightforward, and free from deception. (Paulding 1855: 101)

In this quote, Brother Jonathan becomes an acquaintance who seems strange at first but grows on the spectator over time, "harmonizing" to yield ever "new attractions." Jonathan's roughness inspires a libidinous desire to penetrate the body politic, "soften[ing]," "unfold[ing]," and "ripen[ing]" into a "deep design" in which the onlooker is entangled. Neither the "years of observation" nor the "intimate acquaintance" of a closer look yield certainty about him: "we are in doubt." This strategy appropriates the female form of classical allegory and renders the national body an object of sexual desire and deep understanding of the ever-evasive and shapeshifting figure. While Paulding hastens to ensure Jonathan's honesty and straightforwardness, the impression of performance, even shapeshifting, remains central to the national icon he portrays.

Saint Jonathan thus shows an essential moral and intrinsic ambiguity: Paulding is uncertain about his fitness as national saint and about his "true" character. Jonathan represents not so much a great man or deity as the very body for the entire nation. In the last part of the essay, his Gargantuan hunger and growth are projected onto the scale of national territory in a rhetoric of farming, landgrabbing, and annexation: Jonathan "grasp[s] Canada with one hand and Central America with the other, while he gazes with longing eyes upon Cuba" (105). Jonathan's imperial gesture is legitimized by "the great leading spirit" who will "stand without a rival, leading all and controlling all" (ibid.). Opposite this expansionism is an internal void for national literatures and arts. Jonathan has made "poetry subsidiary to commerce and education by giving the rudiments of science to young learners, in the form of epic poems, and advertising unpoetic commodities in smooth measures and harmonious rhyme" (103). Jonathan's capitalist interest has led him to even put poetry in the service of commerce, not least in the luring words of the Yankee peddler praising his wares (see Chapter 3).

Jonathan's ambiguous "peculiarities" are thus dissolved in a patriotic embrace of the national icon Saint Jonathan. Paulding concludes the article with a call to worship: "We sons of Columbia, descendants of the Pilgrims, the true votaries of Liberty, will invoke no Saint but St. Jonathan [. . .] [who] shall be the patron-saint of the universal Yankee nation—and the Fourth of July, St. Jonathan's Day" (106). Paulding's "Saint Jonathan" transcends the allegorical figure of the state; he has a character, and grows organically and technologically into new territories amidst a sense of national crisis. Whereas in "Brother Jonathan" (1853) Paulding ruled out the possibility of "divorce" in the national family, two years later in "Saint Jonathan" he acknowledges that the conflict over slavery threatens the health of the body politic. The "saint from the people, the saint of the people"[13] impersonates the fascination and ambiguities of the new nation, despite or even because of his weaknesses and calculation. In his closing formula, Paulding invokes the physical and ideological legacy of Americans as "sons of Columbia" and "descendants of the Pilgrims," asserting the superiority of the "universal Yankee nation." Paulding's allegorical texts reveal an increasing sense of political and representational crisis and a libidinous desire for civil religion; his stance develops from criticism to a call to union, from the federal government's club law in "Uncle Sam and his B'hoys" to the desperate invocation of "Saint Jonathan" at a time when the already grotesquely formed national body was under threat.

Brother Jonathan, Yankee Doodle and Uncle Sam were used in allegorical narratives to comment on the state of the nation, for criticism and patriotic messages alike. Variations talk back at England and claim that the "son" has long outdone the "father," while the old man has not yet acknowledged this. For the young nation, cultural maturity, expressed in an internationally admired national literature, is mandatory.

Non-professional writers commented on this lacuna by penning epic or mock epic poems featuring Jonathan as protagonist throughout the nineteenth century (see Pairpoint 1857; Paul 1860; Savary 1899); Colton's *The Americans, or An American in London* (1833) employs the transatlantic kinship narrative to discuss truthfulness in English travelogues. In the twentieth century, when the U.S. joined WWI, a propaganda comic book used Uncle Sam/Brother Jonathan to compare strengths and weaknesses among the nation states involved. These texts perform the cultural work of conjoining national historiography with national literature. The texts I discuss—*The Adventures of Uncle Sam, in Search after his Lost Honor* (Fidfaddy 1970 [1816]), *St. Jonathan: The Lay of a Scald* (Coxe 1838), and *The New Yankee Doodle* (Gay 1868)—sketch Jonathan as superhuman or magic figure by drawing on European literature as a framework for cultural authority.

The Adventures of Uncle Sam, in Search after his Lost Honor offers a different allegorical narrative with shifting notions of the central figure of Uncle Sam: he is at once an impersonation of government, the constituency of voters, and a rendition of public opinion who can be controlled by the members of government, that is, the chief steward (the President) and Uncle Sam's wife, Congress.[14] The author, writing with the pen name "Frederik Augustus Fidfaddy," is a self-described "Member of the Legion of Honor, Scratch-Etary to Uncle Sam and Privy Counselor to himself," thus an allegedly faithful mediator between the Uncle Sam figure and the reader. Next to his own prose account of the events of the war, the narrator also includes renditions of historical events presented in biblical verse form and antiquated language, which were written by his Uncle Zachary, a rabbi (see chapters 2 and 10). Next to this mixture of literary forms, the narrator uses Cervantes's mock epic *Don Quixote* as a paratext to plead the "New World's claim [. . .] to the honors of the resurgent age of chivalry" (Fidfaddy 1970: 6).

In *The New Yankee Doodle*, Jonathan is called "Old Jonathan," a figure who advises his friend "Old Abe"—that is, Lincoln—and who hovers with a quasi-divine presence over the events of the Civil War as told by the fictive author "Truman Trumbull, A.M.," a pen name selected by the teacher and journalist E. Jane Gay.[15] *The New Yankee Doodle* is subtitled "Being an Account of the Little Difficulty in the Family of Uncle Sam" and uses the persona of "Truman Trumbull" to refer to the painter of revolutionary motifs, John Trumbull, whose works became vehicles for national historiography and mythmaking. This telling name emphasizes the narrative's investment in patriotic historiography and the glory of the founding days. In the prologue, the narrator claims to give "a truthful impression of the Rebellion as it appeared to a loyal public," addressing a Northern readership.

The story tells the events of the Civil War as an allegorical narrative with the principal actors shown in their surroundings, including Old Abe, King Jeff, and such superhumans as the Devil and Old Jonathan. With this personnel, *The New Yankee Doodle* engages in historiographic mythmaking, interlinking the Civil War with the myths of the Revolutionary War. This link is procured by the title persona of Yankee Doodle, who permeates the text in two ways. First, its poetic form is modeled on the rhyme scheme and rhythm of the song "Yankee Doodle": the opening stanza tells how "King Jeff," the Southern politician, and later President of the Confederacy Jefferson Davis sat down to plot on "Yankee Doodle Dandy." In the second stanza, King Jeff sings the refrain: "Yankee Doodle, keep it up, Yankee Doodle Dandy; // We'll keep you snoozing, Mr Buck, // Yankee Doodle Dandy" (Gay 1868: 13). The second link to the Revolutionary War is furnished by "Old Jonathan," born in 1776 (16), an impersonation of the Yankee Doodle warrior who marched against the English to the sound of the song. In the text, he first appears after Old Abe writes to "Yankee Doodle," by implication Congress, asking for troops. This awakens Old Jonathan:

> [. . .] Sumter's guns have waked at last
> Old Yankee Doodle Dandy.
> For Jonathan has risen in haste
> His powder-horn to fill, sir;
> (it is the same his gran'sir used
> On famous Bunker Hill, sir).
> He calls his sons to leave the plough,
> The old sword buckles on, sir,
> And side by side with steady tramp
> They march to Washington, sir.
> [. . .] Sound the alarm! Ho! Minute men!
> To arms! the brave are falling;
> The land is cursed by treason's rule,
> The oppressed for aid are calling. (Gay 1868: 25)

Old Jonathan embodies the spirit of the American Revolution who returns in times of crisis. His "sons" are the minute men who now are called to the defense of "the oppressed." Old Jonathan mourns his "lost boys" and implores the President, Old Abe, to strike back (65). His interests are pro-Union, and Northern; he warns Old Abe about the "foe at home, right in the family" and about the interference of strangers: "Some foreigners who've come ashore // Among our honest folks // Make awful discord; John Bull roars // and Johnnie Crapaud croaks" (140). Gay's Old Jonathan also has a wife, Betsy Jane, and a homestead where he keeps his purse. Contrary to the earlier versions of Jonathan's wives, though, Betsy Jane is no nuisance; she cares for the wounded in the Washington hospital.

Jonathan is in control of his money; he "fumbled in his bureau" for the "Commissions" (98, 99).

Jonathan's relationship with Old Abe is described as friendship and counseling ("'Ask Jonathan,' said Abraham, // 'whate'er *he says is law*,'" 230) and the story presents their conversation in letters and meetings. The President is thus shown as a king selected by providence, inspired by the spirit of the Revolution. Lincoln's decision to sign "Order No. 1," the Emancipation Proclamation on September 22, 1862 is triggered by a letter in which Jonathan urges him to "stand steady at the helm" in stormy times: "Don't swerve a hair's breadth from your course" (149). Lincoln's death is his ultimate sacrifice for the union. Jonathan is now deprived of his friend and removed from his citizens. The poem concludes on a note of mourning and concern for the future.

Compared to Paulding's Jonathan texts from the 1850s, *St. Jonathan: The Lay of a Scald* (1838) develops a similarly tainted hero driven by money-worship. The *Lay*, however, shows no educational interest in improvement, but bemoans the state of cultural affairs embodied in a national Saint Jonathan who descends from continental European literatures. As such, the New World is afflicted by the same vices that have been around since antiquity. Published anonymously by New York Archbishop Arthur Cleveland Coxe, the *Lay* delivers an acerbic and self-reflexive commentary on the New York literary market and on literary fashions in the form of a mock epic poem, all despite the fact that epics are outdated and not to the scald's own taste, and that he feels his own claim to artistic achievement is "flimsy" (Coxe 1838: 4).[16] As he tells the reader early on, the epic sells, while poetry doesn't (53, 59). Coxe thus evokes Alexander Pope's posthumous popularity in New England, which eclipsed Pope's legacy in England (Giles 2001: 40). American writers perceived this popularity of Augustan style as a "form of bondage, a surrogate prison from which the native subject must liberate itself" (ibid.). In Coxe's mock poem, the patron Saint Jonathan is installed despite himself and functions as a metageneric and metaliterary commentary.

The text is divided into two cantos, consisting of eighty-eight and 142 stanzas of eight lines each, with an irregular rhyme scheme. The iambic pentameter is soon interrupted by enjambments and mid-line cesuras; likewise, the final couplet which forms an ending for the first stanzas is abandoned after the first pages. The epic poem's irregular form echoes the meandering of the plot. Like the form, the narrative progression of the mock epic is characterized by interruption and deviation, which cater to the impression of the narrator/poet's autocratic persona. In the closing statement, the narrator describes the *Lay* as a Scandinavian version of Homeric epic, asking the muse for inspiration to help in "installing" the hero patron Saint Jonathan (96). The narrator insists on being called a Nordic "scald" instead of a bard, or national poet: "Now *Scald*—and this I mention for reviewers—Meaneth a kind of minstrel, good Messieurs!" (96). The text speaks to its own creation and to its narrator's artistic ambition between artistry, social criticism, and simple misanthropy. His layering of tropes in a thicket of deviations and diatribes ultimately chisels out two entangled readings of the *Lay*: in the vein of the traditional mock epic, it contains both derisional satire and scathing social critique. Hence, the narrator's hint about the minstrel quoted above indicates that his poetic endeavor might well be a sham to avoid critical reviews ("I forbid all publications [. . .] to dish me up at all," 96). On a more serious note, he attacks the soulless habits and customs of the city, which drown out all poetic inspiration.

The narrator has a lot to say to the nation, impersonated in the national allegory of "my Uncle Samuel [. . .] my honored relative." Instead of dedicating his text to an allegorized "Posterity" (4, 6), the narrator reminds the reader various times that he has no interest in profit or literary fame ("I write for frolic, fun is my delight," 16; "The bard before ye // cares not for gold," 38). Instead, he expresses a regionalist and systemic critique of New York society. He addresses "Uncle Sam," the nation, as well as "my tender cousins, the public," as the "gente nova" (the "new people") of Dante's Florence. Citing from the *Divina Commedia*, he compares the place of his dwelling, New York, to Dante's enchanted city, "where men are cheated of long lives in weary slavery of lucre, where they die in the elusive dream that they have achieved the real good and awake to the dread reality too late to amend it" (6).[17] New Yorkers, and by implication Americans, are somnambulists caught in the illusion of capitalist promises, their creativity muted. At the beginning of the text, the narrator describes waking from a dream to being "with business men" (10), "animals" who stifle him: "My harp unstrung // hangs on the willows. When I leave the city, perchance I'll take it down, and play again; // But here I *write*—not *sing*. I live mid business men" (11). Unlike Dante, however, who is lost in Florence, as well as in the middle of his life at the beginning of the *Commedia*, the narrator of the *Lay* neither achieves literary fame (symbolized in Dante's prophet's robes) nor does he return to his life world in the end. Instead, he expresses several farewells to the reader and to the American shores; he will leave for England to have his work reviewed by the literary magazines there, since "the English are, in everything, our mothers" (97). The very final couplet reveals that the narrator intends to continue his resistance to aesthetic and creative paralysis: "Were my mood as meek, this soul of mine // were theirs who stifle song, and drown the dream divine" (98).

The narrator uses Dante as well as American and English poets as a template for his own work, evoking a transatlantic canon in which the American side has yet a lot to achieve: "we have no poets, sir!" (26); "this sweet harp hath for this blockhead age no glory more" (38; see also 23–4). Likewise, the narrator has an axe to grind with the New York literary critics and magazines (e.g. 18–19; "Straining for a great man, yet // ye leash the only great man ye have got!", 23). In U.S. literature, jewels are scarce; its luster results from a kaleidoscope of promise, "made by a few stain'd pebbles, and a gem" (27). The narrator's own literary proficiency is equally pedestrian; he frequently discusses his own deficiencies. For instance, he gets ahead of himself and commits to improvement: "My, here are fifty stanzas! How // did I do this? [. . .] I'm well aware that oft the public deaf is // to poems long. In short, then I intend // to sing awhile" (27–8). At the beginning of canto 2, he stalls the narrative with a long digression (53–9) about his "old ill—*ennui*!", which he also projects onto the reader: "and so, too // dieth your patience; and lest I should bore ye, // so dieth this already longlived proem," 59). Ultimately, he undermines his repeated disinterest in profit by admitting that he is addicted to applause as to delicatessen, such as "cream tarts from Guerelli" (36). His composition thus becomes a "dish" offered for consumption, a "*recherché plat*" that should not be too long, or "too far done" (60–1).[18]

The plot of *St. Jonathan: The Lay of a Scald* tells the allegorical story of St. Nick, the Dutch patron saint, and his wife Katrina, who send their layman St. Jonathan into exile to be the patron saint of the U.S. The origins of the American patron saint are shown amidst marital strife in the Dutch household, in a "farce of lowly life" (62). The wife literally cooks up a plan while talking to her husband over dinner; like Greek gods on Mount Olympus, they receive prayers as smoke messages. Katrina urges her husband to grasp the opportunity:

> Those Hudsonites are sending you petitions
> To be their saint; and blixen! Why they smoke
> Very like Christians! If they're good conditions
> I hope you'll take them, for our league is broke
> With Dutchmen here. I'm fond of foreign missions. (32)

St. Nick, typically slow to make decisions, smokes away the year considering and doubting, caught "'twixt doubts and fear" (32), while the Dutch in New Amsterdam prosper and believe in his patronage. In the meantime, the task has fallen, as the narrator proclaims, to St. Mammon (*"you'll find if you examine his // credentials that our saint, St. Mammon is!"*, 34). The workings of Mammon, of money, are visible in Wall Street, in the elections, and in the slave labor industry: "St. Mammon 'tis that gets the prayers rejected // of those who love not Mammon's love for slaves" (35). For his new function as national saint, St. Mammon is renamed by St. Nick. In the *Lay*, Brother Jonathan thus comes into a literary career as devil and fallen angel (cue to John Milton's *Paradise Lost*), where Mammon is a skilled devil interested in gains who walks hunched over as if he were looking for money on the ground ("So Mammon, Vulcan once, is St. Johnny now!", 80). Coxe's Mammon is an airborne shapeshifter who appears in the North and South of the U.S. (93–4); his transformation from Miltonesque devil to saintly national icon is only his most recent one. He sheds his title as saint and becomes "more republican! He [. . .] is but the Yankee, Brother Jonathan // True brother to John Bull" (93).

Coxe's *St. Jonathan: The Lay of a Scald* wraps the story of a money-ridden exiled patron saint oblivious to his subjects in a self-reflexive and metaliterary narrative about the United States. In an "age of blockheads," it seems that Americans get what they deserve with a money-grabbing national saint who sires their worst fault: "Slavery // Monster more curst than Polypheme, I ween; // Medusa's head, a Fury's heart" (92). Coxe intermingles national, sectional, and regional matters in New York City's urban setting with the politics of cultural mimicry. Coxe's narrator suffers from ennui not least because his environment is driven by money interests only. His position in a postcolonial North American setting is paradoxical: while he embraces the maternal influence of England, he is also saturated, even overstuffed, with European aesthetic forms and contents. While his *Lay* appears as a pastiche of literary forms and citations at first gaze, its narrative representation delivers a much more uniform, if dire, message about writing in the U.S. Coxe's colonial ennui spells out the frustration of the family narrative, an incestuous circle of relations and repetitions. It drains all creativity and leaves only masquerade and minstrelsy. Coxe attributes Jonathan's ambiguity to his kinship, claiming that cultural maturity cannot be reached when European literature haunts the American cultural imaginary.

Allegorical texts employ Brother Jonathan to work through internal crises such as elitist urban ennui, the War of 1812 or the Civil War, and the absence of literary greatness in American literature, but he also serves as a punching ball in the transatlantic scandal of the Great Exhibition at London's Crystal Palace in 1851. *Brother Jonathan's Epistle* (N.N. 1852a), a pamphlet in the form of a mock poem published anonymously in 1852, articulates an American response to the unfriendly reception of the U.S. contribution at Crystal Palace. The event of the Great Exhibition prompted not only allegorical narratives but also cartoons, transitioning Brother Jonathan from narrative into visual culture, where his success and dissemination may have been even greater. In the following, I use the Great Exhibition as a point of departure for looking more closely at the visual renditions of Brother Jonathan and Uncle Sam in magazines.

The scandal of the Great Exhibition prompted the author of *Brother Jonathan's Epistle* to respond to the British ridicule of the Americans. His intention is paraphrased in its full title: "Brother Jonathan's Epistle to his relations, but chiefly to his father, John Bull, Brother Jonathan being a little riled by the remarks made by John Bull at his small wares displayed at the opening of the grand exhibition."

The cause for this "rilement" was such: since the U.S. contribution to the "grand exhibition of the works of industry of all nations" was perceived as minuscule in quality and quantity, it became a laughing stock in the British press (see Cunliffe 1951). The 600 exhibits only filled parts of the allotted exhibition space. Next to somewhat absurd pieces such as a stuffed Ohio squirrel or a Boston gossamer wig, it included such products as McCormick's Virginia grain reaper, a set of daguerreotypes by Mathew Brady, India rubber goods by Charles Goodyear, and revolver guns by Samuel Colt. *Punch* magazine dubbed the Americans "Non-Exhibitors" who left the biggest and most impressive American inventions at home and to the audience's imagination (qtd. in Cunliffe 1951: 119). Among those imaginary goods was also, according to *Punch*, "the tremendous Wooden Style that separates the American from the English fields of Literature" (*Punch* 20, 1851: 20; qtd. in Cunliffe 1951: 122). However, some inventions that seemed ridiculous at the exhibition were later applauded. Again, it was *Punch* magazine that published a reconciliatory version of "Yankee Doodle," acknowledging, in the typically colloquial tone of the song, that Yankee Doodle "licked" all his critics:

> Yankee Doodle sent to town
> His goods for exhibition;
> Everybody beat him down,
> And laughed at his position—
> They thought him all the world behind;
> A gooney, muff, or noodle,
> Laugh on, good people—never mind—
> Says quiet Yankee Doodle.
> [. . .]
> You must now be viewed all
> As having been completely licked
> By glorious Yankee Doodle
> (*Punch* 21, 1851: 17; qtd. in Cunliffe 1951: 125)

Cunliffe observes that the American performance at the exhibition boosted British feelings of superiority, which also led the British press to "temper their observations" of the U.S. (ibid. 126). While for the British, the American presence affirmed the necessity of free trade, the American side felt restored after a bad start. Horace Greeley, the American emissary to the exhibition, maintained that Americans might do better to observe than participate in the exhibition to plan for future contributions (ibid.).

Brother Jonathan's Epistle, the anonymous author's response to the British scolding of the American performance at the Great Exhibition, is a mock poem of 111 stanzas in six verses. The stanzas are divided into two sections; the fourth verse forms a cesura that introduces a new sound rhyming with the last line of the stanza. The rhyme pattern (aaabab) and meter invites a pause after the fourth verse, which is frequently marked by a semicolon and, in terms of the content, by a new or summarizing thought that brings the contents of the stanza to a point. With this composition, the text reads not so much as an epistle, but rather like a scolding of its addressee, the allegorical John Bull. The stanzas allow for exclamations with the shortened lines 4 and 6 and a turnover in the final verse couplet, typically illustrated with stanza 4:

> John Bull, you laugh, in proud emotion
> At our small wares sent o'er the ocean—
> From all our famous clockwork motion:
> So small a sight;
> But to my own plain Yankee notion
> We're in the right.
> (N.N. 1852a: 4; all subsequent references to this edition)

The reception of the American "small wares" is but a trifle of the country's invention (such as the clockworks cited here), but, the narrator holds, from his own Yankee perspective, "we're in the right." The author uses several strategies for speaking and conjuring up the American voice. The poem first addresses a "you" John Bull, in stanza 4, against whose laughter he posits "my own plain Yankee notion [in which] we're in the right." The narrator thus calls himself a representative of collective Yankeedom that talks back at its father John Bull. The Yankee addresses John Bull (as England) throughout the poem, adapting a communal "we" for the U.S. when talking about the "Yankee passion" of American volunteers (25) or asserting, in typical New England diction, that "we've beat you at all that *pays*" or "at all we tried" (6, 7).

The title character only resurfaces at the very end of the poem, in a reminder that John Bull might "need to call for Jonathan [since] he's your son" (24). Here, Jonathan is also called "Young Nutmegs" after the legendary wooden nutmegs sold by the tricky Yankee peddler (see Chapter 4). While the American "we" intersects with the narrator's "I" throughout the poem, the opening (stanzas 6–9) also shows the "Yankee" as an active figure in a transatlantic business relation, in which the Yankee has the last laugh because he is younger:

> To Yankee, when he makes his book,
> The profit has a queersome look;
> Just cipher out by hook or crook
> What Yankee gains,
> By meeting you in yonder nook,
> Beneath the panes.
>
> A lesson to the odd conceit
> That thinks his nation can't be beat
> I'll grant, by gazing at the neat
> Array of things,
> With which, at present to compete,
> Would strain his wings.
>
> [. . .] He'll take a peep at every tray,
> And startle you some future day,
> When your old head is flecked with gray,
> And he but hearty,
> For then, John Bull, the debt to pay—
> He'll give a party. (4–5)

The narrator here abandons the "we" to look at "Yankee's" profit from the exhibition stand ("yonder nook beneath the panes"). The narrator concedes that Yankee's arrogance ("thinks his nation can't be beat") is rightly stumped by the competition, yet his present inferiority will vanish when he learns to outperform his father ("when your old head is [. . .] gray // and he but hearty"). In this section, the narrator spells out the metaphorical family kinship between England and the U.S. to argue that John Bull's position in the world will be replaced by his offshore son Brother Jonathan or Yankee. The plural "we" is exchanged for a singular "Yankee/he," a body for the nation who matures into empire.

Brother Jonathan's Epistle illustrates the transatlantic relationship through various paradigms of a national body that share a narrative of growth. The repertoire ranges from the singular son to the unified body of Yankee fighters who compose a growing tree. They descend from the "thorny shoot" of the Puritans that was expelled from Britain and took "root" at Plymouth Rock and brought forth "stock" (3); later, the young American nation is called a "tree" with "Yankee fruit" (9). With this line of biological descent on foreign shores, the narrator also reiterates the settler colonial narrative and wields an anti-royal statement. Opposite the tree of liberty that grows Yankee minutemen, he employs the cultivation of the land ploughed by the noble farmer and ruler of the land:

> The only line that ought to reign
> The farmer boy that ploughs the plain
> As noble as the thickened strain of Adam's clay
> That dwindles through a monarch's vein
> Its life away. (10)

Compared to the spoiled princes of England, the Yankee boys are of different stock; they sneer at effeminacy and "grind their points and make a show"; likewise American rulers distinguish themselves not by royalty (they are of the "common" mass, 13) but by their use of the blade (11), which ennobles them. In turn, the narrator reminds the English of their inability to feed their own people and of the Irish Famine. In an unfavorable installment of John Bull's body, the narrator warns Bull against infringing on American interests: Bull should not "stretch your arm across the bay," "stay[ing] your busy fingers," and take "your gouty foot" from American territory (9). Most importantly, Bull should not make war in his own family and "stain with kindred gore" the American hearth stone (14). In the ending, John Bull is shown as an old drunk who cocks his "old red nose" and drinks his beer (24), all images which juxtapose Bull's aging and decay with the Yankee's youth and future-steering growth.

Apart from warning John Bull to honor his kinship with the U.S. and not to laugh at his young offspring, the poem makes a self-critical argument about American faults and the need for an American literature. The narrator acknowledges that the U.S. is indebted and shaken by sectionalism, as well as by slavery, a "trouble" inherited from the British (that "your laws begun and ours must end," 13). In stanza 65, he admits that the U.S. cannot boast "a single bard [. . .] [who] knows how to write" (16) and goes on to list fifteen American authors of literary acclaim. This trick echoes his argument about the American performance at the Great Exhibition: despite the absence of one single national poet who would speak "brave and true // For God and Freedom" (16), it becomes clear from the mere number of authors included in the poem that the U.S. is at the threshold of growing into a national culture.[19] But even for this concern, the narrator has an excuse: Yankees are too busy and have no money to spare to raise a poet: "our native land affords // no famous line of haughty lords, // to foster Art with golden hoards" (23; see also 21).

Brother Jonathan's Epistle thus articulates a rather simple message in a poem layered with allegories that all raise an American voice. It uses the Yankee to assert national business sense and the confidence of future growth. To discuss (or rather apologize for) American faults, it puts forward a more complicated argument which is drowned out, in the ending, by a call to a patriotic huzza of "three mighty cheers" that shake the ocean's ground and proclaim the American independence from England.

The Crystal Palace Exhibition of 1851 inspired national spite and self-defense. The printmakers Currier and Ives also defended the American contribution to the exhibition in a graphic satire that shows Brother Jonathan as a taller figure in a white coat explaining American achievements to a bored and stout John Bull (Fig. 1.1). Jonathan points to the American yacht, saying "Mister Bull you can now see the 'American department' of 'the exhibition'" while in the background, English gentlemen cannot contain their admiration for the grain reaper. The subtitles to the image are set to the rhyme of Yankee Doodle.

The Yankee thus resurfaces in Currier and Ives's depiction of the 1876 Centennial Exhibition, the first in the U.S., held in Philadelphia at the centennial of the American Declaration of Independence. Designed to demonstrate America's development, the dimensions of the exposition building (at the time the largest structure in the world) told the story of the U.S.'s growth since the embarrassment of the Crystal Palace Exhibition of 1851. Currier and Ives chose a more gigantic allegorical figure (Fig. 1.2).[20]

Figure 1.1 "The Great Exhibition of 1851. American Department." Lithograph, Currier and Ives, 1851. Library of Congress, Prints and Photographs Division. Popular Graphic Arts Collection.

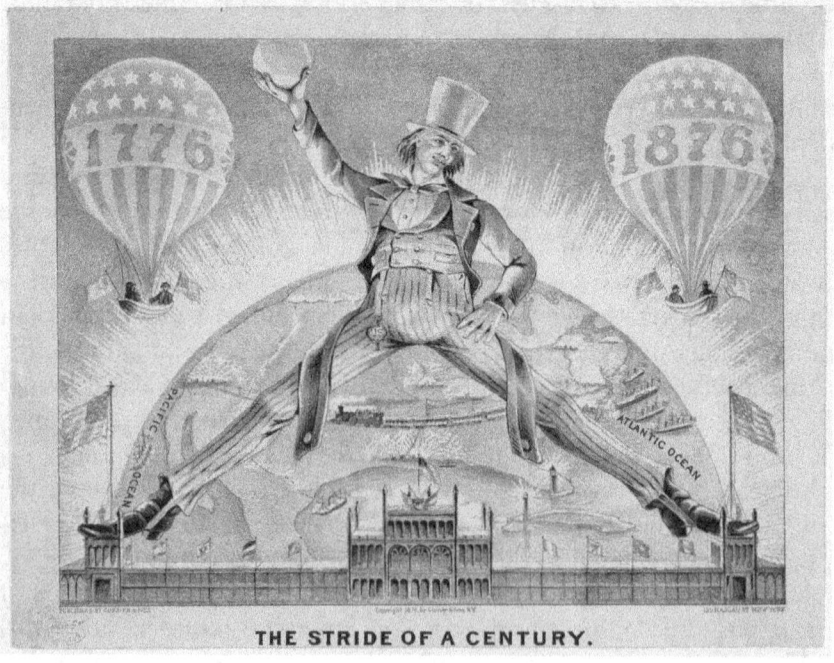

Figure 1.2 "The Stride of a Century." Lithograph, Currier and Ives, 1876. Library of Congress, Prints and Photographs Division. Popular Graphic Arts Collection.

In "The Stride of a Century," the exposition building serves as a pedestal for a Brother Jonathan whose long legs span space and time: positioned before a half-globe that shows North America, he reaches from the American East Coast to the West Coast; the two hot air balloons at his sides indicate that the national territory has grown between 1776 and its centennial. Brother Jonathan is clad in typical Uncle Sam garb (striped pants, top hat, U.S. waistband) and shown as a Yankee with extremely long legs, slightly protruding belly, and youthful face. He is thus inscribed into the visual tradition of Jonathan figures from magazines and from theatric descriptions, as slightly awkward, but lank and sprightly, with a feisty look on his face.

Currier and Ives's Brother Jonathan cites the image of the Greek Colossus of Rhodes, one of the lost Seven Wonders of the World from antiquity. The Colossus greeted arriving ships and commemorated the Rhodesian victory over Cyprus in the third century BC, thus proclaiming maritime power. Unlike Jonathan in the lithograph, the original Colossus did not straddle the harbor entry of Rhodes; this straddling posture was an invention of medieval commentators based on the statue's dedication which mentioned a "dominion over sea and land"; thus Currier and Ives reproduce a figment which nevertheless expresses territorial dominance over North America. Maritime and imperial powers are foreshadowed in the steamships and beacons illuminating the sphere of American influence.

In a larger framework, this Brother Jonathan also cites the classical depiction of allegory. Like allegories of Fortune in classical imagery, this image contains a sphere or ball that symbolizes the slipperiness of luck. Yet while in classical painting female figures balance on this slippery sphere or play with it, signifying the fleetiness of fortune and power, Brother Jonathan is holding it up in a gesture that looks effortless. Fortune is safely in his hand and shines a light in the U.S., while he even looks the other way. His territorial influence is depicted not only in the continental outreach of his legs, but also by two beacons of American imperial influence that are burning bright at the tip of the Florida panhandle and on Cuba. The other nations present at the Philadelphia exhibition, symbolized by the flags on top of the exhibition building, are dwarfed by the two gigantic American flags left and right, as well as by the technological inventions, the railroad that crosses the North American continent, and the steamboat circumventing it. The map also shows a slightly enlarged Erie Canal situated underneath Brother Jonathan's left arm. The celebrations of American independence, symbolized as the light of civilization, are shown as fireworks in the South, the Midwest, and in California, connoting urban growth and industrial prosperity throughout the land. Along the Canadian border, they make a sparkling line that could also be a shiny barbed wire. The world is enlightened by the U.S.; a glowing halo across the northern hemisphere frames Brother Jonathan's head and shoulders, giving him an iconic saint-like look that recalls the allegorical texts cited above. In this image, Currier and Ives capture the centennial history of the United States as one of territorial expansion and growth. Brother Jonathan is still young, even beardless, and his long legs imply not only the titular stride of a century but also the territorial expansions beyond North American shores that foreshadow the rise of the American empire.

In the contest of nations played out at the Great Exhibitions of the nineteenth century, the U.S. was a newcomer. The allegory of Brother Jonathan, or the song *Yankee Doodle*, became a vehicle for telling the story of transatlantic kinship and national growth through space and time. By 1895, the American satire magazine *Puck* (yet another English spinoff, copying the magazine *Punch*) visualizes the transatlantic comparison as an encounter between John Bull and Uncle Sam in the cartoon "Mutual Sympathy" (Plate 2). Both are plagued by their state forms, monarchy and representative democracy. The latter are shown as also male, dressed in royal and nineteenth-century business garb, and weighing down their sweaty characters, with the burden of documents that enable the senate and the king to obstruct legislation. Framed by the two parliament buildings in the background, John Bull and Uncle Sam sympathize with each other's heavy plight, bemoaning the difficulties of governance that the Senate and the Crown subject them to. The two signs by the roadside indicate that there is no change in sight: the British sign says "Commons come, Commons go, but the Lords go on forever," whereas the American one reads "Notice: the 53rd Congress goes but the Senate still remains." The cartoon argues that the institutions of government, self-assured and in control of their constituency, hinder the nation's agency in both countries. The national allegories John Bull and Uncle Sam impersonate the citizenry. Both are in a poor state, worn out and unkempt. The cartoon shows transatlantic allegiance between the peoples (i.e. the constituency of both states) of the U.S. and Great Britain, while their governments ogle each other with an expression of contempt. The bodies of government look different at first view, but the signs on the road to the parliament buildings indicate that their shortcomings are the same. This image/text relation is completed by the handshake that creates a link across the middle of the page, across the Atlantic, and across political bodies. This link, the cartoon argues, does not only exist in the present moment, but will prevail in the future. "Mutual Sympathy" therefore also interlinks national spaces, peoples, and political bodies over time. The cartoon dismisses the myths of the American Revolution by showing two peoples united in suffering.

The National Body as Image and Text: Thomas Nast's Uncle Sam and Humor Magazines

How does Brother Jonathan connect to the more widely known figure Uncle Sam? *Puck*'s "Mutual Sympathy" shows an Uncle Sam as impersonation of the American people, illustrating the transition from the younger Brother Jonathan to the mature Uncle Sam's national manhood; the youngster Jonathan shown in "The Stride of a Century" coexists with the bearded and white-haired Uncle Sam of the 1895 cartoon in *Puck*. Over the course of the nineteenth century, the original allegorical narrative of transatlantic kinship fosters two national characters: the visual icon of Uncle Sam and the textual body of the Yankee in humor magazines. Unlike John Bull's social ascent to complacent country squire, though, Uncle Sam remains a classless figure and performer located outside the social echelons of American society. He maintains his ambiguity and streetsmart obliqueness and literally stays "in character."

Today, Uncle Sam is the most widely known embodiment of the U.S., due to James Montgomery Flagg's 1917 "I Want You for U.S. Army" recruitment poster (Plate 3), which has been replicated and altered in many ways since. It shows Uncle Sam as a hybrid between a masculine *patria* and government, pointing at the viewer with a determined look and calling the citizens to come to the nation's defense.

The creation of Uncle Sam, the bearded, white-haired man, evolves in cartoons alongside the image of Brother Jonathan. As Alton Ketchum (1959: 81) has shown, Uncle Sam's first appearance with whiskers originates in the British *Punch* in 1856; another influence were the cartoons of Abraham Lincoln, with long face and slightly haggard features, wearing striped pants and a star-spangled vest under his coat, in English magazines.

The origins of the Uncle Sam figure remain unclear, but Albert Matthews (1908) proposes three different sources: first, Thomas Chandler Haliburton's literary figure Sam Slick the peddler, who enters the American cultural imaginary in the 1830s (see Chapter 4); second, "U.S." as abbreviation for United States as well as "Uncle

Sam," with reference to nicknaming politicians at the time; and third, the historical army contractor and slaughterhouse owner Sam Wilson of Troy, NY, who supplied the American troops with beef during the War of 1812. Wilson was known as "Uncle Sam," as various newspapers and other sources suggest. Matthews contends that, while the veracity of these sources cannot be ascertained, they are "extremely probable and [. . .] plausible" (59).

In the postbellum era, Uncle Sam was popularized by German American cartoonists Thomas Nast and Joseph Keppler, who commented on transatlantic and national politics. The cartoon as hybrid between art form and political commentary carried a visual appeal that granted its commercial success far and wide, since it allowed for visual reading. As a quick response to events, caricatures are less invested in historical or factual accuracy than in using already familiar designs in a new context to gain readability. In the eighteenth and nineteenth centuries, they influenced the opinion of a public "removed from the scene of political action" (Hunt 2003: 19). The cartoon draws on other, literary, genres and reproduces the Western cultural archive, an "artistic hybrid, combining acidic and witty commentary on a range of political and social issues with an eclectic, multireferential form of pictorial and textual dialogue" (Mark Hallet qtd. in Hunt 2003: 3).[21]

In the 1870s, Thomas Nast used Uncle Sam extensively. A German émigré, Nast became a political figure thanks to his Civil War drawings for the Union army for *Harper's Weekly*. Lincoln called him his "best recruiting agent" (qtd. in Vinson 1957: 339), no small feat for the German immigrant who never became fully fluent in English. Later, Nast's conflict with the corrupt New York Tammany Ring earned him more political fame. Nast is credited with popularizing the party signs of the Republican elephant and Democratic donkey and the figure of Santa Claus. Nast's work spells out the transatlantic formation of U.S. visual culture: he imported a classical European and a German pictorial archive to the U.S. His drawings quoted European folk tales and transformed human figures into other shapes, such as animals from Aesop's fables, steam trains, or money bags, as in the famous case of Boss Tweed. Like medieval emblems, Nast's cartoons combined drawings with texts, titles or slogans; often he included policy names to help his readers decode the message of his cartoons.

Nast's drawings required visual expertise in folk symbols and contemporary political issues. His cartoons sometimes served as embellishment to written text; mostly, however, they stood by themselves as pieces of pictorial journalism, often on the magazine's title page. In

John Bull and Brother Jonathan 61

the 1870s, Nast took on Uncle Sam, a bearded man in striped pants, with long legs and top hat, and a haggard face that made the figure recognizable in all his cartoons. Nast's Uncle Sam is a policymaker, an embodiment of government, as well as an allegorical body for the nation in the international context. He is frequently disgruntled, as in "The Lightning Speed of Honesty" (1877; Fig. 1.3).

Figure 1.3 Thomas Nast, "The Lightning Speed of Honesty." *Harper's Weekly*, November 24, 1877, p. 924. Courtesy of Thomas Nast Verein Landau.

Nast's Uncle Sam shows how American government is slowed down by his "ride," a snail that symbolizes the 45th Congress. Sam carries the Army and Navy payrolls in his hands and the Resumption Act in his back pockets; with these burdens, the cartoon argues, no quick progress in military politics can be made. The Resumption Act of January 1875 returned the U.S. economy to the gold standard and stalled military spending and expansionist politics. Nast blends the Uncle Sam allegory with animal symbolism; the gigantic snail, Congress, has one single defining feature: its slowness. It matches Uncle Sam in size, and there is no alternative to this vehicle for getting ahead. The references to speed in the image (the spurs) and the title ("lightning speed") reiterate Brother Jonathan's most important character trait: hastiness. The cartoon's humor results from the ironic inversion between image and text, the snail's slowness and the Yankee's lightning speed. At the same time, the contrast between speed and "honesty" comments on the history of Uncle Sam/Brother Jonathan in the U.S. If honesty slows Uncle Sam down so much in the present, how did he manage to grow so fast in the past? Only with dishonesty, it seems.

Nast's Uncle Sam cartoons in *Harper's Weekly* intervene in national and local New York politics. In a conflict with the new editor about the political criticism of President Grant in the 1870s, Nast even included himself in two cartoons, as impersonation of the power of the media and of public opinion, opposite an Uncle Sam figure.[22] For his Uncle Sam, Nast used the same face, probably of a person he knew, with a wide range of facial expressions. In keeping with the literary and pictorial representations, Nast's Uncle Sam was no classical allegorical figure with stoic expression, but became relatable as a person. For the wide readership of *Harper's Weekly*, Uncle Sam became an acquaintance whose adventures and turmoils they could follow on a regular basis. Nast installs his Uncle Sam figures in surroundings that concretize abstract concepts such as trade, national historiography, as built architecture.

When addressing transatlantic conflict, Nast turns to Brother Jonathan in a cartoon about the stinted British intervention in the Alabama economy (Fig. 1.4), showing John Bull and Brother Jonathan as businessmen leaving Bull's office, turned towards opposite directions. The two allegorical bodies are recognizable by their appearance (John Bull bulky and bloated, Brother Jonathan lank) and by their vests, embellished with the English lion and

Figure 1.4 Thomas Nast, "Error Wounded Writhes in Pain." *Harper's Weekly*, June 5, 1869, p. 361. Courtesy of Thomas Nast Verein Landau.

the stars of the American flag, respectively. Both look distressed, with clenched fists but restraining themselves. Jonathan's back is turned to Bull, but he looks over his shoulder as if ready to react to a blow, his left hand balled to a fist. Bull's feet show the reason for the conflict. He rests on a walking stick, his right leg in a cast inscribed "national debt," his good foot inscribed with "corn." Bull's office sign shows the U.K.'s privateering enterprise, "built and furnished at shortest notice," implying hasty and questionable business. To illustrate the impending physical ruse, Nast employs the double meaning of "corn": John Bull asks, "Did you mean to step on my corns?" Jonathan replies: "Yes Sir—and if you don't pay me what you ought I will grind your corns for you, and swell that other foot bigger yet!" Brother Jonathan responds to Bull's intervention by stepping on his opponent's feet and threatening to cripple him. Adapting Arbuthnot's cudgel play, Nast shows the transatlantic protectionism as a brawl, sketching minor trade conflicts and war as different phases in a continuum of manly contest among national bodies.

Nast's most striking usage of the Uncle Sam character for commenting on the state of the nation is "The Two Georges" (Fig. 1.5), published on April 6, 1878. Nast's America has become a "Union of Debts": a rascally Uncle Sam overlooked by his disappointed ancestors, the English King George and George Washington, is slouching on his chair next to a column of many parts bound by the U.S. motto "E Pluribus Unum," which is here linked by a tape of debt. Uncle Sam rocks his chair back, smoking with a smug smile on his face, his right leg caught in a bear trap and resting on another column, his left leg sustaining his laid-back posture. He enjoys his cigar and shows no sign of pain or remorse. His upward-turned face looks beyond the title characters of the cartoon, the two Georges in an oil painting who look down at him from the past.

The monarch, who looks a little bullish opposite an ennobled Washington, addresses the latter: "I say, George—Daddy—is that the free and enlightened Cherub for whom you fought? Don't you think you had better write another Farewell Address to him?" Nast links the revolutionary history of the U.S. to the adolescence narrative; both "fathers" are disappointed with their offspring's development. The English king has the last laugh, since despite Washington's good hopes, the ex-colony is unfit for self-governance. Washington consequently assumes a bent posture, with downcast looks and disappointed expression.

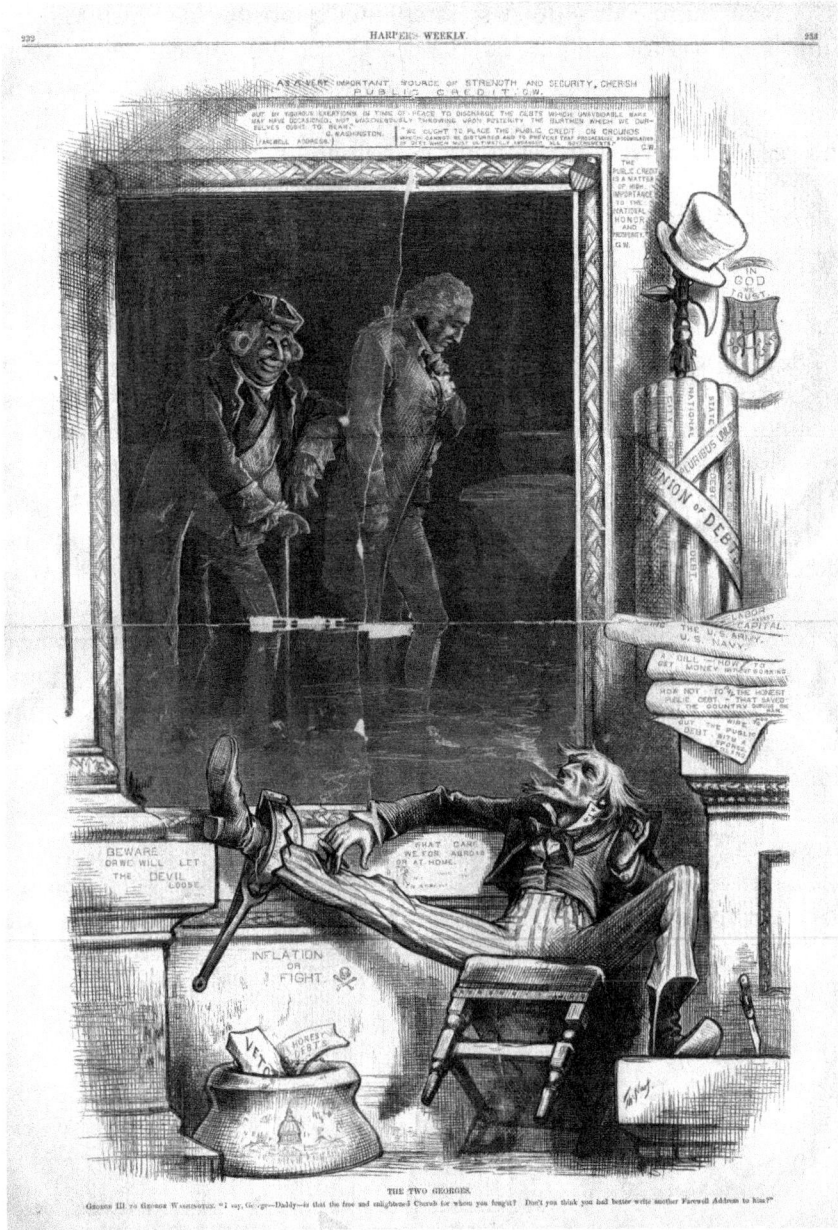

Figure 1.5 Thomas Nast, "The Two Georges." *Harper's Weekly*, April 6, 1878, p. 235. Courtesy of Thomas Nast Verein Landau.

Uncle Sam, who impersonates the opposite of Washington's angelic hopes for the U.S. as "Cherub," remains unscathed by such criticism. The cartoon's composition meditates on history's imaging with the nation's founding on the wall, in a painting that Sam has no regard for. The setting could be a government building, a classical architecture adorned with oil paintings of the founding fathers among pedestals, into which the crude insignia of U.S. power are thrown (note the debt column with the hatchet on top as holder of Sam's top hat, and the plaque proclaiming "In God We Trust" ornamented with the dollar sign). Sam governs from here, surrounded by folded paper bills and a Congressional dustbin for vetoes. From top to bottom, the wall is covered by graffiti, pinpointing both the words symbolically engraved into the governmental edifice, and the defilement of the noble institution by scoundrels. Around the oil painting are quotations from Washington signed "G. W." that link the American's credit to credibility, for instance on the top right: "The public credit is a matter of high importance to the national honor and prosperity." Below, and closer to Sam, the graffiti changes in tone and measure. "Beware or we will let the devil loose" and "Inflation or Fight" next to a skull and crossbones abandon Washington's moral guidance and threaten the Union as well as the government. Sam's posture of comfortable arrangement among these threats shows he has long broken with Washington's tenets; his whittling knife stuck to the right reveals that he is an idling storyteller, whittling politics down to nothing.

Next to this criticism of economic policies, Nast also shows Uncle Sam as home body in a domestic setting with Liberty or Columbia. The female allegory conjures nationalist sentiments of patriotism and pride, specifically in Nast's many cartoons about the Civil War or in the mourning portrait after Lincoln's death. Uncle Sam appears in the transatlantic family narrative as well, as the benevolent paterfamilias of the American family, protector of his children and his wife, Columbia. In "Let the Good Work (House Cleaning) Go On" (Fig. 1.6), a cheerful Uncle Sam and a dismayed Miss Columbia clean out New York City politics with the help of reform soap. Columbia has to rub out the stains of the ring judges on the bench in front of her; in the background is the washboard inscribed "Board of Health," and next to the broom used on November 7, the open door shows the swept-out debris of Tammany Hall, including a portrait of Boss Tweed. "Romish Ingratitude" (Fig. 1.7) shows Uncle Sam about to chop off the head of a snake symbolizing the Catholic Church. The snake has entered

Figure 1.6 Thomas Nast, "Let the Good Work (House Cleaning) Go On." *Harper's Weekly*, December 16, 1871, p. 1172. Courtesy of Thomas Nast Verein Landau.

Figure 1.7 Thomas Nast, "Romish Ingratitude." *Harper's Weekly*, July 13, 1872, p. 557. Courtesy of Thomas Nast Verein Landau.

the house and is coiled up before the family hearth, with the fire of (Protestant) enlightenment burning. As Sam lifts the axe which is inscribed "order," we see Columbia in the background, shielding her children from the bloodshed and the possible attack by the Roman snake.

Uncle Sam and Brother Jonathan coexist throughout the nineteenth century; with Nast's postbellum reinvention of Uncle Sam for *Harper's Magazine*, Uncle Sam becomes the predominant impersonation of the U.S. government. The transition of the family bond from Brother Jonathan, the prodigal son, to Uncle Sam as every American's kinsman marks the passing of dependencies from the transatlantic into the national arena. Compared to the father figure, the nepotic filiation with "Uncle" Sam provides a little more freedom, while making space for some good-willed mockery, as I will argue in Chapter 3.

Like Brother Jonathan, Uncle Sam in story and image is first and foremost an agent and performer, whose actions are driven by questionable morals. The novel *Uncle Sam at Home* (Brydges 1888) similarly interlinks an allegorical narrative of Uncle Sam's homestead with boys (i.e. "grandsons of Englishmen in the U.S.," 34) and daughters, such as the Boston girl who excels European maids. The narrative alternates between braggadocio and a matter-of-fact correction of this tone, which still affirms American exceptionalism, such as when talking about the U.S.'s (phallic) size: "Bulk is the measure of superiority; and as Uncle Sam has the biggest things in creation, he has no superior" (8); "Exaggeration aside, the American continent is not only a marvel of immensity but of wealth and beauty" (11).

The best case in point to illustrate the double-edge function of nationalist showboating may be the brief "Portrait of Uncle Sam" (N.N. 1852b) published in the *German Reformed Messenger*. The text quotes the "pen and ink sketch" from "a writer in the Southern Literary Gazette"; the hybrid version of Uncle Sam sketched out in the *Messenger* therefore prevails across sectional boundaries, and is deemed interesting enough to be reproduced for German immigrants. "Portrait of Uncle Sam" mingles the roles of national saint, national character, and frontier screamer who brags he can "out-run, out-jump and whip any man on the hill." It opens with a description of Uncle Sam's physique and youthful looks despite his age ("tall, boney, healthy looking man, apparently of 45 years, though born in 1776"). Uncle Sam owns a farm and hosts his allies, in this case the gray-headed fighters of the Revolution. Like Brother Jonathan, he has considerable but excusable character flaws: he "makes himself ridiculous" with braggadocio; he acts compulsively, shouldering his cane and acting out "maneuvers," and, like John Bull, he will "cudgel his best friend." All these weaknesses are "excusable," however, because of his inclination to peace and "generous virtues." The references to painting and sketching in the "Portrait" relate Uncle Sam's image and story and highlight the importance of the reader's gaze upon the figure: the "Portrait" requires a viewer, and it caters to the desire of the American public to view itself as a unified body despite this particular character's odds.

Uncle Sam's success may be attributed to two interrelated reasons: first, his mass dissemination in weekly magazines; and second, his embodiment of a mature image of the nation which brought the narrative of the prodigal son to a conclusion and gestured at futurity. Despite his beard and white hair, Uncle Sam is no old geezer running out of power, like the Knickerbockers' John Bull. "[A]pparently of 45 years" (N.N. 1852), he displays Yankee endurance and virility. His prowess is ingrained in his male potency, and his policies are driven by an expansionist male desire for an effeminate object, as in W. A. Rogers's 1900 cartoon about the Panama Canal, "No Other Arm Around this Waist," that served as *Harper's Weekly*'s cover illustration in the December 29 issue (Fig. 1.8).

"No Other Arm Around this Waist" depicts U.S. expansionist politics as Uncle Sam's firm grip around the middle of a female figure whose lower body is shaped as South America and whose hair and scarf represent Canada and Alaska. She is pulled over by Uncle Sam, her arm thrown up and her leg tipping underneath her skirt as if he would carry her off screen to have his way with her. The two upper bodies are fused as the territory Uncle Sam already has under firm control. The woman's body and features are portrayed in a blurry, hatched style, her face half turned towards the viewer with a disconnected look. Uncle Sam is drawn with more detail, as a more realistic figure, with no visible pen-strokes. His face shows a contented grin as he sweeps the rest of America off her feet. The different styles of drawing employed for the two figures oppose a fully articulated and powerful male U.S. allegory with a yet undefined, unincorporated female land mass North and South: Canada looks cloudy, consisting of female hair or a veil; South America, the woman's skirt and site of her reproductive organs, is recognizable only by its shape. Neither North nor South shows a recognizable feature of national character; the woman is cast exclusively as Uncle Sam's prey. Her neutral face directs the viewer's attention away from her and towards Sam's lecherous smirk, casting U.S. imperialism as ravaging greed that meets no resistance.

Figure 1.8 W. A. Rogers, "No Other Arm Around this Waist." Pen and ink drawing, publ. 1900. Library of Congress, Prints and Photographs Division.

With this projection of an ideal, if belligerent and lecherous, masculinity, Uncle Sam follows the same lines of development as John Bull in English national iconography, but he has no upward social mobility. Instead, his social standing and acceptability remain ambiguous, as paterfamilias/tyrant of an American Union, as head of government embroiled in sectional conflict, and as matured imperialist who "goes ahead" at the expense of other nation states' and people's rights.

Like the postbellum icon of Uncle Sam, the Brother Jonathan allegory remains a deliberately vernacular version of American humor, fun, and subversion, specifically in the 1840s when U.S. print culture experienced a brief carnivalesque and experimental stage, which included a new and short-lived format: the mammoth newspaper. The megalomaniac dimensions of these papers played out not only in their size but also in their intent to include, like the mammoth newspaper *Brother Jonathan*, "all the literary world of the New World." A literary magazine, *Brother Jonathan* was subtitled "A Weekly Compend of Belles Lettres and the Fine Arts, Standard Literature and General Intelligence." The advertisement for the 1843 subscription claims nothing less than the superlative of primacy and quality in print production: "The Publishers of this Mammoth Weekly Newspaper can now with pride [. . .] [claim] that the Brother Jonathan must stand FIRST BEST of the literary productions of the day" (N.N. 1843). The folio editions of *Brother Jonathan* appeared in six square feet size; special numbers for Christmas or Independence Day came as "double double sheet," "quadruple sheet," "mammoth quarto," or even "leviathan." No wonder that the mammoth newspapers soon "collapsed" (Lehuu 2000: 61).

Another magazine that sought to embody national print culture was *Yankee Notions, or whittlings of Jonathan's Jack-knife*, published by T. W. Strong between 1852 and 1875, the longest-lived satire magazine of the Civil War period. Furnished with cartoons by artists John McLenan and Augustus Hoppin, *Yankee Notions* interlinks the "notions" of the Yankee peddler with the non-purpose activity of whittling. The shards he whittles while talking symbolize the trifles included in the magazine, a horn of plenty in the best sense, a heap of debris in the worst. The frontispiece of the first edition shows a Jonathan figure with striped pants and top hat in an urban setting, whittling away while waiting for his wife Jemima, as the caption below his feet indicates (Fig. 1.9). In the illustration, Jonathan looks out for the passers-by who are oblivious to him. The city is a threatening place, with a male figure to the left of Jonathan collapsing on a lamp post. In this hostile environment, Jonathan is a smug and streetsmart persona who observes while whittling, a strategy for passing time; yet, as the magazine title suggests, whittling also represents the production of trifles of entertainment, storytelling and vignettes, that is, the contents of the magazine itself. The frontispiece thus gains an additional meaning: Jonathan's whittlings are the little curiosities of city life collected in the magazine, and he embodies American urban society, which produces these trifles. The second number, from February 1852 (Fig. 1.10), shows Jonathan at his desk, hard at work trying to write a love letter to his dear Jemima. He is about to be stabbed in the back by the satirist's knife hanging above

Figures 1.9 and 1.10 Frontispieces of *Yankee Notions*, vols. 1.1 (January 1852) and 1.2 (February 1852). Library of Congress.

his head like the sword of Damocles, implying that his expertise in whittling obstructs any other kind of sentimental writing. Despite the help of classical literature, represented by the tome of Ovid's *Art of Love* next to his desk, Jonathan is at a loss for words. The caption, in Yankee dialect, quotes his longing for "soft sodder to express my sentiment." *Yankee Notions* therefore fuses the character of the hapless country bumpkin with the satirist of the city. A professional writer himself, Jonathan is limited to one genre and would have to commission a hack writer for anything else. As hyperbole for the young literati of the U.S., Jonathan simply cannot get out of character and is unfit for a literature of sentiment.

As this chapter has shown, the American national character Brother Jonathan/Uncle Sam is adapted from the English John Bull and attributed with a coming-of-age narrative that makes this allegorical narrative into an epitome of the modern nation state. Harking back to the opening of this chapter and the critique by Garance Franke-Ruta, present-day feminist writer for *The Atlantic*, of Uncle Sam's lack of "classiness," it seems that for Uncle Sam, it is impossible to rise to a respected middle-class position like his English predecessor John Bull. First, of course, Jonathan remains a vernacular character representative of humor and everyday culture. Second, with regard to the semiotics of this figure, his ability to embody the United States is questionable: he remains outside the class system of the new republic and is deeply ambiguous with regard to both his morals and his plausibility. American authors are uncertain if he is a fitting candidate for national saint, and whether they need such a figure at all. Overshadowing this problem of representation is Jonathan's third type of ambiguity, his theatricality and the tremendous success of the stage Yankee in antebellum America, which will be discussed in the next chapter. Audiences can never take the Yankee at face value, since he talks to them from the stage and the page at the same time, and since his talk is typically braggadocio. They have to stick to the entertainment aspect of his performance and postpone the definition of what an American man is (not).

Notes

1. Hanlon (2013) discusses references to England in American sectional rhetoric to defend the Northern or Southern cause, respectively. Clark's study *The American Idea of England* (2013) includes a chapter on allegorical narrative that will be explored further below.

2. Arbuthnot's characterization blends medieval humorism (in describing Bull as choleric and inconstant) with the modern tradition in his focus on social relations and interactions.
3. Eighteenth-century readers were familiar with the character craze from such formats as the character sketch. As McGirr maintains, the character is "an attempt to define social and moral types," i.e. it speaks to the distinctions of class and type (2007: 2).
4. For the history of the depiction of John Bull, see Hunt 2003: 121–69, Taylor 1992, Matthews 2007, and Mellini 2012. Caricature as an art form was adapted from Italian artists; the artist would visualize sitters' character traits in their faces; caricature was employed as a propaganda weapon (Vinson 1957; see also below).
5. See also Daisy Delogu's study of the invention of the female allegory of France in times of crisis, which maintains that "France" "took a geopolitically unstable category [. . .] and transformed it into a bounded, coherent, and autonomous whole, one that provided the basis for an emergent and distinctive French identity founded upon birth or (figurative) kinship, political allegiance, law, and a shared history and set of beliefs" (2015: 7). Susanne Scholz's 2000 study on the reciprocal relation of individual and political body in early modern England historicizes the body narrative and focuses on the body of Queen Elizabeth I, but does not discuss allegorical representation.
6. My reading of allegory in European rhetoric and poetics draws on Eggs 2015, Freytag 1992, Machosky 2013, Kelley 1997, Tambling 2010, and Whitman 2003.
7. Kelley also identifies, in the modern reinvention of allegory, the use of "fantastical allegorical agents in a realistic or historical narrative" and an "excess of rhetorical pathos that those agents often bring to verisimilar situations and characters" (1997: 73), which applies to the texts examined here.
8. Regarding the creation of national figures in the eighteenth century, compare, for instance, the meaning of the French Marianne in revolutionary iconography, or the history of Nicolas Frog, as well as the German figure Deutscher Michel, which dates to the Thirty Years' War but is flowered in caricatures of the 1840s. Daisy Delogu's (2015) study on the female allegory for the nation in late medieval France also contrasts the exclusion of women from the succession of power to their conceptual presence in iconography of the French realm during a time of crisis.
9. As Heinrich Plett (1979: 325, 326) has shown, in Renaissance England, the performance of masque plays in which courtiers and even kings participated intermingled the social role of the courtier and the allegorical meaning of the plays. The casting thus deliberately added another social framework to the allegorical story, and performance became a mark of professionalism, when the courtier performed a persona in order to be accepted at court, hiding his "real" self behind the mask.

For instance, Ben Johnson's allegory plays hid the court society behind a plethora of images and narratives (shepherds' plays, *tableaux vivants*, the king posing as the sun). Aristocracy thus was presented as artifice, as make-believe captured in the French fashion of "faire semblant" or the Italian "sprezzatura." The full achievement of this artistic performance meant that the mask would become invisible and it would be taken, literally, at face value.

10. Hastings argued that English nationhood and nationalism provide a prototype well before the modern period, with a climax in the sixteenth century (1997: 5). This makes my own reading even more important, since the transatlantic gaze that directs the formation of American nationhood creates an "offspring" from the prototype of nations. Hastings comments that "it was this English model [. . .] which was then re-employed, remarkably little changed, in America and elsewhere" (ibid.).
11. Fliegelman notes that this forced chastity places "personal virtue [. . .] over the greater good of society," an argument used by Protestants against the sentimental novel (1982: 120). Kramer links the family narrative of biological and cultural reproduction to sexual behavior, with "nonreproductive" sexual activities posing a threat to nationalist concerns. On the meaning of the family narrative for nationalist thinking in general, see Kramer 2011: 102–24.
12. Paulding's stance on sectional conflict in the 1850s is reflected in other pieces published in the *Democratic Review*; he defended the Southern rights, which earned him little appreciation in the North.
13. This formula anticipates Lincoln's 1863 Gettysburg Address; Paulding may have adapted it from Daniel Webster's Congressional speech in 1830 about democracy as "the people's government, made for the people, made by the people, and answerable to the people."
14. The text includes stories about the events leading up to the war, the declaration of war, as well as sectional dissent, embodied in "Tom Boston," the "wicked" "insolent Yankee" (Fidfaddy 1970: 46, 47) who expresses the New England refusal to participate when called to arms.
15. Elizabeth Jane Gay (1830–1919) worked as a Yankee schoolteacher in the South. In the Civil War she nursed wounded Union soldiers, and she worked for seventeen years at the "Dead Letter Office" in Washington, until 1883. She was involved in the English suffrage movement and emigrated to England with suffragette Caroline Sturge in 1906.
16. All subsequent references are to this edition; instead of indicating stanzas, I refer to page numbers. The following analysis reads the autopoiesis of the narrator or poet based on the text only, since biographical information on Coxe is scarce. His literary endeavors appear to be minuscule and invested in personal expression.
17. The prologue quotes the phrase from Dante's *Commedia* about the new people and their sudden profits ("La gente nova, e sùbiti guadagni [. . .]

Fiorenza, in te, sì che tu già ten piagi"). In this part, Dante bemoans the moral degeneration of the city and the collapse of the authorities of Church and Empire; see Brand and Pertile 2001: 67.

18. The narrator uses the culinary framework as a motif for describing the production and ingestion of literature; not only does Katrina convince her husband to send St. Jonathan to the U.S. over an extended dinner, he describes the classical epics *Iliad* and *Odyssey* as cookbooks, "recipes [. . .] mixed with fights, and boasting [. . .] to make them more instructive." About the ingredients of epic, the narrator concludes: "I took this turn to prove to you there must be // Cooks, as well as gods, in every epopée" (69).
19. N.B. the New England authors that are today canonized under the complicated term of the American Renaissance, and that are found to represent a national American literature independent from Europe, are not listed in this poem. As European models an American bard should aspire to, the narrator names John Milton and Edward Burns.
20. See also Astrid Böger's chapter on the Philadelphia Exhibition (2010: 61–108).
21. My discussion of Nast's Uncle Sam cartoons builds on Hunt (2003: 1–22) and Banta (2003, esp. 1–3), who emphasize the cultural function of cartoons and caricature to enforce and deviate from norms and their satire's intent to instruct and punish; on caricature in the U.S. in the eighteenth century, see Nevins 1975.
22. In the first cartoon, Sam is holding Nast down in a chair that symbolizes policy, with a sign on the wall saying "give the President's policy a chance." The next cartoon shows the bottom of Nast's chair falling out and the artist crashing into the frame, while Uncle Sam runs out of the room in despair and haste (see Ketchum 1959: 90).

Chapter 2

Theater of/for the Nation: The Stage Yankee as Metatheatric Sign

Among the renditions of Yankees in nineteenth-century texts and media, the stage Yankee is certainly the most embodied one. The figure was immensely popular on the antebellum American stage and has received more scholarly attention than other Yankee types discussed here. My own reading of the stage Yankee as a metatheatric sign contextualizes antebellum theater culture and the performance of American character in the public sphere. Building on the literary nationalist debates of the nineteenth century discussed in the previous chapter, the present part first addresses the lacuna of Yankee scholarship and the persisting discomfort with the "earthy" figure which leaves little wriggling room for a "high brow" and elitist concept of American literature. I then examine the theatrical codes that frame Yankeedom on the stage to argue that the Yankee participates in the making of symbolic spaces for the nation, including the make-believe of the national stage.

Yankee Theater and Drama Scholarship

The *Cambridge History of English and American Literature*'s (1907–21) definition of "Yankee Theater" foregrounds the Yankee's authenticity:

> These plays are usually of the same type, a comedy or melodrama into which a Yankee comic character has been inserted. He bears little relation to the play, but it is this very detachment that makes him important, for he is the one spot of reality among a number of stage conventions, and it is no doubt this flavour of earth that secured the warm reception which these plays received. (Ward and Trent 2000)

In this entry, the Yankee's importance hinges on his detachment from the plot and on his alleged "reality" and "flavour of the earth." An allegedly authentic "earthiness" also forms the core of two influential historical studies, Francis Hodge's *Yankee Theater: The Image of America on the Stage, 1825–1850* (1964), and Walter J. Meserve's *Heralds of Promise: The Drama of the American People in the Age of Jackson, 1829–1849* (1986). Both trace a diachronic narrative of Yankee theater undergoing a rise and fall, until 1850, with four popular Yankee actors: James H. Hackett (1800–71), George Handel "Yankee" Hill (1809–49), Danforth Marble (1810–49), and Joshua Silsbee (1815–55). Hodge claims that Silsbee's passing in 1855 marked the ending of this theatrical tradition, with a latent afterglow in the postbellum appearance of aged Yankee figures. Hodge's interest in the four American Yankee actors maps a semi-biographical reading of theater culture in which the Yankee part became a career ticket for star actors. The stage Yankee was tied to a distinct type of actor: New Englanders who came to acting after trying other businesses and cutting out a path for themselves. The star system featured troupes organized around an actor touring the East Coast and down South. The stars would often act as protagonist and stage managers, exporting renowned New York productions to playhouses in the growing urban centers around the country.[1] The Yankee impersonators therefore brought considerable biographical experience to their part, creating the stage Yankee as a type taken straight from the New England village.

Yankee Theater also collects a corpus of eighty-five Yankee-theater plays (Hodge 1964: 273–83) that has been largely ignored by more recent drama scholarship. The list shows the Yankee's prevalence across many theatrical subgenres and entertainment forms and the versatility of the Yankee actors; the popular figures of Major Jack Downing, Sam Slick, and Sam Patch, who jumped down Niagara Falls in a tub, were all rendered on the stage by Yankee actors. However, Hodge's corpus of Yankee plays exclusively lists plays that starred the selected Yankee actors. Some of the plays included do not feature a Yankee figure, while other Yankee plays are obliterated because they were never acted by his stars. A case in point is the image of G. E. "Yankee" Locke (1817–80), a New York comedian originally from New Hampshire, who first appeared in New York as Solomon Swap in *Jonathan in England* (1858) but mostly acted on smaller provincial stages after that. He impersonated a number of Yankee roles, including Jedediah Homebred from *The Green Mountain Boy*, Jonathan Ploughboy from *The Contrast*, and Curtis Chunk from *The Stage-Struck Yankee* (see Fig. 2.1).

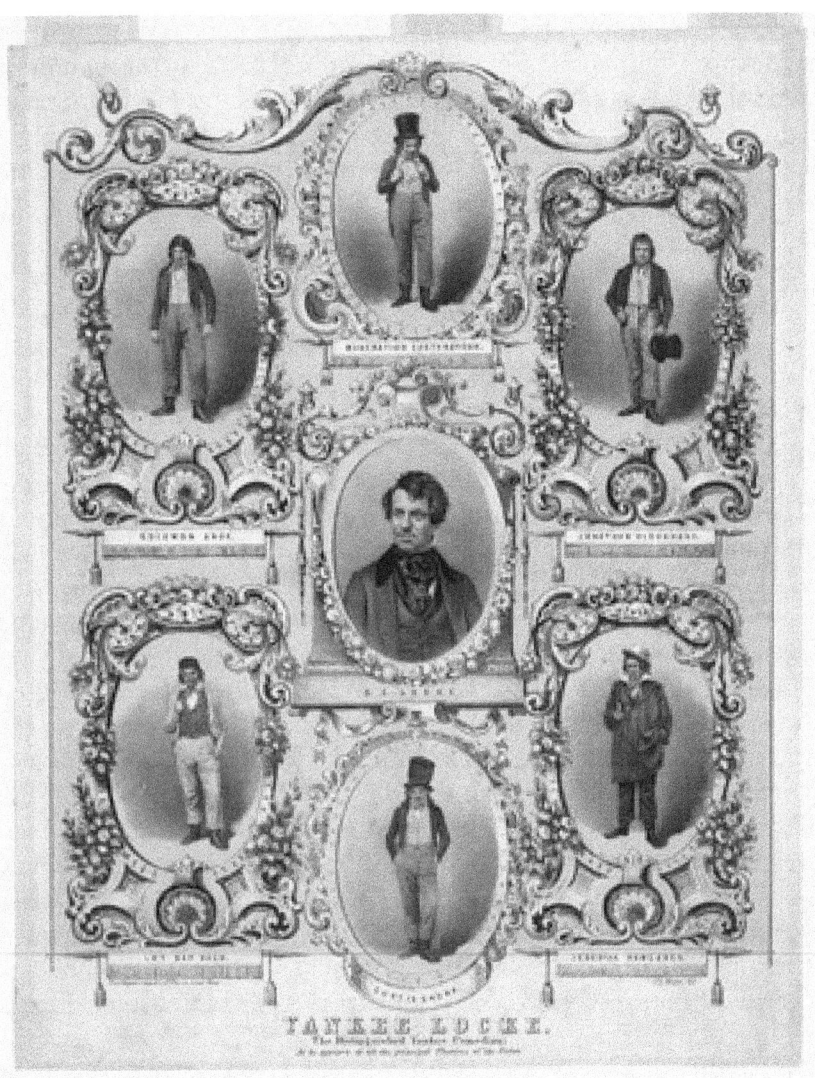

Figure 2.1 "Yankee Locke. The Distinguished Yankee Comedian; As he appears at all the principal Theatres of the Union." N.d. Library of Congress, Prints and Photographs Division, Popular Graphic Arts LC-DIG-pga-03943.

Locke's posture in these characters showcases the stage Yankee's expression: with hands in pockets and cocked hat, he expresses cunning and smugness. While the conventional Yankee costume of striped pants and top hat is only used for Tyler's Jonathan Ploughboy in this image, it is Locke's body posture which shows the Yankee's essence; ready for action, looking straight at his audience, he impersonates a precocious version of American character.

But Hodge's revered list shows more gaps: John E. Owens (1823–86) successfully took over the part of Solon Shingles in J. S. Jones's *The People's Lawyer* after George Handel Hill's death in 1849 (Bank 2010: 103). Matthews (1879: 331) observes that Owens's "ownership of the character has never since been disputed." The career of star actor Joseph Jefferson included title roles of popular plays, such as Newman Noggs in *Nicholas Nickleby*, or Caleb Plummer in *The Cricket on the Hearth* (both adapted from novels by Charles Dickens) and, finally, as the Yankee Salem Scudder in Dion Boucicault's *The Octoroon*, which will be discussed below (see Jefferson 1890: 209). Other noteworthy actors include Alexander Simpson, Henry Placide, John E. Weaver, and Louis F. Mestayer (see Moody 1966a: 149–50).

Like Hodge's *Yankee Theater*, Meserve's *Heralds of Promise* focuses on the promulgation of the Jacksonian common man on the American stage. Meserve argues that playwrights felt compelled to write "vehicle plays more notable for quantity than quality" (1986: 89) for the star actors. He links the Yankee to other Jacksonian figures like the frontier hero Davy Crockett and Mose the Fire B'hoy, a Bowery lad from Manhattan in a rough and rowdy working-class typology. And indeed, the Yankee's defining quality is his masculinity. Rosemarie Bank (2010: 38, 42), for instance, mentions "female stage Yankees," but observes that "[n]o actress of the antebellum period made a starring career of female staged Yankees, but few escaped playing them, some notably (e.g. Catherine LeSugg Hackett [wife of Henry Hackett])" (ibid. 204 n. 28). My research has uncovered no female Yankee title heroines or Yankee plays in which female Yankees are given a central part. Rather, they serve as foils and love interests to the male Yankees and often ridicule their love-struck boobyness. In these cases, the only person who can outperform a Yankee might be a Yankee girl. Conversely, there are just as many Yankee girls who become objects of a Yankee suitor's bartering and trading.[2]

The "earthy" Yankee proved hard to stomach for drama historians Meserve and Hodge. Both scholars reveal a tacit discomfort with the "low brow" and folkloristic figure. For Meserve, the Yankee's storytelling was hard on the audience's ears, a "cacography for the reader and a twangy accent for the listener" (1986: 87).³ Similarly, Hodge bemoans the Yankee theater's "gross impoverishment, naiveté" and calls it "very poor stuff," an American *commedia dell'arte* (1964: 3). Hodge's and Meserve's studies read Yankee theater as a necessary step in the development of an artistic coming-of-age of the U.S.; Meserve bemoans that "there was a [. . .] rising sun of dramatic literature in America [. . .] clearly visible, even radiant, and then it disappeared" (1986: 3). In their view, theater and audience need to educate each other to reach cultural maturity. Progressive Era theater critic Brander Matthews exculpated viewers' tastes and called for greater artistry in playwrights in his polemic "The American on the Stage" (1879: 322). For Matthews, the stage Yankee is a mere caricature stripped of its originality:

> [I]n nearly all of [the Yankee actor's plays] is to be detected a strong odor of wooden nutmegs and shoepeg oats, in nearly all of them is to be heard much bragging and tall talk and much sharp practice is to be seen. [. . .] The stage Yankee was coarse, exaggerated and extravagant; the real Yankee, if he ever had been like the attempt at reflecting him, had long ceased to bear any recognizable resemblance to the caricature of succeeding actors. (Matthews 1879: 325)

Matthews's typology links the stage Yankee to the Yankee peddler's "wooden nutmegs," a counterfeit commodity which can hardly possess a smell in the first place (see Chapter 4). Matthews thus relegates the Yankee to the realm of the folkloristic and fantastic, reiterating a striking unease with the stage Yankee in literary criticism. He appears unbearable, and critics attempt to excuse or mitigate his existence. According to Matthews, he is only a caricature, a reduced version; for Meserve and Hodge, he is too real, earth-flavored, but a precocious and half-baked version of a fully fledged American character. The developmental narrative persists in contemporary analyses of antebellum theater (see e.g. Bank 2010).⁴

Reading the stage Yankee thus proves a tricky task. The first problem comes with the generic label "Yankee theater." The stage Yankee appears in a multitude of dramatic subgenres, sparing only the tragedy in a failure to fill the part of comic relief. The Yankee figure reflects the material conditions of American drama, with its star system evolving around signature performances of New England men. Whereas, by mid-century, the star system is replaced by local troupes with an extended repertoire for middle-class entertainment, the stage Yankee was latently present in oral culture and travelogues before the rise of the Yankee actors, and he easily survived beyond the passing of the last famous Yankee actor. The Yankee was the title character of many plays, yet his place in the plot was sometimes marginal, scarcely central to the action. Instead, his typicality hinges on cameo behaviors, dress, and language features, as well as on frontier humor and tall tale storytelling.

Second, the Yankee as a theatrical figure is ambiguous. He is neither a hero nor a complete country bumpkin, but he commonly accomplishes his agenda in the plays. His mission may be business scheming or courtship, yet it is commonly linked to a progressive "going ahead." Depending on the logic of the play, this may be laudable or despicable. If he succeeds, it may be the rightful harvest of his hard labor—or by mere accident. He may chicken out of a duel or take a stand; he may be the butt of a smart Yankee girl's joke or win her over with his sweet talk. He impersonates the region of New England and America as a nation at the same time and yet he can hardly be tied down to one definitive style of speech, behavior, or social background.[5] He also reveals himself as an outsider to the *dramatis personae* with regard to regional provenance, class, or profession: a "downeaster" among Southerners, urbanites, or even New Englanders, a newcomer to the city or the village, a trader among farmers.

In light of the figure's ambiguity described here, I propose to read the stage Yankee as a metatheatric sign. His behavior is most commonly marked by an emphasis on performance; he sings and dances, uses asides, addresses the audience, or comments on the events of the play as well as on his own character. The appearance of the Yankee figure transforms all kinds of dramatic plots into theatrical narratives of national identity, satisfying what Heather Nathans has called an "impulse to define difference" (2014: 98). He fuses politics and entertainment, articulating an unstable, embodied national identity. Karl Kippola has examined the "reciprocal relationship of entertainment and masculinity identity" (2012: 189) throughout the nineteenth century. Yankee actors such as James Henry Hackett would carefully distinguish their professional self-presentation as managers and troupe leaders from the laughable masculinity they impersonated on the stage. I would argue that this need for distinction emanates not primarily from the Yankee's ridiculousness, but from the era's culture of fraudulence and performance which permeated the theater business. With a biographical background like Yankee Hill's, who started out as a New England storyteller, shopkeeper, and peddler, the part of a professional star actor commanded yet another performance of business smarts and of what Kippola calls "mannerly manhood" (2012: 181). The masculinities star actors displayed on and off stage thus represent not so much a change of professional acumen as a continuum of Yankee ambiguity. In dramatic entertainment, the Yankee ridiculed women and cultural Others, as many drama historians have shown.[6] The Yankee affirms hegemonic whiteness, as Bruce McConachie comments: "Although accommodating the values of republican simplicity and sentimental virtue, the stage Yankees actually advanced the cultural system of rationality and the whiteness it assumed" (1998: 154–5).

Because of his ambiguity, however, theater audiences had to take the stage Yankee's fitness for representing America and American arts with a grain of salt. Rather than defining national character within the play, the stage Yankee interlinks the fictional world of the play with the social code of the theater and with antebellum debates around American character. The term "Yankee theater" operates in a broader sense, as a corpus of plays and performances in which the Yankee evokes and creates an American cultural imaginary. Yankee theater employs the Yankee as a mediator of an ambiguous white American masculinity and of different spheres of American social life. The stage Yankee thus constitutes American theater in various ways: wherever there's a Yankee, there is a theatrical arena for displaying and negotiating American manhood, manners, and social spaces. Looking at present-day politics, this phenomenon might pertain to the performance of American presidents, as Matt Fotis (2011) shows in his discussion of George W. Bush in office.

After redefining Yankee theater, the present chapter illustrates his ambiguity by reading together popular and lesser known dramas and shorter performance pieces. I examine first how the Yankee creates national spaces (i.e. the country and the city), and second, when he finds himself aboard, international cultural relations. This structure extrapolates the hyperbolic and performative link between the Yankee's body and the national space. The stage Yankee's presence transforms the stage into a laboratory for national entertainment and identity.

Due to the ephemeral nature of the performance in drama, my analysis focuses on the texts available in print and the stage space and descriptions provided in the primary (dialogue) and secondary (stage directions, *dramatis personae*, position sketches) texts of the plays to examine how the Yankee figures constitute and are constituted by the spaces of the stage. My approach follows Erika Fischer-Lichte's semiotics of drama (*Semiotik des Theaters*, 1994 [1983]) and Patrice Pavis's *Semiotik der Theaterrezeption* (1988). Pavis's theory of reception esthetic argues that the theatergoer's reception depends on her own codes, psychological, ideological, and esthetic-ideological, which I briefly relate to the history of Yankee theater here.

From today's perspective, the psychological code for viewing Yankee plays can only be assessed speculatively; there is no way of reconstructing immediate reactions and thoughts, but a look at audience composition indicates the audience's dispositions.[7] From the Early Republic to the 1820s, the theater witnessed a shift in audience composition from the urban elites toward a broader range of class background. Shaffer (2007: 12) contends that theatergoers in the Early Republic predominantly belonged to the propertied class and had access to the stage and the pulpit, the printing press, and political platforms; Bank (2010: 95) notes that young city migrants from the 1820s onwards increasingly went to the theater in the urban hubs. The playhouse itself, however, was a composite "tripartite class-containment system" (ibid. 50), with a pit, seating space, and boxes (also offering entertainment by sex workers). With the playhouse as a microcosm of class distinctions, the shift from a well-to-do audience towards a younger and predominantly masculine crowd reflects a turn towards entertainment and participatory theater culture. Jeffrey Richards has argued that "[t]he stage functioned as a supracommunity, whose traditions in some ways superseded those of the culture immediately outside its doors, even as they acknowledged them, in the syntax and diction of the theater" (2005: 6). By the 1820s, American theatergoers would boo or applaud, ask for popular songs, sing along and generally participate in the entertainment (Grimsted 1987: 58–63; Levine 1988: 192), a behavior that appeared barbaric to foreign visitors. David Grimsted maintains that audiences "controlled, as well as contributed to, theatrical entertainment" (1987: 62). The 1849 Astor Place Riot, according to Grimsted (1987: 68–75), marked the end of the era of audience control. On May 10, the feud between the British actor William Charles Macready and the American working-class star Edwin Forrest, who represented different types of masculinity and social divides (Kippola 2012: 89–116), escalated and killed twenty-five people.[8]

Considering Pavis's psychological code of reception, we can observe that audiences of the day conceived of the playhouse as a site of participation, even showmanship in performing the part of theatergoer, as will become more obvious below. Pavis's ideological code describes the knowledge of the reality shown on the stage and the "real world" the audience inhabits; esthetic-ideological codes pertain to the theater itself. The ideological code of Yankee plays latches onto the nationalist desire for cultural independence from Britain and for the proclamation of an American "native" character. From its beginnings, American theater, just as American literature, functioned as "a provincial stage of the British empire" (Richards 2005: 2). The task for the nascent cultural industry was threefold: to consolidate the national space of the U.S., to negotiate tropes of wilderness and cultural contact, as well as to call forth an imaginary rural space that would symbolize home to urban work migrants and distinguish the U.S. American "country" from the "city." With audiences consisting largely of those most likely to engage in politics, the theater became a "temple" that replaced the agora as a locus for politics, as star actor Joseph Jefferson claimed:

> [N]ow, in nearly all of the new and rising cities, the theater or the opera-house is centrally located; and it is generally the finest building, both in point of size and architecture, to be seen—heated with steam, lighted by electricity, and provided with every comfort. Within these temples, actors, opera-singers, minstrels, and ministers hold forth, and the same audience goes to hear them all. The desire for dramatic entertainment was resolved itself into a tidal wave that nothing can stop, particularly as there is no desire to impede it. It has not the fleeting character of a political movement that might change with the new influence of the next Administration; it belongs to no party; it is born of no sect; but it is the outcome of a universal passion. (Jefferson 1890: 427)

In the U.S., politics and the theater are entangled in a relationship that dates to colonial times. In *Theater Enough*, Jeffrey Richards defined theater as a rhetoric device in colonial America, arguing that the *theatrum mundi* trope was used to emplace the U.S.: the American "ideology of theater [...] carries with it the weight of history and cosmology" (1991: xviii). From the American Revolution onwards, the theater was seen either as play or as serious matter, as a means of inward self-definition as a nation and presentation to the world.

In this setup, the stage Yankee amalgamated transatlantic identity politics with the theater from the very beginning. On the English stage, the formation of English identity in contrast to cultural and ethnic Others (including Jews, Scots, and Yorkshiremen) reached a peak in the second half of the eighteenth century (Ragussis 2000). It is therefore no surprise that the stage Yankee was invented by an English actor: Thomas Wignell created the original Jonathan character in the first Yankee play, *The Contrast* (1789). In the 1810s, Charles Mathews, England's most popular comedian, took to the Yankee. Mathews was renowned for his performance of types across a national, social, and racial range. In *Trip to America*, he impersonated as many as fourteen of these types, included in George Cruikshank's caricature "The Mathew-O-Rama for 1824" (Plate 4). Punning on the state-of-the-art theatrical technique of the panorama that put stage landscapes on display for nineteenth-century audiences, the "Mathew-O-Rama" parades a roster of national and stage types and their stage speech, including an English landlord, a Dutch damsel, a French taylor, a Kentucky shoemaker, and an escaped slave. The subtitle's mimicry of Yankee speech and expletives ("'Pretty considerable d—d particular' Tit Bits from America") pinpoints the performative reception of this panorama that hinges on body, behavior, speech, and dress. Mathews's "real Yankee," Jonathan Doubikin, is positioned prominently third from the left, clad in brown homespun. He makes his appearance in *The Yankey in England*, a play Mathews commissioned to playwright David Humphreys. Mathews's craft in acting out types aimed not so much at authentic reproduction but at "exceed[ing] the original," to bring out its essence (Ziter 2010: 212). Mathews enacted these types in a one-man travelogue revue and claimed that he was interested not in "the precise height of a mountain or the depth of a cave," but sought after "PECULIARITIES, CHARACTER, and MANNERS" (qtd. in Pethers 2013: 95). At the very core, Mathews's Yankee is a panoramic caricature created by anthropological interest. This origin provided the blueprint for the stage Yankees of American actors, not least thanks to the documentation Humphreys provided in the print version of the play: a glossary of Yankee words (Hodge 1964: app. B) and characteristic behavior which became, in turn, the basis for dialect studies (see e.g. Killheffer 1928; Spingarn 1958). Humphreys's Yankee typology runs as follows:

> Inquisitive from natural and excessive curiosity, confirmed by habit; credulous, from inexperience and want of knowledge on the world; believing himself to be perfectly acquainted with whatever he partially knows; tenacious of prejudices; docile, when rightly managed; when otherwise treated, independent to obstinacy; easily betrayed into ridiculous mistakes; incapable of being overawed by external circumstances; suspicious, vigilant and quick of perception, he is ever ready to parry or repel the attacks of raillery, by retorts of rustic and sarcastic, if not of original and refined wit and humor. (Qtd. in Hodge 1964: 54)

The stage Yankee thus sprang from the minds of theater professionals who viewed Americans from an English perspective. This transatlantic meandering becomes obvious, for instance, in *The Yankey Pedlar*. In the 1830s, Yankee actor George Handel Hill commissioned the English playwright William Bayle Bernard to write a Yankee play. Bernard was the son of John Bernard, an

English actor who recorded his American sojourn in his autobiography *Retrospections of America, 1797–1811* (Bernard 1887). For the creation of the Yankee character Hiram Dodge, a thief and trickster, the son turned to his father's memoir. *The Yankey Pedlar* premiered at London's Drury Lane on November 1, 1836, and granted Hill a successful run in England. Hill's Hiram Dodge was entertaining to English audiences, but after Hill failed in New York, he had to be rendered more sympathetic for American audiences (see Jortner 2013; Pethers 2013). Just as Hill's *Yankey Pedlar*, the three earliest American plays that feature Yankee figures are set in the transatlantic sphere: Royall Tyler's *The Contrast* (1787), James Nelson Barker's *Tears and Smiles* (1807), and Abraham B. Lindsley's *Love and Friendship* (1809), which splits the Yankee figure into three characters and includes the first Yankee story told in dialect.

The Yankee's esthetic-ideological origins are steeped in the era's theater industry.[9] The quest for American character started with the Yankee, who "appeared to his best advantage [...] when contrasted against different ethnic types" (Nathans 2014: 101). The Yankee would appear several times per night. A typical playbill included about five hours of theater entertainment, starting with a canonized English or European play, followed by a short interlude, minstrelsy performance, or Yankee farce, moving to a second, lighter comedy, and concluding with another skit. Versions of the stage Yankee could appear in all of these, except for the imported canonized plays. The same actor would play the Yankee in the farce and the second long piece, the comedy, so the boundaries between the pieces dissolved. An advertisement in *Scribner's Magazine* for a playbill at the Broadway Theatre on the eve of August 19, 1853, features the actor Joshua Silsbee twice, in two Yankee plays: as Jedediah Homebred in *The Green Mountain Boy*, and as Hiram Dodge in *The Yankee Pedlar* (see N.N. 1853). A playbill for New York's Bowery Theatre announces the appearance of George Hill in several plays, among which only *The Green Mountain Boy* features a Yankee figure.[10] The typical stage Yankee costume is prescribed, for instance, in the secondary text of George Colman's *Jonathan in England*, as "Yankee coat; striped trowsers and vest; shoes; red wig" (Colman 1828; see also the Yankee costumes in Fig. 1.1 and Appendix III).

Royall Tyler's *The Contrast* illustrates the concoction of theater culture with national historiography and mythmaking. Tyler's Jonathan Ploughboy, the "ur" version of the American on the stage, has been discussed extensively by theater critics and scholars.[11]

Ploughboy interlinks the metageneric debate about transatlantic theater with a self-conscious performance that breaks down the fourth wall and plays with audience knowledge about the theater. Tyler's Jonathan calls himself a "true blue son of liberty," a "true born Yankee American son of liberty" who was "never afraid of a gun yet in all my life" (Tyler 1997: I, 1, 15; II, 1, 35). Ploughboy plays a janus-faced part, since he is positioned as a country bumpkin between the American military talent Colonel Manly (whom he serves diligently, but not as a valet, of course, rather as a footman to make a living) and the foppish continental Dimple. The British actor Thomas Wignell created this "first American," and in the play, Jonathan has a few lines about this actor's skills, thinly disguised as one "Darby Wag-all" (Tyler 1997: III, 1, 35). *The Contrast* stages a mélange between history and theater; Jonathan harbors patriotic tastes but, unlike Manly, he did not fight in the Revolutionary War. As a walking "repository of American patriotic mythology" (Shaffer 2007: 177), Jonathan sprinkles his dialogue with references to pre-revolutionary street theater and political upheavals, such as Shays' Rebellion or the Battle of Bunker Hill. Jonathan's sightseeing in New York includes colonial and revolutionary monuments, but his description of "two marble-stone men and a leaden horse" (Tyler 1997: II, 2, 26) speaks directly to New Yorkers: the statue of the colonial Pitt the Elder was demolished by British soldiers in 1776, and as a response, the "Sons of Freedom" beheaded the statue of King George III. Finally, Jonathan, the country bumpkin, recounts his own relation to the theater in a metatheatric comment; despite his fears, he goes to see the two London plays that served as sources for Tyler's *Contrast*: Richard Sheridan's *School for Scandal* (1777) and John O'Keeffe's *The Poor Soldier* (1783; see Tyler 1997: III, 1, 35). Jonathan's fear of the "playhouse where the devil hangs out the vanities of the world upon the tenter-hooks of temptation" (Tyler 1997: III, 1, 33) quotes the Puritan rejection of the stage, while at the same time acknowledging the widely felt need, among American writers, for theater in a free society.[12] Charlotte, the heroine, describes the playhouse as a place of social performance in which the action on stage is mimicked by the audience:

> Everything is conducted with such decorum. First we bow, then [. . .] we have so many inquiries after each other's health [. . .] then the curtain rises, then our sensibility is all awake, and then, by the mere force of apprehension, we torture some harmless expression into a double meaning, which the poor author never dreamt of, and then we

have recourse to our fans, and then we blush, and then the gentlemen jog one another, peep under the fan, and make the prettiest remarks; [. . .] and then the curtain drops, and then for nuts and oranges, and then we bow, and it's pray, Ma'm, take it, and pray, Sir, keep it and oh! Not for the world Sir; and then the curtain rises again, and then we blush and giggle and simper and bow all over again, Oh! The sentimental charms of a side-box conversation! (Tyler 1997: II, 1, 23)

Theatergoing of itself functions as the performance of spectatorship in the public sphere. Hence, it is no surprise that the country bumpkin Jonathan, ignorant of such urban masquerades, fails to understand the plays he attends. The two other male figures of the play, the British impostor Dimple and the American revolutionary fighter Manly, symbolize conflicting functions of the theater in the U.S., representing "life as a historical social performance versus life as an antihistrionic acting in history" (Richards 1991: 272). The relationship between the nascent American theater tradition and its English forebears was a political topic; the first U.S. theater historian William Dunlap, in *A History of the American Theater*, called for a theater "induced by our republican institutions" but also claimed "the works of the [British] dramatists [. . .] as *much ours*, being the descendants of Englishmen, as if our fathers had never left the country in which they were written" (1832: 85–6). Shaffer argues that patriotism was instilled in American theater through familiarity with British (theater) culture, even though "American nationalism [. . .] used British culture against itself" (2007: 7). Thus, Tyler's Jonathan Ploughboy initiates a tradition of American self-performance deeply mired in theatric culture on the levels of acting *and* producing. Ploughboy's performance acknowledges his theatrical origins and constructedness. His skeptical indulgence in the thespian art proves the theater's claim for producing—that is, embodying and staging—the new nation. The esthetic-ideological code of Yankee theater builds on the Yankee actors' careers as storytellers. Last but not least, the theater is one site in a continuum of a theater culture invested in national performance, alongside republican festivities, processions, and parades (see Bank 2010; Shaffer 2007). The Yankee plays boasted tall talk or "strong personal narrative" (Meserve 1986: 86), drawing from an archive of Yankee stories circulated in humor magazines. This relates the playhouse to popular oral and print culture and to the regional varieties in the storytelling performance.[13]

My new look at the stage Yankee suggests a linkage between Yankee plays and the nationalist discourses of the American public. The Yankee as metatheatric sign reminds audiences of the theatrics of identity formation and transforms the stage into contested national spaces (social, political, geographical, and symbolic). His presence reverberates with the nineteenth-century spectacle culture of displaying U.S. landscapes on stage or in museums; Susan Tenneriello has examined the usage of dioramas and landscape painting in theaters and museums as multimedial storytelling, which demonstrates at once territorial possession and the engineering of superiority (2013: 2). A good example for the linkage between Yankee theater and the display of American landscapes to American and foreign audiences is William Dunlap's play *A Trip to Niagara* (1828, Dunlap 1966; for a discussion, see Schäfer 2015). Installed in such diverse settings as the urban city parlor or the pastoral village, the Yankee plays into the desire for myths and fantasies that become important for the cultural imaginary and that engender symbolic landscapes for the nation.[14] The following analysis therefore examines Yankee plays that contrast the American pastoral with the city, before following the stage Yankee abroad to foreign shores and different national identities.

Tales of Country and City: From Jonathan to Uncle Nat

On the antebellum stage, the stage Yankee interlinks the village and the city, putting on display their respective manners and customs. In expanding Raymond Williams's (1975) exploration of the relationship between the country and the city as mutually constitutive, I argue that the presence of the stage Yankee transforms the spaces shown on stage into sites of national imagination. A similar expansion applies to the figures of the plot: the male figures become foils to the Yankee in an overarching ideology of national manhood; the female figures are commodified by wooing and entrepreneurship into receptive fertile bodies that hold the future of the nation. The Yankee country rube fuses the Jeffersonian yeoman farmer with the Jacksonian self-made man and the entrepreneur.

The stage Yankee is often a marginal figure unfamiliar with urban life. His forays into the city represent a vignette that is included, for instance, in narrative poems such as "The Yankee in New York" from *Boston Weekly Magazine* (1817; see Appendix I). The plot of antebellum Yankee plays follows the comedy of manners: love conflicts are dissolved in happy marriages, and several couples form despite the interventions of greedy fathers, love-sick spinster aunts, or European impostors who pose as lords. In this setup, the Yankee frequently serves as comic relief on the lower social scale, a rustic who encounters the house servants or valets, black or white. Compared to the city folk, he appears clumsy, but he usually has the last laugh, when he plays tricks on them or saves the heroine from an unhappy marriage. This makes him stand out from the conventional comedic *dramatis personae* as a figure of lower social status with upward social mobility, or as a newcomer to a close-knit community. Unlike the fool or villain figure of the comedy of manners, however, the Yankee is not shown as "moral reprobate and social deviant" (Hokenson 2006: 34; see also Martin 2014). He somehow gains the upper hand, be it in terms of audience sympathy or as specimen of the go-ahead man who strives to make a living.

Next to the comedy, the farce became a platform for the Yankee: the short play time and crude humor painted a character sketch in between longer plays on a theater bill. The genre traditionally condenses or crams (French "farcir") meaning into grotesque exaggeration. As Bentley contends, farce also represents a "theater of the body [. . .] far from the natural [state]" that is related to "the actor's art" (1991: 251, 252). Farce thus offers a perfect setup for the Yankee to play out his theatricality and allegorical meaning as national character.[15] While the genre comes in many forms, its humor typically plays out in words rather than action (Stephenson 1960), catering to the Yankee storyteller. Also, farcical characters are funny "in advance": they are known to the audience as stock characters that put forth labels and masks for the sake of entertainment. This forgoes dramatic tension or surprises and allows instead for immediate audience participation (ibid. 86, 87). In a typical New York or Philadelphia playbill, the Yankee farce wedged between a lighter play and a tragedy would serve as denouement of the catastrophe. Authors would advertise their pieces as farce on the title page, such as *Ebenezer Venture* (LaBree 1841), *Jonathan Postfree* (Beach 1807), *The Vermont Wool-Dealer* (Logan 1844), *The Stage-Struck Yankee* (Durivage 1847), and *The Yankee Duelist* (Field 1883).

The stage Yankee represented an addition to and variation of well-known plot lines and predictable conflicts. Moreover, he acted as mediator between the action and the audience, breaking down the fourth wall and performing in both worlds. The print versions of Yankee plays frequently provide a final tableau of figures facing the audience, in which the Yankee is positioned center stage. He often has the last word, addressing the audience to ask for applause, such as in the print versions of *Tarnation Strange* (Moncrieff 1825), *Jonathan Postfree*, or *The Stage-Struck Yankee*.

The Yankee's performance conventionally displayed long monologues, replete with Yankee dialect, Yankee witticisms, and descriptions of New England communities, such as in *Ebenezer Venture, or Advertising for a Wife*. The play was intended as a "farce, in one act, written expressly for the Peculiar Powers of Mr. D. Marble." The part of Ebenezer was therefore designed to fit the Yankee persona Marble had already created. Ebenezer's speeches are the longest monologues in the play. The monologue cited below is Ebenezer's self-presentation to his potential love interest: a braggadocio run-on narrative interrupted by non sequiturs. It links Ebenezer's biography to the tight-knit Yankee community in which Ebenezer stands out with talents such as animal-like strength and performance skills with various instruments, dancing, singing, and "make[ing] poetry":

> *Ebenezer*: Well now, I can tell you about [what I came here for] as quick as anything, I guess; now I think jest as like as not you don't know who I be neither; well as the world has got to hear from me, in some way or other, I may as well begin with you; I was born down East, in Rockingham County, New Hampshire, and that was about the first that was hearn of me. When I was born, uncle Zeb said of me—you know uncle Zeb—heern tell on him? Get out; you have though? No! du tell. Look here, did you ever study jeography and 'stronomy? Never did? Well, I thought so. Guess you ain't never read Thomas's Almanac? Never did; well, I thought so! Not know uncle Zeb! Well. If these New Yorkers ain't the most ignorantest nation of people ever I did see, then smash my onion bed—not know uncle Zeb, I du declare. Why, he raised the biggest turnip in his garden ever did grown, not excepting any. Why, it was so big, nobody wouldn't believe it was turnip, and no livin' soul believes it to this day; it was so big, it took all the strength of the earth to bear it. Well, uncle Zeb said, when I was born, that he kinder reckoned, as noar as he could make out, that Miss Natur had done her puttiest that time, any how. I guess she did tu; there was a thunder storm when I was born—I'll tell you what, if it didn't roar more than amazin' and all the folks said they never saw the like afore. I'm the youngest of seventeen children, all boys except one, that's a gal, she's next to me, and the handsomest critter you ever set your eyes upon; folks say she and I look jest alike—the gals used to say, that I was proper handsome, but I never thought so; I never liked myself much, no how, some way or other. Well. My mother named me Ebenezer, that's my name, Ebenezer Venture, Esquire;—I was educated in school, the school marm always called me her little genus, but it didn't make me proud; my father was selectman of the town, my mother was President of the Benevolent Society, and Secretary of the Foreign Board of the Charitable Society

at home; my aunt Nabby, she was a snorter—a screamer—she conducted the singers in the core of the meeting house, Sabbath days; as for me, I'm a team by myself, twenty oxen and a stallion; I come down to New York to see the place, and tell the folks a thing or two; I can play the jews harp, fiddle, fife, drum and bugle horn, the sweetest; I can dance anything from the college hornpipe to Jim Crow—I can read loud, sing, and sometimes make poetry. (LaBree 1841: I, 4)

Ebenezer's run-on narrative engages a dialogue with his audience: he uses question tags and responses; he repeats petty details and exaggerates them to implausibility, as in the case of Uncle Zeb's turnip that was so huge nobody believed it was a turnip. He also mimics a superficial modesty, pretending not to be proud of his looks or of the teacher's praise of his "genius." His family appears to be near royalty in the village, involved in the running of affairs, and with overbearing female figures (mother, aunt, sister). The ending of his monologue quotes the formulas of the tall tale: Ebenezer describes his own strength as superhuman and animalistic, with masculine properties of oxen and stallions. His choice of words "I'm a team by myself" plays on the double meaning of "team of oxen" and "team of two," the latter of which shows his absurdity: how can one person be "a team by themselves"? Likewise, his refined musical skills clash with his beast-like physical prowess: it is hard to imagine someone as strong as a stallion as a fine musician and dancer. Finally, his dialect and half-wit ("jeography and 'stronomy") undermine the learning he brags about. However implausible they may seem, these formulas refer to popular entertainment and performance types: the animalistic strength is usually attributed to frontier heroes, and the singing and dancing "Jim Crow" relate Ebenezer to the minstrelsy show with its versatile performers in blackface. Ebenezer's self-advertisement therefore showcases that the stage Yankee is just as good a performer as his rivals in the entertainment industry.

Ebenezer directs his show at the audience and his on-stage love interest. In the play, his intention is to gain an inroad into a community, by marrying a girl and establishing a business. True to his last name, Ebenezer Venture epitomizes the typical go-ahead Yankee, in the world of the play as well as in the theater business. The Yankee's wooing of the audience was controversial not only among critics, but also among actors. The star actor Joseph Jefferson, for instance, denounced the "unnatural trick of speaking soliloquy and side speeches directly to the audience. We should act *for* the audience, not *to* the audience" (1890: 430). Jefferson proposes to let the audience observe and dismisses "guying," that is, improvisation with figures and stage types:

> "Guying" was formerly a slang term, but it has of late years become a technical one for trifling with a part upon the stage. [. . .] The practice of guying is unpardonable, and the indulgence on it unworthy of an artist or a gentleman. The leisure hours passed in the dressing-room or the greenroom afford ample time for an actor's amusement without inflicting the exuberance of his personal humor upon the audience. The rehearsals and subsequent performances of a play are not his property, and he has no right to mutilate them. Managers and leading actors are altogether too lax in their rebuke of this senseless and ruinous practice. (Jefferson 1890: 215–16)

For Jefferson, guying was ungentlemanly and unprofessional. He asks that actors practice self-effacement and focus on the dramatic production which is "not [the actor's] property." Jefferson's diatribe illustrates that Yankee actors had a distinct "business model": they established a trademark Yankee performance, self-advertised as Yankee, and bartered for audience sympathies while on stage. This compulsive exhibitionism may well be characteristic of every comedian, as Eric Bentley (1991) holds: the actor's desire to be watched is found, on the one hand, "socially inappropriate and mentally unhealthy" (150–1); yet, on the other hand, comedians are "gifted compulsive talker[s]" (233).

However, the Yankee actors made special show of it. They spoke to a double audience on stage and off stage, to theatergoers who paid to see a Yankee performance. The following close readings explore the wooing country bumpkin and businessman-performer from his rural origin in the poem *The Country Lovers/Jonathan's Courtship* (Fessenden 1795/1806) to Samuel Woodworth's *Forest Rose* and Abraham B. Lindsley's *Love and Friendship, or Yankee Notions* (1809). The second part links the young Yankee to a mature version in the postbellum plays *The Old Homestead* (Thompson 1889) and *Shore Acres* (Herne 1966 [1892]).

Thomas Green Fessenden's *The Country Lovers*, later called *Jonathan's Courtship*, is one of the earliest texts published after independence. It portrays a Jonathan figure which is remodeled, by 1806, as Yankee character. The earliest preserved version of this poem was published as a broadside in Dartmouth, New Hampshire, in 1795 (see Fessenden 1925: 33–5).[16] The poem is subtitled "Mr. Jonathan Jolthead's Courtship with Miss Sally Snapper; an excellent New Song, said to be written by the author, and really founded on fact" (Fessenden 1925: 192; all subsequent references to this edition). The protagonist's telling names prefigure the plot: one night, Jonathan is told by his mother to woo Sally, who has good prospects; he is insecure and afraid of "getting the bag," but eventually manages to confess his love. When she makes a joke at his expense, he is embarrassed into a fit ("His chin began to quiver // He said he felt so deuced droll // He guessed he'd lost his liver," 192), so she throws a bucket of water on him and sends him running home. In the final couplet, the narrator concludes: "I've heard him brag, sir, // That though the jade did wet him some // He didn't get the bag, sir!" Fessenden's Jonathan Jolthead is outwitted by the smart but squeamish Sally Snapper; the country lovers are an awkward couple who parody romance narratives.

Porter Gale Perrin's appendix includes a version of the text which shows the changes between the 1795 broadside and the 1806 version Fessenden included in his *Original Poems* (see Fessenden 1925: 186–92). The revised version illuminates how Fessenden, a mere decade after the broadside was published, emblazons the original country bumpkin as Jonathan the Yankee. The 1806 poem's new title, "Jonathan's Courtship," is programmatic: the poem is expanded from an original twenty-eight to fifty stanzas and frames Jonathan's wooing as Yankee business. As Jonathan mounts his horse to seek out Sally, he has an inner monologue of four additional stanzas the narrator deliberately shares with the audience ("I'll tell you every word, sir," 187). Jonathan wonders about the "stuff" girls are made of and thinks about the ideal housewife, who should be "clever," like Sally. Yet he dreads the wooing and implied sexual intercourse: "I'd rather lie in stacks of hay // In coldest winter weather." When the two are alone by the fire and Jonathan is paralyzed in embarrassment, in the new text, Jonathan "wish[es] himself at home"; he awkwardly "thinks to smack [kiss] her // [but] [. . .] he did not dare attack her" (190). In the newer version, the audience thus gains more insight into his inner conflicts. However, the 1806 Jonathan is also more effeminate than his older avatar. Both are "fors[aken] by their courage," the older Jonathan "though he was a spunky lad," while the more recent Jonathan "hung his under lip [. . .] like a heartless hen" (191, 192). The image of the hanging lip and the flustered animal disfigure Jonathan. In the end, Sally straightens him out with a pail of cold water, and the prospects for a happy marriage are shaky.

The other additions to the 1806 version also support this image of the effeminate country bumpkin and the strong Yankee girl: Jonathan avoids Sally by engaging in a lengthy conversation with her brother about "sheep, and cows, and oxen" and a "witch, in shape of owl //who stole her neighbor's geese" (189). Sally plays along with Jonathan's gossip when she asks him:

> Are you the lad who went to town,
> Put on your streaked trowsers
> Then vow'd you could not see the town
> There were so many houses? (191)

In the 1806 version, it is this question that triggers Jonathan's nervous fit; he is exposed as the laughing stock, the Yankee who went to Boston in his country dress. Likewise, the narrator describes Sally's dress as provincial ("One stocking on one foot she had, // on t'other foot a shoe," 189) which "a Boston lady" would find "monstrous [. . .] [and] quite shocking" (ibid.). In the 1795 version, *The Country Lovers* merely ridiculed country custom; in the 1806 version, "Jonathan's Courtship," the city is cast as the opposite of the rural backwaters. In the metropolis, fashions and manners rule, and even a smart country girl like Sally inspires raised eyebrows.

The scenario of the Yankee lost in Boston reappears as a vignette in many Yankee plays which show the country rube as honest and upright farmer (Thompson's *The Old Homestead*), as provincial comic relief (LaBree's *Ebenezer Venture*), or as a mixture of both (Jones's *Solon Shingles, or The People's Lawyer*). Fessenden's corrections to his 1795 mock poem therefore provide the earliest transformation from general country rube to a distinct cultural type, the Yankee. Fessenden completed the "Yankeefication" of *The Country Lovers* by proposing that it be sung to the tune of "Yankee Doodle" (186). He adapted the meter by adding "sir" at the end of the verses and inserted the original refrain after the first stanza:

> Yankee doodle keep it up,
> Yankee doodle dandy
> Mind the music-mind the step
> And with the girls be handy. (186)

As Fessenden uses "Yankee Doodle" to chisel out his Jonathan figure, he foregrounds the performance of courtship in the U.S. The original "Yankee Doodle" is more invested in the Revolutionary War; amid this bustle, Yankee Doodle seems to have little trouble with dancing and "being handy" with the girls. By comparison, Fessenden's Jonathan performs very poorly, even in the private space of Sally's home. Fessenden's ballad therefore mocks Yankee

Doodle's provinciality. The "country lovers" are exposed as "doodles" in the sense of the Dutch original term. Fessenden's mockery introduces the rural Yankee as a go-ahead man looking to settle down and establish himself.

Samuel Woodworth's *The Forest Rose, or American Farmers* (Woodworth 1966) adapts Fessenden's *Country Lovers* Jonathan and Sally. The "pastoral opera" ranks among the most popular plays of the antebellum period. It became a vehicle for the rise of Yankee actor George Handel Hill, who took over the part of Jonathan Ploughboy in 1832 and played it in the U.S. and in England for fifteen years. Likewise, Joshua Silsbee took the part with great success on both shores, creating an iconic Yankee (see Appendix II). A newspaper clipping for the Adelphi Theater in 1851 celebrates him as "the only living successful delineator of Yankee Eccentricities":

> This evening, Thursday Dec 11th, 1851 and during the week will be performed (for the 69th, 70th and 71st time) the laughable Comic Drama, in two acts, by Samuel Woodworth, The Forest Rose and the Yankee Plough-Boy. [. . .] During the piece, the story of the Yankee courtship! And a Yankee Country Dance, called the Cape Cod Reel. (Harvard Theater Collection, Playbills and programs from London theaters, 1700–1930)

In Louisville, KY, *The Forest Rose* was staged in 1857, with "Yankee Bierce" starring as Jonathan Ploughboy, who also danced a "Kowtillon" (read: cotillion):

> First night of the popular Yankee comedian Yankee Bierce who will appear in his great character of Jonathan Ploughboy (in The Forest Rose)
> The performance will conclude with the Beautiful American Drama, from the pen of S. Wordsworth, author of "the Old Oaken Bucket," etc and entitled the Forest Rose during the piece, A Kute, Keen, Kurious, Komikal, Kape Kod Kowtillon, **Yan K. Bierce** & Ko. (Harvard Theater Collection, Playbills Louisville, December 12, 1857)

The plot of Woodworth's "pastoral opera" revolves around the romance between two couples as well as Jonathan's own courtship of Sally Forest, the deacon's daughter. Harriet Miller and Lydia Roseville are the young villagers hoping for love: Lydia has been snubbed by the family of her city courtier, Blandford, and is now pining after his return; Harriet is destined to marry her long-time friend William (Lydia's brother), but is tempted by Blandford's rake friend Bellamy, an Englishman who comes to the country to hunt for animals and for female prey. Blandford eventually wins back his Lydia, while Bellamy plans to ruin Harriet, but his scheme is exposed by Jonathan and Sally. In the end, love and honesty prevail over temptation and fleeting fashions, and the rural community presented in this pastoral opera prospers.

Woodworth's play offers a tongue-in-cheek rendition of the pastoral (as defined by Gifford 1999, Williams 1975, and Marx 2000), based on the stage composition as well as the self-conscious acting of the figures. The pastoral tradition is questioned, most prominently, by Jonathan Ploughboy, who comes to the New England village from another Yankee dwelling, Taunton, MA. His Yankeedom is set against theirs: he is the only trader in a community of farmers and the only male character who has no particular love interest but who tests various ladies. He is also the only character who displays an inner conflict between negative and positive traits, with an agenda to gain a foothold by marrying a girl and establishing a shop.

But even before Jonathan enters the action, the ideal of rural life is revealed as construct in the primary and secondary text. In the overture, Woodworth describes the countryside's awakening, with noises eventually orchestrated into a musical portrait of village bustle:

> *The overture expresses the various sounds which are heard at early down, in the country, commencing at that hour of silence when even the ticking of the village clock is supposed to be heard. It strikes four, and a gentle bustle succeeds, indicating the first movement of the villagers. A confused murmur gradually swells on the ear, in which can be distinguished the singing of birds, the shepherd's pipe, the hunter's horn, etc.etc. until the united strength of the band represents the whole village engaged in their rustic engagements.* (Woodworth 1966: I, 1, 155; all subsequent references to this edition)

Woodworth's village features the props of the rural ideal: birds, shepherd's pipe, and hunter's horn. Village life appears as preordained in an Aristotelian unity of time and space: the play begins in the morning and ends with a harvest dance at night of the same day. But this dramatic unity is ordered by the striking of the village clock, with its "dial plate" that looms in the background of the scene on a "village spire" (ibid.). The vision of village life is one of modern times, where the work begins even before the arrival of daylight, and in the stage directions, the clock remains the timekeeper as the action unfolds. The face of the clock thus literally oversees the activities of the villagers.

It transforms the rural ideal of the remote New England village into an industrialized work space where the workers are subjected to the dictate of the clock. In combination with the invention of electric light, the replacement of daytime labor hours by the clock compartmentalizes labor in hours and minutes (see e.g. Marsh 2005 and O'Malley 1990, as well as Chapter 4). The image of the village clock paints an American pastoral in the sense of Leo Marx's *Machine in the Garden* (Marx 2000; see also Erbacher et al. 2014). Woodworth's pastoral opera is set in the tamed landscape of a "farm-yard, separated from a field by a pale fence, with a gate" and a "cottage" (I, 1, 155). Harriet, Lydia, and William arrive on the scene to get their work day started. They join in with a joyful expository song about their country life of "sweet seclusion, far from bustling towns" that is colored by the "rich profusion [of] Autumn's yellow bounties [. . .] mellow gold lands" and vines that "court the hand" (ibid.). In the harvest season, Nature spoils them with riches yellow and gold, lovingly returning their cultivation efforts with caresses that "court the hand." The song ends:

> All the day, to recreate us,
> Strains of music freight the breeze,
> Healthful sports at eve await us—
> What are city joys to these? (Ibid.)

In this song, Nature as pantheistic mother nourishes and replenishes the villagers. They do not tire from their toil but look forward to "healthful sports" that are much more inspiring than the urban "sports" temptations of the tavern and the gambling table. The pastime dance and song of the workers returning from work at the end of Act I similarly finds "[s]weet the hour when freed from labor lads and lasses thus convene [. . .] nymphs with all their native graces, swains with every charm to win" (I, 4, 164).

Against this bucolic vision of singing and dancing village workers stands Harriet's first utterance: "This may all sound very well in song, Lydia, but, for all that, I should like to have an opportunity to judge for myself" (I, 1, 155). Harriet's curiosity takes a turn to coquetry at the first occasion. Her ticket out of the village would be "a beau with gallantry enough to take me [to the city]" (156), so she hopes to attract a "city beau" by affecting simplicity. She pretends in an aside "not to hear him," and sings a country song even louder to make herself noticed. Her newly arrived interest, the cunning Englishman Bellamy, likewise plays a double game by commenting on this display in asides: he calls her singing "tolerable, but damn'd little science," and finds Harriet a "fine girl" and "simpleton." Bellamy starts speaking figuratively to her about "hearing a nightingale," which immediately brings her to her wit's end ("I do not understand you sir"). Harriet thus reveals herself as a real "simple artless" country girl (II, 1, 165), while Bellamy's courtship is shown as devoid of real affection; the village girl is indeed threatened by the worldly tempter ("We change [the girls] once a fortnight," ibid.).

The opening scene of *The Forest Rose* consequently paints the pastoral scenario as a staged illusion in which the figures act as players with the sole aim of finding a love interest. The rules are known to the players, and they do not hide their real intentions behind a mask of make-believe and affectation. The humor of the play results from different conventions of performance: Bellamy is unable to read Harriet's coyness as real ("No city belle could perform better," II, 2, 167), and Harriet, overwhelmed with his city manners, starts to reconsider the honest country boy William. Their pretense is contrasted with the real devotion that makes Lydia and Blandford so unhappy; Lydia's pride is hurt not because she feels inferior but because of the "haughty" and "purse-proud" behavior of Blandford's father, whom his own son calls an "Englishman with foibles" (see I, 1, 156; II, 4, 170 and 171). This constellation, like the befuddlement of Harriet and Bellamy, critiques social pretense and city manners. The songs of the play express the real suffering of the lovers Lydia and Blandford or the romantic charade Harriet and Bellamy get engaged in. Woodworth clashes musical and spoken language, the poetic expression of rustic romance and courtship as a business transaction. This becomes most obvious when Jonathan, after being refused by Sally, is urged by Granny Gossip to court Harriet instead (I, 4, 162–3).

Because Harriet is impatient with Jonathan's awkward proposal, the two sing a duet in which Harriet asks him to display his love ("You'll have to lie and flatter, and swear, my lad [. . .] Declare you even love, sir, the ground on which I tread"). Jonathan focuses on the bartering ("I love the ground you walk on, for 'tis your father's farm. // Could that be mine without you, I'd be a happy man, // But since you go together, I will love you if I can"). But Harriet's dream of a city life ("a coach and horses [. . .] footmen all in livery, // And when you don't attend me, I'll get another beau") is too much for Jonathan; he decides to go for Sally, since "I will not live in town."

In the course of events, romantic love is replaced by marriage business. Gender norms are tied to commodity discourse, in which the exchange value of men and women is linked to animal or plant imagery. This is true, for instance, for the male dandy: the farmer William, who feels threatened by Bellamy, compares English "dandies" to "donkeys," because they have the "same root," even though the American version appears to have more (masculinity) value: "The real genuine dandy is an imported animal; and the breed having been crossed in this country, the fullblooded bucks command but a low price in the market at the present time" (I, 1, 157). The "dandies" Bellamy and Blandford admittedly come to the country for leisure and to forget business, but their hunting activities concentrate on female "game," "[b]lushing like Innocence, and smiling like Venus" (II, 1, 164 and 165). Bellamy's plan to return to town with a "Forest Rose" (II, 1, 165) encapsulates the play's main theme and pinpoints the sexual value pinned onto the country in this pastoral opera. While Bellamy's image of the forest rose implies an innocent rustic beauty blooming in the forest out there for his taking, the play's actual "Forest Rose" is the young black slave Rose Forest, property of Deacon Forest. The deacon's daughter Sally abuses Rose twice to repel male lovemaking: in I, 2, Sally has Jonathan close his eyes and kiss Rose instead of herself; in the finale, she uses the same trick, disguising Rose as Harriet, whom Bellamy is planning to take away. Bellamy's embarrassment, when he discovers his error in front of everyone, results in the racist wordplay cautioning against "love in the dark" (II, 5, 172): the slave girl's dark complexion makes her repulsive to the white men, whether they are seeking true love like Jonathan, or sexual entertainment like Bellamy. Jeffrey Richards (2000) has explored the racist logic of the play with Toni Morrison's trope of "playing in the dark" about the muted African presence in American literature and culture that makes whiteness shine. Richards argues that this mechanism is enacted by the humiliation and dehumanization of Rose. Like black figures in other plays of the antebellum stage, Rose would be played by a white actress in blackface, with exaggerated physical features. In *The Forest Rose*, Jonathan is disgusted by Rose's alleged odor of garlic and onions; when Blandford inquires about Lydia, Jonathan thinks he is talking about Rose Forest ("They call her the black Rose," I, 4, 161); this misunderstanding turns Blandford's romantic hope from a "bud of hope" into a "clove of garlic" (ibid.).

Richards focuses on Jonathan's formulaic quip "I wouldn't serve a negro so": whenever he is doubted by another figure, he defends his virtue with this motto, but of course he tolerates Sally's abuse of Rose and discriminates against the girl whenever he can, which may be the best proof against his self-defensive "I wouldn't serve a negro so." Given the central pun around the forest rose in the play, I propose to shift Richards's argument about the presence of black characters on the stage towards the commodification of the female body, both black and white: Rose is employed to highlight white female sexuality as a luxury commodity. Rose, technically the title character, represents the grotesque and most extreme disfigurement of the romantic love concept of the forest rose.[17] The combination of her floral name and the stench of garlic and onions is oxymoronic; the rose bud resembles the layered shape of the onion. Both are consumed, but where the rose represents a (sexual) luxury, the garlic is a mundane ingredient that should not be overdosed. The racist trope of *The Forest Rose* becomes a vignette; it is cited, for instance, in *Blanche of Brandywine* (Burnett 1858), a Revolutionary War play which was adapted for the stage by the author and by actor Joseph Jefferson. In the first scene, the Yankee figure, Seth Hope, is playing blind man's bluff and is led to kiss the black character Sampson instead of his love interest Rose; he complains of her "smelling of onions," and the other figures joke about making "Love in the dark" or "to the dark" (Burnett 1858: I, 1). *Blanche of Brandywine* contains a hodgepodge of genres and theatrical entertainments; next to Rose's funny trickery of Seth, the play draws heavily from Cooper's novel *The Spy* (1821; see Chapter 4), with a spy plot, skirmishes between the front lines, two damsels in distress who are abducted and saved, and a shipwreck. Its revolutionary plot line culminates in the battle cry "Vengeance, Washington, and Right," and the final tableau has all-American figures wrestling British soldiers to their knees.

Woodworth, in *The Forest Rose*, ambiguates not only the oxymoronic Rose but also the other female characters of the play: Lydia and Harriet wear the same dress and appear from the same farm door in the play; even their lovers confound them. The men talk about female beauty in dark hair and eyes several times. Blandford talks about Lydia's "black hair, dark eyes, pouting lips," but Jonathan mistakes this for Deacon Forest's Lid Rose (I, 4, 161), which withers Blandford's dewy-eyed adoration quickly. In the next scene, Harriet asks Jonathan to "tell me all about my beautiful eyes, auburn hair, rosy cheeks, pouting lips and ivory teeth," to which Jonathan replies dryly: "That's just what a fellow said today about the deacon's wench" (I, 5, 163). In the wake of this confusion, the beauty value of dark features seems questionable. By implication, its opposite, whiteness of complexion and presumably blonde hair, shines even brighter, but none of the country ladies possesses this exquisite look.

In this blur of hearsay and adoration, the romantic lover Blandford literally gets lost in the woods: "Involved in the mazes of this intricate forest, every step increases my perplexity and adds to my fatigue" (II, 3, 168).[18] Woodworth's usage of forest imagery contains a nod to the pastoral view of Shakespeare's Forest of Arden in *As You Like It* or the night-time forest of *A Midsummer Night's Dream*, with its playful disguises and confused lovers. Yet, ironically, the village setting is hardly a sylvan idyll. The romantic symbolism of the forest rose is undermined by the marriage economy, in which those beautiful "forest roses" are prized like cattle. This is also shown in the deliberately confusing names: apart from the oxymoronic Rose Forest/Forest Rose, there is Sally Rose, the deacon's daughter, and Lydia Roseville, the country girl. Harriet Miller has no floral reference in her name, but is obsessed with courting and romance. Among the female figures of the play, only Sally's looks remain nondescript, since she is an important figure for the resolution of the plot: she exposes Bellamy, saves Harriet, and assures that the order is maintained. In the end, Lydia is off to city life with her bourgeois American beau Blandford, while Bellamy weakly threatens to pen a derogatory travelogue about his American experience. Woodworth's pastoral opera entangles the opposite spaces of the village and the city in a national narrative.

The Forest Rose opposes two modes of the pastoral: the idealized forest where lovers may carelessly indulge in their whims and city lads abandon their business to love's follies, and the American pastoral as vision of a social order; the stage mostly shows the village backdrop with the steeple and the clock as a reminder of the work that needs to be done to sustain the community. The Yankee Jonathan Ploughboy brings this second meaning of the pastoral to its fullest expression. His last name marks the country's transition from the rural dwelling towards a capitalist economy: Ploughboy describes himself as "[a] little in the marchant way, and a piece of farmer besides" (I, 3, 160). He is typically focused on trading, inquires about bargains, and repeats the formulas "I calculate" and "by way of trade" (see e.g. II, 2, 167). As the only businessman of the village, Ploughboy prevails over the urban businessmen Blandford and Bellamy, if involuntarily so. During their first encounter, Jonathan and Blandford misunderstand each other and Blandford is frustrated by Jonathan's provinciality and inquisitiveness:

Jonathan: [. . .] If I may be so bold, sir, what may I call your name?
Blandford: Stupid—Pshaw! I will keep my temper!
J: Stupid Shaw, 'spose you an't any ways related to Squire Shaw of Taunton, are you? He that married the widow Lovett, mother of Ichabod Lovett, who was tried for horse-stealing?

> B: [*Aside*] I must humor this fellow, or find the Eagle Tavern myself. [. . .] What do you sell?
> J: Everything, whiskey, molasses, calicoes, spelling-books, and patent gridirons.
> B: With which you contrive to shave the natives?
> J: No sir; everybody shaves themselves here.—There is no barber nearer than Paris.
> B: You don't understand me. By shaving I mean making a *sharp* bargain or what your parson or deacon might denominate cheating.
> J: I wouldn't serve a negro so. But as to the parson or deacon, folks say they are pretty cute that way themselves. (I, 3, 160–1)

With his asides, Blandford appears as superior to the country bumpkin in this scene. By asking about "shaving the natives," he links the ignorant Jonathan to Yankee shrewdness and the peddler's ability to sell anything. This exchange contrasts the urban businessman and the aspiring country entrepreneur. In Blandford's eyes, Jonathan oscillates between provinciality and smartness: "Confound your stupidity, or your shrewdness, I know not which to call it!" (I, 3, 161; see also Joshua Silsbee as Ploughboy, Appendix III).

Woodworth's Jonathan Ploughboy is an ambiguous stage Yankee, naïve and shrewd at the same time. He is tricked by Sally, who puts a samp mortar on his knee when he falls asleep and exposes his ineptness as a lover. He is also snubbed by Harriet, who dreams of a city life he cannot offer her. He fails to read the initials of Lydia and Blandford on the locket, proposing that they mean "C. for cows, and B. for Bulls, and L. for Lambs, and R. for Rams" (II, 3, 171). However, in the end, he lures Sally into consent by promising she may wear Lydia's locket at the dance, and he keeps the money Bellamy offered him for assistance in the elopement, arguably a dishonest act. Jonathan wins the money and gets the girl. In the play's only soliloquy, Jonathan argues with himself about the moral conflict tied to the elopement money:

> Jonathan: I don't calculate I feel exactly right about keeping this purse; and yet, I believe I should feel still worse to give it back. Twentythree dollars is a speculation that an't to be sneezed at, for it an't to be catch'd every day. But will it be right to keep the money, when I don't intended to do the job? Now if I was at home, in Taunton, I would put that question to our debating society; and I would support the affirmative side of the question. "Mr. Chairman! Hem! If A. gives B. a sum of money to do an unlawful act; and if A.—no, if B. instead of doing that wicked act, exposes A., then B. prevents a crime, and deserves a reward; while A. having intended, with malice aforethought, to do a wicked action, is justly punished;

and that, Mr. Chairman, which punished the aggressor, ought to reward the-the-the *informer*." No—stop, I don't like that word, informer. (II, 3, 169)

Jonathan's soliloquy engages the audience in a staged dispute about his honesty and reputation. By imagining his appearance at the debating society, Jonathan plays out a New England community ritual and shows his shrewdness: he is concerned about being an "informer" and wants to be perceived as keeper of good morals and order. As newcomer, Jonathan needs a good reputation as well as capital to start his business; at the end of the play, he retains both and can thus start to enact his new part as village shopkeeper.

In the final scene, the modernization of the New England village goes full throttle. Lydia leaves for city life and William can save and modernize his farm. In the play's final spoken word, Deacon Miller affirms the importance of American farmers to the wealth of the nation: "while we are lords of the luxuriant soil which heeds us, there is no lot on earth more enviable than that of AMERICAN FARMERS" (II, 3, 173). All characters join in a song about their fate, with individual stanzas and a chorus "For lords of the soil, and fed by our toil, American farmers are blest my boys, American farmers are blest" (ibid.). Jonathan's stanza links the play to the national and transatlantic arenas:

> By girls we may be thus cajoled,
> But not by any dandy blade,
> Whatever price be paid.
> But tempters are told, as we pocket the gold,
> It's all in the way of trade, my boys,
> It's all in the way of trade. (Ibid.)

Jonathan argues that Bellamy, the "dandy blade," fails because "a Yankee's honor" is not for sale. Instead Jonathan "pockets the gold" and insists on "the way of trade." In *The Forest Rose*, the Yankee performs business ambition and capitalist masculinity. Jonathan displays a fraternal contest of national manhood among young white men that occurs in a number of plays. In the logic of the American pastoral, Jonathan occupies the middle ground between farmers and businessmen in the village, and between "honest" (or would-be honest) village business and the big/transatlantic business of the city.

A different take on this contest surfaces in Abraham Lindsley's *Love and Friendship, or Yankee Notions* (1809), an early Yankee play that transports Tyler's *The Contrast* into the urban setting of

Charleston, South Carolina. In *Love and Friendship*, the Yankee Jonathan oscillates between revolutionary New Englander and country half-wit. Lindsley designed the play "for a farce, but being considered too long, [it] has been printed as a comedy" (Lindsley 1809, author commentary, n.p.), and his sketching of Yankee figures may be the strongest clue to his farcical interest. The play revolves around the love of the Bostonian Seldreer for Augusta Marcene, the daughter of a rich Charleston merchant, who is saved from an unhappy marriage to the fop Dick Dashaway. The love plot's resolution maps sectional conflict between honest and virtuous Northerners and a Southern elite corrupted by greed and learning: Mr. Dashaway freely admits to his own corruption ("I got my fortune by cheating and lying, and it's cursed hard if I can't lie a little to help my son to a rich wife," I, 3, 17); his son Dick is a half-wit drunk and gambler softened by education who clings to the formula "I learned it all in college" (see e.g. I, 2, 14; II, 1, 27 and 28).

Compared to the Southerners corrupted by greed and college learning, the male Yankee figures are ideal businessmen and romantic lovers. Seldreer, the Bostonian "gentleman Yankee" (II, 2, 30), comes into a fortune which makes him marriageable. Jonathan, the country bumpkin, travels south as valet to Captain Horner and as trader looking to sell his "Yankee notions." A salesman, he advertises New Jersey cider as national drink, produced by the "true blue" Revolutionaries "from the Jarsays, and somehow folks think its better'n ourn, for its true jarsay blue, made arter the pattern'f seventy-six" (I, 1, 8). Jonathan meets the seafaring Yankee figure Jack Hardweather, who appears smarter at first sight. The two figures are distinguished by their speech; Jack employs seafaring metaphors ("Shiver my topsails and chain plates," II, 4, 37), while Jonathan uses dialect and Yankeeisms ("it beets the very rot and all anter! [. . .] I swow I believe I am raked before and aft, from stem tewe starn," II, 4, 38). Jack characterizes Jonathan as "my blue skin Presbyterian Eaton and Decatur! [. . .] pass the grog brother blue skin!" (II, 4, 38–9). And indeed Jonathan reveals himself as a Puritan when he asks Captain Horner not to swear ("what would our parson say?", I, 1, 10). A patriotic New Englander, Jonathan also sings stanzas of "Yankee Doodle" (I, 1, 11) and blurts out patriotic mottos ("Huzza! Bunker Hill forever tewe the enemies of Columby, and the sweet kisses of her pretty girls tewe her galyant sons," II, 2, 30; "bunker hill and the yankee boys forever! (*steps off*)," II, 4, 40).

Predictably, Jonathan the country Yankee and Jack the seafaring Yankee try to trick each other (see II, 4). Jack Hardweather may appear more worldly, but it is Jonathan who ushers in the happy ending. Before exiting, he describes to the audience the two happy couples and the reformed Dashaway men:

> Jonathan: I'm not off yit. (*views the company with much satisfaction*) What a nation fine thing it is tewe have a pretty wife, by gum! Darned 'f I don't git straight along back tewe Suffield agin, and marry along'f my sweet Polly Perkins, and we'll kick up sich a rotten dust on't, never fetch me! Bunker hill and the yankee gals for ever, for the yankee boy, says brother Jonathan. (*exit*) (III, 2, 57)

Even though Jonathan does not get the very last word, he performs the part of chorus who explains the clash between romantic love and matchmaking. Jonathan emphasizes that a love match holds a happy future not only for individuals, but for the nation: his quip about the "nation fine thing" only makes sense in connection with the "Yankee notions" he sells. As I show below, the "notions" have a double meaning, as objects of trade and as Northern virtues. In the end, honesty prevails over greed, Yankee men over Southern rakes and manipulating dames. All Yankees are off to find women to ensure the dissemination of "Yankee notions" in the world, and poetic justice grants a future only to those who deserve it. In *Love and Friendship*, the Yankee is not only a trader and suitor himself: as theatrical figure and embodiment of New England smartness, he installs national prosperity as ulterior aim to the wooing business.

From his beginnings as country bumpkin, the stage Yankee develops into a Jacksonian go-ahead man. On the postbellum stage, he reappears as mild old man, chock-full of memories, and as preserver of good morals, a remnant of the antebellum era. The aged Yankee looks back at a life of achievement and interlinks the rural past with the industrialized present. Where the young Yankee related the country to the city, the old Yankee stands at the threshold to modern America, carrying a nostalgic value of identity and belonging. He continues the normalization of a white masculine perspective on life and serves as a guardian to the young men fending for themselves. The aged Yankee is an uncle figure whose kinship to the conflicted young men is at one remove from fatherhood. This nepotic relation alleviates intergenerational conflict: the uncle acts as counsellor and paternal friend and amalgamates the clownish awkwardness of the country bumpkin with the guidance of the rustic Yankee. He reverberates with folkloristic comic uncle types of the New England rural community such as Uncle Zeb, cultivator of gigantic turnips, from Ebenezer Venture's monologue cited earlier in this chapter (LaBree 1841). As embodiment of national character, he impersonates a (New England) home and history at the same time. On the verge of modernity, the Yankee uncle serves as a reminder of better (rural) times and places and as carrier of New England community virtues into an uncertain but ambitiously imperial future. Like his younger version, he retains a key position in the resolution of the central conflict in plays that employ nepotic filiation across genre boundaries: Denman Thompson's *The Old Homestead* (1889) mixes the folkloristic character sketch with the sentimental novel, and James A. Herne's realist play *Shore Acres* (1892) endows the Yankee with a personal past and psychological depth. Further Yankee uncle figures that cannot be considered here include Uncle Hosea Biglow from James Russell Lowell's humor writings *The Biglow Papers* (1885), and the farmer Adam Trueman in Anna Cora Mowatt's broadway hit *Fashion, or Life in New York* (1845; Mowatt 1997).

In Denman Thompson's play *The Old Homestead* (first perf. 1886, Boston Theater), the union of a romantic couple is imperiled because the young man, Reuben, leaves New Hampshire to make a living in New York. His Uncle Josh, the Yankee figure, goes to look for him and, after some city adventures, brings him back and sees him united with his country love Ruth. Thompson developed the play from the original sketch "Joshua Whitcomb" he performed successfully in the 1870s. The Uncle Josh figure therefore holds a central position in the plot, representing moral authority, old rural ways of life, and the good soul of the story. The *dramatis personae* draws from local characters of Thompson's hometown of Swanzey, New Hampshire. Thompson acted the part of Uncle Josh himself and received praise for his "naturalism" that distinguished Uncle Josh from the flamboyant stage Yankee of earlier times (Miller 2007: 154). The New York production featured "real oxen, hay [and] well water" and transported city dwellers back to their country origins, *The Spirit of the Times* maintained, like "an old cradle song, heard again in later life" (qtd. in ibid.).

In 1889, Thompson transformed the play into a sentimental novel (Thompson 1889 in the following), which will be discussed here because the author molds his experience as actor and playwright into the narrative. Like the play, the novel's "homespun" quality literally ennobled the American plot: "there was *nobility of soul* under *homespun cloth*, such as is not often found under the finest product of the foreign loom" (ibid. vii, emphasis added). Thompson's prose version catered to the literary fashions of the day; whereas the play allegedly did not have enough room "for all the facts of this true and wholesome story [. . .] [and] there is no love [in the play]" (vii), Thompson added a double love plot with the star-crossed lovers Ruth and Reuben, who get their happy ending, and the unhappy couple Ben and Sue Eastman. Ben, an American farmer, cannot compete with the businessman Reuben, and Sue falls prey to the temptations of the city and to her own jealousy and plotting. Against this sentimental love trouble, the clumsy wooing of Cyrus Prime, a country rube who pursues the old spinster Aunt Matilda, provides comic relief and village curiosity.

The success of *The Old Homestead* continued beyond Thompson's death; it was made into a film in 1915 and, to this day, is performed regularly in Thompson's hometown of Swanzey. With its nostalgic image of the rural past, it has become a fixture in the community's regional identity. The website of "The Old Homestead Association" projects the play's poetic justice onto New England character and the very essence of the nation:

> In a word, "The Old Homestead" epitomizes not merely the New England in which its scenes are laid, but the nation as well. It stands for those rugged qualities that have made this nation great. It stands for all that is clean and worth-while in our life.[19]

Denman Thompson thus created a signature rural image that developed its own economy throughout the ages. Like Woodworth's *Forest Rose*, the production of *The Old Homestead* with sounds and smells from the New England village evoked a synesthetic authenticity and a pastoral landscape in which the farmers happily toil away. Likewise, the novel opens with a landscape view during haying season with a female traveler nearly scorched by the heat:

> It was late in the afternoon of a warm July day, but the glowing sun, still at a white heat, was sufficiently high in the heavens to make the shaded side of the dusty New Hampshire road very grateful to the traveler by foot; even though that traveler carried her own protection against the sun's rays in the guise of a hat with a brim so broad that it drooped with languid curves about the sweet, rosy face of its owner. (Thompson 1889: 8; all subsequent references to this edition)

The New England summer threatens the white skin of the young woman, who is subjected to a physical description that also pays heed to her unmarried state: "she was pretty, and winsome [. . .] lissome and free, with the grace of youth and robust good health [. . .] hands that honestly wash dishes and make butter" (9). Her hair, it is further described, has a curly "coquettishness" to it, but her personality, "in simplicity of thought and directness of expression, abhorred coquetry" (11). Ruth Stratton, this young woman walking, is observed by a man looking for her qualifications as country wife: her body promises healthy offspring and fitness for labor; her hair inspires flirty intentions, but she shows no interest in such engagements. With this gaze and reflection as to her character, Ruth is viewed as a commodity, a trophy wife for the American farmer Ben Eastman, who turns out to be the voyeur in this scene:

> A pair of keen eyes had [. . .] been watching her for more than five minutes [. . .] a strong, sun-browned hand shaded the blue eyes [. . .] [and] the man [. . .] strode with a long, plough-learned step to a big, black-cherry tree and waited [. . .] so that he could easily watch the approach of the young girl. (10–11)

Thompson's narrator adapts the gaze of a man who knows he will need a wife to get ahead in life. Eastman's desiring gaze links the body of the young woman walking "with furtive shyness" (10) to the land. To build a future, he has to cultivate both the virginal female body and the sundrenched farmland. Compared to *The Forest Rose*, *The Old Homestead* articulates more explicitly what Annette Kolodny has called "land-as-woman" (1975: ix). Woodworth's pastoral opera toyed with the pastoral ideal and exposed the strain of farming that would be simplified by industrialization, anticipating the modernization of agrarian society. By comparison, the Progressive Era narrative of *The Old Homestead* suggests a similarly simple rural world, with the able-bodied farmer looking out for wife and land. However, the story is more complicated: despite being ogled and courted by Ben, Ruth stands by her man, Reuben Whitcomb. Ben and Reuben are cast as different evolutionary types of American masculinity, the farmer and the banker. In this story, it is the banker who gets an outlook at a prosperous future. As David Danbom has shown, by the end of the nineteenth century, even though "rural and America were no longer coincidental, [. . .] farmers remained essential to the Republic's political and social health" (2015: 13). Ben Eastman's only trouble is his unrequited love for Ruth; Reuben, however, navigates an identity crisis and loss of reputation as well as the temptations of the city before returning home.

Reuben impersonates a city migrant: he starts as a bank clerk in the nearby New Jersey town of Keene with a positive outlook that is spoiled when a false witness accuses him of bank robbery. Even though his innocence is proven quickly, his name is tarnished and he seeks to rehabilitate himself by "making it" in New York. The central conflict develops around Reuben's failure to see he really belongs in the country, with Ruth, but the narrative does not provide Reuben's point of view. Instead, Ruth is the sentimental heroine, who fights her fears after Reuben leaves and, when in New York, resists the plotting of her rival, Sue Eastman. The sentimental plot invites an allegorical reading of Ruth as romantic lover and fertile body, who bestows a future on either the farmer or the banker. Her struggle to choose between them showcases simultaneously the value of American womanhood and of a cultivated landscape. Ruth's choice displays the shift to modernity, when the farmer's function shifts from "bedrock of the Republic" (Danbom 2015: 13) to impersonation of a pre-industrial past. Returning from New York, the couple looks toward building the capitalist future from their settlement in Swanzey. There, they remain firmly rooted in the "old homestead," their childhood home and their provincial New England identity.

The New England farm evokes rural neatness and order, just like its inhabitants Uncle Josh and Aunt Matilda. They are cast against a babylonic image of New York. All the characters of the novel save young Reuben perceive the city as a "wicked place" with "lots of poor folks, an' lots o'young men with nuthin t'do" (60, 63).[20] Uncle Josh's sojourn to New York reiterates the vignette of the country rube lost in the city. This episode is told from Josh's naïve but good-willed perspective; he experiences estrangement and rudeness first hand: "He tried always to do it right, according to his notion of it. He was perfectly free from self-consciousness; and he was as generous in his feelings as he was direct and simple in his manner" (169).

In the city, Josh is disoriented and overwhelmed. Shopkeepers and businessmen repeatedly mistake him for a rural trader and shush him away when he asks for directions ("we don't need any taters," 170, 171). He realizes he cannot feed all the poor and help all the needy. Apart from poverty, Josh also witnesses moral decay; at the hotel, he puts an ailing young girl to bed for recovery and looks for her father, who arrives but approaches his daughter's bed with sexual intent. Scandalized by this lewd behavior, Josh throws the geezer out of the window (192). The old farmer is a fast learner and typical Yankee; he is naïve at first but quickly adjusts to the situation, adapting the social Darwinist imperative of city life by saving whom he can while maintaining his dignity. The novel offers a split perspective: the longest part of the story is dedicated to the love conflict as perceived through the eyes of Ruth, Reuben, and Ben. For the city episode,

Thompson chooses Uncle Josh as focalizer, blending the country bumpkin narrative with the nostalgic image of the mature Yankee. Josh impersonates both the awkward bumpkin and the moral senior who lets Reuben go, hoping the young man will eventually return.

The Yankee uncle in *The Old Homestead* is funny, authoritative, and a replacement father who embodies the white American farmer whose masculinity stems from cultivating the earth and building the nation, from the Revolutionary War onwards (see e.g. Fitz 2010: 81–93; Inge 1969). Strong enough to throw a man out of the window, he is also manly in his physical prowess, an aspect which distinguishes him from the feminized African American Uncle Tom figure. A paragon for African American masculinity to the present day, the friendly and harmless stock figure Uncle Tom juxtaposes the equally hurtful hypermasculinized stereotype of the black rapist.[21] In contrast to these stereotypes which relegate black men to the sidelines of the family and of society, the Yankee uncle not only retains his sprightly posture even at an advanced age but, more importantly, is ready to step in and act as father of the family, as in James A. Herne's *Shore Acres*.

A Progressive Era narrative like *The Old Homestead*, *Shore Acres*, set in 1891, links moral virtue and true love to financial prosperity. It is built around Uncle Nat, a Civil War veteran who lives with the family of his younger brother Martin at the Berry farm in Bar Harbor, Maine. *Shore Acres* brought Herne economic success and critical acclaim because of its "charming [and] [. . .] poetic realism" (qtd. in Moody 1966b: 669). Compared to his play *Margaret Fleming* (1890), in which the protagonist sacrifices herself for her own baby and her husband's illegitimate offspring from an extramarital affair, *Shore Acres* seemed "more realistic and attractive" (ibid.): the unity and property of the New England farmer's family are preserved. The happy ending and the Uncle Nat figure stress the play's nationalist symbolism. Herne's aged Yankee, a defender of home and nation, might have been the secret of the play's success. Over this part, Herne even had a falling out with his long-time partner, New York manager Abraham Erlanger, who wanted star actor and Yankee impersonator Joseph Jefferson as Uncle Nat (see ibid. 668, 669). Herne staged *Shore Acres* for the first time at the Boston Museum on February 20, 1893, and himself starred as Uncle Nat until 1898.

Herne's Uncle Nat transforms the stage Yankee into a substitute paterfamilias when the real head of the family, Martin Berry, falls prey to the temptations of the Gilded Age. Uncle Nat develops from comical country bumpkin to caretaker. In the beginning, he consoles his niece Helen, who is secretly in love with Samuel Warren; he plays horse with young Millie and lends his gun to a neighbor trying to kill a fox. Yet he soon becomes a heroic figure when he volunteers to keep the family lighthouse running and saves the ship *Liddy Ann* from hitting the rocks when his brother Martin wanted them to crash. Martin is neither fit to run the family farm nor a good husband to Ann, whom he embarrasses in front of their guests (Herne 1966: 699–700).²² Herne's description in the secondary text casts Nat as stage Yankee, "of the soil," endowed with "much sly, quiet humor":

> *A man of sixty, and his large sturdy frame shows signs of toil. His eyes, of a faded blue-gray, have the far-seeing common to sailors. He wears his yellow-white hair rather long, and he is clean-shaven save for the tippet of straw-white beard that seems to grow up from his chest and form a sort of frame for his benevolent, weather-beaten old face. Uncle Nat is of the soil, yet there is an inherent poise and dignity about him that are typical of the men who have mastered their environment. He has great cheerfulness and much sly, quiet humor.* (I, 673)

Herne's Yankee has "mastered his environment," and in the end saves the Berry family and their estate. Herne's figures differ from the stock personnel of the antebellum Yankee plays; they have psychological depth and experience inner conflict, which Herne chisels out in the secondary text with narrative strategies. When Nat first learns about Martin's plan to sell the farm, his thoughts change his character from comic good-hearted Yankee figure to warden of the family fortune. Herne uses free indirect discourse to paint the beloved land in Nat's mind and before the reader's eye:

> *Slowly it comes to him that his brother is saying "Sell the farm." He grows cold—there is a heavy lump where his heart was beating a moment ago. His eyes grow dim and tired—there is no sunshine—no more music in the day. Sell the farm—the dear fields with all their slopes and undulations, the great old silver birches guarding the orchards from the pastures, the gnarled oaks along the rocky shore. He knows in a thousand aspects this old farm, summer and winter, always affable and friendly to him, and it is here he has learned to know God and love him.* (I, 686–7)

Nat's thoughts feminize the land ("dear," "affable and friendly to him") and assert its emotional and economic value and need for protection from enemies ("birches guarding the orchards"). This pastoral image in Nat's mind reiterates the opening description of the Berry farm in Maine. Herne's narrative visualization of the land recalls landscape painting: he writes about "picturesque hills," "mountains veiled in mist," "birds sing[ing], flitting to and fro" (I, 673). The settlement is organically entwined in nature, the "farmhouse [. . .] hidden in profusion of shrubs and flowers," "trees overhang[ing] the roof" of the house and barn (ibid.). Such harmony canvasses the prosperous agricultural tradition at the Berry farm, where the land has been adorned with "old fashioned flowers." This description reiterates the pastoral ideal of *The Forest Rose*, and just like Woodworth's play, Herne includes the Marxian machines in the garden:

> *A tiny steam launch appears once, about the middle of the act, and is seen no more. A mowing machine is heard at work in the distance off left. It stops, turns, goes on again, while the voice of the driver is heard guiding his horses [. . .]. (All this must be very distant.)* (Ibid.)

Herne's agrarian pastoral is a modernized one. The sounds of birds and insects ("the one distinct note of the scene," ibid.) blend with the bustle of the mowing machine; the plough lying "against the lower end of the fence" harmoniously coexists with the "steam launch." Herne uses the landscape to establish a link between the property and its owners in the first scene of the play. Uncle Nat chats with Helen and little Millie, but soon the farmer Gates arrives to borrow Uncle Nat's gun. Their talk about the army gun recalls the perils of the past: Uncle Nat calls his gun "Uncle Sam'l" and uses the female pronoun to describe "her," who was "fit all through the war" and "never kicked me" (I, 675). In the present of the play's setting in 1891, the gun epitomizes Uncle Nat's role: it sits in the kitchen corner, always loaded, ready to defend the house and family. As a second reminder of the Civil War, Uncle Nat's army coat and cap are hanging next to the kitchen door (II, 688). These props of Nat's biography link the Berry family history to the fate of the nation. In the past, the Union was preserved, thanks to the efforts of Uncle Nat and others—even though Uncle Nat does not brag, he lets on that he "used to jus' p'int 'er, shet both my eyes 'n let 'r do her own work" (I, 676). On the one hand, the fighting was thus done by "Uncle Sam," i.e. the government itself embodied in Uncle Nat's gun. On the other hand, the comradeship of the two "uncles" represents their unity in purpose and effort.

Like the imperiled republic, the Berry family in the past had to face threats to their unity; young Nat nursed his baby brother Martin and later left his part of the farm to him. When Martin showed interest in Ann, Nat went off to war (III, 1, 704–6). During their fight in the lighthouse, Nat also confesses his love for his brother's wife Ann and that their first child, Helen, is really his own. Nat thus atones for his sins by saving his family. He has matured into a moral authority, quite literally a "keeper of the light" of tradition in stormy times. His moral authority jars with his actions, such as when he helps Helen elope with Sam. Helen is under age and disobeys her father, who wants her to marry the land speculator Blake. Uncle Nat encourages her to follow her true love and takes money from the family savings. He gives Helen his mother's wedding band, in good faith that she will not be ruined by Sam.

Herne's postbellum stage Yankee has a personal and national history. With this variation on the well-known comic persona, Herne affirms the Yankee's hyperbolic relation to the nation. Whereas the antebellum stage Yankee would save the young heroine from elopement and from corruption by a greedy impostor, Herne's realist Yankee relies on Helen's innate virtue and education. Helen's two fathers act in opposite ways: Nat hands over the responsibility for her life and body to herself; Martin claims she is his possession and has to do his bidding, a traditional conception of the female body and sexuality that will be discussed below. For the two men, Helen represents an investment in the future. Martin wants her to marry Blake, to whom he mortgages the farm. He has the lands surveyed and cut up into building lots, dreaming of moving his family to Bangor or Boston and getting "rich as Jay Gould" (I, 686). Conversely, Nat's investment in Helen pays out in many ways. Helen gets her true love, and the two return after a year as a married couple with a newborn son, and with a small fortune that saves the farm. Additionally, Sam, an avid businessman, has commissioned Nat's veteran war pension, without Nat's knowledge. The letter with the happy news arrives at Christmas Eve, when the family is reunited. Despite his old age, Herne's Yankee remains a keen schemer.

With the double conflict about Helen's love interest and the land scheme, Herne articulates a critique of traditional gender roles that clashes with the rural nostalgia. As explained above, Uncle Nat proves himself the better provider of the family than Martin. Nat's success also stints the ambitions of the townsman Blake, a character in a *"gray business suit, 'store-made' [. . .] he is portly, well to-do, but jovial [. . .] [and] has the air of a contented, cheerful businessman, shrewd, but not conning or mean"* (I, 676). Blake's projects fail because he only focuses on money. He seduces Martin with fantastic riches that go bust within a year and loses his own fortune ("I tell yeh, the boom's a-comin here jes' as sure as you're born," I, 677). To woo Helen, he offers her a piano (I, 679) and "half of every dollar

I make for the next twenty years, if you marry me" (II, 695). In the end, Blake faces bankruptcy *and* loneliness and is ashamed ("I've ben s' busy all my life makin' *money* I hain't hed time to git lunsome. Now I'm gettin' old, I begin to see p'r'aps I might [. . .] I'm ashamed" (IV, 712, 715).

While Blake's regrets at the end of the play grant the small-town businessman a sympathetic turn, the unleashed capitalism of the Gilded Age is literally fenced in. The land boom is linked to the Gilded Age mansions erected between 1870 and 1900 in New England ("it'd make a great buildin' site fer Vanderbilt 'r Rockenfeeder 'r any 'o them far-seein' fellers," II, 699). Impressed by the careers of railroad and steamboat tycoon Cornelius Vanderbilt and John D. Rockefeller, founder of Standard Oil, Martin hopes to become a nouveau riche himself. Instead, the land is preserved and remains the Berrys' property. Big business fails to gain a foothold in *Shore Acres* because the Berry family prospers. Herne's motif for this conflict was a land dispute he witnessed in 1888, when he vacationed with his family at Galt House near Bar Harbor, Maine (Moody 1966b: 668).

Where greedy speculators fail, the career man in the play is young Samuel, Doc Warren, who is driven from the backwards village community because of his controversial beliefs. He is an avid reader of Swedenborg and proponent of Darwinian evolution theory (I, 679), but feels that "[a] fellow that knows some things his great-great-grandfather didn't know is an object of suspicion here" (I, 680). Sam shares his love of books with Helen, and the two read William Dean Howells's novel *A Hazard of New Fortunes* (1890) together, which was published shortly before the production of *Shore Acres*. This reference completes Herne's critique on Gilded Age speculation: the readers Helen and Sam abandon the village with its backwards ideas. They "make it" by themselves out West by virtue of their learning. Herne's ideal American man is thus reflected in the shared qualities of Uncle Nat and young Sam: modesty, honesty, and self-reliant perseverance govern their actions, and they support Helen's independence and progressive views of female gender roles.

As in Thompson's *Old Homestead*, it is the young woman's choice of husband that venerates American masculinity. Herne's heroine, however, is driven less by sentimentality than by intellectual stimulation. In the stage direction, Helen is described as *"the modern girl"* opposite her mother Ann, *"the old-fashioned, submissive wife, awed and frightened at Helen's daring to oppose her father"* (II, 701). Helen impersonates a version of the New Woman opposite Ann's Angel of the House. Her benefactor Uncle Nat advertises for women's independence in other instances. When little Millie hangs up her petticoat instead of a stocking for Santa Claus, he tells her that she will be able to wear pants before she dies: "Things is comin' your way mighty fast" (IV, 707). Likewise, Nat buys the farm back under the condition that Martin make Ann the proprietor (IV, 719). In act II, Nat takes to the stove, preparing the meal for Ann and Martin's wedding anniversary. He asks Helen to tie the apron "in a bowknot so that when the company comes, I can get it off handy" (II, 690). Once in the kitchen, however, he acts in a bossy way that differs from his usual modesty: "I'd rather have I don't know what around me than a lot of women when I'm a-cookin a dinner [. . .] Upon my word, a man can't leave a stove out of his hands five minutes without somebody a-foolin' with it" (II, 691). Nat claims the kitchen for himself, and declares it "man's" territory.

His cooking efforts are thwarted, however, by the hired girl Perley, who sets the potatoes on the back of the stove, turns the turkey in the oven, and throws the giblets out to feed the chickens. When he discovers this, Nat throws a tantrum, while the women stand quietly around him and avoid eye contact. This scene shows an ambiguous authority: on the one hand, they let him boss them around; on the other hand, they ignore him. With his foray into the kitchen, Nat crosses over into the (sole) realm of female power in the house, but remains the odd one out. The aproned Yankee recalls the comic depiction of his war effort (aiming the gun with eyes closed) and adds a new facet to the stage Yankee turned wise uncle: Nat is mother and father to the children of the household; he nourishes and provides for them. His act in the kitchen also draws a line between the inside of the family household and the outside community, presented with the arrival of the guests to the silver wedding. Inside the family, his caretaking may well extend into the female realm of the kitchen; to the outside observer, he upholds the role of friendly family man.

With Uncle Nat's versatile role inside and outside the family home, Herne completes his transformation of the Jacksonian go-ahead Yankee's rough masculinity into a matured and wise guardian of the homestead. Anderson (2006: 6) reads Uncle Nat's performance in the kitchen as an "androgynous flexibility," akin to the regional malaise of the New England decline.[23] I would argue to the contrary. The preservation of the family farm and Nat's Yankeedom update the masculinity model for the challenges of big business and new gender roles alike. As keeper of the light, Nat saves his own daughter from drowning, fights his brother "with almost superhuman strength" (III, 1, 706), and struggles to reconcile his past mistakes with his present wisdom.[24] At the end of the play, he also acts out a long silent episode. On Christmas Eve, after everyone else has gone to bed, he extinguishes the lights, clears up the table, and leaves the dark stage lit only by the "firelight flickering through the chinks of the stove" (IV, 720). The contest of masculinities of *Shore Acres* ends with this tableau. The greedy businessman is defeated by the progressive young thinker, and the old-fashioned patriarch loses out to the husband-partner of a modern woman who can think for herself and have her own property. The Yankee Uncle Nat interlinks generations, lifestyles, and gender norms. The New England farm is similarly versatile, an invaluable nostalgic home or a stifling cage from which young generations have to escape. In *Shore Acres*, both the Yankee and the farm withstand the challenges of modernity and persist as emblems of American national mythology.

The Stage Yankee at Large: International Projections and Yankee Ambiguity

As a transatlantic fantasy of English comedians and American patriotic playwrights, the stage Yankee also occupies an intercultural contact zone. When the Yankee goes abroad, his New England regional markers may get mixed up with other regionalisms and contrasted to Englishness, while he remains a social and cultural outsider. Whereas before he was the odd one out in the New England rural community or the urban parlor, he now becomes the foreign newcomer to an English and mostly upper-class social universe. He performs Americanness in his speech and behavior, and thus engages hearsay, myths, and stereotypes about Americans. Yankee plays that tell stories of the stage Yankee abroad routinely employ the contrast between explicit figural commentary by other characters and the Yankee's (non)conformity with these expectations as a tool for characterization. Suspense increases when other figures talk about him before he finally enters the action.

Such is the case in *Tarnation Strange, or More Jonathans!*, by an English author (Moncrieff 1825). Set at General Popham's mansion in fictional Popham Park, England, the play focuses on the debutante Amelia's love match. Amelia's suitors include the sprightly young officer Wimbleton, the old greedy town clerk Dawkins, and one Jonah Goliah Bang. The last represents a mixture of the frontiersman and the stage Yankee; he is "from Kentucky" (I, 1, 3) but also called a "Yankee" (I, 2, 44, 46, 48). His biggest fan, Aunt Swallow, introduces him with an anecdote about how Bang captured the panther she now uses as a hearth rug; the beast was preparing to attack him when, by merely grinning at the animal, Bang provoked the panther so much that it jumped into the pit and broke its neck (see I, 1, 3). The story describes Bang's hunting skills as psychological manipulation instead of marksmanship. It defines masculinity as performance rather than physical power or hunting expertise. Mrs. Swallow goes on to praise Bang as "sportsman [. . .], hunter [. . .], intellectual man, full of anecdote" with "a novelty about all he says that is quite reviving" compared to the "bores" of her countrymen (I, 1, 4) and the "monotony" (II, 1, 50) of England. Even before Bang arrives, Mrs. Swallow portrays him as an ambiguous performer. Of course, this characterization is biased because it is expressed by the spinster aunt of the play.

To the English characters, Bang represents a "foreigner" who is yet strangely related to them: "he is English in language and sentiment, while in customs and manners he is [. . .] an American" (II, 1, 50). Bang confirms this image with a braggadocio about his physical abilities à la Crockett. Bang's "Americanness" becomes a bone of contention in the play; Mrs. Swallow's excitement about the Yankee's "freshness" (I, 1, 4) seems obnoxious to Amelia, who marries Wimbleton instead. His national identity boils down to "newness" and "haste":

> Bang: We Americans don't do things like other people—we are born in a hurry—are educated at top speed—make a fortune with the wave of the right hand, and lose it with the move of the left [. . .] our bodies are locomotive, we travel ten leagues an hour—our spirits are high pressure—our life is a shooting star, and we go ahead till death comes like an electric shock, and surprises us in the middle of it [. . .].
> Mrs. Swallow: That I know is true, for I saw it in the paper myself; but there it was headed a Jonathan, what did they mean by that?
> Bang: Called it from me—I gave them the information, and I am so awfully smart, so tarnation cute I reckon, that they call all my articles after me—"jonathans"—you can't scarcely see a paper now, but you'll find two or three Jonathans in it, I calculate. (I, 1, 11–12)

Bang paints Americans as machines in movement, traveling as locomotives at top speed. Instead of organic decay and death, they are electrocuted. When Mrs. Swallow inquires about the appearances of "Jonathans" in the newspapers, Bang develops a second disfiguration of the American body, as narrative or text. Both the machine and the newspaper articles are phenomena of a modern world order, which is opposite the "old Europe" epitomized by the characters of the play and their actions. This is spelled out in Bang's reaction to a duel, that feudal practice defending masculine honor. Instead of facing his enemy with guns, Jonah engages his opponent in a contest of words and animal voices: "'I can neigh as well as you can crow!' (*neighs and crows*)" (I, 2, 39).

American ridicule of dueling occurs in various Yankee plays. When forced to fight, the Yankee usually prevails, proving himself more able-bodied than the European rakes. Yet American masculinity does not simply vanquish European manliness, it takes the battle to a new arena defined by business rules and streetsmart talk. In this vein, the courtship plot is equally reconfigured: romantic happiness is more important than material comfort, but often true love is financially rewarded, when the sympathetic young lovers gain social status and a surprise heritage. In this way, the transatlantic marriage plot differs slightly from the rural version. In the plays discussed above, young American ladies have to be saved from marrying European pranksters; they choose the promising young Yankees instead. In the international setting, of course, the situation is reversed: young American men seek a match and find English women bored by the mannerisms and constraints of class. The marriage plot symbolizes the transatlantic economy, reconciling Americans with their English "relatives" only a few generations after the Revolution.

At the same time, the transatlantic courtship narrative contributes to a transatlantic market culture of mobility and exchange, "actively schooling audiences in how to negotiate the marketplace" (Pethers 2013: 87) and positing the theater as site of cultural trade. This European genre with its sentimental heroines and love-struck beaus is ironically broken by the insertion of spinster aunts and fake lords. American plays contain the melodramatic notion of female purity by the absence, in the U.S., of stilted customs and mannerisms, and by the awkwardness of Americans in European upper social circles.[25] James Kirke Paulding, a nationalist member of the Knickerbocker School, employs this plot line in his two plays *The Bucktails* (1812) and *The Lion of the West* (1831). Young Henry Tudor, the American visitor to England in *The Bucktails*, applauds the alleged purity of American gender relations in a monologue about love in the North American "wilderness," claiming that the relationship between men and women in the U.S. makes for

> mutual affection and happy marriages. [. . .] 'Tis not the light of the moon, the sacred quiet of a calm evening, the repose of a country scene, nor the pure beauties of nature, nor the innocent intercourse

of a lonely walk that inflame the senses, or corrupt the heart. It is at midnight balls and masquerades, where lascivious music assails the senses, where dazzling lights confound the imaginations, and wines and costly viands pamper the heated appetites. It is there that virtue melts like wax, and female beauty is most successfully assailed. (Paulding 1993: III, 1, 36)

In William Dunlap's *A Trip to Niagara* (1828), a similar logic propels the relationship between the young English traveler to the U.S., Amelia, and her countryman John Bull, who only wins her heart after curing her brother of his English snobbishness when he makes him see the natural beauty and technological progress of the U.S. (see Schäfer 2012 and 2015).

Such is also the case in *Jonathan in England* (Colman 1828), a play adapted from the comedy "Who Wants a Guinea?". Colman rewrites the original character Solomon Gundy as the Yankee Solomon Swap, who is sympathetic even though he belongs to the servant class. After being captured from an American ship in the Revolutionary War, Solomon works as a footman in England. Compared to the Yorkshire servant Andrew, Solomon is benevolent; saving the heroine from abduction and arranging for her marriage to a virtuous American, he is patriotic ("As to my being a Yankee, I'm proud of it"; "I'm what you call a Yankee in the rough," II, 3) and honest ("I'm always on hand for a trade or a swap of any kind; but darn me if ever I *sell* my *humanity*," ibid.). After its London premiere, *Jonathan in England* met with tremendous success in the U.S., where Solomon Swap was played by important Yankee actors—Hill, Hackett, Marble, Silsbee—as well as G. E. Locke between 1840 and 1859. Solomon remains true to the stock figure regarding his social place; as footman, he belongs to the lower caste. The ending projects his remaining in England, to work. He refuses to settle down with an English girl in England but also declines when asked about a return to his native U.S. ("there's so many Yankees there already, that it's dog eat dog," III, 3). Solomon is a Yankee without an outlook to a positive future, which makes him stand out from the bulk of Yankee characters. As in the country to city plays, the Yankee works toward upward social mobility, which sets him apart from other ethnic types on the antebellum stage.

Among the stage Yankees that are put in the hot water of international relations, Tom Taylor's Asa Trenchard in *Our American Cousin* illustrates the Yankee's aspiration to upward social mobility and his self-conscious playing to the expectations of what an American might be. By 1858, when the play premiered at Laura Keene's Theatre in New York, the Yankee became a symbol of transatlantic relations, while his humor and backwoods character persisted. Set in England, at the fictional Trenchard Manor, *Our American Cousin* shows the old Trenchard family, "one of the first families in the country" (Taylor 1858: I, 1; all subsequent references to this edition), on the verge of ruin because Sir Edward, the baronet, failed to pay attention to his business agents and is now threatened by their attempts to take over his property. Florence Trenchard, Sir Edward's bright daughter, becomes a pawn in the game for the estate, but finally marries her love interest, the businessman Harry Vernon. Trenchard Manor is not only home to the Trenchard family but also hosts Lord Dundreary, an idiotic nobleman, and Mrs. Mountchessington, who is looking for husbands for her daughters Augusta and Georgina.

The action matches no fewer than five happy couples, including even the less sympathetic characters and the servants. This happy matchmaking is administered by a single character, Asa Trenchard, the American cousin from the title, about whom his creator Joseph Jefferson wrote:

> While [*Our American Cousin*] possessed but little literary merit, there was a fresh, breezy atmosphere about the characters and the story that attracted me very much. I saw, too, the chance of making a strong character of the leading part, and as such I was quite selfish enough to recommend the play for production. (Jefferson 1890: 194)

Asa Trenchard kicked off Jefferson's career and foreshadowed his creation of the iconic American figure of Rip Van Winkle in the play by William Bayle Bernard. Jefferson developed Asa opposite E. A. Sothern's Lord Dundreary, whose malapropisms and non sequiturs became a fashion trend ("dundrearies" being long sideburns that echoed the ridiculousness of the figure). Taylor encouraged improvisation to exaggerate the contrast between these figures with "*ad. lib.*" marks in the stage directions. The clash between the idiotic aristocrat Dundreary and the stage Yankee Asa ridicules the alleged American lack of civilization. To stage this clash, Taylor uses explicit figural characterization: the figures talk about each other. When they first meet, Taylor sketches a "*business of recognition, ad. lib.*" in the stage direction (I, 1). Asa comments on Dundreary: "Concentrated essence of baboons, what on earth is that?"; the latter merely quips about Asa: "He's mad" (ibid.).

Throughout the play, Dundreary speaks as an imbecile, knocking his knees and twisting every word. His performance peaks in III, 5, when he reads a letter to himself, or in the ending, when he is given the final 'word'. Throughout the play, he tries to sneeze, but the other characters spoil this by addressing him; in the ending, Dundreary finally gets his gigantic sneeze, after which he happily exclaims: "That's the idea" (III, 7). The final sneeze is absurd, of course, but it also marks the play's emphasis on performance. Dundreary's character hinges on non-verbal features that are supported in his speeches. In *Our American Cousin*, enactment precedes verbal expression, and this also holds true for the stage Yankee Asa. At the end of I, 2, Asa has finally arrived in his room at Trenchard Manor, and he starts by testing the appliances unknown to him. He examines the shower ("what on airth is that? Looks like a skeeter net, only it aint long enough for a feller to lay down in," ibid.) and rings the bell for help, but ends up drenching himself in the shower ("Murder! Help! Fire! Water! I'm drown"). The servants arrive and stand laughing until the curtain falls, replicating an on-stage audience. Asa's behavior in acts I and II reiterates the situation of the rural Yankee in the big city. The American is unaccustomed to the comforts of civilization and behaves roughly, trying to kiss his cousin Florence right upon his arrival, and sporting the conventional theatrical self-presentation: "I'm Asa Trenchard, born in Vermont, suckled on the banks of Muddy Creek, about the tallest gunner, the slickest dancer and generally the loudest critter in the state" (I, 1).

In the beginning, Asa is shown as a mixture of the stage Yankee and the frontiersman. During the hunt held at the estate, he wins the first prize and confirms the characterization by Mrs. Mountchessington as "Apollo of the Prairie" (I, 1) and "American savage" (II, 1). However, Asa also exposes such stereotypes and evades Mrs. Mountchessington's attempt to lure him into a marriage trap. When she asks him about the dress "in which you hunt the buffalo," he comments in an aside: "Buffaloes down in Vermont. [*Aloud*] Wal, you see, them dresses are principally the natural skin, tipped off with paints, and the Indians object to parting with them" (II, 1). The Yankee thus plays the part of savage American to the ignorant English ladies while mocking them in his asides, illustrating that the "American cousin" is construed mostly by the expectations of the English. Mrs. Mountchessington's interest withers quickly when she finds out he will not inherit the Trenchard fortune. She instructs her daughter: "I think if you read up Sam Slick a little, it might be useful, and just dip into Bancroft's History of the United States, or some of Russell's Letters; you should know something of George Washington, of whom the Americans are justly proud" (ibid.). With these references, the play interlinks with the debate about American character in the public realm, beyond the embodiment of the stage Yankee.

Apart from these second-hand descriptions, Taylor advocates for the American pastoral ideal, notably through Mary Meredith, the designated Trenchard heiress, who is at the center of the play's transatlantic kinship web. Since Mary's mother married against old Mark Trenchard's will, the grandfather went to the U.S. to seek out the American branch of the family and made his property over to young Asa, making the "American cousin" closer kin to the English Trenchards than the Mountchessingtons or Dundreary. With his cousin Florence, Asa forms a duo: both have a large portion of stage presence and frequently comment on the evolution of the plot; both oppose ignorance and greed; and finally, both have an amorous plight that ascertains the future of the Trenchard estate, in England (with Florence as keeper) and in the U.S. (with Asa and Mary as renewal of the American branch). This kinship moves Asa into the inner circle of the Trenchard family. Thus, Mary, the impoverished and disinherited lady, is the perfect match to keep the fortune in the family. Mary's simplicity is virtuous and graceful, she "presides over her milk pail like a duchess playing dairymaid" (I, 1), and her image of the U.S. is a scenery evoked before the mind's eye:

> I can shut my eyes and almost fancy I see your home in the backwoods. There are your two sisters running about in the sunbonnets. [. . .] Then I can see smoke curling from the chimney, then men and boys working in the fields. [. . .] The girls milking the cows, and everybody so busy. [. . .] And then at night, home come your four big brothers from the hunt laden with game, tired and foot sore, and covered with snow. [. . .] Then how we lasses bustle about to prepare supper. The fire blazes on the hearth, while your good mother cooks the slapjacks. [. . .] and then after supper the lads and lasses go to a corn husking. The demijohn of old peach brandy is brought out and everything is so nice. (III, 1)

Mary's image of New England farm life sketches a rustic ideal of work and play in which the entire family returns home at night; she even pictures herself as part of this ("*we* lasses bustle about to prepare supper"). Asa authenticates this voyage of the mind by affirmative comments and asks Mary to become a part of it: "You ought [. . .] to pack up and emigrate to the raring old state of Vermont" (ibid.). This rural ideal forms the opposite to Mrs. Mountchessington's American "savage" sketches; it is not the lonely hunter who embodies the nation, but the extended family working together and sharing a community feeling at the homely hearth. The "real" America thus resides in Mary's pastoral reverie.

Swept away by this realistic idea of America, Asa Trenchard changes. From stage Yankee and country rustic, he turns into gallant lover and fighter for Mary's "golden heart." Before, he compared his cousin Florence to Mary in typical frontier vocabulary, equating the women with the revenue of field work. Flo's "feminine accomplishments" amounted to a mere "small potatoes, and few in a hill" and "some pumpkins"; Mary, by comparison, seemed to him like a "regular snorter" and a "squeeler" (II, 1). All of these are unintelligible to the women, of course. After Mary's revery, however, Asa performs another role, that of storyteller and performer of a short play-within-the-play. He informs Mary about how old Mark Trenchard made the fortune over to him, Asa. In the story, old Trenchard lights a cigar with a sheet of paper, the will which makes Asa heir to the Trenchard estate, telling him "that act disinherits you, but it leaves all my property to one who has a better right to it" (ibid.). As Asa tells this to Mary, he also lights a cigar, using the same will and thus burning up his claims to the estate before Mary's eyes.

After giving up his fortune to Mary, Asa saves Florence from marrying the villain Coyle. He achieves this with smartness and strength, staging his resolution with wordplay:

> Asa: [*Re-enters with axe*] Why here's a key that will open any lock that Hobb ever invented.
> Murcott: What key?
> Asa: What key, why, Yankee. [*Shows axe, breaks open cabinet*] (III, 6)

Taylor's stage Yankee behaves in a typically brutish manner, but he comments on his doings with a pun that fuses his own Yankee body with his instrument, the axe, which to him is a mere "key." With this specimen of tall tale humor, he acts the Yankee part and ridicules it at the same time, not least while facilitating single-handedly the happy ending of the play. Taylor's "American cousin" layers the frontiersman, the noble savage, and the awkward backwoodsman of English travelogues into one fabulous simulacrum of the stage Yankee, whose performance saves the day. Ultimately, Asa's true character is revealed in a romantic twist that turns all sympathies to him; faced with Mary's purity, however, he drops his mask in a confessional scene: "I know what a rude, ill-mannered block I am. [. . .] I'm rough, Mary, awful rough" (ibid.). Mary herself happily chooses "rough-spun, honest-hearted Asa Trenchard" (III, 7).

The stage Yankee of *Our American Cousin* is seasoned by performance and aware of his deficits. He readily gives up a fortune for true love and uses power to right wrongs. These traits make him sympathetic compared to earlier, rustic and speculating Yankees. Most importantly, Asa Trenchard transcends class boundaries regarding property and social refinement: he hopes to have his roughness corrected by the virtuous English Lady Mary. Taylor thus concedes the English view of uncouth Americans and argues for a transatlantic reconciliation that is mutually beneficial. He shows the Yankee as hyperbolic American in the making.

On a final note, *Our American Cousin* is best known today not for its multifaceted Yankee Asa, but as "the last play Lincoln saw" at Washington's Ford's Theatre on April 14, 1865. John Wilkes Booth, a confederate sympathizer, used the laughter of the scene when Asa calls Mrs. Mountchessington a "sockdologizing old man-trap" (III, 2) to shoot Lincoln in the back of the head. This incident endows *Our American Cousin* with a specific irony. While the play reconciles transatlantic differences and presents the U.S. as good-willed rough Yankee, the Civil War violently disrupted the theater that night. It shattered the comedic illusion and exposed the Yankee as fictional figure in need of audience agreement: for the play to work, its viewers must not only accept the many facets of the stage Yankee presented; they must also assert the fact that a singular "national character" existed against all odds of sectional conflict. Lincoln may have found a premature death that night, yet the circumstances of his passing in Ford's Theatre added to his larger-than-life status as American icon and preserver of the Union. In 2008, the Lincoln assassination was transformed into an opera by Eric. A Sawyer titled *Our American Cousin*, which presents the events from the point of view of the actors on stage.

Taylor's Asa Trenchard travels to England to claim a bride and a fortune he can take back to his American farm in a typical representation of American individualism. This individualist agenda is linked to the pro-American fight of the last stage Yankee I discuss here. In Silas Steele's *The Brazen Drum* (1846), Calvin Cartwheel partakes in the Polish rebellion of 1831 against the "tyranny" of Russian annexation. He fights to bring American values to foreign shores and invites immigrants from Poland and elsewhere to a better life in the U.S. Calvin is captured twice and breaks free from the Russian fort, helping the Polish Lady Rowina and her love interest, the English nobleman Nelson Murdale, escape to a free country. The Vermont Yankee Cartwheel is brave, smart, and almost superhumanly strong. He tells stories in typical Yankee dialect and uses tall talk to provoke and trick his adversaries. To facilitate his first escape from the Russians, he "entertained [the Count's] ear by his tales and drolleries, and gained [his] indulgencies" (Steele 1846: I, 1; all subsequent references to this edition).

In the *dramatis personae*, the Yankee is contrasted with the romantic lovers Rowina and Nelson, whose high register of speech indicates their nobility, and with the comic Russian couple of the Blusterdoffs, who both fall prey to Calvin's plotting. Blusterdoff's telling name captures his ambition and cowardice in the face of threat. He proclaims himself governor of the fortress but refuses to hunt down the fugitives ("I'm afraid [. . .], I mean the fortress may be assaulted in my absence," I, 2). Adding to the awkwardness of the Russian commander Blusterdoff, Calvin ridicules the Russians' names; he calls Count Ruffenhoff "Roughenough," and treats the soldiers according to their names "Yermanoff, Whiskeroff, Chokenoff" (I, 3). Calvin has no respect for these "rustycrats" (II, 3) and calls them "bears," "dogs," "bulldogs," or "wolves" throughout the play. Opposite these wild beasts, the Polish "patriots" are sympathetic. The noble Lady Rowina has to be protected from Count Ruffenhoff's beastly desires, and her father, "the brave old Count Poloski" (II, 1), fights valiantly against the foreign oppressor. The fights that preceded the play's action are told by Calvin, but the grand narrative of the Polish rebellion is told by Poloski himself in a melodramatic monologue. He mourns his "native land—dear, lost, ill-fated Poland" that is "usurped" by "tyrants" who "trampled" the Constitution, "butchered" the nobility and leave the Polish in "despair and desolation" (ibid.). Poloski's speech culminates in his decision to leave: "When hope of liberty is gone in his native land, the patriot becomes worse than an exile—the *slave* of his oppressors" (ibid.). Stripped of their belongings and of their freedom, Poloski and his ilk escape tyranny and slavery. Their narrative reiterates the rebellious vocabulary of the Declaration of Independence. The American Calvin and his drum form a physical liaison between the Polish rebels and the free American people. Calvin joined the Polish rebellion spontaneously in return for Polish support in the Revolutionary War:

> I was a carpenter, carter and drum-major in the State of Varmount, and was reckon'd at trainin' and the like, a purty considerable of a critter—well, then the news come over that the brave Poles had struck against tyrant Nick [Russian tsar Nicholas], and wanted help, I thought of Rusciosko and Pulaski helpin' us—and think I one good turn deserves another, so here goes for Poland. (II, 3)

"Rusciosko and Pulaski" refers to the Polish general Thaddeus Kosziusko, who helped fortify the strongholds of the Continental Army in 1776, and to Casimir Pulaski, who emigrated to the U.S. after the failed Polish uprising, fought as a general in the Continental Army, reformed the cavalry, and saved Washington's life.

Calvin the soldier displays a belligerent version of the stage Yankee. He is a trained fighter, but his most important skill lies in charming his way out of trouble. He talks about his fighting actions as if they were events of farm life: when he feels provoked, his "cornstalk was up" or is "raised," making him "a little bit fiercer than a steam saw mill"; his fighting is "slick as a Varmounter in corn cuttin' time" and executed "in regular pitchfork fashion" (I, 3). He is also provoked by the intrusion of Russians into what he calls his territory: "this is none of your ground anyhow, and if you begin mowing about me, darn me if you don't cut up a bumble bee's nest" (ibid.). His motto, "by the forewheel of old Phoebus' cart," conjures the rising of the sun over his farm. To describe traveling, he uses the image of maneuvering his cart, such as when he plans for the ship to come up to the fortress (II, 1). Calvin's rustic vocabulary absurdly fuses the American farm and the Polish battlefield, stressing the stage Yankee's theatricality. He is the odd one out in this plot, but he is more able-bodied than the Polish rebels or the English lord (who nearly drowns in a well). *The Brazen Drum* transports the American pastoral into a European Revolutionary War by means of a typical stage Yankee fighter. The joke is not only the Yankee's, it is also on the Yankee himself. For instance, Calvin's tale of his escape from the fortress with Rowina hidden in the drum is told in tall tale fashion, with farming vocabulary aggrandizing the narrative to absurdity. The "planification and roundaboutation" of the plan includes him getting worked up in his prison cell, so much that his risen "cornstalk," a phallic manifestation of his anger, almost carries him to the top window. When this fails, he tries self-flagellation and drum beating:

> So I took out my cartwhip, pulled off my coat, and begun lickin' myself, but it wan't the thing; I next went to work upon this 'ere brass kittle, and I beat Yankee Doodle at sich an allstormin' rate, as you hain't heer'd me do since we left Boston; in come old Ruffenough and the rest of the Russian dogs [. . .] and [. . .] they promoted me right off to be beater of the great drum. I crawled clear into their affections like a black snake into a stone fence. (I, 4)

Calvin's story mixes fantastic elements with cunning manipulation. Where autosuggestion and self-flagellation fail, he takes to beating

"Yankee Doodle" on the kettle until the Count and his entourage are entranced, as the rats in the fairytale of the Pied Piper of Hamelin.

The Yankee's superhuman abilities are provided by his magical weapon, the drum. As beater of the drum in the Polish army and later in the fortress, Calvin directs the fight. He also beats a false alarm and puts Lady Rowina inside the drum to smuggle her out. As instrument used on stage, the drum recalls the myth of the American Revolution to American audiences. When Calvin beats it in the Polish rebellion, the drum symbolizes the plight of oppressed peoples around the world. Thus, Calvin's drum-beating and farming speeches evoke the amateurish revolutionary fervor of the mythical minute men, who picked up their pitchforks and joined the war for independence (Fitz 2010).[26]

Calvin's provenance from Vermont also plays a specific part in his embodiment as militiaman. His militarism also echoes the uprising of the Green Mountain Boys of Vermont in the 1760s (Nuquist 2003). The Green Mountain settlers resisted claims of New Yorkers to their lands; they would dress up as Indians or women and publicly embarrass their adversaries. After the Green Mountain Boys assisted in conquering a British Fort in 1775, a Green Mountain regiment was created in the Continental Army. To following generations of Vermonters, the Green Mountain Boys symbolized grassroots resistance, and Yankee theater shows its own Green Mountain Boy tradition, such as in Logan's *Vermont Wool-Dealer* (1844), in which Deuteronomy Dutiful is set upon courting a rich girl above all other things (including peddling). He has "respect for military men—I was pretty near being made a major once" (I, 1) but is now interested in making money. In the end, he returns to Vermont empty-handed, accomplishing only his sales in wool. Similarly, the title hero of Jones's 1833 play *The Green Mountain Boy*, Jedediah Homebred is no fighter but a country rube who finds himself embroiled in an urban microcosm under the influence of romantic literature. Homebred's name points to his New England origins; he boasts grammar learning and being "the smartest chap at a huskin' or a log-rollin'" (I, 2). At the prospect of a fight, he goes to "get [his] fighting clothes" (II, 5), but his main Green Mountain quality is awkwardness. In the end, he seeks work in the city.

Vermont is tied to Yankee whiteness throughout the nineteenth century and is, to this day, referred to as the "whitest state" (see Vanderbeck 2006). Opposite the industrializing coastal region, Vermont retained its rural image. In *The Brazen Drum*, Calvin's rural Yankeedom is defined against other notions of whiteness (Polish or

Russian) and of Americanness (non-white American Others). Calvin is the only American on stage and, like many stage Yankees, has to answer the foreigner's questions about the U.S. and its inhabitants. In *The Brazen Drum*, this interview occurs between Calvin and Mrs. Blusterdoff, the commander's foolish wife. Mrs. Blusterdoff is easily swayed by the Yankee and shares strong liquor with him, until she is intoxicated and gives up her keys to him in a symbolic act of sexual and territorial surrender. In response to her naïve ideas, Calvin offers an overdue lesson about the greatness of the U.S. The subject of this intercultural debate is color, and, by implication, racial identity. Mrs. Blusterdoff asks if Calvin really is "a Yankee savage," since she heard they were "of a copper color, and all alike." While Calvin lets on that "some parts of the nation are pretty considerably speckley with all sorts o'skin," he insists:

> Calvin: Why ma'am we're all alike, but not all of a color—most of us are of no color.
> Mrs. Blusterdoff: How? (*with surprise*)
> C: That is *white*—that you know ain't any color. (II, 3)

Steele's Yankee defines the logic of race relations in the U.S. antebellum, to the ignorant stranger as well as to American audiences. He postulates white supremacy by setting the norm of "white" as colorless status quo against which all other identities are defined. In the same vein, Calvin responds to Mrs. Blusterdoff's question about intermarriage between "white and black Yankees." He acknowledges that, while "some queer old critters do go in for 'malgamation,'" "true blooded Yankees" refrain from this, lest "the country'd be so eternally dark" (ibid).

The legacy of the "true reg'lar bred Yankee" (II, 3) and the purity of his racial identity has to be maintained. In *The Brazen Drum*, Silas Steele uses the stage Yankee to paint a white supremacist image of the United States; he makes no mention of slavery, but equates dark skin color with corrupting forces that endanger the American project. Calvin Cartwheel from Vermont acts as Revolutionary War fighter and American farmer. He saves the victims of Russian tyranny and renews the kinship between the U.S. and "granddad" England (I, 3), accommodating American and international audiences in various ways. Calvin welcomes immigrant newcomers to the land of liberty and defines white American superiority over other nationalities and other American identities. The stage Yankee's fictional foray into a foreign revolutionary conflict defines Americanness within and without.

Of all the stage Yankees examined here, Calvin is the most racist, but also the most theatrical and superhuman specimen. Compared to the rural upstart Jonathan Ploughboy, the Anglophile Asa Trenchard, or the docile Uncle Nat, Calvin Cartwheel is less relatable as a character. He appears instead as a rendition of the American superhero/saint negotiated by the literary nationalist movement discussed in Chapter 1. His magical weapons are the Revolutionary War myth (represented by the drum) and his ambiguity (represented in cornstalk superpowers).

As this chapter has shown, the stage Yankee's vernacular and folksy character distinguishes him from the *dramatis personae* of the plays; his Yankeedom disturbs the social order and accelerates the plot. Reading the stage Yankee as a metatheatrical sign thus reveals that national character was perceived as theatrical performance which occurred in the village, the city, the English manor, or the theater itself. In this sense, the stage Yankee's crashing into these spaces transforms them into staged arenas of "American life." Furthermore, these stage settings hinge on literary plots and tropes, such as the transatlantic marriage, the pastoral, or the comedy of manners. As unprecedented character, the stage Yankee interrupts these narratives and ridicules their formulaic patterns. Aware of his own theatricality, he emblazons a new and ambiguous American masculinity on an imaginary super-space that spans such disparate scenes as revolutionary Poland and rural New Hampshire. Finally, to theatergoers who would indulge in an evening playbill, the Yankee plays and farces were a reminder of their own contribution to the making of an American national and cultural tradition. The scenario of Yankee entertainment reaches beyond the playhouses, as the following chapter argues, and into the daily life of community and trading in the U.S., in a continuum between the stage Yankee and the Yankee peddler and storyteller.

Notes

1. Bank writes about the labor conditions of the antebellum period, in which companies of twelve to eighteen men and four to six women would do long runs (40–130) of a wide range of plays in a season of thirty-nine weeks (2010: 95–6); on structure and management of the antebellum stage, see also McDermott 1998, specifically on the star system (191–210).
2. On the Bowery B'hoy, see e.g. Bank 2010: 84–90. Matthews (1879: 325) places the Yankee alongside Rip Van Winkle, the Dutch colonist.

Actresses in antebellum America were morally scrutinized; many married actors or stage managers to sustain their position. Given this condition of female professional actors, the rascally part of a Yankee girl would necessarily be inferior to a male version.

3. Meserve's conflicted perspective on the Jacksonian roughness is spelled out in his introduction: "During the Age of Jackson, essentially the 1830s and 1840s, theater audiences experienced a flurry of playwriting in America that not only reflects the attitudes and dreams of Jacksonian America in farce, spectacle, and heroic melodrama but provides a vision of the American playwright's potential, a potential that might have reached golden heights of achievement had the character of that period of history been different" (1986: 3). Similarly, German Americanists have treated the Yankee as a nationalist and low-brow character; see e.g. the writings of Jürgen Wolter (esp. Wolter 1979).

4. Exceptions include, for instance, Pethers 2013, which interlinks theater with the business of international (cultural) relations (see below). Likewise, Heather Nathans (2014) has acknowledged the Yankee's central role in the representation of ethnic identity on the antebellum stage, and Karl Kippola (2012) uses Tyler's Brother Jonathan as the starting point for his discussion of American masculinities represented on stage. Yet both Nathans and Kippola focus their discussion elsewhere.

5. See for instance the article "Yankeeisms" in *The New England Magazine* (1832), which represents a linguistic discussion of typical Yankee speech but concludes that regional differences and literary invention by native writers as well as misconstrual by ignorant foreign writers prevent any systematic insight. In its provocative conclusion, the author strikes back at English critics of American speech. He maintains that "many Yankeeisms might be found to be legitimate *bloatings* of the calves of John Bull" ("Yankeeisms" 1832: 381).

6. From the 1820s onwards, cultural Others (the stage Indian, the stage Negro, the stage Irishman) served as stock figures who persist well into contemporary popular culture. Wilmer (2002) reads hegemonic nationalism together with counter-hegemonic and subaltern versions of American identity formation on the stage. Roach conceives of the stage Yankee's interaction with other cultural types as a liminal relationship: "The concept of liminality—the threshold betwixt and between the inside and outside of a culture—is basic to the understanding of how performers mediate in a process that includes or excludes candidates for assimilation, while at the same time it also works to shore up the necessary fiction of a core identity around which boundaries can be fixed and controlled" (1998: 345).

7. The following overview of late eighteenth- and early nineteenth-century U.S. theater culture draws from Bank 2010, Grimsted 1987, Nathans 2003, Shaffer 2007, Richards 2005 and 2014, Roach 1998, and Wilmer 2002.

8. The riot escalated a rivalry that had been cooking on both sides of the Atlantic and across class divisions. Forrest was popular among the working class; Macready catered to the tastes of the urban elites and the English audiences. When both acted the title character of *Macbeth* in New York on the night of May 10, 1849, supporters of Forrest disturbed Macready's performance at Astor Place Opera House. In the ensuing tumult, the National Guard started firing at the crowd, leaving twenty-five dead.
9. To define the esthetic-ideological, Pavis draws from Ubersfeld's emphasis on the dramatic text's relation to pre-existing and culturally specific theatrical codes: "The text would not have been written without a pre-existing theater convention [. . .] authors write for, with, or against a pre-existing theatrical code [. . .] often, in direct view of a distinct theater" (Ubersfeld 1991: 395–6, my translation). Similarly, Richards (2005: 6) argues that in the Early Republic, plays were influenced "more by other plays than by current events."
10. On the entertainment offered on a playbill, see also Grimsted 1987: 99. An announcement on the playbill for Thursday, November 20 (no year) runs: "The manager with the universal desire of his patrons, has effected an engagement with the universally popular comedian Mr. Hill who will, during his short engagement, perform a round of his most favorite characters, these peculiar to himself alone and in which he stands unrivalled in the world!! The Comedy of the Green Mountain Boy—The Comedy of A Wife for a Day—and the Popular Drama for Ugolino or the Innocent Condemned!" (Harvard Theater Collection, Bowery Playbills, call #TCS 65).
11. See e.g. Shaffer 2007, Kimmel 2012: 11–14, Richards 2005 and 1991, esp. 272–9.
12. Cf. Shaffer 2007. In the U.S., the debates of the 1790s between the Federalists and the Democratic Republicans brought forth a clash between pro-British Federalist class distinctions on the one hand and Democratic Republican egalitarian values of French origin on the other. This also played out in English and French characters on the stage. Wilmer (2002: 53–79) examines the controversies between Federalists and Democratic Republicans in four plays of the 1790s: John Burk's *Bunker-Hill* (1797), *Female Patriotism* (1798), William Dunlap's *André* (1798), and *The Glory of Columbia* (1803).
13. Hodge includes such a corpus of Yankee stories as an appendix in his study *Yankee Theater* (1964: 283–4); for an example, see "The Yankee in New York" (app. I). Shaffer notes that the colonial cultural industry imported from Britain featured "live theatrical performance and playbooks, [. . .] newspapers [. . .] almanacs and political pamphlets" (2007: 15) that founded the cultural industry of the Early Republic.
14. I take the notion of symbolic landscapes from Caroline Rosenthal's study of North American cityscapes. She argues that symbolic spaces are "spaces in which a nation sees its myths, narratives, and beliefs

most accurately represented and reproduced; spaces which have held a specific importance for a nation's self-conceptualization; spaces which have functioned as spatial meta-narratives and which—just like historiography—inform a nation's image of itself" (2011: 5). In the U.S., these spaces include the West and the frontier, which are emerging at the time the stage Yankee enters the scene, and which are linked to the frontiersman and the Southwestern Screamer. Contrary to these figures, the Yankee disturbs the creation of the New England pastoral as symbolic space, as I argue in Chapter 5.

15. Hokenson (2006: 155) emphasizes the relation between farce and the cultural archive: "Farce and fabliaux thus transfer into the comic register of caricature the noble matter of allegorical characters, epic combats, courtly adultery." On farce, see Bentley 1991, esp. 219–56; Davis 2003. Bermel (1990) explores the genres resurfacing in American popular culture and film.

16. The broadside is available from the *Early American Imprints* database (series 1, no. 47420) at the American Antiquarian Society. The following commentary examines the version Perrin includes in the appendix in *The Life and Works of Thomas Green Fessenden* (Fessenden 1925: 186–92).

17. Female beauty is often linked to the rarity and frailty of the rose in literature in general. Note for instance the French medieval "Roman de la Rose" in which the rose symbolizes the admired court lady, her sexuality, or even her vagina, or the symbolism of the rose as flower of romantic love in the Western world. Charles Saunders's melodrama *Rosina Meadows, the Village Maid* (1855, perf. 1843) also uses the rose symbolism and the pastoral narrative (see Grimsted 1987: 242–8).

18. Another possible reading of the woods, by Annette Kolodny (1975: 9), projects the feminized landscape as threatening to the male explorer. In this sense, Blandford's quest for "real" love is successful only after he has resisted temptations and "mastered" the dark and exotic jungle of female sexuality and desire.

19. The Old Homestead Association, <www.oldhomesteadswanzey.com/history.htm> (last accessed October 20, 2020). The play is performed by Swanzey amateur troupes annually to the present day at the local amphitheater, the "Potash Bowl," including a cameo appearance by two Swanzey oxen and a hay cart. The seventy-first revival of the play, in 2012, is advertised as "A taste of Old New England in 1880's. Outdoor amphitheater, Third Oldest Outdoor Drama in the Country." The Swanzey tradition is also featured in Eric Jones's regional guide New Hampshire Curiosities: Quirky Characters, Roadside Oddities and Other Offbeat Stuff.

20. This negative image of the city is necessary to highlight the pastoral idyll of the New England homestead, but it does not prevail in American antebellum theater; the city could be "the paradise of the future or the inferno itself" (Bank 2010: 43).

21. On black masculinity and stereotypes, see Richardson 2007, Kimmel 2012, and Lemelle 2010.
22. All subsequent references are to this edition. Herne divides only act III into two scenes.
23. In his reading of *Shore Acres* and a second play, Alice Brown's *Children of the Earth* (1915), Anderson adapts a tacitly ecocritical stance; he argues that the plays "demonstrate that land itself could be more than a surface to walk upon or to speculate upon financially" (2006: 2). Conversely, I would argue that Herne's nostalgic pastoral view of the (modernized) New England farm and the play's allegorical staging of U.S. national history are far from bemoaning the economic decline of the region. Rather, those who stick to self-reliance and true love are rewarded and may restore the old family business.
24. Herne stages Nat's struggle as a contrast between inside and outside in two scenes from different viewpoints in act II. After the family fight and the hasty departure of Helen and Sam on the ship *Liddy Ann*, Martin and Nat fight in the lighthouse (II, 1). At the end of this scene, Nat seems too weak to light the torch. In II, 2 the travelers on the ship amidst the stormy seas look towards the lighthouse. Suspense rises as a small light "wavers, then slowly rises from window to window, as Uncle Nat climbs the stairs to the tower." Nat manages to light the beam and guide the *Liddy Ann* safely among the rocks.
25. On the sad fate of melodrama in the American dramatic and critical discussion, see Postlewait 1999. Grimsted (1987: 248) reads melodrama in the U.S. as paragon of cultural history and the promulgation of "female purity [...], man's upward progress, and a benevolent providence that insured the triumph of the pure" in the first half of the nineteenth century.
26. See also the ridiculous "Soft Pumpkinheads" militia which is formed spontaneously by the Yankee Seth Hope in *Blanche of Brandywine* (Burnett 1858). Seth invents this force, assumes command, and recruits bystanders, having them march back and forth rather ineffectively. In these comic scenes, Seth uses democratic vocabulary to act as tyrant commander of the muddled crew. His amateurish awkwardness contrasts with the noble military comportment of George Washington, whose Continental Army gets little help from the Pumpkin regiment.

Chapter 3

The Yankee Peddler Conjures an American Marketplace

On September 21, 1964, the *Hartford Courant* reported a major mix-up at Paris airport Charles de Gaulle, caused by Hartford's pride, the "Yankee Peddler" (Shoaff 1964b: 23). Carrying fifteen Connecticut businessmen and samples of their wares, the airplane was a "flying showcase" chartered by the city officials to establish business relations. The "Yankee Peddler" visited European capitals to advertise Connecticut industries and Yankee thrift. The report claims that the "Yankee Peddler [. . .] [made] history as the new flying ambassador of Greater Hartford business and industry" (ibid.).[1]

The *Courant*'s coverage of the tour taps into nostalgia for a rural past epitomized by the Yankee Peddler, a larger-than-life American trader who has been enshrined in folklore but largely overlooked in U.S. cultural history. The Connecticut business on board is as diverse as the famous "Yankee notions" peddled by itinerant vendors in the eighteenth and nineteenth centuries: it comprises "Hi-G electronic components, J.M. Ney's Dental Gold Alloy, C-Thru Ruler Co.'s drafting equipment and supplies and Royal McBee industrial products," as well as "cigars from Nuway Tobacco and [. . .] Polaroid Color Cameras." The "Yankee Peddler" "pioneer[s]" in an "intrigu[ing] [. . .] American dress" and meets his allegorical transatlantic relatives abroad, such as in Munich, where "the Yankee Peddler, symbol of New England ingenuity, saluted the Frau Kirchen [*sic*], symbol of Munich, with a dip of silver wings" and "cement[ed] relations with the most popular and coveted American memento in Europe, the Kennedy half-dollar [. . .]." The Hartford wares are harbingers of New England inventiveness that dazzle the Europeans.

In reviving the mythical Yankee peddler, Shoaff recalls a set of typical peddler behaviors; he imitates his charm and echoes his storytelling capacities. Shoaff's travelogue includes observations about the Munich Oktoberfest follies, the *tristesse* of Berliners in a divided city, and the correspondences between Zurich and Hartford: the "happy yodeling people" of Zurich "have a tourist's paradise, a land of lakes and mountains, but they also have electric trains, castles, old age pensions and dial long distance telephones. Like Hartford manufacturers, they have a deep pride in Swiss quality."

Like the coverage of the Hartford business venture, the stereograph "The Yankee Peddler at the Parsonage" (1889; Fig. 3.1) links the present moment to a pre-industrial past and the origins of American society

Figure 3.1 "The Yankee Peddler at the Parsonage." Stereograph. Littleton, NH. Photographed and published by Kilburn Brothers, 1889. Library of Congress, Prints and Photographs Division, LC-USZ62-50934.

with the arrival of a Yankee peddler. It shows a staged scene of sixteen persons in the yard of a house arranged around a peddler's cart. Fifteen women and children surround the cart, facing the viewer, with children standing next to the horse, on top of the coach box and in the back, and two pairs of women engaged in examining linen wares left and right of the image's center, in which the peddler is holding out a shining tinplate to the only man in the image. The peddler is easily recognizable in the composition: he is facing the customer, but looking down at the plate; he is tall and wears a top hat and long coat. Even though there is no additional information about this stereograph available, its title and arrangement speak for themselves. The peddler represents the center of the scene, with the other figures grouped around him and the wares on his cart. He carries wares attractive for all, including dolls for the little girls standing next to his horse. The scene depicts the business the peddler brings to the house, even though he does not go inside. A figure is looming in the background, in the open doorway, maybe the husband in his shirtsleeves, guarding the entrance against the temptations of the peddler. The peddler's customers, judging from their dress, represent a range of social class, from a lady to household maids, and the only man facing the peddler looks small and old in an oversized hat and coat and with a grayish beard.

"The Yankee Peddler at the Parsonage" shows its 1889 viewers an image of the past. By the Progressive Era, Yankee peddlers had long been replaced by freight technology, and the carefully staged arrangement would be known to the young participants only from hearsay. Moreover, the medium used for this still life, the stereograph, promised an enhanced experience of the scene derived from a modern technology of the day. As early form of three-dimensional photography, stereographs consisted of two prints put on top of each other. "The Yankee Peddler at the Parsonage" revives the days of Yankee peddling with a focus on the inspection of the peddler's wares by young and old, a community constituted by curiosity and pre-industrial consumerist bliss.

These two examples from the 1960s and the 1880s reiterate the Yankee peddler's linkage to national myths of mobility, individualism, and upward social mobility. The Yankee peddler became the embodiment of a society "going ahead" in geographical and social economic terms throughout the nineteenth century.[2] Historically, the Yankee peddler was a precursor of and an opposite to the urban pushcart peddlers who took over the cities towards the end of the nineteenth century. The street vendors were mostly immigrants who would get food from the big markets and sell it during the day in the overpopulated streets, most famously in New York City (see e.g. Bluestone 1992).

My analysis of the Yankee peddler's representation in historiographic and literary sources shows that, despite his ambiguous salesperson character, he is imbued with a nostalgia for a pre-industrial past that was replaced by a progressive future. The peddler himself is cast as a thrifty and unsentimental figure installed in a pastoralized vision of trade. In attributing sentimental value to the peddler, writers embrace the settler colonial narrative of progress and market capitalism and reinforce the gendered epistemology of trade. The itinerant vendor helped establish the importance of mobility as "the core of American foundational mythology" (Paul et al. 2012: 11). The peddler's mobility had two effects: first, his own upward social ascent, and second, the transformation of the frontier into a trading space that was connected to the East seaboard. In this sense, the peddler's trade circuits mapped a national marketplace, engendering a "nationalism brought forth by the consumption of goods" (Jaffee 2011: xii).

As David Jaffee (2011: x) has shown, peddling was instrumental in developing New England manufacturing businesses into industrial enterprises. In the colonial period, peddlers worked for the producers, but after independence, they broke away and "inserted themselves into previous systems of distribution and extended them" (ibid. 157) by marketing New England products and increasing the demand. Among the popular products were not only tin wares and household goods, but commodities that marked the advent of industrialization and a new national consciousness. Detailed maps of Vermont, among the first maps produced on U.S. territory, provided self-location in authoritative spatial and political structures, such as the regional and state levels. They also quelled territorial influence by neighboring states. Furthermore, the invention of the Yankee box clock replaced timekeeping by sandglass and introduced the rhythm of the modern work time into the American parlor; as a humorous article from the *New York Spirit of the Times* claims, after the clock entered the house, "everything about the house was done by the clock" ("Yankee Clock Pedlars in the West" 1846: 2; see below). The Yankee peddler is instrumental in the formation of the American citizen consumer, an identity intricately bound up with nation-building in the nineteenth century. As Joanna Cohen has shown, "citizens' understanding of their relationship to the nation state" is operated through consumerism as "civic belonging" (2017: 11). This pertains specifically to the politics of consuming domestic and foreign wares and to women's consumer agency and patriotic abstinence from imported goods.

The first part of this chapter examines the origins and conflicting views of the Yankee peddler in travelogues, folklore, and historiographic texts. The second part zooms in on literary depictions of the Yankee peddler and of trading as nation-building operated by "patriot-consumers" (Cohen 2017: 38), as in James Fenimore Cooper's *The Spy* (1821; Cooper 2006), Thomas Chandler Haliburton's folklore stories *The Clockmaker Series* (1836–40; Haliburton 1995), and the temperance novella *The Life and Adventures of William Harvard Stinchfield, or The Wanderings of a Traveling Merchant* (Robinson 1851). They locate the peddler amidst sectional and economic conflict, as representative of a coercive North long before the eruption of the Civil War, and extrapolate the relation between the male trader and the female consumer. The final part analyzes the materiality of trade by turning to the merchandise, the tricky "Yankee notions," exemplified by the Yankee clock and by wooden nutmegs.

Monster, Wizard, Founding Father: The Yankee Peddler in Cultural and Economic Historiography

The Yankee peddler is a figure at the crossroads between fact and fiction. The historical circuits of young traders setting out from New England were enhanced and influenced by literary representations of the Yankee peddler. A plethora of publications draw him with negative or positive traits, making him out as a national symbolic figure. The roots of the Yankee peddler's representation and his lasting image in American cultural and economic historiography are considered here with four historic studies that view the peddler either as haunting figure or as harbinger of civilization and standard-bearer of American exceptionalism.

The earliest portrayal of the American Yankee peddler I found is John Bernard's travel memoir *Retrospections of America, 1797–1811*. An actor and stage manager from Britain, Bernard was positively inclined toward his subject of study and lauds "the idea of the physical sublime [. . .] merged in that of the spiritual" in America (Bernard 1887: 1; all subsequent references to this edition). His travelogue comprises remarks on Americans of all walks of life, from the New England Yankees to Quakers, Germans, Indians, Irishmen, planters, and sailors, as well as recollections of George Washington and Thomas Jefferson. However, his description of American character focuses on the Yankee and returns to various appearances of the figure, as a Connecticut or a Vermont farmer (240, 324–5). In the introduction, he talks about the New England Yankees in great detail, but from a foreign perspective: "The first writers on the subject were chiefly immigrants [. . .] flitting visitors [. . .] miscellaneous adventurers who, failing in their speculations, devised the scheme of paying their expenses home by writing books in dispraise of the country, knowing that England's irritation at American sympathy with France would readily welcome their perversions" (14). Bernard contrasts the English travel writers' disinterest and for-profit mentality to his own approach. His narrative strategy aims at a double effect: he exaggerates their prejudices, only to debunk this image. The travelogues are a negative foil to make his own authority shine—after all, his almost fifteen-year presence in the U.S. is anything but fleeting. Bernard's *Retrospections* provide the earliest depiction of the Yankee. Mimicking the superficial English perspective, he asks:

> What classification, for instance, could be given to the animal called Yankee? He was a decided Sphinx. No two persons in England, who had read accounts of him, could agree upon his conformation [*sic*]. Some imagined him to be a native magician who could conjure the money out of your pocket by muttering six words of a peculiar cabala; others that he was an ourang-outang or the American satyr, with the brains of a man and the claws of a brute; while the greater portion set him down for a crocodile with a large development of jaw, prowling about the shores and wharves to pounce upon the unwary stranger. However they might differ upon the point of form, all were agreed that it was his nature to rob, and moreover to strip. The experience of all travellers had gone to prove that Puritan New England had set up anew the office of the Inquisition, where strangers were treated as heretics and put, without distinction, to the "question." The Yankee then was the American "Familiar," who not only plundered but tortured you. (Bernard 1887: 16)

Bernard argues that the English ridicule the Americans as a less-than-human species, as "animal," as a mythical creature, or a sorcerer, all thirsty for money. Bernard's mock-rhetoric thus climaxes in the effect the Yankee has on others. In the above quotation, he reproduces not the travelogues per se, but the English gossip about the Yankees, after "read[ing] accounts of him." This gossip is included verbatim towards the end of the quotation with indirect speech ("it was his nature to rob") and the inclusive second person pronoun (he "plundered [and] tortured *you*," emphasis added).

Bernard thus comically depicts how the English colonizers ostracize their former compatriots as scary monsters. Against this shortsighted view, he then positions his own account in chapter 2, which offers comments on "Boston's Resemblance to Old England—Why New England goes Ahead, Its Method of Progress; not Understood by the English [. . .]." His portrayal includes the first typology of American character, "The Yankees; the Swapper; the Jobber; the Pedler" (23). Like the monsters that shocked the English readers, all three types of this "curious class of mammalians" share a characteristic: "love of prey" (37). The swapper, Bernard holds, suffers from a pre-capitalist compulsion to trade anything; he does it for the sake of swapping. The jobber, a "man of genius [. . .] [is] among the most useful in the Union" (40–1), even though he looks ridiculous:

> A jobber is generally a red-faced, yellow-haired man, with light-blue eyes and a capacious mouth, dressed in a nankeen suit which was made for him when a lad, and from whose expressive restrictions his republican frame is now freeing itself at back, elbows and waistband. (Bernard 1887: 41)

Bernard's jobber is recognized by his ethnic identity and comic simpleton dress, a nankeen suit he has long outgrown. The euphemism of the jobber's "republican frame" casts the individual as republican national[1] body and distinguishes it from the English. The swapper and jobber pale in comparison to the peddler, who has "no inventive ingenuity, save in the art of puffing, and [. . .] not the slightest taste for swapping" (42):

> He considers his own goods so much superior to his customers' that nothing but hard cash can represent their value. To buy cheap and sell high comprehends for him the whole circle of knowledge; the supreme excellence of northcountry stuffs is his religion; and science has taught him to believe that the world itself would not go round but to the tick of a New England clock. The same spirit which carried his ancestors into the backwoods with their train of teams and children sends him every spring on a voyage of discovery to the South. (Bernard 1887: 42)

The most prominent of Bernard's downeasters is thus distinguished by his capitalist interest, described as "knowledge," "religion," and scientific conviction. His knack for movement is hereditary, a legacy of pioneer spirit.

In the following, Bernard embellishes his own characterization of the Yankee peddler with a perspective from a Southern point of view, from the victims of the Yankee's scheme. Their "Yankee-phobia" paints the

Northerners as invading barbarians ("commercial Scythian, a Tartar of the North") and as divine punishment; they suppose that "a shower of Yankee was the crowning pestilence which made Pharaoh give up the Israelites" (42). The Yankee is also compared to crabs, mosquitoes, and wasps, all minuscule but obnoxious infestations. Finally, Bernard illustrates the Yankee with a series of anecdotes of "Yankee cuteness" in a vivid scene:

> Suppose a village in one of the rich Virginian or Carolinian valleys [. . .] A pedestrian is seen wandering down the hill, his legs, in the slanting sunbeams, sending their shadow half a mile before him. By the length of staff he might be taken for a pilgrim, but the sprawl of his walk awakens anything but sacred associations. Gradually his hull looms into distinctness, they perceive he is a long-backed man, with a crouching head and loaded shoulders; suspicions are excited; and at length one who may have suffered more than the rest, perhaps, from the endemic recognizes its symptoms and exclaims "I'll be shot if it ain't a Yankee!" At these words if there is not a general rout, or springing-up or banging-of-doors, it must be because their faculties are prostrated by the surprise, and they lie spell-bound, as cattle are said to do on the approach of the anaconda. (Bernard 1887: 43)

The Yankee is a predator in disguise, but once the villagers recognize him, they are doomed. The Yankee is marked by his long legs and long back, as well as the "sprawl" of his walk. In the course of the nineteenth century, this typical gait is used by authors to conjure up the image of the Yankee peddler. Coupled with the physical features, the signature walk of the peddler shows the figure in action, a traveling man carrying his wares to the next village to make business. The peddler is a man on the move; his stride beats the rhythm of progress, the slow advancement of capitalism across the continent.

Bernard's *Retrospections* fan out a multifaceted description of the Yankee. In the scene quoted here, the agents are generic, the villagers are described as animals and easy prey, or defenseless victims of the peddler's expert warfare (see 44–5). Interestingly, though, the peddler is not so much a business agent, but rather the master of a "conjuration over the counter by which the money seems to leap out of the till into the peddler's pocket" (43). While Bernard uses metaphors of the animal kingdom and of militarism for the encounter between the downeaster and the Southerners, he also veils the money transaction as a kind of magic. Trading itself is marginal to his interest and merely a side effect of their encounter. Bernard's Yankee is an irresistible and almost superhuman force.

Bernard's vividness and humorous take on American character can be accused of the same strategies he criticizes in English travelogues. His Yankees are infestations, predators, and skilled warriors. The narrative authority Bernard evokes is the same as the English travelogue's gaze at a seemingly barbarous new nation; yet, his deliberate play with exaggeration and metaphors also carries a subversive strategy: he hardly condemns the Yankees from a moral point of view but stresses the desire for otherness that defines the travelogue's pseudo-anthropologic gaze.[3] Bernard inflates the Yankee for his audience's entertainment, replacing the moralizing tone of the travelogues with ebullient storytelling. He creates types rather than individuals, acting as a cultural mediator. With gothic motifs, he exaggerates "the Americans" to translate them into a language his fellow countrymen back in England can understand.

At the same time, Bernard acts as a cultural ambassador at the onset of a U.S.-American theatric tradition. His professional background as actor and stage manager represents a key stimulus for his narrative choices. He helps foster the beginnings of American theater, material and imaginative, in addressing stage construction and personnel. His theatrical description of American character becomes the kernel of the stage Yankee in nineteenth-century American theater. Bernard's son William Bayle Bernard probably updated the *Retrospections* for the 1887 publication. Bernard junior, a theater professional himself, popularized the stage Yankee figure in his plays written for the Yankee actors Joshua Silsbee and Dan Marble (see Chapter 2). Given his experience with the stage Yankee, William Bernard may have enlarged his father's humorous parts on the peddler to increase the marketability of the *Retrospections*.

Bernard's legacy reaches into the twentieth century; his text represents a platform for Constance Rourke's *American Humor* (1931), which develops a programmatic view of the folk hero on this basis. Rourke saw herself primarily as an American cultural historian/ anthropologist (see Rubin 1980: 66–9). Like many American intellectuals under the impression of the rise of anti-democratic regimes, she was interested in American national literature and character, but she approached this from a different angle than the founders of American Studies at Harvard and Yale: Rourke argued that "accomplishments of the 'folk' were more important than isolated masterpieces" (ibid. 74). Rourke took issue, for instance, with Van Wyck Brooks's (1918) claim, in "On Creating a Useable Past," that there was no tradition in America for artists to build on, bemoaning that Brooks and others only discussed literature and published articles on folk heroes (see Rubin 1980: 42–61). She disagreed with scholars who dismissed nineteenth-century American theater as culturally irrelevant (see Schlueter 2008: 530) and, in *Trumpets of Jubilee* (1927), a collective biography of the Beechers, Horace Greeley, and P. T. Barnum, offered a "revision" of Ralph Waldo Emerson's more elitist *Representative Men* (1850): "In [*Trumpets*], Rourke put forth popular figures who, she tacitly claimed, were more truly representative of their time and place than the usual pantheon of poets and painters" (Schlueter 2008: 532).

Rourke examines folk, performance, and popular culture products and emulates a distinct writing style to go with her subject.[4] The beginning of *American Humor* thus opens up a "rogue's gallery of American self-invention" (Schlueter 2008: 536), a portrait of the most prominent American character, the Yankee peddler:

> Toward evening of a midsummer day at the latter end of the eighteenth century a traveler was seen descending a steep red road into a fertile Carolina valley. He carried a staff and walked with a wide, fast, sprawling gait, his tall shadow cutting across the lengthening shadows of the trees. His head was crouched, his back long, a heavy pack lay across his shoulders. A close view of his figure brought consternation to the men and women lounging at the tavern or near the shed that clustered around the planter's gate. "I'll be shot if it ain't a Yankee!" cried one. The yard was suddenly vacant. Doors banged and windows were shut. The peddler moved relentlessly nearer, reached a doorway, and laid his pack in the half hatch. The inhabitants had barred their doors and double-locked their money-tills in vain. With scarcely a halt the peddler made his way into their houses, and silver lept into his pockets. When his pack was unrolled, calicoes, glittering knives, razors, scissors, clocks, cotton caps, shoes, and notions made a holiday at a fair. His razors were bright as the morning star, cut quick as thought, and had been made by the light of a diamond in a cave in Andalusia. (Rourke 2004: 15; all subsequent references to this edition)

Rourke's text echoes Bernard's most directly in its wording and plot, but in contrast to Bernard's Southern "cattle" awaiting the strike of the peddler-anaconda, Rourke's villagers vacate the premises, yet to no avail; the peddler enters and goes about his money-conjuring business anyways.[5] Rourke has the salesman advertise his wares with unlikely comparisons: razors can hardly shine by themselves like the morning star, they reflect light; their cutting can hardly be as quick as (Yankee) thought; and while the Southern regions of Spain are famous for Toledo steel, there are no diamond caves where razors are produced.

Over a century after Bernard's observations were written and several decades after they were published, Rourke emphasizes the same physical features, but sketches the Yankee figure as a cultural, well-maintained myth. The "long-legged wizard," a "sly thin ogre [. . .] greater than human size" was a "myth, a fantasy. Many hands had joined to fashion his figure, from the South, from the West, even from New England. What the Yankee peddler was in life and fact can only be guessed" (16, 17). Rourke's Yankee differs substantially from Bernard's: where his version is a curious and strange animal, hers is somewhat tamed, more human, albeit mythical.

Rourke's strategy in dealing with the Yankee echoes her depiction of the frontier rogue Davy Crockett, whom she "domesticated" by focusing only on the less shocking "conventionally respectable stories" (Rubin 1980: 93). In her attempts to include popular and folk culture in the nation's cultural pantheon, she mollifies Bernard's Yankee peddler and rounds off his edges. Rourke's Yankee is not an unprecedented, uniquely American character, but he bears "racial strains [. . .] that were well-mixed" (Rourke 2004: 19). Bernard maintained: "The Yankee is the Yorkshireman of America; the same cunning, calculating, persevering personage, with an infusion of Scotch hardiness and love of wandering" (1887: 37).[6] In Rourke's genealogy, this loose analogy ("same cunning"; "infusion of") becomes kinship: "Many of the original pilgrims came from Yorkshire, but the strain cannot be proved as determining the Yankee character, for numbers of others came from the south of England; and Ulster, France, Scotland, and Wales added their elements" (Rourke 2004: 19). Rourke thus abandons both American uniqueness and Anglo-Saxon roots for the sake of forging a multinational, white European family, which even unites the arch-enemies England and France. Her Yankee is not only more agreeable, but also more multicultural than Bernard's.

The striking similarity between Bernard's and Rourke's texts is their usage of "yarnspinning" (Rubin 1980: 136) strategies to describe an American national character. This bears witness to their shared interest in the (theatrical) performance of national character. Bernard and Rourke perceive Americanness as embodied in the popular and the theatrical, though from different historical viewpoints. Where Bernard wrote to entertain and advocate his own theatricals, Rourke defended the popular theater against the argument of the newly flourishing American Studies' veneration of high-brow literature. Rourke's text thus carries a political message that is central to the study of the peddler and to the history of American culture at large: *American Humor* presents a revisionist stance of American mythology which glosses over the Yankee's worst faults, links him to a mixed Anglo-Saxon legacy, and embraces his enigmatic ambiguity.

Cultural historians Bernard and Rourke draw a negative and entertaining image of the Yankee peddler, defining him through the eyes of his customers/victims in the South. Historically, this sectional clash holds more truth than anecdotes about Yankees traveling to London or shipping warming pans to the West Indies, as young men from New England would spend their summers peddling in the South throughout the 1800s and early 1900s. In economic history, the Yankee peddlers are harbingers of trade and civilization. Historians are hard at work to debunk the image of the beastly peddler-wizard. Richardson Wright's *Hawkers and Walkers in Early America* (1927, repr. 1965 in an "American Classics Series") and J. R. Dolan's *The Yankee Peddlers of Early America* (1964) both attempt to restore the peddler to historical and ideological glory, with antisemitic overtones and masculinist bravado. Their studies are the authoritative sources widely quoted in recent studies of peddler history.[7]

The argumentative thrust of *Hawkers and Walkers* and *The Yankee Peddlers* is similar. The former focuses on the history of mobility and progress, but dedicates about one third of its argument to the rise and decline of Yankee peddling, while the latter, subtitled *An Affectionate History of Life and Commerce in the Developing Colonies and the Young Republic*, takes an exclusive interest in itinerant vendors. Both are illustrated popular history books that chronicle peddling as a historical phenomenon, from its eighteenth-century beginnings to the Civil War (Wright) or the 1920s "motor age" (Dolan).[8] Wright's *Hawkers and Walkers* opens with a time-travelling gaze through the centuries:

> Look down upon a road and you see people endlessly coming and going. Stand a moment and watch them. Where are they going? Why are they travelling? What do they carry? Whence have they come? [...] through the hastening and obvious tides of to-day's traffic weave the slower and almost ghostly tides of all the past. Let the eye pierce this palpable and vivid scene before it to the more deliberate panorama of a hundred years ago! (Wright 1965: 7; all subsequent references to this edition)[9]

Wright claims that the past is built into the modern cityscape, detectable in small signs. When looking back, the peddlers appear, with wagons or afoot: "Hawk-nosed New Englanders most of them are, with an occasional Jew or German and Dutchman" (8). Another century earlier ("Once again peer through the tides of traffic—to two hundred years ago"), almost everyone is walking, including the peddlers with their packs. People "all have the same racial look, save where a band of Indians, their squaws bent beneath loads, trudge towards a settlement" (8–9). The remotest image is a pioneer settler cabin in the woods, with a man leaving: "These are times when men go into the forest and never appear again. These are days when, coming back to their homes, they find them in ashes, their women and children slain or carried away. [...] The first trader. The first peddler. The first faint movement of commerce" (9).

Wright's foreword proclaims the peddler as a founding figure of modern America: he is the torch carrier of progress and commerce. *Hawkers and Walkers* heralds American masculinities in a progress narrative in which Native Americans are first an invisible threat and, within a century, reduced to "trudging towards a settlement." Wright's first peddler is generic, fused with the settler to portray the struggle of mankind with hostile wilderness as American Adam: "Both young and old, these peddlers played an unforgettable role in the romance of our early widening frontiers" (25). Wright's text reiterates the lore of American individualism and progress, with the peddler as self-made hero. In the book's concluding future vision, people fly in airplanes, and the peddler also has his place, alongside the pastoral: "Workmen fly from job to job. Peddlers go their rounds awing. Parsons shepherd their scattered sheep from the heaves" (see 270–2).

The "hawk-nosed New Englanders" are the perfect stock for the perilous undertaking of peddling. In the section "What made the Yankee peddler sharp" (40–1), Wright lists the New England climate as stimulator of "keenness and a quicker pace" (40). The Southern climate, by contrast, makes for "easy living and a slow pace in life," so that the poor Southerners really cannot resist the Yankee, who has "sharpened his wits against the wits of his fellow Yankees." The peddler "laid the foundations of the big business of our present times" (42) and "played a role in the building up of other great industries besides his own" (74).

In his attempt to preserve the Yankee's integrity, Wright spells out his "business conscience" (38) and foregrounds "trust":

> Here were hundreds of young men *trusted* with a stock, *trusted* with a team, *trusted* with bartering, and *depended upon* to make *honest* reports and *honest* returns. In the light of their legendary reputation for dishonesty and slick dealing, this would seem almost expecting the impossible of the peddlers [...] for the Connecticut Yankee has never enjoyed the reputation of having confidence in any one except

himself. Doubtless there were fraudulent and absconding peddlers in these first days, but the greater part of their evil reputation lies not in their dealing with their employers but in their overreaching of uninformed customers. (Wright 1965: 4, emphasis added)

The peddler's national meaning also becomes obvious when Wright addresses itinerant vendors from Europe in an antisemitic gesture. The section "The Coming of the Jews" holds them responsible for the "decline" of the Yankee peddler, whom they "crowd[ed]" out (91, 93). While the peddler, in Wright's story, has been overrun by foreign hordes and by the force of modernization, his legacy, then, persists in his social upward mobility, which removes him from this invasion; Wright points out that many American tycoons started out as peddlers (and, of course, among his list of businessmen, there are no Jews).

J. R. Dolan's *The Yankee Peddlers of Early America* tells the origin story of the American economy "From Peddler to Big Business" (Dolan 1964: 229–65; all subsequent references to this edition). Dolan describes the peddler as "thrifty" (17, 258) and "more practical than sentimental" (40), a hero of modernization. He created the supply and demand chain (70) and pushed the "frontier of commerce further into the continent" (109), as standard bearer of such abstract categories as "civilization" and "culture" (10). In Dolan's account, the peddler was nurtured by the war for independence, forming a "commercial army [. . .] building the nation and its business" (29). Once returned from the war, these soldier heroes take to the adventure of peddling:

> But with the return of the soldiers to the hometown the business of peddling suddenly took on a whole new appeal. Instead of settling down into the old rut of working on the family farm or learning a trade, here was a way that offered high adventure, a chance to go places and see things, of possible romance, of being one's own boss and earning a living at the same time. [. . .] Athirst for adventure, freed from the trade restrictions imposed on the colonies by England, the young peddlers broke loose from the narrow provincialism of the colonies, and one of the most important things they did was to get roads built. (40)

Dolan reiterates American mobility myths by celebrating that the peddlers cut out their own paths, had roads built for their business, or invented a credit system that urged farmers to maintain the roads near their property (see 31, 56). Dolan talks about "us Americans"

(47, 53), a group of Yankee peddlers and future businessmen, "with foresight and ambition and industry [who] became the backbone of the nation's commerce once they established a business and made it grow; some of our largest and most respectable enterprises were founded by peddlers" (241).

Against this glistening example of Yankee thrift, of course, all other perspectives must pale. Dolan strategically makes the peddler shine by disavowing other cultural types, including the less business-smart fur trader (76), the pioneer farmers (11), and various cultural Others. He credits Native Americans for their knowledge of trails and the land, but hastens to show them as inferior in racist social Darwinist terms (32–3); likewise, he stereotypes Irish immigrants with derogative wording (58).

Wright's and Dolan's economic origin narrative elevates the peddler as founding father of corporate America whose spatial mobility enabled his social ascent.[10] They attempt to redeem the peddler from his demonization in popular culture by ennobling his typical markers (cunning and business sense). Peddling as historical practice becomes a national characteristic, handed down to the modern-day traveling salesmen and corporate captains of the business industry. As "walking directories" Yankee peddlers explored a new national economic space, using indigenous knowledge to build "the white man's road" (Wright 1965: 95, 96).

Despite historiographic efforts to gloss over the peddler's negative image, in the American cultural imaginary, the peddler is related to talk and fraud. His fame may be due to the fact that he had to make a sale on his first passing; among his difficulties were, next to his bad reputation, the many currencies of paper money and the introduction of peddler licences (see e.g. Friedman 2005; Kline 1939). In comparison to the previous Yankee figures, Brother Jonathan and the stage Yankee, the Yankee peddler's theater of action is first and foremost a national one. All sources examined here portray the peddler as a national symbol. They show trading as a ritual in which the settlers inscribe themselves into a distinct vision of the U.S. as marketplace and consumer industry. However, the encounter between the hawking seller and the naïve customers resembles more a coercion than a voluntary engagement in the trade. The settlers are seduced into the role of consumers not so much by the Yankee's wares but by his appraisal and magic powers. As the following readings show, the popular imagination views the peddler controversially. Consumerism allowed participation in the national project and entailed partisanship in international conflict, but it also corrupted and incapacitated prospective citizens, increased sectional conflict, and coerced Southerners in a national marketplace ruled by the Northern agenda.

The peddler is the most controversial Yankee figure in the American cultural archive. His reception oscillates between admiration and disgust, like his twentieth-century offspring, the businessman: "One minute he's a greedy sinner, the next an inspirational saint; here he's all that is wrong with America, there he embodies the country's greatest egalitarian ideals" (Greteman 2010: 177). Greteman's analysis of historical texts and biographies about businessmen, like Wright's and Dolan's, aims to rewrite a negative conception and show the individualism and "soul" of the salesmen. Similarly, Matthew Josephson's collective biography *Robber Barons: The Great American Capitalists, 1861–1901* (Boston: Houghton Mifflin/Mariner Books, 1962 [1934]) features a chapter on national character and touts the Yankee heritage of the tycoons discussed (32). While the peddling experience was but a short stint for many New England men, this cultural practice became a period of apprenticeship in the American way of life and a tool for building an American masculinity. Latter-day entrepreneurs with this experience include the Concord radical Bronson Alcott (founder of the utopian Fruitlands community and absent father of writer Louise May Alcott), the stockbroker Jim Fisk (whose father was a peddler), and P. T. Barnum, who took his trading and swindling as Yankee shopkeeper to his New York curiosity circus. The Yankee peddler is thus heralded as the predecessor of the American businessman.

What is the peddler's role in nineteenth-century literature? The following section provides the first comprehensive reading of peddler fiction, the figure's political meaning, and the trading plot.[11]

The Secrets of the Yankee Peddler in Nineteenth-Century Literature

> Reader, did you ever know a full-blooded yankee clock pedler? If not, imagine a tall lank fellow, with a thin visage, and small dark grey eyes, looking through you at every glance, and having the word *trade* written in his every action, and then you will have an idea of Mr. Slim.
> *Sketches and Eccentricities of Col. David Crockett of West Tennessee*

Davy Crockett's pseudo-autobiographical narrative *Sketches and Eccentricities of Col. David Crockett of West Tennessee* includes a sketch of the "full-blooded yankee clock pedler," a fixture of the remote landscape of the U.S.-American frontier. (Crockett 1833: 151; all subsequent references to this edition). The peddler is a business pioneer, a type belonging to an "itinerant class of gentry, now identified with every new country [. . .] I allude to the tribe yclept Clock Pedlers, which term implies shrewdness, intelligence, and cunning" (150–1).

In *Sketches*, the narrator asks the (Eastern) reader to send the peddler on his voyage out West: "if you will then fill up his wagon with yankee clocks, throw in a package or two of horn combs, and give him a box of counterfeit jewelry, he will be ready for a trip" (151). The Yankee peddler vignette animates the Yankee's trading with the settlers, the Baines family, not as a visit, but rather as a siege. Mr. Slim spends the night at the Baines farm, winning the support of the women of the house who assist him in "volleys" attacking the old man, who "parries, with the skill of an expert swordsman, the various deadly thrusts." The siege is ended when the old man's resistance "for a moment totters, then falls, leaving a clear breach" through which the Yankee "enters" (154). The peddler's attacks continue the next morning (with a pause for breakfast) and the poor old man finally finds himself in the possession of two clocks, an older one and a new Yankee clock. Importantly, the story does not describe the details of the peddler's "attacks" but relies on reader knowledge about Yankee sales tactics.

The short sketch of Mr. Slim's business in a book that portrays Davy Crockett establishes the Yankee peddler alongside, if not as forerunner of, the frontiersman in the American popular tradition. Both use performance and tall talk, transformed in this example into paradigms of conquest and siege. Another figure close of kin to the Yankee peddler is the confidence man, a petty gangster who would steal pocket watches by involving their owners in a confidential talk, pretending to be their acquaintance.[12] All of these figures originate from historical events and media scandals and rise to fame in literary and visual representations. Yet, compared to the con man and the frontier hero, the Yankee peddler does not exaggerate or fake his own persona with braggadocio and make-believe. He hides his own identity for the sake of animating his merchandise; he emphasizes the value and exquisiteness of his wares, which gain a life of their own in his expert presentation. The peddler's charade marks his ambiguity and indistinctness. While, as I have shown above, biographies stress the importance of peddling for nineteenth-century businessmen, peddling is not a vehicle for character development in the sense of the *Bildungsroman*. Rather, it is an apprenticeship of self-restraint,

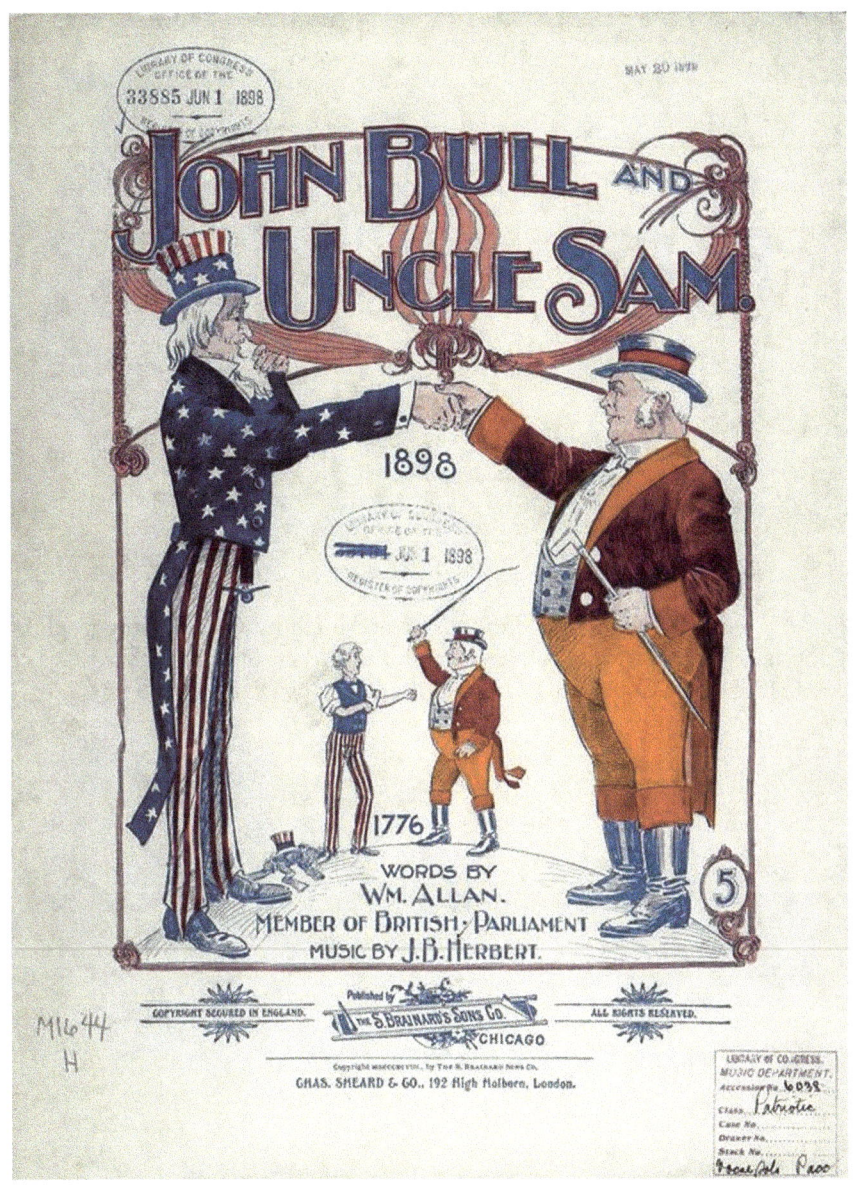

Plate 1 William Allan and J. B. Herbert. "John Bull and Uncle Sam." Chicago, S. Brainard's Sons, 1898. Sheet music cover. Library of Congress, Prints and Photographs Division.

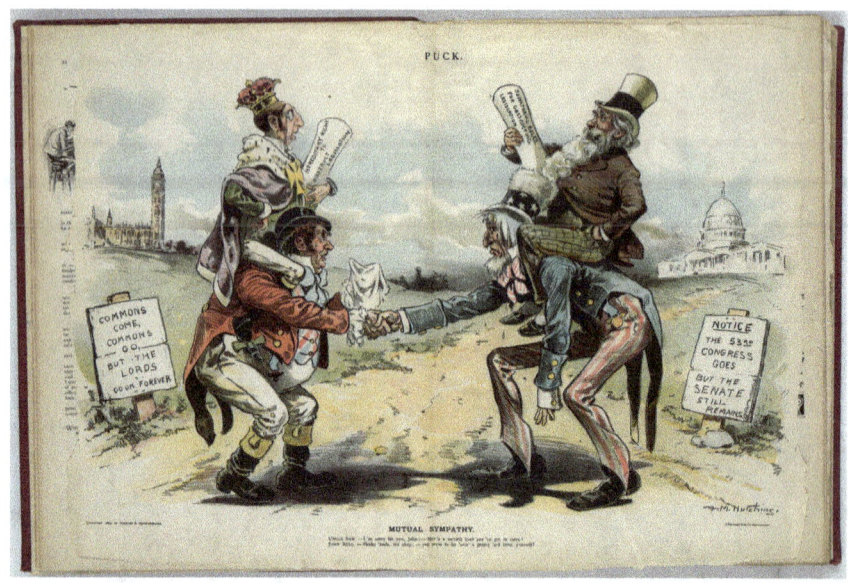

Plate 2 "Mutual Sympathy," Frank Marion Hutchins. Chromolithograph. Published by Keppler and Schwarzmann, *Puck* Magazine, February 27, 1895. Library of Congress, Prints and Photographs Division.

Plate 3 "I Want You for U.S. Army." James Montgomery Flagg, 1917. Print/Poster. Library of Congress, Prints and Photographs Division.

Plate 4 "The Mathew-O-Rama for 1824." Aquatint etching by George Cruikshank. First published April 15, 1824, by G. Humphrey. Library of Congress, Prints and Photographs Division, Cartoon Prints British.

of talk and trading skill that engenders what Dana Nelson (1998) describes as a manhood of fraternal competition that echoes the warfare trope used by Crockett.

Just as the clock peddler is entrenched in business warfare in *Sketches and Eccentricities*, the romance hero of James Fenimore Cooper's first "professedly American" novel (Cooper on *The Spy*; qtd. in Lee 1993: 31), *The Spy: A Tale of the Neutral Ground*, fights as a peddler and spy in the Revolutionary War.[13] A historical romance, the novel centers on the fate of the genteel Wharton family, whose members are caught in a network of loyalties and love interests while the colonial army faces the English troops in Westchester County, NY, one of the most embattled territories of the war. Cooper's title character also provides the central plot of the novel. Harvey Birch works as an informant for General Washington himself, but he is suspected to be an English partisan and prosecuted by American troops. Throughout the novel, he appears in masks and disguises, but his true allegiance is only uncovered in the last chapter, set thirty-three years later, when he is killed while fighting with the American troops in the War of 1812. On the dead body, young American soldiers discover a note from Washington himself which redeems Birch as true patriot and martyr. My reading of *The Spy* focuses on Harvey Birch's masquerade: to disguise his undercover activities, he employs the persona and occupation of a Yankee peddler, and Cooper's narrative strategies emblazon the struggle for independence and national self-definition. The clash, in one character, between the peddler, the spy, and the war hero stages a literary fight for the nation, as the following will show.

The Spy portrays the fate of civilians and soldiers in the Revolutionary War. Harvey Birch secretly works for Washington as a spy. He meets the American commander in chief twice in the novel, first when Washington visits the Whartons in disguise as Mr. Harper, and later when Harvey refuses to be paid for his services, declining the only recognition he can hope for. Washington is a spiritual father figure for the unlucky Harvey, who suffers badly from being a suspected English spy. The American militia hunt him down and burn down his house.

Harvey's spying and life in disguise are cast opposite the explicit debate over allegiances in the Wharton household: the British loyalist Mr. Wharton wants to protect the family estate, his son Henry enlists with the royal troops, and the daughters Sarah and Frances support the English and American camps respectively. The "neutral ground" of Westchester County is a place where "Nothing 'holds'"

(Peck 1977: 99). It is affected by fighting during the daytime, and by night partisan marauders (English Cow-Boys and American Skinners) pass through this proto-national lawless space, where pandemonium can break loose at any time and appearances are deceiving. Amidst this danger, Harvey is not so much a brave fighter as a cunning shapeshifter masquerading as Irish washerwoman or priest.

The figure of the spy Harvey Birch's heroism is negotiated from the very beginning of the novel. Cooper's historical romance is framed by a preface that offers to the readers "the facts connected with [the book's] original publication" (Cooper 2006: 9; all subsequent references to this edition). Written in 1831, a decade after the publication of the novel and as a response to a scandal in which an impostor claimed to be the spy from the title (Walker 1956: 411), the preface clarifies the origins of the story in historical events. Cooper claims to have heard the story of the spy from a high-ranking congressman. The spy's task was to "learn in what part of the country agents of the crown were making their efforts to embody men, to repair to the place, enlist, appear zealous in the course he affected to serve, and otherwise get possession of as many of the secrets of the enemy as possible" (10). The author characterizes the chosen agent as "least reluctant to appear in so equivocal a character. He was poor, ignorant, so far as the usual instruction was concerned; but cool, shrewd, and fearless by nature" (10).

Cooper's title character is thus sketched out as a commoner of low social status and little means, both financial and intellectual, but also "cool, shrewd, and fearless." The "making" of Harvey Birch begins in the preface of the novel, with an ominous claim to historical truth: Cooper's character is deemed authentic because he is based on an eyewitness account. At the same time, this commoner's character is linked to the framework of forging American citizens. Cooper recalls his own dealing with the congressman's anecdote: he initially transformed it into a novel about England, his first historical romance, *Precaution* (1820). After feeling justly criticized for his look abroad, he recycled the story with an American setting and "patriotism for his theme" (12; see Lee 1993: 31–3; Wallace 1985). Cooper maintains that struggling through allegiances is necessary to make American citizens; his story, he claims, illustrates "the effects which great political excitement produce on character, and the purifying consequences of a love of country, when that sentiment is powerfully and generally awakened in a people" (9). The simple man's unrecognized sacrifice is glorified in retrospect. While in the novel itself, Harvey at first sight occupies a marginal position, overshadowed in terms of narrative quantity by the Wharton family troubles, the preface and final chapter posit him as elusive symbolic hero. He is given a double role to play, both as the emblem of the commoner molded through hardships and struggle into the new American man, and as quiet maker of the nation he will inhabit.[14]

Before discussing Birch as Yankee peddler type, I want to note the paradigms employed in analyzing this enigmatic character. Birch's status as revolutionary and spy has been examined by various critics. Margaret Reid (2004) and Andy Trees (2000) relate Harvey, and Cooper's novel as a whole, to the cultural production surrounding the legendary hanging of Major André in 1780. The British soldier was caught helping the American Major Benedict Arnold desert to the British; Washington condemned him to the gallows in a controversial decision. Trees and Reid highlight the importance of secrecy and indeterminacy in the novel and show that it is deeply indebted to the popularity of the André legend.[15] Similarly, duplicity as a matter of the law is discussed by Charles Adams (1985), who illustrates the difficulty Harvey faces between the warring camps and picket lines. Barton Levi St. Armand (1978) reads the peddler as American rendition of the Wandering Jew, a magical creature. He claims that, eventually, Harvey is "elected" in Calvinist fashion to a mythical American patriotic afterlife. These readings grapple with the clash between Birch's masquerade and his protagonist/hero status, due to their failure to examine his peddler masquerade.[16] Yet, the peddler figure interlinks the historical content with Cooper's poetological project to "invent 'the American novel,' [and] also [...] invent an audience for it" (Wallace 1986: vii).

After the publication of *The Spy*, readers speculated about the real people behind the story. The question gained so much traction that an impostor, Enoch Crosby, attempted to claim the part of Harvey Birch for himself, in a fake autobiography published by H. L. Barnum and quickly pirated and published in London (1828/29).[17] After a long period of speculation, Warren S. Walker's 1956 article puts forward a plausible explanation of the origin of Cooper's Birch, arguing that the secret agent probably never uncovered his civilian identity. Walker argues that the revolutionary spy corresponding with Washington was one "Samuel Culper," a pen name employed by two agents, Abraham Woodhull and Robert Townsend, who would sign their letters respectively with "Samuel Culper, Sr." and "Samuel Culper, jr." (Walker 1956: 402). While details of the lives of both remain largely unknown, Walker states that "Townsend was a travelling merchandiser, usually buying rather than selling, for the wholesale grocery, clothing and building supplies business of his father Samuel Townsend. Although he was not actually a pack peddler, like Birch, he was an itinerant merchant" (403). Townsend's profession possibly figured in Cooper's writing, especially since Cooper's wife's cousin was a member of the Floyd family which served as a model for the Whartons (Walker 1956: 411). Thus, Cooper had two sources for the story, his wife's family connection as well as his friend and neighbor, Congressman John Jay, whom he quotes in the Preface (ibid. 399). In transforming the spy story into a historical romance, Cooper must have considered the station and cultural potential of the Yankee peddler, and decided to transform Townsend's business from travelling buyer to seller. Most obviously, Townsend's occupation provided a good cover. In 1779, Washington wrote:

> It is not my opinion that Culper Jr. should be advised to give up his present employment. I should imagine that with a little industry, he will be able to carry on his intelligence with greater security to himself and greater advantage to us under the cover of his usual business, than if he were to dedicate himself wholly to the giving of information. It may afford him the opportunities of collecting intelligence that he could not derive so well in any other manner. It prevents also those suspicions which would become natural should he throw himself out of the line of his present employment.[18]

Cooper drew Birch from the Yankee peddler type and inserted him into the plot of his American historical romance. Harvey Birch's peddler type is increasingly complicated in the novel, when the peddler becomes a "star-spangled paradox" (Fink 1974: 152). In his first appearance, the Whartons assert his lowly social status before he even enters, and Sarah apologizes to their visitor Harper for the "presence of a peddler" (40). The narrator introduces Harvey as follows:

> Harvey Birch had been a peddler from his youth; at least so he frequently asserted, and his skill in the occupation went far to prove the truth of the declaration. He was a native of one of the eastern colonies; and [. . .] it was thought [Harvey and his father] had known better fortunes in the land of their nativity. Harvey possessed, however, the common manners of the country, and was in no way distinguished from men of his class, but by his acuteness, and the mystery which enveloped his movements. (Ibid.)

At first sight, the distinction between Birch and the Whartons is one of class. The peddler is not, as in Bernard's text, a traveler from somewhere else but a next-door neighbor, but at The Locusts, he remains a stranger.[19] While the quotation above describes the peddler's expertise and long-standing experience in his business, no further detail is given. The narrator is more interested in the Birch family history, stressing that Harvey and his father are outsiders from New England and "down east"; the Whartons' relationship with them is limited to Harvey's trading and a faint interest in hearsay that conceals snobbery.[20] The class contrast between the genteel Whartons and the Birches hinges on economic inferiority and on Harvey's occupation. Yet, if the peddler business makes him inferior, paradoxically, it also awards him a distinctive "acuteness."

Yet Harvey, as the commoner-turned-modest-hero of the republic, cannot be captured as a typically lowly, cunning peddler type. He epitomizes what W. M. Verhoeven (1993: 81, 83) has called the "ideological tensions" of the novel: Cooper "realign[s] Birch's social status in order to make him a more likely companion for Washington." Harvey is the first of Cooper's lonely pioneer figures, like Hawkeye and Natty Bumppo, an outsider whose existence questions the social order (see also Ringe 1988: 11–12). In the spatial and temporal setup of *The Spy*, Harvey occupies a morally and socially "neutral" ground.

Morally, Harvey remains a cipher to the other characters who suspect him to be a British partisan. In contrast to the Whartons' family debates over the pros and cons of independence, Harvey does not give away his opinion. Socially, Harvey declines from a status inferior to the landed gentry of the Whartons to impoverished outcast when he is robbed of all his business profits and condemned to hanging by the American soldiers. Yet, the Whartons also face decline, when their house goes up in flames and their daughter loses her wits after almost entering a bigamous marriage. The war thus uproots and unsettles the entire social order, pairing moral obscurity with visual obscurity (Peck 1977: 98). Importantly, the title's "neutral" ground designates no zero neutrality, but a contested, proto-national space, maybe "the most threatening and dangerous landscape in [Cooper's] fictional world" (ibid. 97). But it also carries great future potential that is realized in the ending, in the War of 1812, with the redemption of Harvey Birch as American founding father. He gives away his secret to a young American officer, Wharton Dunwoodie, whose full name labels him the son of Frances Wharton and the American Major Dunwoodie. After all the uncertainties and threats of the 1770s, poetic justice rewards the American patriots: Frances, who supported independence, has been granted a happy and fruitful marriage with her true love; her sister Sarah, who vainly gave in to the pursuit of the wicked English Colonel Wellmere, dies childless and mentally deranged.

In this proto-national contested space, Harvey Birch's peddler masquerade is written into the Yankee tradition, tall and wiry:

> In person the peddler was a man above the middle height, spare, but full of bone and muscle. At first sight, his strength seemed unequal to manage the unwieldy burden of his pack; yet he threw it on and off with great dexterity, and with as much apparent ease as if it had been filled with feathers. His eyes were grey, sunken, restless, and, for the flitting moments that they dwelt on the countenances of those with whom he conversed, they seemed to read the very soul. (43)

The double mention of false impressions in this section—about the peddler's physical competence and his psychic abilities to peer into the soul—echoes a description of the peddler's interests; Harvey is "acutely" interested in "traffic," but when the conversation turns to "Revolution and the country," he feigns a carelessness which seems affected to his observers (43, 44). Harvey thus distinguishes himself from the common peddler: he has a secret passion for politics.

After the description of Harvey's passions—an openly enacted one for money and a hidden one for the war—the peddler's torn character is represented with telling and action. What is more, like the narrator's first introduction of the peddler, his second appearance also focuses on the peddler's looks, this time with a commentary on his gait: "Heedless of wet or dry as it lay in his path, with arms swinging to and fro, and with his head bent forward of his body several inches, Harvey Birch approached the piazza, with a gait peculiarly his own. It was the quick, lengthened pace of an itinerant vendor of goods" (60). Harvey's walk recalls Bernard's peddler walking along the Southern hills (Bernard 1887). The peddler's "stride for which he was famous" (418) resurfaces at the end of the novel, when he frees Henry Wharton and guides him through the territory: "Birch led the way, with the lengthened strides that were peculiar to the man and his profession; his pack alone was wanting to finish the appearance of his ordinary business air" (410). The "peculiar" gait, coupled with the "appearance" of his peddler business, reveal Harvey's skill at peddler masquerade. He is always seen on the move, his knowledge and physical prowess allowing him to traverse the territory almost magically:

> He wound among the hills and vales, now keeping the highways and now avoiding them, with a precision that seemed instinctive. There was nothing elastic in his tread, but he glided over the ground with

enormous strides, and a body bent forward, without appearing to use exertion, or know weariness. (412)

Harvey covers the territory faster and better than anyone else, a snakish "pilgrim through life," as his father calls him (145). Much in the vein of the original spy Townsend/Culper, his profession comes in handy for spying. At the Whartons', in the presence of his secret commander Washington (disguised as Mr. Harper), Harvey impersonates his role perfectly. His eyes "twinkle" at the sight of money, and he pleasures himself with the sound of the coins: "not satisfied with the sound of [the dollar's] fall [into his hand], the peddler gave each piece in succession a ring on the stepping stone of the piazza, before he consigned it to the safekeeping of a huge deerskin purse" (64).[21] After Harper has left and the atmosphere changes from light-hearted banter to war, Harvey advises Henry Wharton to return to his English command that same night, since The Locusts is located behind the colonial picket lines. After Harvey's departure, the Whartons puzzle about him. Henry is unsettled by "his knowing and portentous warning" but finds him "faithful in matters of business"; Frances finds him "not without good feeling; at least, he has the appearance of them at times" and even lauds his loyalty, but Henry and his father find this goes too far: "Love of money is a stronger passion than love of his king [. . .] no love will withstand the temptation of money, when offered to avarice" (67). This dialogue illustrates the enigma surrounding the novel's title character. His act as peddler is so convincing that the other figures perceive him as churlish and predictable, even though they do not know if he acts as a spy or not. Their debate about Harvey interrogates his hero potential: can a peddler be a spy? And can such a figure be sympathetic, even a hero in a historical romance? Contemporary readers and critics of the novel appear to have negated this possibility; Maria Edgeworth pointed to the difficulty of making a spy into a hero in 1823: "Neither poetry nor prose can ever make a spy an heroic character [. . .] it has been found impracticable to raise a spy into a hero" (qtd. in Dekker and Williams 1997: 68).

The lowly character of the spy and the peddler type thus contrast Harvey with the other figures, such as the well-bred but naïve Henry Wharton, the dashing but evasive Major Dunwoodie, and the masochistic Virginia turncoat Captain Lawton. While Wharton and Dunwoodie are renditions of the youthful genteel romance personnel, Lawton develops into a quasi-magical counterpart to Harvey. His eyes "flashed fire"; his "voice reached the heart of his dragoons [. . .] His presence and words acted like magic" (108). Harvey warns

Henry about Lawton: "Beware of a tall Virginian, with huge whiskers; [...] the devil can't deceive him; I never could but once" (66).

Harvey's peddler persona and love for money are staged, and the narrative indicates that his appearance might be deceiving (see e.g. "To a superficial observer, avarice would seem his ruling passion," 44). As the story unravels, the narrative contrasts external views of the peddler with insight into his feelings. In the beginning, he is characterized as a "mysterious being" (101, 139), spotted only from the distance: "there were those who studied him closely, in his moments of traffic, and thought his only purpose was the accumulation of gold. He would be often seen near the Highlands, with a body bending under its load" (139). This outside view is best illustrated in the character of his housekeeper Katy Haines, who also has a soft spot for him. She recalls his fall from semi-respectable man to "despisable [sic], poverty-stricken wretch" (149). Reducing him to the literally worthless peddler type, she expresses her own disappointed hopes for a late marriage.[22] Katy's repetition of the peddler's devastation after his house and fortune are taken away implicitly interrogates the concepts of social class and status: if merely seen as a lowly peddler, Harvey definitely has to be regarded as a failure. But Katy's bickering clashes with the peddler's almost superhuman abilities on the one hand, and with his inner turmoil and fate on the other.

Harvey possesses not only the typical peddler stride; his ability to navigate the dangerous neutral ground seems to go beyond human ability. He appears and vanishes suddenly, "like the winds in the good book" (327).[23] His skills are much remarked upon. The washerwoman Betty Flanagan repeatedly calls him "Beelzebub" (246, 276, 278); when he saves Sarah from the flames, he is described as a "spectre" (297); he "glides" into the room where he meets Washington (436); and observers can hardly distinguish him from his surroundings, thinking him "an animal [...] by its hump, 'tis a dromedary!" (129). The American judge presiding over Henry's trial, upon hearing his name, "turn[s] pale, and shrink[s] as if stung by an adder" (339); he describes Birch as the arch-enemy: "A more dangerous man, for his means and education, is not ranked among our foes than this peddler of Westchester. He is a spy—artful, delusive, and penetrating beyond the abilities of any of his class" (ibid.). In the course of the novel, Harvey becomes a haunting figure.

Contrary to this perspective, he is also endowed with features that are uncommon for a peddler. Despite his alleged materialistic desires, Harvey is modest: he uses iron spoons instead of silver ones (143), he sells his wares well below value (77), and he does not seek revenge even when tempted (132). When he escapes from the American dragoons, his inner turmoil is spelled out: he watches his foes "with a beating heart"; "despair seize[s] his heart"; his "heart beat high with hope"; and "fear, exhaustion and despair seized his heart" (129, 130, 131). The mention of his anxiety makes the peddler seem human and sympathetic, a stark contrast to his uncanny reputation. The narrator portrays Harvey's despair with the same animal/human paradigm when Harvey finds himself, in the most terrifying moment, "Hunted like a beast of the forest!" (130).[24] As a result, the narrative condemns rash judgment and the corrupting effects of hearsay. After his father's death, Harvey goes through a period of forlornness and despair, during which he talks about his secret commander Washington as "him" (221, 226, 242), conflating the military chain of command with a divine guidance and consolation (198, 226).[25] His despair foreshadows his fate: he will not be redeemed but instead will wear the masks of peddler and spy throughout the war. His most heroic deed, however, is his refusal to be paid for his services by Washington: "not a dollar of your gold will I touch; poor America has need of it all!" (438). The entire novel thus hinges on presenting the untold story of this revolutionary martyr, whose service Washington reads as symbol for America's divine calling: "That Providence destines this country to some great and glorious fate I must believe, while I witness the patriotism that pervades the bosoms of her lowest citizens" (439).

Cooper employs the peddler figure to create a scenario of uncertainties and deception during the Revolutionary War. Significantly, the spy's masquerade as peddler builds on the peddler's intrinsic ambiguity which makes the community distrust him, most fervently the figures who are types themselves: Katy Haines, the Birch's spinster housekeeper, and Betty Flanagan, the Irish washerwoman, who is such a well-known character that Harvey can imitate her perfectly and escape from prison in her clothes. In keeping with the peddler type, the novel lays out his performance and social mimicry. The Whartons mistrust him because of his all-too-obvious love for money, but they become his customers nonetheless, as I will show below.

I would argue that Cooper's ironic take on the Yankee peddler foreshadows the figure's fate in the American cultural imaginary: by opposing the typical peddler as viewed from the outside with the heroic account of his inside feelings and secret story, he asks his readers to check their preconceptions about the peddler. By making his spy into a peddler, he enhances the figure fantastically. Up to the very end, Harvey Birch remains strangely intangible, at the same time less and more than human, a beast-like shapeshifter in the American landscape and a glorified "martyr for her liberties" (448). Finally, fusing the spy and the peddler emphasizes mobility; thanks to their fast gait, the peddler and the spy travel undercover and at magic speed. They use the territory for their own purposes and act as agents of nation-building, politically and economically.

Cooper's golden-hearted secret agent peddler differs significantly from Mr. Slim, the gentleman who subjects the frontier home to a siege in Crockett's *Sketches and Eccentricities* only a dozen years after the publication of *The Spy*. By 1833, the Yankee peddler had become a fixture in the American cultural imaginary. Yet, like the stage Yankee and Brother Jonathan, the peddler's most memorable development emanates from the pen of a foreign writer, the Nova Scotian Thomas Chandler Haliburton. Slick became famous well beyond the national borders: "For fifty years after 1837, Sam Slick the Clockmaker was the most celebrated literary Yankee of the day" (Davies 2005: 3). Haliburton's *Clockmaker* series offers an engrossing self-reflexive view of North American identity formation across and between national borders and colonial legacies; as Canadian author Robert Kroetsch terms it, "I cannot bear to look, and I cannot bear to look away."[26] Haliburton draws on the craze for national character as well as on the hysterics of fraudulence, layering narrative perspectives and sketching the Yankee peddler as agent of business civilization.

Haliburton's Sam Slick might well have been inspired by Mr. Slim in the *Sketches and Eccentricities*, since the telling names of these two Yankee peddlers refer to their physique and character.[27] The Yankee is a hypernationalist type opposite the blurry British North American colonial. Published initially in the *Novascotian* magazine between 1836 and 1840, these humorous stories became immensely popular and founded Haliburton's career as colonial writer of international renown. The first series was pirated by a London publisher; it was soon followed by a second and third series (published 1838 and 1840), as well as a volume in which the title character makes a career in England, *The Attaché*.[28] The Sam Slick stories chronicle the travels of the narrator, an unidentified squire of middle to old age, with the clockmaker Sam Slick, an American itinerant vendor on the "Eastern Circuit." Thematically, the stories of the first series focus on the development of Nova Scotia; the travelers traverse the province and discuss the people and manners they meet on their way. Sam praises the province's beauty and resources but bemoans that its progress is so far behind the U.S.—and, of course, Sam also has a recipe for advancing it, namely by implementing the railroad (which the Squire agrees with; see Haliburton 1995: 35–6, 73; all subsequent references to this edition) or by a U.S. takeover:

> What remedy is there for all this supineness, said [the Squire], how can these people be awakened out of their ignorant slothfulness, into active exertion? The remedy, said Mr. Slick, is at hand, it is already working its own cure. They must recede before our free and enlightened citizens like the Indians—our folks will buy them out, and they must give place to a more intelligent and active people. (64)

In the narrative setup of the stories, the Squire initially appears as a quiet recorder who very rarely interrupts the Yankee's ramblings. When they part at the end of series one, the Squire maintains that he is "amused" by the "valuable and interesting" conversation: "There are many subjects on which I should like to draw him out and I promised myself a fund of amusement in his remarks on the state of society and manners at Halifax, and the machinery of the local governments, on both of which he appears to entertain many original and some very just opinions" (202). The Yankee becomes a counselor and a spectacle for the observing Squire.

The two characters pit the clichéd New England Yankee type against the largely nondescript, unidentifiable British North American subject. As Oana Godeanu-Kenworthy has argued, "[t]here is no Canadian equivalent to Sam Slick"; the colonial self remains faceless and unidentified, "ambiguously located between the two aggressive parent cultures, Uncle Sam and John Bull" (2009: 212). Opposite the faceless North Briton, the Yankee as typified American is an "artificial construct originating in the colonial space" (231).

I develop this relation further by close-reading the narrative situation and the Squire's roles as reporter and focalizer. As a backdrop for Haliburton's stories, he uses the controversial English travelogues of the early 1800s.[29] Yet, his look at the national and cultural Other is fractured in a kaleidoscope of interaction, cultural positions, and territorial vantage points. The debate over the U.S. is conducted north of the 49th parallel, a neutral ground beyond both the U.S. and the English mother country; the peddler tests the Squire's double role of narrator and experiencer; and finally, the mixture between kinship and rivalry between the U.S. and British North America complicates the relationship with England. The Squire's curiosity in the U.S. is stimulated by a stronger sense of competition than might be harbored by a cross-Atlantic visitor to North America. Throughout the first series, it is Sam who stresses repeatedly that the Nova Scotians and the New Englanders are "first Cousins" (61) and of the same "old stock [...], and the breed is tolerably pure yet, near about one half apple sarce and tother half molasses; all except to the Easterd, where there is a cross of the Scotch" (58). Likewise, the Squire remains largely unfazed by Sam's bashing of the English, who appear as common whipping boy, while there is still hope for the Nova Scotian bluenoses.[30] Slick takes up more room than the Squire; his long stories are included verbatim, without the Squire's mediation, so the peddler talks back, both at the Squire and at the English travel writers, becoming even a second narrator (Vincent 1985).

The first story, "A Trotting Horse," opens with a short retrospective by the Squire, who talks about being proud of his horse's trotting capacity and his own resulting ability to "tak[e] the conceit out of coxcombs" by simply leaving them behind on the road (8). This pride is stunted, though, by the arrival of a "tall thin man, with hollow cheeks and bright twinkling eyes" (ibid.), whose mare effortlessly outperforms that of the Squire, who decides that this stranger cannot be an American ("in a dialect too rich to be mistaken as genuine Yankee," ibid.). Thus, the Yankee peddler tricks the Squire, and a little later even talks down to him: "What, not enough, I mentally groaned, to have my horse beaten, but I must be told that I don't know how to ride him, and that too by a Yankee?" (11).

The narrator offers his direct thoughts as well as a commentary on his own behavior in retrospect, which presents him as a sensitive man. First the Squire distances himself from his former impatience, arrogance, and weaknesses which the Yankee rightfully mocks. Secondly, he reveals himself as a generally virtuous, pious, and self-critical character, who strives for self-improvement and living up to his ideals. And last, of course, his narrative mediation positions him as observer, removed from the events. He spins the situation so he does not lose face: "To continue this trotting contest was humiliating; I yielded, therefore, before the victory was palpable, and pulled up" (10).

The Squire's authority is undermined further when, a little later, Sam tells him he actually planned the trotting conquest to "go ahead" on the Squire: "Never *tell* folks you can go ahead on them, but *do* it; it spares a great deal of talk, and helps them to save their breath, to cool their broth" (59). Sam retells his own version: the Squire's attempt to resort to virtue ("Pride must have a fall," 10) is shattered by the Yankee's explanation of his "going ahead" strategy. The Squire is doubly duped, on both the plot and the storytelling levels.

In the Sam Slick stories, the audience can examine opposing and competing masculinities at play: the Squire as a loyalist gentleman of British hue, and the Yankee as smart(er) stranger in a strange land. While this refers to Haliburton's own standing as gentleman loyalist,[31] reading the Squire as a simple representation of Haliburton ignores the complexities that make the text so entertaining. The Squire's secrecy is his single defining character trait. The narrator explains his preference to "travel incog." (54) in one of the very rare narrator commentaries:

([. . .] no person knows, nor do I intend they shall [know my name]; at Medley's Hotel in Halifax, I was known as the stranger in No. 1. The attention that that incognito procured for me, the importance it gave me in the eyes of the master of the house, its lodgers and servants, is indescribable. It is only great people who travel incog. State traveling is inconvenient and slow—the constant weight of form and etiquette oppresses at once the strength and the spirits. It is pleasant to travel unobserved, to stand at ease, or exchange the full suit, for the undress coat, and fatigue jacket. Wherever too there is mystery there is importance—there is no knowing for whom I may be mistaken, but let me once give my humble cognomen and occupation, and I sink immediately to my own level, to a plebeian station, and a vulgar name; not even my beautiful hostess, nor my inquisitive friend, the Clockmaker—who calls me 'Squire'—shall extract the secret!) (54–5)

In this quotation, the Squire reveals a taste for social mimicry, achieved by dressing down while acting mysteriously. He focuses on appearances and trickery, the same strategy he employs to keep face when the Yankee beats him at trotting.[32] The Squire's tacit self-inquiry has been dubbed "pragmatic" and (proto) "Canadian";[33] at first sight, it clashes with the Yankee peddler's self-confabulation, his use of a national, American "we" and of blatant generalizations about the U.S. Yet, both North Americans are putting on a show, even if the Yankee trumps the Bluenose. While the Squire attempts to emulate "mystery" and "importance," his nebulousness is exposed by the peddler Yankee. The American is shown as, literally, calculating his (inter)actions. The Squire corrects himself only in retrospect, but the Yankee admits to his braggadocio.[34] Sam's thoughts are hidden but his comments reveal that he is much smarter than he makes us believe.

The performance of "Yankee" and "Squire" in the *Clockmaker* series links the figures to the theatrical tradition and the stage Yankee—not least in Sam's own criticism of "hav[ing] been used scandalous, that's a fact" (5), a "fool [. . .] for folks to laugh at" (7), uttered in a letter to the publishers which opens the series.[35] The fleeting boundaries between theater and popular literature were well known to reviewers of Haliburton's sequel novel *The Attaché*. Commentators from Britain and the U.S. acknowledge the fabrication of the Sam Slick character. The English reviewer points out that since Sam converses "in the fashion of the aside, the soliloquy of the stage has no objection in the world to satisfy so natural a curiosity" and includes him in a list of "friends containing the names of Tristram Shandy [. . .] and other rhapsodical discoursers on time and change" (Anon. 1845: 156, 161). The American reviewer Cornelius Felton is disappointed about *The Attaché* and the character of Sam Slick:

> Mr. Slick is designed by the author to be a representative of the common New England character. The keen pursuit of gain, the eagerness for driving a bargain, the resort to trickery and even downright fraud, which have been charged upon the Yankee, are drawn out at great length in the character of Mr. Slick, the peddler. That very apocryphal personage, the Yankee peddler, with his clocks and wooden nutmegs, is the most common object of the jeers and jokes of our Southern brethren, whose mythical and highly imaginative notions of the men of the North it seems quite impossible to correct. These myths have been taken up, apparently in good faith, by the provincial judge, and with a still more poetical coloring, drawn from the gentleman's own lively fancy, presented in the person of Mr. Slick. No doubt there is some foundation for these representations; something approaching a type, by the gross exaggeration of which these distorted and scarcely recognizable images are produced. [. . .] Sam Slick is no proper representative of the Yankees. He is [. . .] an incongruous mixture of impossible eccentricities. We can distinguish the real from the counterfeit Yankee, at the first sound of his voice, and by the turn of a single sentence; and we have no hesitation in declaring that Sam Slick is not what he pretends to be; that there is no organic life in him; that he is an impostor, an impossibility, a nonentity. (Felton 1844: 211–12)

The success of Sam Slick appears to hurt Felton's pride as a member of the New England Whig elite. The clearly negative depiction of the Yankee peddler provoked the self-perception of the Whigs' desire for a competitive "marketplace in which self-restraint and more responsibility, not the seduction of wealth, would guide commercial relations" (Laird 1993: 73). Sam's popularity, coupled with the common belief in the didactic effects of literature (ibid. 78), provoked an outcry among Americans fearing for their positive vision of commerce, and for the success of popular literature over more high-brow ideals.[36] Felton's review taps into these fears, but also reiterates stereotypes about the Yankee peddler. He casts Sam Slick as the result of the incorrigible Southern mind given to myths and imagination. The Yankee's fantastical quality was not only adopted but further embellished by Haliburton. To Felton, this Yankee peddler is an "incongruous" and "impossibl[y] eccentric [. . .] counterfeit," that is, clearly less than human if not monstrous. His enraged enumeration "impostor," "impossibility," "nonentity" proceeds from fraud to denying Slick human quality. He degrades Slick's theatrical fakery to nothingness.[37]

Felton also attacked the author Haliburton himself: the provincial judge speaks from a culturally marginal position like a "village belle, who apes the fashions of some great city, and [. . .] overacts the part, adopting all that is absurd and extravagant, and failing to acquire the grade and dignity with which they are worn in the proper circles" (1844: 213–14). In comparison to this colonial effeminacy and impotence, "[a] full and complete national existence is requisite to the formation of a *manly*, intellectual character. [. . .] The intense national pride, which acts so forcibly in the United States, is something vastly better than the *intellectual paralysis that deadens the energies of men* in the British American provinces" (ibid. 214, emphasis added). Ironically, the reviewer here reproduces the exact same topos Haliburton's Sam Slick uses to equate progress with movement.[38]

Haliburton's Yankee defines the peddler as embodiment of the budding U.S. economy. In the *Clockmaker* series one, the Yankee gives away the secrets of his business strategy, revealing the details of the business interaction between the trader and his customers/victims. He thus exacts the message of the epigraph of the first series, "*Garrit aniles—ex re fabellas*. The cheerful sage, when solemn dictates fail, conceals the moral counsel in the tale" (1). Sam Slick explains to his audience the American philosophy of "going ahead," consisting of the "knowledge of *soft sawder* and *human nature*" (15, emphasis in original), which is illustrated in the second story, when Slick sells a Yankee clock to Deacon Flint. The peddler's strategy of flattering the Flints and then leaving the clock with them to lure them into keeping it against their will is played out *in situ* for the Squire to witness: Sam lectures on his actions while the Flints are outside ("That is what I call *soft sawder* [. . .] That I call 'human natur'!", 15, 16). Sam explains how he sold the clock after telling Mrs. Flint her neighbor Mrs. Steel was interested in it:

> Now that clock is sold for forty dollars; it cost me just six dollars and fifty cents. Mrs. Flint will never let Mrs. Steel have the refusal, nor will the deacon learn until I call for the clock, that having once

indulged in the use of a superfluity, how difficult it is to give it up. We can do without any article of luxury we have never had, but when once obtained, it is not in "human natur" to surrender it voluntarily. Of fifteen thousand sold by myself and partners in this province, twelve thousand were left in this manner, and only ten clocks were ever returned; when we called for them they invariably bought them. We trust to "soft sawder" to get them into the house, and "human natur" that they never come out of it. (16)

Slick's strategy enacts a confidence game and relies on gender stereotypes, such as the jealous wife or the gullible husband. On the one hand, he is a connoisseur of "human natur" and a sweet talker; on the other hand, he poses as an expert in sales numbers and the statistics of his business, emphasizing that he is a keen performer. His business sense is exhibited further in "Go Ahead" (32–6), which demonstrates the activity of "cyphering": "'*Cyphering*' is the thing— if a man knows how to cypher, he is sure to grow rich. We are a 'calculating' people, we all cipher" (33). Sam presents two strategies of cyphering, according to numbers and according to "human natur," the latter as a non sequitur calculation that yields a call for a railroad in Nova Scotia, trying to "sell" another business scheme to the Squire. Sam's tour de force in "*Yankee Cyphering*" culminates in the observation that the railroad not only "*goes ahead, but nullif[ies] time and space*"; in Sam's narrative of progress, it "*makes the child a giant. To us it is river, bridge, and canal, all at once. It save what we haint got to spare, men, horses, carts, vessels, barges, and what all in all—time*" (35, 36). The cultural contrast between "go ahead" Americans and the Squire here resides in training; the Yankee realizes that the Squire cannot "count in [his] head" (34) and hardly follows the Yankee's tribulations because, as Sam claims, his reliance on classical education is useless: "I see you don't cypher, and Greek and Latin won't do, them are people had no rail-roads" (34).[39]

Sam's advocacy of the railroad reiterates the progress narrative; in the logic of the peddler's role as cartographer of the national marketplace, it paradoxically supports his own replacement by a better means of transport. However, with this argument, Haliburton portrays the peddler as spearhead of the development of North America that is needed in Nova Scotia as well (note the Squire's general support of the idea of developing the region). The peddler's famous quip of "going ahead" works in various dimensions, as motto for development, but also as the peddler's mobility. Tracing the paths of Native Americans and trappers, the walking trader on his circuit prepares the ground for more advanced technologies. Where the hunters and trappers explored the territory, the peddler's "going ahead" fuses his own physical foray with the transit of the railroad; his body, like Brother Jonathan's body politic, is an early version of the machine, growing, huffing and puffing (see Chapter 1).

In this context, the act of walking also connects to pace and travel through time. The Yankee's gait, operated by his long legs and the weight he carries, is frequently commented upon; his steps resemble the ticking of the clocks he sells, the timekeeper of the industrialized world. And even peddlers on horseback or in wagons may be related to this; while Sam himself does not walk but ride, the logic of the pace propels his vanquished trotting contest against the Squire. When Sam talks about the "nullification of time and space," he argues that technological progress ushers in a new age, collapsing spatial and temporal measurements of travel and growing the national body by "making the child a giant." Sam's reference to the national adolescence narrative echoes his linkage between the peddler and the railroad: U.S. progress means an accelerated process of growth in leaps. As the nation explodes from child to giant (not a figure associated with maturity or wisdom), so is the peddler's gait replaced by the rhythm of the steam engine, his body developed into the locomotive and the steamboat.

In the *Clockmaker* series' contest among North American political "Others," the colonists lose out to the newly independent republicans. Even though the Squire tries to belittle the Yankee ("a Yankee what? Perhaps a half-bred puppy, half yankee, half blue nose," 11), the peddler is the better performer of the two. Sam's resemblance to the fabricated stage Yankee supports American calls for an "authentic" American character. His letter of protest to the publisher cautions against exhibiting oneself in Slick's manner, arguing that his persona is a commodity put on sale by the publisher. Ironically, Sam's insistence on the revenue for his performance cements his money-grabbing character:

> now there's one thing I don't cleverly understand. If this here book is my "*Sayins and Doins*," how comes it yourn or the Squire's either? If my thought and notions are my own, how can they be any other folks's? According to my idee you have no more right to take them, than you have to take my clocks without paying for them. (5)

Haliburton's popularizing of the Yankee peddler tethers the figure to nationalist discourses of growth, progress, and commodification.

As we have seen, Sam Slick lives up to his name; he is a slick and ambiguous figure from all points of view, whether seen through the eyes of the equally ambiguous Squire or judging from his own verbatim storytelling.

Opposite Haliburton's embrace of the Yankee peddler's ambiguity and of his commodification, the Yankee peddler, as protagonist, is compromised by his profession. John Hovey Robinson uses the figure of the Yankee peddler as a didactic vehicle in his temperance narrative *The Life and Adventures of William Harvard Stinchfield, or The Wanderings of a Traveling Merchant* (Robinson 1851; all subsequent references to this edition). Published for the author in 1851, the novella warns "of the gaming table and the bowl," a temperance narrative with an account of the victim's bad awakenings and tearful remorse, and reform towards a happier, quiet life with his love interest out in the country.[40] The narrator dedicates the text to temperance orator John B. Gough and expresses his didactic interests frankly in the introduction:

> May [the reader] learn from the past [. . .] May the events of his life prove a salutary warning to the young and inexperienced, about commencing the world, and induce them to shun the "*gaming table* and the *bowl*." May it be production of good to all, and evil to none—amuse all, while it displeases none. I have embellished it in many places, and given it in some parts the coloring of a romance, but I hope without the sacrifice of any of the principal truths connected therewith. But in the following pages, you will see in their true light, the evil of intemperance and gaming. (viii)

In this quotation, the narrator also explains how he strives to achieve his didactic aim: *The Life and Adventures of William Harvard Stinchfield* is a fictional exemplum biography with romance elements. Its narrative scenario differs from the autobiographical temperance narratives; in Robinson's story, the narrator only records the reform life story of the victim Stinchfield. In this setup, the use of the Yankee peddler figure offers an additional key for the text's cultural positioning between popular culture and didactic intention. Upon closer scrutiny, the Yankee peddler, presented with all his ambiguities and typical markers, functions perfectly as a struggling hero in antebellum America.

The subtitle "The Yankee Pedlar or Traveling Merchant, 'an owre true tale' of the Gaming Table and Bowl [*sic*]" links the peddler story to the temperance narrative and claims historical authenticity. The "Yankee Pedlar" of the title is Harvard Stinchfield, who, as the epigraph claims, "is extensively known in the State of Maine, and is now living at Farmington Falls with the object of his youthful heart." The first meeting between the narrator and the peddler as recounted in the "Introductory" (v–ix) shows Stinchfield as a typical representative of his trade, even though time-worn. He is a six-foot-tall "good figure, with a face far from ugly, although it was bronzed" (vi), and after a quick exchange, the narrator realizes

> I had fallen in with an original character [. . .] the man of adventures amused me with his conversation as well as his original manner. I found him a man of good sense and natural abilities of no mean color. Joined to an athletic frame and an iron constitution was a heart not deficient in boldness, and a restless energy which no circumstances could control. Physically, he was a fine specimen of a man [. . .] His expression was open and manly, although there was much in his eye which would escape the casual observer. (vii–viii)

The narrator's description gestures towards the sinewy New England peddler type. Stinchfield's speech portrays the typically talkative peddler demeanor, but with a self-conscious note towards the toll peddling has taken on him:

> I have peddled sixteen years in the States and in the Provinces, in the heat and cold. I have been rich as a Jew and poor as an Indian. I have met with more adventures in my wanderings than any person in existence. [. . .] You think me a very singular individual—a sort of wild-man or nondescript, and perhaps a little unsettled in the upper works [. . .] but you are not quite right, sir, it's my way—natural as is breathing. Mixing with the world for so many years has made me familiar with it—too familiar, perhaps, for that matter—and confirmed the habit which singles me out from all other men and makes me a wonder. (vii)

Robinson's reform narrative thus hinges on the peddler profession. Hailing from rural New England, he has traveled "all over the United States" (ibid.). He has transgressed from the countryside to the city, portrayed as pastoral habitat of the reformed peddler, and as abyss of temptations and sin.[41] He is described as "an inveterate talker, [and] never neglected an opportunity to indulge in his loquacious powers. Talking was a part of his business" (29). Even before he falls prey to the bottle, Stinchfield's youthful enthusiasm is checked by an external power, Nature, or the landscape he travels through. When the inexperienced hotspur leaves his New England home, he soon becomes weary of traveling: "He climed [sic] hills which seemed to lengthen as he went—he trudged across valleys that mocked his efforts, he toiled through woods that appeared interminable" (17).

Nature obstructs the peddler's profession and resists the coercion that comes with his peddling; the peddler as agent of commerce disturbs the bucolic ideal. At the beginning, the narrator provides a pantheist description of his travels through New England in midsummer, in which he sheds his city life and recovers, resembling Emerson's transparent eyeball:[42] "It is good to commune alone with Nature in her summer mood, and become a part of the great whole whose sum makes up the Universe—comprises all" (v). All is order and harmony, and the narrator's own inspiration foreshadows Stinchfield's return to this state of being after "mingl[ing] with the world" (19). Stinchfield has been corrupted by too much knowledge of the country and the city, but he also pulled himself up by the bootstraps (see below); he is both an actor on and an object of fate.

Robinson's text taps into the debate about heroes and genres that claims that the peddler is no hero material. With its didactic intent, the temperance narrative relies on a life story and romance hero who can be cast as reformed wretch. When Stinchfield leaves his parents' humble New England farm, the narrator sketches out his white supremacy before the reader's eyes. He is "the most prominent figure of the group, [. . .] his figure was symmetrical, well-knit together, displaying thews and sinews of great power. His features were regular, with a nose of the Anglo-Saxon mould, and a mouth denoting firmness and resolution" (12). Equipped with the alleged New England hardiness and the "quick, sanguine temperament" (ibid.), Stinchfield is a fine downeaster. He plans, as he explains to his parents, to "follow my fortune," "seek a broader field of action," and "battle with the world" (13, 14). In this scene, young Stinchfield is made out as Anglo-Saxon American romance hero, thirsty for adventure. He departs from his humble home with a sentimental tear in his eye, but full of hope.[43]

While at first sight young Stinchfield looks like a perfect romance hero, the fact that he is a peddler jars with this role, as the narrator acknowledges:

> He did not choose the progression of the law [. . .] He did not take to physic [. . .] He did not even rush into the ministry [. . .] He did nothing of the sort. He became a—a merchant—a wandering merchant,—mounted a box, cracked his whip, and whistled

"God Save America," and traded with old ladies, many of whom, no doubt, wished him at their antipodes or a hotter vicinity. I am aware, dear reader, that I have made the above revelation, to the great detriment of the romance of the whole performance, [...] but the collateral of the case required it. (20)

In describing the hero's profession, the narrator grapples for words and uses pauses. He hints at the peddler's dishonesty by reiterating the old ladies' wishes that the trader best go to hell. Robinson's narrator apologizes to the reader for shattering the romance image of the "hero," but defends this particular trader by claiming that he has an "honest heart" and "sterling principles" (ibid.), observing that Stinchfield is "more real than is often found in works of fiction" (ibid.), and "sensible," not given to rash and futile "Quixotic mission" (40). The peddler is not fit to be a romance hero, but he can be reformed and used for the temperance narrative's teaching.

Stinchfield's "mingling with the world" (19) happens effortlessly at first, "whistling himself up the Connecticut and down the Merrimack" (22). He enacts different religious beliefs to lure his customers into trading, as "promising Universalist," "confirmed Calvinist," and "flaming Infidel" (22, 23),[44] adapting Sam Slick's mode: "And this, reader, is the world and what is termed 'human nature'" (23). Like many peddler stories, Robinson's narrator focuses on an "illustration of the 'way of trade'" in which the peddler invokes a pious personality to make a sale to a young lady (24–6). The responsibility for being "gulled" (26) is the victim's own, ever since the fall of mankind: "Sin has come into the world, and so have peddlers and Indian doctors. Eschew evil and mountebanks" (ibid.). Robinson's peddler is a phenomenon of a post-lapsarian world.

After one of Stinchfield's drinking episodes, he returns to business with an ingenious invention: he discovers in his pocket a "recipe for putting shoes together without stitches or pegs!" (72). The narrator praises this recipe to the reader as if trying to sell it, only to trick us:

> Think of this idea, reader: shoes, real shoes without stitches or pegs! Beware ye gullible ones; beware lest ye wear shoes without stitches or pegs; and if ye do wear them, trust not yourself upon such a treacherous foundation from the shadow of the door-step, and shun the water as ye would wet feet or a severe cold, or as ye fear returning to your homes barefoot! Shoes without pegs! Did you buy the wonderful recipe, reader? If you did was you not most wonderfully "sold" when you bought it? (72–3)

Robinson excuses his protagonist from being a peddler, even if he outperforms everyone in his "shrewdness" (73). The narrator criticizes not the peddler's demeanor, but his customers' hypocrisy. This is expressed by Stinchfield's only friend, Ned the sailor. Ned travels incognito, but when his full name "Ned Buntline" is given, readers of the period would have understood the reference to the temperance promoter and author of *The Mysteries and Miseries of New York: A Story of Real Life* (1849).[45] In Robinson's novella, Buntline serves as a mentor to the depressed drunkard Stinchfield, telling him to "arouse yourself with the strong energy of a man, and resolve to make the only amends that are in your power. Meet the world with a bold front and an honest heart, and fight bravely the 'battle of life'! A *man*, Harvard, a MAN!" (59). Ned reminds Stinchfield of his manly ideals and makes him promise to "become a MAN, and live for some object; to atone for his youthful errors" (70), but Stinchfield never stops peddling. Thus, while Robinson critically assesses the peddler profession, he also finds the peddler more fit than the romance hero for affirming imperialist "manhood" and manifest destiny.

The Yankee peddler unifies the eclectic genre mix of Robinson's text. Stinchfield embodies the "go ahead" man as well as the con man/magician Bernard writes about, a personified postlapsarian punishment to all mankind. Robinson pits the bucolic agrarian idyll against the urban cesspool, the agrarian past against an industrialized "worldliness," and he negotiates the peddler-as-hero conflict. To fulfill the purpose of the temperance narrative, the peddler has to be cast as the poor sinner. Stinchfield therefore oscillates between the peddler-as-predator and the reformed wretch, a versatility that attributes the peddler with an emotional depth the cultural peddler type does not carry.

The peddler as national figure hinges on performance; his skill of "soft sawder" and knowledge of "human natur" can only be shown in action. The peddler is a *perpetuum mobile* national icon. The texts discussed present him as a transgressive figure, his traveling the nation's development narrative. Cooper's Harvey Birch transgresses between a host of forms and camps, real and symbolic: between disguises, between the picket lines of British and American troops, between allegiances to either, between the characters representing each (he helps both American and British partisans, his allegiance being governed by a sense of compassion). Symbolically, he oscillates between noble fighter and commoner, between enigmatic marginal figure and focalizer/protagonist, and, finally, between singular national icon and American everyman. Sam Slick takes the

Squire along on his Northeastern circuit through the British province, enlivening the backwater landscapes with his visions of industrialization and "going ahead." Harvard Stinchfield has been lured into the city by his profession; even though he could have remained a country peddler, he is outsmarted by the urban villains who take his money. His return to country life nourishes the pastoral image of the Early Republic, but, importantly, his peddler business is unscathed by this. His individualist New England spirit allows him to become a successful peddler, and ultimately leads him back to the right path. The peddler as a messenger and go-between maps the imaginary and real grounds of the American nation, and, most importantly, he lumps together the (yet imagined) national space with the individual, domestic space Americans inhabit, as the following will show.

Yankee Clocks and Wooden Nutmegs: "Yankee Notions" and the Making of a National Marketplace

Like the historiographic texts examined at the beginning of this chapter, the literary texts foreground the business transaction between the peddler and his customers, illustrating the peddler's performance and his wares. This scene blends the textual world with the reader's gaze; as the Yankee peddler praises his wares to his fictional customers, the readers may imagine themselves as customers and test the reliability and quality of his offer. The peddler texts thus duplicate the scenario of trade and allow readers to make up their own minds, opposite the fictional figures who are rapt in the Yankee's soft sawder. Consumerist pleasures in the text reverberate with reader experience, addressing her as a consumer citizen and participant in the national economy.

The peddler's entrance into the social sphere kicks off the banter. The photograph "The Yankee Peddler at the Parsonage" (Fig. 3.1), which appears at the beginning of this chapter, typically shows the peddler positioned next to his wagon, with his potential customers grouped around him, outside and in front of the house. The peddler has made it into the garden of the parsonage but not inside (a person appears to be guarding the door). The setting of trade is thus public but the primary actors in this arena are the women who are lured out of their houses. This process is also shown by nineteenth-century genre paintings focusing on the Yankee peddler advertising his wares to potential customers. John Whetten Ehninger, Thomas Waterman Wood, Abbott Fuller Graves, and Edward Lamson Henry use the peddler as a nostalgic subject of the pre-industrial past of the U.S. in paintings of the second half of the nineteenth century. They show the peddler outside the settlement or in the market square, talking with grand gesture. In the paintings, his customers are all women, their gaze fixed on the merchandise they are holding (mostly some kind of fabric), while children are playing around the peddler's cart.[46]

The gender politics at work in the genre paintings show that the peddler's arrival makes the frontier housewife leave her home and become a consumer in the marketplace. Harking back to the siege executed by the peddler Mr. Slim in the *Sketches and Eccentricities of Davy Crockett*, the mother and daughter's assistance mean disloyalty towards the head of the family, who ultimately gives in to the peddler's attacks. The Yankee peddler thus becomes a threat to the frontier settler's masculinity. Since his seduction of the women may well include sexual innuendo, his entrance into the house, where allowed, is a critical transgression. In Cooper's *The Spy*, Harvey trades not only goods but also news with the Wharton daughters. The fact that Harvey is let into the family's parlor proves that the family trust him more than they would an unknown peddler, and that his trade visits are a regular event. In this scene, the women take over the action, while the men of the family silently look on and listen to the barter and the news.

Upon Harvey's arrival, Sarah is fascinated with his wares, giving "little time for the usual salutations, before she commenced her survey of his pack [. . .] The tables, chairs, and floor were soon covered with silks, capes, gloves, muslins, and all the stock of an itinerant trader" (Cooper 2006: 44). Sarah's anticipation nearly makes her forget her manners; when she asks him about war news, the peddler ignores her request and tempts her with fine things:

> The question could not have been heard; for the peddler, burying his body in the pack, brought forth a quantity of lace of exquisite fineness, and, holding it up to view, he required the admiration of the young lady. Miss Peyton dropped the cup she was engaged in washing, from her hand; and Frances exhibited the whole of her lovely face, [. . .] beaming with a color that shamed the damask which enviously concealed her figure. (Ibid.)

The display of his wares becomes a still life; the women abandon their positions as if invisibly drawn towards the lace. Their movement toward the goods highlights the peddler's role as agent of civilization and tempter. His trade allows the women to model themselves according to fashionable gender identities that make them desirable for the men, and to thereby keep up the customary social norms—an act of preservation that is all the more important in the uncertainties of the Revolutionary War period. Yet the imported damask also recalls the U.S.'s dependence on England for luxury wares. The comparison between the coloring of Frances's face and the color of her dress magnifies this symbolism; like the damask she is wearing, the lace Harvey offers to the women represents a means for ornamenting the natural beauty of the frontier damsel whose luminous complexion outshines the color of her dress. The peddler's wares preserve social conventions and decorate the female body, while gesturing towards the transatlantic trade conflicts of the nineteenth century. The luxurious damask that "enviously concealed her figure" hides and reveals Frances's body at the same time, showing off her silhouette and sketching out the female consumer's part in the making of the patriot consumer.[47]

In the next scene, the examination and appraisal of wares continues, but the conversation shifts to the peddler's other valuables, news and gossip. The trading of material objects is equated with the passing back and forth of intelligence in the following:

> "I repeat but what I hear," said Birch, offering a piece of cloth to the inspection of Sarah, who rejected it in silence, evidently determined to hear more before she made another purchase.
> "They say [. . .] that Sumter and one or two more were all that were hurt, and that the rig'lars were all cut to pieces, for the militia were fixed snugly in a log barn."
> "Not very probable," said Sarah, contemptuously, "though I make no doubt the rebels got behind the logs."
> "I think," said the peddler, coolly, again offering the silk, "it's quite ingenious to get a log between one and a gun, instead of getting between a gun and a log."
> The eyes of Harper [Washington] dropped quietly on the pages of the volume in his hand, while Frances, rising, came forward with a smile in her face, as she inquired, in a tone of affability that the pedler had never before witnessed from the younger sister:
> "Have you more of the lace, Mr. Birch?"
> The desired article was immediately produced, and Frances became a purchaser also. (Ibid. 46)

Harvey Birch brings intelligence to his commander unnoticed, by performing his peddler business. Birch's typical interweaving of "soft sawder" and knowledge of "human nature," usually intended for trading, becomes an activity of national importance in this scene. Robinson's drunkard Harvard Stinchfield is also shown in a scene which the narrator includes as "illustration of the 'way of trade'" (Robinson 1851: 24). Harvard poses as a pietist to a "good lady [who] purchases tin whistles, Jew's harps, pine hams, wooden nutmegs, together with damaged pieces of calico, and a half dozen other things which she might never want, or could not use if she should" (ibid. 25). Upon the return of her husband, "her other and stronger half," the naïve customer is scalded with "a most icy frown, and has the pleasure of hearing her acuteness called in question, together with sundry unique and not endearing epithets" (ibid. 26). Robinson sketches women as easily tricked victims. The peddler uses the absence of a man in the house to go about his seductive business. In "The Yankee Peddler at the Parsonage" (1889), the only man in the front is the person touching the other side of the tin plate the peddler offers, as if to guard the household from the influence of the peddler, while another man in shirt sleeves suspiciously blocks the entrance to the house.

Robinson not only criticizes the hypocrisy of religious fanatics, he also hints at the devilish role of the peddler as tempter who re-enacts original sin over and over. In the short stint about the Yankee peddler included in the *Sketches and Eccentricities of Col. David Crockett*, the trading business of Yankee peddler Slim is shown with theatrical devices, such as a mixture between narrative telling and showing, or the peddler's asides.[48] Like Harvey Birch, Slim communicates almost exclusively with the women of the house. In an exercise of "soft sawder," he lauds their beauty, and his words even penetrate the women's dreams at night: "The daughter dreams of tortoise shell combs and jewelry. The mother, from Slim's compliment, believes herself both young and beautiful" (Crockett 1833: 156–7). Slim's sweet talk wins over the women as partisans in the following "war" over the selling of a Yankee clock to the head of the household, old Baines (see ibid. 154). The women consumers in *Sketches and Eccentricities* are backwoods people and cannot afford damask dresses or lace; they buy fake tortoise shell combs that are really made of horn. The (male) voice of economic austerity is drowned in the women's desire for the objects that ornament their natural beauty or make them feel pretty.[49]

In the "soft sawder" talk of the Yankee peddler, his wares are transformed into objects of great value. Historically, the peddlers indeed "helped to pull the outlying rural world into the orbit of a more modern and urban print culture" (Cohen 2008: 12). Itinerant vendors would trade small household wares like buttons, combs, or needles, but also tin ware or books. The peddlers disseminated print culture products, broadsides, almanacs, sermons, and other ephemeral texts. In a study on the material and cultural life in New England in the Early Republic, William Gilmore finds that peddling "had a definite ecology [and] [. . .] circulated the widest variety of printed matter available in America, a selection broader than all but the most bookstores sold" (Gilmore 1989: 176). For Gilmore, the geographical reach of peddlers equals the spread of commerce between 1780 and 1830, when "[s]ome families did have their first experience with market products, and with money as a commodity, in dealing with peddlers" (ibid. 177). In rural Vermont, during the winter, a literary "cabin fever" broke out: "Those possessed by it later founded religions and utopias, invented gadgets, prophesied industrial strife, became presidents, or lost their minds" (ibid. 2). Jonathan Plummer, one of the earliest book peddlers, was also a "balladmonger" who wrote poems on commission from the 1790s onwards.[50] The peddlers emulated a memorable salesman persona. The 1879 girlhood memory of Sarah Emery from Newburyport described the "old lame peddler named Urin" as "quite a character":

> He would stump in, usually near dusk, with a big basket, and sinking into the nearest chair, declare himself "e'en a'most dead, he was so lame!" Then, without stopping to take breath, he would reel off, "Tree fell on me when I was a boy, killed my brother and me jest like him, here's books, pins, needles, black sewing silk all colors, tapes varses, almanacks and sarmons, thread, fine thread for cambric ruffles, here's varses on the pirate that was hung on Boston common, solemn varses with a border of coffins atop, and Noble's sarmon preached at his wife's funeral, the 'lection sarmon when the guv'ner took the chair, Jack the Piper, Whittington's Cat, Pilgrim's Progress, Bank of Faith, The History of the Devil, and a great many other religious books." [. . .] As I had an eager avidity for books, the peddler's advent was hailed with delight. (Emery 1879, qtd. in Cohen 2008: 14)

Urin's sales pitch pinpoints the specific relation between storytelling and sales. The nonsensical memory (how can he have been killed by the tree if he's sitting in the parlor now?) is uttered in the same breath as the sales talk, making the storytelling and the offering of wares episodes parts of the same (peddler) show. The enumeration of goods on display has a monotone quality, with the objects being repeated ("thread," "varses") and their diversity praised. With her spelling of the words "varses" and "sarmons,"

Emery also reproduces the New England dialect and authenticates the peddler's performance. The peddler's goods are a part of his persona, animated and beautified. The wares make the man and vice versa: "And every article he parts with will carry with it a lasting impression of the 'clock peddler'" (Crockett 1833: 152).

The peddler's wares in the frontier household therefore bear witness to the arrival of modern times in remote areas. Two goods are particularly iconic: Yankee clocks and wooden nutmegs, both of which are part of the concept of "Yankee notions." This term articulates the materiality of peddler narratives. The "Yankee notions" galvanize the peddler business by designating his salesman's performance as well as his (animated) merchandise.[51] While the polysemous nature of "Yankee notions" has not been explored in great detail, I found further evidence of its usage, for instance, in a short notice in the *San Francisco Call* in 1895, which reports the provocative behavior in court of one acquitted John Smith: "When Smith was discharged he proceeded to shake hands with the jury, on advice of his counsel, but the Judge stopped him and ordered Smith out of his sight, saying that he was a Yankee notion" ("A Yankee Notion" 1895, n.p.). In another piece by anonymous author "Q.Q." entitled "Yankee Notions" (1834), the whimsical British author imagines a roguish Yankee Jonathan traveling to Sicily and swapping with a Neapolitan, concluding, "yet, if the Neapolitan would not make a profitable swap by the exchange, mine is no true 'Yankee notion'" (Q.Q. 1834: 167). The Yankee notions are chosen as title in the story collection *Yankee Notions: A Medley by Timo. Titterwell, Esq.* (Kettell 1837) and in the New York-based popular humorous magazine *Yankee Notions*, discussed in Chapter 1.

I return to *Yankee Notions* to discuss an 1861 frontispiece which links the meaning of Yankee notions as consumer goods animated by Yankee salesmanship with the sectional depiction of Brother Jonathan. The June edition of the magazine shows a Brother Jonathan figure going South to the Civil War, framed by a plethora of Yankee notions (Fig. 3.2). The little objects range from animated apples (top right corner) to cider kegs (low right corner) that continue the reference to their original material meaning. Among the trifles are the jackknife for whittling (on the right), and symbols of industrialization and progress, like the railroad on the bottom with "Yankee" written on the steam machine, and the hot air balloon on the left side with a Yankee signaling "Goodbye" to the viewer as he ascends. The head of the page is overcrowded with figures and fruit

Figure 3.2 Frontispiece of *Yankee Notions*, June 1861. "Jonathan, Going South." Library of Congress, Prints and Photographs Division.

and vegetables and other things hard to discern, but all the plenty shown here is organized around a centerpiece, the round, smiling face that extends its hands left and right as if to present everything to the reader. Most notably, a Yankee clock is positioned as a centerpiece among the letters of the magazine title, a heavy burden carried by a long-legged peddler, located between two coats of arms toting the magazine's philosophy: "Liberty" and "Fun."

The comic universe of Yankeedom represented in the frame is checked by the topic of the frontispiece. Only two months after the Civil War began, *Yankee Notions* selects a Jonathan figure for showing the Northern engagement, using the top hat flying an American flag, striped pants, and characteristic long legs as well as determined expression on a haggard face. Jonathan is armed to the teeth; the weight of his load indicates that this is not a human figure but the allegory of the North going South, with all the materials the North has available. With the allegorical figure, the magazine also declares its partisanship. The caption "Jonathan Going South" is subtitled with his battle cry: "South's the word, and South I'm going! Hurrah for the Star Spangled Banner! The Union must and shall be preserved! Our war cry is death to Traitors! God bless our country!" The dog, small and sweet-looking, equipped with sunglasses and equally heavy armor, provides some comic relief to the war image. It may even be a nod to John Bull's bulldog, yet it also indicates Jonathan has allies and true friends that accompany him. The progressive impact of the image hinges on the direction the figures are going, from right to left and slightly turned towards the viewer. This implies they are walking uphill with a long and heavy stride; also, given the viewing convention from left to right, the viewer feels engaged since her gaze is directed first to the front of Jonathan's body and his face. His coattails are flying, his body is on the move, his gaze fixed upon his aim, physical (the South) and ideological (saving the Union). The furrowed brows and focused look conjure an expression of determination and seriousness that runs contrary to the huzza of the jubilant subtitle. His concern and firmness also echo cartoons of Abraham Lincoln, adding another level of meaning, of presidential leadership, to the figure in war garb. Comparing the 1861 frontispiece to the 1851 beginnings of *Yankee Notions* discussed in Chapter 1, the artistic refinement is noticeable not only in the cover illustration, but also in the masthead and frame. By 1861, the visual design has amalgamated the urban Yankee figure with the material culture of the Yankee peddler, the New Englander, and the figure's ambiguity. The cover mixes images of consumerism, mobility, and progress, creating an iconography of Yankeedom.

The Yankee peddler's (con)fusion with his merchandise also reiterates the ambiguity related to Yankeedom. As deceiving as the Yankee peddler's stories are, so are his wares. The Yankee clock as timepiece symbolizes modernization; as in Samuel Woodworth's play *The Forest Rose*, it replaces the rhythm of daylight and defines work hours in an industrial society (see Chapter 2). Yankee clocks "engendered a new culture of speed or 'freneticisim'" (Marsh 2005: 260) of physical growth and expansionism linked to the national allegory of Brother Jonathan. In the frontier household, the clock is given an honorable and central place, on the mantelpiece of the hearth, expressing its (alleged) value and establishing a symbolic presence of Yankeedom and the national imperative of "going ahead."

The sketch of Yankee peddler Slim portrays the itinerant vendor's business as revolutionary upheaval. Slim sells a clock to the Baines family, although they already own one. He puts up his merchandise next to the Baineses' clock against the host's will. The two rival clocks come alive in the Yankee's salesman comportment:

"I don't want you to buy it. I only want to put it up."

Still asking permission, yet having it denied, Slim is seen bustling about the room until, at the end of the dialogue, his wooden clock having encroached upon the dominions of an old family time-piece, is seen suspended with all the beauty, yet bold effrontery, of a yankee notion—while the old family time-piece, with a retiring yet conscious dignity, is heard to cry out "Oh tempore! Oh mores!" And concludes her ejaculations by thundering anathemas against this modern irruption of the Goths. (Crockett 1833: 155)

Slim is not so much an agent as a distraction, and his clock finds its way to the mantel magically, invading it like a barbarian. The old clock comes to life in this tryst and, like an old person, condemns the misbehavior of the young generation. The narrator smartly weaves generational conflict into this "battle of the clocks," in which the Yankee clock stands for the progressive, self-enamored "Yankee notion."

Historically, the Yankee clocks were smaller than the conventional stand-up "grandfather clock" and easier to transport. The peddler's success is linked to the progress in clockmaking technology, such as Eli Terry's (Yankee) idea to reduce the clock size and weight.[52] Nevertheless, the clocks would suffer on the long traveling circuits the peddlers went on, and stories about broken clocks abound.[53] Some merchandise became famous for being fake. In a defense of the itinerant vendor, Wright argues that this bad reputation might have served as a conversation opener:

> The reputation the early peddler won was enjoyed by chapmen of even so late a date as the Civil War. In fact, it was shrewdly turned to account as a bit of humor in the introductory remarks that preceded the bargaining. A peddler would drive up to a house and blithely address his prospective customer in some such pattern as this: "Madam, are you in need of any pocket saw-mills? Wooden nutmegs? White oak cheeses? Tin bung-holes? Or calico hog troughs?" And having gained the smile of the lady of the house, he proceeded to recite what he actually did have in his wagon—tinware, mats, glassware, brooms, washboards, clothes pints, rolling pins, matches, paddy irons, kettles, and pots. (Wright 1965: 22)

Among the fake wares catalogued are the renowned wooden nutmegs, which surface in many texts about peddlers. An imported spice from the Pacific Banda Islands, nutmeg was traded along the New England coast and brought inland by the peddlers; it is featured in many traditionally "American" foods today, such as pies, hot toddy, mulled cider, or eggnog. In the peddler texts examined here, the wooden nutmegs appear in Wright (1965), in Robinson (1851: 25), and in Bernard (1887: 45). In 1928, the *Hartford Courant* published an anecdote about the original misunderstanding of an ignorant Southern customer who "took it for granted that he was being cheated and spread the report that the Connecticut Yankees were manufacturing wooden nutmegs with which to cheat the Southerners. This report travelled faster than the denial" ("Wooden Nutmegs," Newton 1928, n.p.). The trader prepared a crate of nutmegs for sending to his Southern customer by adding hickory nuts to the half-filled box to prevent the nutmegs from rolling around, but, importantly, he only charged for the nutmegs. The Southerner "had never seen any hickory nuts" (ibid.) and suspected the worst. Like many others, this story avenges the negative image of the peddler by claiming the incompetence of the Southerners. The wooden nutmeg anecdote might well be derived from Haliburton's Sam Slick, who recalls talking with a congressman, Professor Everett, about the wooden nutmegs and concludes, "Well its been a standing joke with them Southerners agin us ever since" (Haliburton 1995: 37).

Today, the legend of the wooden nutmegs is a marker of Connecticut identity.[54] A hoax article from 1952 proclaims "Drought Will Not Affect Wooden Nutmeg Harvest" (Griggs 1952). The article attributes the myth of the wooden nutmeg to the Yankee peddler but insists on the provenance of this rare fruit from the New England state. Interviewees include the Committee of the Yankee Fair of the Wilton Congregational Church, the State Department of Farms and Markets, and the State Development Division, who celebrate the "original product of Connecticut" while acknowledging difficulties in recognizing it: "It is not until the product is retailed, not until it is in the hands of the housewife, that reports are heard" (ibid.). In the conclusion, the secret fruit is cast as token of state identity: "Carping, bitter people will doubtlessly doubt forever. But in the farmlands of the Nutmeg State you'll find that everyone knows just how much truth there is to the story" (ibid.). Similarly, a 1964 contribution revisits the olden days and hails the Yankee peddler as "forerunner of modern sales and distribution setups" ("Noted for Wooden Nutmegs," N.N. 1964: 22F). The article relocates the traveling salesman in the present of the 1960s, with a nod towards the "Yankee Peddler" European tour initiated by the Hartford business chamber quoted at the beginning of this chapter: "The system still works, and the Yankee peddler is back—except that now he travels by jet and if he says it's a nutmeg, it's a nutmeg" (ibid.).

As native fantasy fruit and counterfeit merchandise, the wooden nutmeg materializes peddler performance. Even Haliburton's Squire is familiar with the fakery of the itinerant vendor:

> I had heard of yankee clock pedlars, tin pedlars, and bible pedlars, especially of him who sold the Polyglot Bibles (*all in English*) to the amount of sixteen thousand pounds. The house of every substantial farmer had three substantial ornaments, a wooden clock, a tin reflector, and a Polyglot Bible. How is it that an American can sell his wares, at whatever price he pleases, where a blue-nose would fail to make a sale at all? I will enquire of the clock-maker the secret of his success. (Haliburton 1995: 13, emphasis in original)

As early as the 1830s, the peddler's tricky merchandise was as famous as his selling skills, and, as in Haliburton's text, a distinction of national character. The Yankee peddler impersonates the young nation, seen from without. Within the U.S., the peddler frequently transports a ubiquitous sectional message, because it takes two to cheat. The peddler profits from naïve customers who have themselves to blame. The Englishman Bernard joins in with accusing the Southerners of their own demise:

> it can be no wonder that the Virginians indulge in occasional vituperations, insist that the Yankee cheats them in every transaction, and that, however he may vary his commodities from the traditional

wooden nutmegs and red-flannel sausages, swindling is still his talent, his stimulus, and local distinction. (Bernard 1887: 45)

In this chapter, historiographic, literary, and visual sources have shown that the boundaries between real peddlers and the imagined character are blurred. The legendary figure tinges historiographic studies, and the peddler's wares have gained a strange material life of their own. Among the Yankee figures discussed in this book, the Yankee peddler articulates a staunch sectional identity, propelling industrialization and the formation of a national economy. He is shown as hybrid man-machine precursor of the steamboat and railroad and shapes where Americans live and what Americans do, namely, produce and consume their own domestic products. He enables people to participate in an American economy and perform the cultural routines of buying and selling.

Like Brother Jonathan and the stage Yankee, the peddler is not to be trusted. As "spokesman for an industrial marketplace filled with sham products and dubious imitations" (Marsh 2005: 261), he is admired for his cunning and shrewdness. The Yankee peddler is no positive allegory, no national monument, but an aggressive upstart and node of action. His mobility is transformed into a transgression between different worlds: the wilderness, the city, the village public sphere, and the homely parlor as the American family's inner sanctum. Literary texts fictionalize the trade scenario with fantastic devices for the reader's entertainment, but they also have a didactic effect. The last laugh about the peddler's customers/victims is reserved for the audience who look on while frontier women and naïve villagers fall prey to the peddler's magical soft sawder. By warning his readers against doing as the backwoods buyers do, the peddler educates Americans in the art of buying and selling.

Notes

1. The following quotations are taken from the article series covering the visit, listed in the bibliography as Shoaff 1964a, 1964b, 1964c, 1964d, and 1964e.
2. Itinerant vendors were also familiar figures in England. For instance, William Wordsworth in 1798 wrote about a peddler in a fragment that was to be included in *A Ruined Cottage*; he then decided to publish it individually as a poem titled "The Pedlar," only to later change the title to "The Wanderer" and incorporate it in *The Excursion* (1814). The

poem was published individually only in 1969 (see Wordsworth 1985: 19). Hieronymus Bosch shows a peddler with a pack as early as 1510 in his painting *The Wayfarer*, a figure that has been read as a wanderer between the worlds of gluttony and the spiritual realm. On Christian figures that relate to the peddler, see St. Armand 1978.

3. Bernard's design of the Yankee as monstrous "crocodile [. . .], prowling about the shores and wharves to pounce upon the unwary stranger" (16) can also be seen as a reference to depictions of America from the pre-colonial period; as Mario Klarer (1999) has argued, cannibalism looms large in early travelogues and imaginations of the Americas.
4. About Rourke's writings, Schlueter observes: "Rourke intended to create a study that maintained the ebullient flow of American humor itself: a book that talked big and stood tall, a book that, in short, *performed*" (2008: 541; see also Rubin 1980: 135–70).
5. In the entire section on the Yankee peddler, Rourke draws heavily from Bernard's text, retelling the same anecdotes and peddler tricks, such as the story of a Yankee tricking some Englishmen in London, handing them "a Yankee handle for their London blades" (Bernard 1887: 47; Rourke 2004: 17), or the coup of a Yankee trader exporting a shipping of warming pans to the (tropical) West Indies (Bernard 1887: 48; Rourke 2004: 16).
6. The Yorkshireman in turn is himself not so much real as imagined, a clownish figure on the English stage in the seventeenth and eighteenth centuries. Regional identity, linked with provinciality and a specific behavior, frequently becomes the foil for comic figures on the stage; see for instance the labeling of Davy Crockett as "our national Gascon" in Paulding's *Lion of the West*. The French gascon figure refers to inhabitants of the Southwestern region of France, as well as to a distinct way of joking (Schäfer 2012).
7. As of March 25, 2019, Wright's *Hawkers and Walkers* yields ninety citations on Google Scholar, Dolan's *The Yankee Peddlers* forty-one. Recent contributions focusing on peddling also use these sources; see e.g. Jaffee 1991.
8. From a scholarly perspective, both books appear as semi-academic. They include unreferenced images and etchings to illustrate the text; they feature anecdotes and literary cameos loosely attributed to sources; they provide a bibliography of works cited, but do not give page indications in the texts. Wright's and Dolan's texts are directed at a general reading public and occupy a middle ground between academic and essayistic writing. Given this getup, it is all the more striking that they serve as the basis for contemporary research.
9. Dolan, meanwhile, describes "history as everyday living"; he claims that people collect antiques and memorabilia because they represent "a direct link to our near past. We like to have history recreated for us for our pleasure" (1964: 9–10).

10. While Wright's and Dolan's rhetoric strategy is heavily infused with progressivist ideology, the point itself is well taken. Paul Uselding (1975) examines the effect of peddling on industrialization and economic development before the Civil War; he examines the link between itinerant vending and entrepreneurship and finds that, for newly arrived immigrants, peddling entails an important cultural "schooling" function for marketing for immigrants. This last observation supports the importance of the peddler as a representative of American (business) culture from a sorely needed economic history perspective.

11. In contextualizing the role of the peddler in literature, I draw from a number of studies in economic and cultural history, specifically Jaffee 1991, which looks at peddlers transforming the rural North, and Atherton 1945 and Jones 2000, which address peddling in the antebellum and postbellum South respectively. Jaffee (2011: 156–68) offers a historical overview of the New England peddling industry.

12. On the confidence man and the workings of identity fraud, see Rosenthal and Schäfer 2014 and Bergmann 1969. The figure of the confidence man is based on the scam of William Thompson, who would approach strangers in New York in genteel dress and ask them to entrust their watch with him for a day as a sign of their trust in him. His trial, in 1849, caused a stir across the country and inspired Herman Melville's novel *The Confidence Man* (1857), published on April Fool's Day, which remains controversial among scholars.

13. Cooper wrote about this novel to Andrew Thompson Goodrich on June 28, 1820: "I confess I am more partial to this new work myself as being a Country-man [. . .] The task of making American manners and American scenes interesting to an American reader is an arduous one" (qtd. in Lee 1993: 31). W. H. Gardiner, who reviewed the novel for the *North American Review*, also comments extensively on the question of a new national literature (Gardiner 1822; a reprint is available in Dekker and Williams 1997: 55–66).

14. The spy's importance has been overlooked by commentators; Trees (2000), for instance, finds that Harvey's story pales in comparison to the turmoil of the genteel Wharton family (see e.g. 268). Verhoeven (1993) also discusses the seeming discord between Cooper's choice of title and Harvey's marginality in the story, arguing that, in casting Harvey as a "gentleman in disguise" (84), Cooper "attempts to smooth out hitches in the novel's hidden ideology [of quasi-egalitarian principles and social elitism]" (83). Verhoeven argues that Harvey serves as a projection of the author's self-image "isolated and misunderstood, yet full of great potential" (84).

15. Trees argues that Major André's (genteel) heroism contrasts with the republican virtue of his yeoman captors (who resisted his attempts to bribe them); he argues that Cooper's *The Spy* takes a different approach to the André story, criticizing Washington's decision to hang him and

advancing a more complicated account of loyalties with the Wharton family. Reid discusses secrecy in the making of an American national literature and traces Cooper's use of the revolutionary legends of Major André and of the 1777 murder of Jane McCrea, who hoped to meet her British fiancé in the woods.

16. An exception is Robert A. Fink's 1974 essay published in the *New York Folklore Quarterly*, "Harvey Birch: The Yankee Peddler as American Hero." Commentators have either ignored the peddler paradigm or treated it as secondary to other cultural influences. Reid (2004), for instance, emphasizes that the spy is "ubiquitous on the land" (46), and in her following description of this well-known type, she employs terms that are equally characteristic of the Yankee peddler: "[A]s a character type, he would have been familiar to Cooper's audience. Throughout the romance tradition were many hermits and spies who moved 'from one place to another' [. . .] teaching them far more than the settled American could know" (47). Both Lee (1993: 39) and St. Armand (1978: 367) talk about the peddler's pack. They agree that the pack is a Bunyanesque symbol of the spy's sins and heavy burdens, sidelining the peddling aspect. Similarly, Verhoeven (1993: 81, 82) only comments on the social status of the peddler in a footnote, relying on J. R. Dolan's *The Yankee Peddlers of Early America*.

17. Crosby was a soldier and spy in the Revolutionary War, and he reported to John Jay. After the publication of H. L. Barnum's fraud biography *The Spy Unmasked: or, Memoirs of Enoch Crosby Alias Harvey Birch, the Hero of Mr. Cooper's Tale of the Neutral Ground* (New York, 1828), Crosby was generally accepted as the blueprint for Birch. The hoax was only exposed in 1930 by Tremaine McDowell in "The Identity of Harvey Birch," American Literature 2: 111–20. For an overview of Crosby's biography, see Pickering 1966. Further sources addressing Crosby's identity as Birch include: Guy Hatfield, "Harvey Birch and the Myth of Enoch Crosby," The Magazine of American History 18 (1887): 431–5; James Deane, "Enoch Crosby Not a Myth," ibid. 73–5; Guy Hatfield, "Harvey Birch Not Enoch Crosby," ibid. 431; Harry Edward Miller, "The Spy of the Neutral Ground," New England Magazine 18 (1898): 307–19.

18. Qtd. in Walker 1956: 403–4. The full text of Washington's letter is accessible at <dspace.sunyconnect.suny.edu/handle/1951/52522?show=full> (last accessed November 2, 2020).

19. Wallace maintains that the Whartons' home is a metonymy for the British colonizer and that its telling name, "The Locusts," insinuates that this presence is a plague to the new republic; similarly, he reads Wellmere as defunct representative of England (Wallace 1985: 44, 47).

20. The Birch family (Harvey, his elderly father, and their nosy housekeeper Katy) are the Whartons' only neighbors (138), but the two families keep to themselves. The Whartons only spare their domestic servant

Caesar to help Katy tend to Mr. Birch on his deathbed (143), and when Harvey's home is plundered by Skinners and his father torn from his dying bed, they "slept, or watched, through all the disturbances [. . .] in perfect ignorance of their occurrence" (154). The combination of "slept, or watched" hints that the Whartons might have turned a blind eye to the injustice done to the Birch family. After Mr. Birch's death and Harvey's departure, Miss Peyton, the head of the Wharton household, mercifully hires the desolate spinster Katy (161).

21. The peddler's dedication to his business is also described as uncommon and potentially dangerous in war times, when he carries on his peddling to "seize the golden opportunity which the interruption of the regular trade afforded, and appeared absorbed in the one grand object of amassing money" (43).
22. Katy creates a formula: "A peddler without goods, and without money, is sure to be *despisable*"; "Harvey will be nothing but an utterly *despisable*, poverty-stricken wretch"; "Harvey is little better now than a beggar, and a beggar [. . .] is the most awfully *despisable* of all earthly creatures"; "He is nothing more than *despisable*, or, what's the same thing, a peddler without house, pack or money" (148, 149, 153, 155, emphasis added).
23. See e.g. the scene when he meets Dunwoodie (241–2), when he suddenly stands before him and is gone when "surprise and smoke allowed Dunwoodie to look again," or the anecdote included by the narrator about his capture and "unaccountable disappearance" from the American forces, which had occurred "under too mysterious circumstances to be easily forgotten" (78), or his vanishing from Betty Flanagan's sight (278–9).
24. Another scene that illustrates the peddler's inner turmoil is during his father's funeral, when the muscles on his face "were seen to move," his "frame was for an instant convulsed," his body "bent"; "there was an expression in his countenance that seemed to announce a writhing of the soul; but it was not unresisted, it was transient" (194). The detailed description of Harvey's features highlights his ability to restrain himself.
25. Washington became a mythical character and national icon in literary texts after Mason Locke Weems's hagiographic biography *The Life of Washington* in 1800. For a reading of Washington's appearance in *The Spy*, see Adams 1985, or the 1822 review by Gardiner, esp. 252. St. Armand (1978) establishes a useful reading of Harvey as spiritual Bunyanesque pilgrim wandering towards the heavenly kingdom. The dark, satanic aspect of Harvey's wanderings, St. Armand claims, refers to the European legend of the Wandering Jew, reminiscent of the Flying Dutchman, or Dr. Faustus, who is condemned to cross the earth after selling his soul to the devil.
26. Kroetsch 1989: 95. Kroetsch compares his own dealing with the question of violence with Haliburton's view on the American Sam Slick. On the twentieth-century afterlives of Sam Slick, see also Blackington (1954).

27. Richard A. Davies (2005: 54–5) cites the *Sketches* as a source but also observes that Haliburton probably drew from Seba Smith's Major Jack Downing or from an imitation of Smith's figure by Charles Davis.
28. On the transnational publication history of the *Clockmaker* series and its reception, see Davies 2005: 62 and Ruth Panofsky's research (1992, 1993a, 1993b). The third series was popular in the U.S. between 1837 and 1863, but "[a]fter 1863, [. . .] Haliburton's readership was primarily British" (Panofsky 1993a: 16). Panofsky also chronicles the rift between the author and his Halifax publisher Howe (see 1993a: 12, 14).
29. The travelogues are an important reference in the opening part. Sam's diatribe on the English military travel writers resonates with Bernard's criticism in *Retrospections* (see Bernard 1887: 16): "Your friends, Ensigns and Leftenants, I guess from the British marchin regiments in the Colonies, that run over five thousand miles of Country in five weeks, [. . .] and then return, lookin as wise as the monkey that had seen world—when they get back, they are so chockfull of knowledge of the Yankees, that it runs over of itself, like a hogshead of molasses rolled about in hot weather—a white froth and scum bubbles out of the bung, wishy washy trash they call tours, sketches, travels, letters and what not, vapid stuff, jist sweet enough to catch flies, cockroaches, and half fledged galls" (57). Critics have mitigated the travelogue in the Sam Slick stories; see e.g. Davies (2005), who explicitly cites Haliburton's dictum "I visit men, and not places" (57) in this vein.
30. As Sam makes his demeaning comments on the English ("The British can whip all the world, and we can whip the British," 60; "we speak English better than the British," 172; see also 57), the Squire never interrupts. However, his ire is sparked when Sam associates him with "your friends," the English travel writers who misrepresent the U.S., and he is irked by the Yankee's "tone of [such] ineffable contempt, that I felt a strong inclination to knock him down for his insolence" (57).
31. Haliburton was "torn between fascination with and rejection of the new American center" and of "two minds about the necessary evils of modernization" (Godeanu-Kenworthy 2009: 220, 224). The bicentenary review of his oeuvre capitalized on his misogyny and racism; see for instance George Elliott Clarke's articles "Must We Burn Haliburton?" in the *Chronicle Herald*, October 15, 1993, and "White Niggers, Black Slaves: Slavery, Race and Class in T.C. Haliburton's *The Clockmaker*," *Nova Scotia Historical Review* 14.1 (1984): 13–40. See also Davies 2005: 3–5.
32. Smurthwaite (1997: 39) points out that the reception of the *Clockmaker* stories hinges on a paradox: the Yankee is deemed too stereotypical to be true, while at the same time critics find him to be too eclectic and multilayered "to be a flat character."
33. Tom Marshall has argued that the text's politics are "pragmatic," that "the ability to see two or more sides to every question [. . .] is 'Canadian'" (1976: 137). Commentators have remarked extensively on Haliburton's

own critical views on the U.S. and on his fascination with it (see Godeanu-Kenworthy 2009: 220 and Smurthwaite 1997: 40; for more detail, see Marshall 1976: 134). The different reactions of the Yankee and the Squire to judge Pettifog illustrate this contrast: both are appalled by the judge's lack of professionalism, but whereas the Squire tacitly takes sides and "concur[s] in the opinion, though not in the language" (28), it is the Yankee who calls Pettifog by his telling name, a "prime superfine scoundrel" (29).

34. Sam admits, for instance: "Brag is a good dog, but hold fast is a better one" (61). He also seems fair in his distribution of criticism. When talking about the travel writers, Sam acknowledges: "Our folks have their faults, and I know them (I warnt born blind I reckon)" (59); about the *Clockmaker* series as a whole, he states: "[The book] wipes up the blue noses considerable hard, and don't let of the Yankee so very easy neither [. . .] and although it ain't together jist gospel what's in it, there's some pretty home truths in it, that's a fact" (6).

35. Commentators have applied multiple genre labels to the series; Vincent (1985) relates the first series to British satire, arguing against an oversimplified reading as humorous stories; Godeanu-Kenworthy (2009) calls it a hybrid between "moral essay and picaresque novel" (211); Royot (1985) links it to the U.S. humor traditions of the Southwestern tale, but fails to acknowledge the Northeasterners, most notably the peddler and stage Yankee.

36. Laird describes the double threat as follows: "The *Clockmaker* was in the vanguard of a new popular literature which appeared to herald the disintegration of an elite belletristic, social, and cultural hegemony; Sam Slick's suspect values and shady dealings, meanwhile, made a mockery of Whig faith in self-restraint and morally conditioned commerce in an expanding medium which possessed an enormous potential for shaping the popular attitudes and behavior" (1993: 80).

37. In looking beyond Haliburton's Slick, the reviewer points to James Fenimore Cooper's "bad attempts" at creating American character and observes that Sam Slick can hardly live up to his American precursor Major Jack Downing's "wit" and "sagacity" because he is so "improbable" (Felton 1844: 215). The *Athenaeum* also comments on Slick's authenticity, maintaining that while the *Clockmaker* series is a "*Down Eastern* book with a vengeance [. . .] [w]e do not however think, rich as some of the stuff is, that so huge a mass of slang, slyness, and bitter bad words, will be relished by the ordinary palates of readers on this side of the Atlantic" (*Athenaeum* 494, Saturday, April 15, 1837; qtd. in Davies 2005: 63, emphasis in original).

38. In a metanarrative twist, Sam himself becomes a commodity for the reading public of the *Clockmaker* series. The prologue includes a letter by Sam to the publisher which complains about his unfavorable depiction and, in a typical twist, demands that he receive the revenue for being exploited in such a way. Slick writes: "I don't know as I ever felt

so ugly afore since I was raised; why didn't he put his name to it, as well as mine? When an article han't the maker's name and factory on it, it shows it's a cheat, and he's ashamed to own it. If I'm to have the name I'll have the game" (5).

39. Sam's canon is governed by an American interest in profit and an urge for competition, as the following quotation shows: "As for Latin and Greek, we *dont valy it a cent*; we teach it, and so we do painting and musick, *because the English do, and we like to go ahead on em*, even in them are things. As for reading, tis well enough for them that has nothing to do, and writing is plaguy apt to bring a man to States-prison" (32, emphasis added).

40. The temperance narrative in the U.S. is most prominently related to the efforts of the Washington Temperance Society; Crowley maintains that confessional texts represent "one major type of temperance literature, on the generic cusp between the novel and autobiography, in which inebriates recounted their enslavement to, and subsequent emancipation from, King Alcohol. [. . .] all of them had something in common with sentimental and sensational novels, and also with spiritual autobiography, especially the themes of religious awakening and conversion" (Crowley 1999: 3–4).

41. The country is the place of Stinchfield's childhood, symbolized in a "rude hearth stone" (11), and the place he returns to live in a "vine-clad cottage," "[r]omantically situated upon the banks of the 'Sandy river,' [. . .] where peace and contentment shed their choicest blessings" and he "cultivates the soil and warns the young to 'Beware of the gaming table and the bowl'" (81). The reformed drunkard in Robinson's narrative thus takes to settling and farming, i.e. he becomes a builder of civilization. The city is the place of his major downfall into drunkenness and gambling, where the able-bodied countryman is seduced by dubious characters described in a rogue's gallery as "he of the Roman noes [*sic*]," "he of the eye sinister," "he of the long ears and sore eyes," and "he of the genteel figure" (47). After his drunken and gambling bouts, Stinchfield awakes each time to remorse and leaves the city to make up for his lost money and to get sober. Likewise, he meets his love Imogene first in the country, then again in the city in dubious circumstances, and he eventually settles down with her on a farm.

42. The narrator observes that the river is "smil[ing]" and a water lily "nodding," while the leaves from the trees are "protecting" the river from the sun. All nature, he finds, is in "mutual understanding," and the "traces of human industry" in this pastoral induce a "spirit" that makes the narrator feel like a "happier and better man" (v). Likewise, clear water is the cleansing treatment that eventually quenches Stinchfield's "unnatural" thirst for alcohol (60, 64, 76).

43. The link between romance and real life as commented upon by the narrator is triangulated further with frequent references to the theater. The

story opens with Shakespeare's *theatrum mundi* quote from *As You Like It* (11); Harvard's father warns him "You know but little [. . .] about the stage in which you are now becoming an actor" (14); there are two dramatic brawl scenes described in great detail (54–5, 65–7) and an "old stage manager who was passing at this crisis [of the fistfight] remarked that the imitation was most felicitous, though far from musical" (55). The narrator thus weaves metanarrative references to drama into his story, recalling theater entertainment; he also uses the device of comic relief, especially in the fight scenes.

44. Robinson's text here mocks and condemns religious extremism, revealing that practitioners of all denominations are hypocrites when it comes to consumerism. Note also the scene with the corrupt deacon: "Even deacons, reader, are willing to avail themselves of a good bargain!" (74).
45. Buntline, whose real name was Edward Zane Carroll Judson, Sr., would eventually become a reporter and author of dime novels about the West, most importantly as author of the myths of Wild Bill Hickock and Buffalo Bill, which he is most widely known for today.
46. Witkowski (1996) offers a close reading of the process of selling and buying shown in nineteenth-century genre painting; he argues that this depiction functioned as education of the audience in consumer skills (99). The earliest and most iconic of the genre paintings is John Whetten Ehninger's (1827–89) "Yankee Peddler" (1858, Newark Museum, New Jersey), which shows the peddler at the center of the image in front of his wagon, holding up a coffee grinder to a couple of women and children. Ehninger's peddler is young and tall, the center of the composition. In front of the trading group, a little boy, the only other male figure in the image, is seen playing with something while carrying an American flag. In the background are several houses; a similar arrangement of figures is seen in Abbott Fuller Graves's (1859–1936) "Yankee Peddler," which has an aged peddler next to his cart talking to a woman and children in a garden. Edward Lamson Henry's (1841–1919) "The Itinerant Peddler Displaying His Wares" (1879) divides the image into a darker front porch area (to the left) and the bright road with the peddler's cart, next to which the peddler shows fine linens to the women of the house. As in the photograph "The Yankee Peddler at the Parsonage," a person is seen on the porch, in between inside and outside, either guarding the entrance or about to join the trade scene. Thomas Waterman Wood's (1823–1903) "The Yankee Peddler" (1872) shows the peddler next to his cart in a shed, hitting closer to home.
47. Joanna Cohen has analyzed the double standard female consumers are faced with, which "valued their taste but [. . .] did not provide them with access to capital" (2017: 226) and demanded self-sacrifice through abstinence from European fashions in the Early Republic.

48. The text uses narrative voice for general action but renders the peddler's selling formulas verbatim, such as "Now let me sell you a clock worth having"; "Let me sell you the clock" (Crockett 1833: 153, 157); or when he "feeds his 'cretur'" (ibid. 157)—note how "cretur" is even highlighted by inverted commas. Likewise, his cunning is embellished with asides in which he comments on the action. He "chuckles to himself 'I've got that fellow'"; see also "'not so bad a beginning,' said Slim to himself" (both ibid. 153).
49. The peddler histories by Dolan and Wright also reiterate this stereotyping. Dolan talks about the "age old feminine joy that today we call shopping" and about the wares that "dazzle [her] eyes [. . .] Did she dare use up all her egg money on this bit of finery?" (Dolan 1964: 79, 63). In a vignette about pious New England, Wright applauds the peddler's "way with the ladies. [. . .] What possibilities that picture opens up!—[. . .] What a relief on market days was the garrulous chapman! He may even have gone so far as to have exchanged a wink! Let's hope he did; for the Pilgrim wives deserved every little iota of enjoyment a merciful Providence might spare them, even if it came from the peddler!" (Wright 1965: 95).
50. Cohen (2008) chronicles Plummer's life as one of the earliest American poets; he quotes Redford Webster's call for a literary profession instead of leaving literary production to the seductions of the peddler: "Let us not therefore any longer leave the composition of songs and ballads, to the journeymen of the Pedlar. For lo! He no longer keepeth in a corner, but under the eye, and even under the license of the police; he spreadeth out his verses, and his tales, full of superstition, of horror, of immorality; thus corrupting the innocent youth, and confirming the abandoned" (1822, qtd. in Cohen 2008: 38).
51. General interest in the term remains unbroken. The online "New Hampshire Glossary," a non-academic internet base, includes a definition of "Yankee notions" as peddler wares; see <www.cowhampshire-blog.com/2006/08/18/new-hampshire-glossary-yankee-notions> (last accessed November 2, 2020). The term is also used as a band name by a New England folk duo whose concerts include a set called "The Peddler's Pack"; see <timvanegmond.com/yankee-notions-folk-duo/> (last accessed November 2, 2020).
52. See Wright 1965: 78–9 and Jaffee 1991: 517. In his historical overview of peddling, Jaffee also examines the spreading of the Yankee clocks, quoting an Arkansas traveler in 1844: "in every cabin where there was not a chair to sit on there was sure to be a Connecticut clock" (qtd. ibid). See Jaffee 2011: 172–87 for details on the invention and distribution of Eli Terry's box clock.
53. See e.g. Dolan 1964: 166 on clock repair tricks, or the short piece "Yankee Clock Pedlars in the West" (1846).

54. The Connecticut State Library offers two explanations for the state's label as "Nutmeg State": first, the Connecticut peddler's shrewd ability to sell wooden nutmegs, and second, the incompetence of the buyers to grate the hard nut into a powder to use, so they felt tricked; see <http://www.ctstatelibrary.org/node/2333> (accessed November 2, 2020). Connecticut also gives out a "Nutmeg Award" for children's literature; Griggs (1952) claims that the state also gave out wooden nutmegs as souvenirs on its tercentenary celebration in 1935.

Chapter 4

New England's "Homespun Yankee" in the Cultural and Literary Imagination

[M]odern nations and all their impediment generally claim to be the opposite of novel, namely rooted in the remotest antiquity, and the opposite of constructed, namely human communities so "natural" as to require no definition other than self-assertion. (Hobsbawm and Granger 1983: 149)

New England's principles spread at first to the neighboring states; later they gradually won out in the most distant, and in the end, [. . .] they *penetrated* the entire confederation. They now exert their influence beyond its limits, over the whole American world.
 The civilization of New England has been like those fires lit in the hills that, after having spread heat around them, still tinge the furthest reaches of the horizon with their light. The founding of New England offered a new spectacle; everything there was singular and original. (Tocqueville 2000 [1831]: 32)

In 1831 Alexis de Tocqueville imagines the relation between "New England's Principles" and the rest of the United States as a fire that warms and lights up its surroundings. Where its warmth cannot reach, it still illuminates the darkness with a glow. Yet the sensation does not stay on the surface; it "penetrates" the yet-to-be-defined "American world," slipping under its skin, dissolving in the proto-national space and altering the very essence of whatever it touches. Tocqueville's New England is a locus of civilization, a hearth in the darkness of an uncivilized continent. To this observation he adds, in the very last phrase, another quality: New England is powerful because it is unique.

Tocqueville's image of the homely fireplace reiterates a well-established master narrative of American cultural history: New England, "the nation's smallest region, may also be its most studied one" (Conforti 2001: 10).[1] It is perceived as the cradle of the nation. Like the fires burning in Tocqueville's vision, its characteristics spread all over the map. From the Frenchman's perspective, New England's "newness" requires no mention of transatlantic or colonial legacies. He rejects the historiography New Englanders created themselves at the time, namely New England's legacy from English Puritan and Pilgrim stock. While the French traveler thought New England was unique, the New England elites were hard at work in crafting an English heritage narrative. New England originality and English heritage represent rivaling epistemes in the settler colonial construction of New England as "home" and of the Yankee as national homebody.

This chapter argues that the Yankee interlinks discourses of national performance and material culture in New England texts and negotiates national heritage narratives. Literary history has sidelined him as a marginal comic figure (see e.g. Buell 1987),[2] overlooking the Yankee's cultural work in embodying the nation state as fabricated and performed. My reading looks, first, at the Yankee schoolmaster as a mobile figure who acts out an imaginary New England identity; the second part relates the schoolmaster to the depiction of the New England communities in the village novel and the romance and shows how the pastoral tinge clashes with Yankee progress and "going ahead." The Yankee disturbs conceptions of region and nation alike, for instance in Sarah Hale's novel *Northwood* (1827 and 1852). John Neal's unsuccessful historical novels *The Down-Easters* (1833) and *Brother Jonathan* (1825) are contemporaries to Hale's *Northwood*, but by parading a gallery of Yankee types, they differ fundamentally from her conservative but popular views. In reading these texts together with satirical writings such as *A Yankee Among the Nullifiers* (Greene 1833) and *The Hypocrite* (Aesop 1844), I advance a critical regionalist reading of New England's "genius loci" (Buell 1987: 293) through the ambiguous Yankee figure.[3]

The third part combines the literary motifs of the schoolmaster, the village, and the romance narrative to examine the Yankee homespun. Building on feminist literary criticism's assertion that "[v]irtue is seen as developing sequentially through the three levels of community organization—family, village, country" (Gossett and Bardes 1985: 19), I argue that the homespun embodies, masculinizes, and commodifies the nation state, and that it interrogates the ideology of separate spheres (Kaplan 2002; see also Baym 1993). As polysemous concept, the homespun amalgamates white male bodies, trade as cultural performance, and storytelling. The homespun tethers the sentimental value of nostalgia to the anti-sentimental performance of the Yankee. It transports feelings of civic belonging in a narrative that disavows sentiment and prioritizes "going ahead." Finally, Yankee homespun shows how the "invention of tradition" (Hobsbawm and Granger 1983) in U.S. literature is administered deliberately, with the Yankee's embrace of confabulation and trickery.

Fantasies of New England in Regional Historiography

Cultural historians have described the invention of New England from historical and imaginative processes, arguing that, over the course of the nineteenth century, the locus of the alleged "real" New England moved north into the rural spaces, as southern urban New England was industrialized and diversified.[4] As a result, the region was pastoralized; after the "demise of New England triumphalism" came the postbellum "rise of the nostalgic colonial revival" (Conforti 2001: 9), which showed "America in flux, New England at rest" (Brown and Nissenbaum 1999: 1). Between the Civil War and 1945, this memory work was continued in American art, as the 1999 exhibition *Picturing Old New England: Image and Memory* at the National Museum of American Art has shown (Truettner and Stein 1999). Imagined New England thus represents a rural and pastoral antidote to the bustle of the industrialized metropolis.

New England invented itself early in the political arena, in the constitutional debates of the 1780s when it became "by far the most self-consciously distinctive region in the country, its delegates to Congress most likely to act in concert with one another" (Onuf 1996: 24). Its political unity was consolidated by two interrelated phenomena: the Northern Federalist movements (1804 and 1815) and the 1830 congressional tariff debates between Robert J. Hayne and the New England "mascot" Daniel Webster (January 19 to 27, 1830).[5] In his responses to Hayne's attacks on New England, Webster defended Massachusetts as the original site "where American Liberty raised its first voice, and where its youth was nurtured and sustained, there it still lives, in the strength of its manhood and full of its original spirit." Webster's story follows the allegorical troping outlined in Chapter 1: the male Liberty has been nurtured into manhood by a female New England and is now expanding into "the west, one monument of her intelligence in matters of government, and her practical good sense." After the debate, Webster was held as champion of New England and sectionalist conflict (Onuf 1996: 11).

New England Federalism, organized in the American Whig Party, was founded on discontent with the Jeffersonian model in 1804 (see e.g. Gannon 2001) and revived in the Hartford Convention of 1815. The Federalists had opposed the War of 1812 and debated a separate peace with Britain that would break away New Hampshire, Rhode Island, and Massachusetts from the Union. The Southern states read these secessionist tendencies as treason and used them to attack New England.[6] After the failure of the Hartford Convention and the victory of General Andrew Jackson in the Battle of New Orleans, the Federalist cause died a slow death. The conservative New England elites opposed Jacksonian democracy and economic policies; they feared a mob rule while their own cultural and political authority was waning. Their loss of political power spurred New England literary and critical production, for instance with the new *North American Review* in 1815 (Levine 1998: 223; see also Matthews 1978). The Whigs' cultural politics became instrumental in the development of a national and regional mythography.

Upon exploring their history, the Whigs discovered the Puritans. The idea of a cultural legacy and character passed down from New England's first settlers became a political vehicle for the invention of a "usable past" (Matthews 1978), combined with a promotion of self-restraint as republican virtue and masculinity ideal (ibid. 194–5). They celebrated Forefathers' Day and the Mayflower Compact, as well as Plymouth Rock as allegedly the first point where the Puritans touched American soil (an alternative to Virginia claims of first settlement in Williamsburg; see Conforti 2001: 176, 182). Daniel Webster's bicentennial speech at Plymouth Rock in 1820 capitalized on a feeling of the "genius of the place" and the New World as home for body and spirit, encapsulated in its "hearth" and "altar": "We feel that we are on the spot where the first scene of our history was laid; where the hearths and altars of New England were first placed; where Christianity and civilization, and letters made their first lodgment" (qtd. in Conforti 2001: 185). In Whig historiography, the pious Puritans were "Pilgrimized," their intolerance mitigated in favor of their "republican kinship with the virtuous, unvarnished founders of Plymouth" (ibid. 172). By 1807, the image of the Puritans had fused with that of the pioneer, battling the hardships of founding the settler colony (ibid. 180).

Next to the myth of the Pilgrims, the Whigs also nurtured the image of the New England white village in the antebellum period, developing a "cult" which Laurence Buell (1987: 305) has called "the most distinctively New Englandish contribution to the American social ideal."[7] As a locus of "pastoral Yankee stability" (Nissenbaum 1996: 39), it occupies a key function in literary and visual culture, yet just like Plymouth Rock, its colonial history is entirely fictional. Nissenbaum (1996: 45–56) argues that the town centers built around the church and school arose only in the 1790s as a response to capitalism and the influx of shopkeepers, creating a village "core" with a green grazed by livestock, which probably did not look very green most of the time. Secondly, the "white village" did not exist before the nineteenth century. Houses were traditionally painted green and blue, but outsiders and businessmen started whitewashing them in attempts at beautification (ibid.).[8]

Timothy Dwight's *Travels in New England and New York* (1822) describes a citizenry organized in a close-knit settlement with a center school, church, and meeting house. In Dwight's view, the citizenry of New England forms the kernel of the nation:

> Almost the whole country is covered with villages, and every village has its church and its school. Nearly every child, even those of beggars and blacks in considerable numbers, can read, write, and keep accounts. Every child is carried to the church from the cradle, nor leaves the church but for the grave. All the people are neighbors: social beings, [they] converse, feel, sympathize, mingle minds, cherish sentiments, and are subjects of at least some degree of refinement.
> (Qtd. in Nissenbaum 1996: 49)

Whig cultural politics created a collective memory for Americans; against the Jacksonian rugged individual, they posited republican self-restrained masculinity weaned from the imagined Puritan legacy. For the centennial celebrations, ballads like Daniel March's *Yankee Land and the Yankee* (1840) lauded Connecticut thrift and republican virtues. Echoing Webster's feeling of homeliness at Plymouth Rock, Whig orator and politician Rufus Choate in 1833 called for a national literature that would instill national(ist) sentiment in Americans. One year later, Choate's speech "The Colonial Age of New England" at the centennial of Ipswich, MA, moved Daniel Webster to tears.[9] Choate argues that factual historiography is inferior to the imaginative quality of literature and of a nascent national romance (Choate 1849b, esp. 324–6).

In New England historiography, Puritanism muted other narratives, such as the influence of Virginia and the Tidewater gentiles, the Virginia model of the Williamsburg colony, or indigenous and African American voices and presences.[10] And yet, historians agree that Puritan mores provided a decisive impulse for New England's development. The English settlers were committed to literacy and learning in institutionalized settings, schools and universities; their interest in history built a market for New England print products (Conforti 2001: 4–6). The Whigs' insistence on their Puritan ancestry percolates in twentieth-century historiography such as in Wright's racist portrayal of immigrants as a social and economic disturbance of a nascent market society (Wright 1965), which chimes in with Richard Bushman's influential study *From Puritan to Yankee* (first published 1967). Bushman's Puritans "value order above all other social virtues"; they are "driven to work" and have difficulty discriminating between "praiseworthy industry and the 'Cursed Hunger of Riches,'" a problem that roots in their "avarice and shrewdness" (1967: 3, 23, 24, 87). Bushman goes to great trouble to excuse these moral flaws, such as when he develops a semantics of (economic) desire to euphemize greed for social and economic recognition (ibid. 25). He concludes that the Yankee revolutionaries inherit the "cultural genes" of the Puritans:

> [A] defensive independence, cupidity tempered by regard for the public good, and yearning for the divine underlying hardheaded rationalism, was securely embedded in the cultural genes of the generation alive in 1765. No sudden mutation had caused them to appear. [. . .] In the century after the Revolution, Yankee society produced a flowering of individualism, a magnificent display of economic and artistic virtuosity. (Ibid. 288)

Because New Englanders carry Puritan DNA, so the story goes, the Revolution was not a violent rupture but a "natural" coming-of-age of republican virtues after a long gestation in New England soil. Bushman here reiterates the settler colonial logic of Whig historiography (Sheidley 1998; Appleby 2000), and the DNA model was revived in David Hackett Fischer's influential *Albion's Seed: Four British Folkways in America* (1989), a "genetic" history that replaces the narrative of a holistic U.S. with an equally monolithic understanding of a New England thriving on East Anglian folkways (Conforti 2001: 5, 6). Bushman therefore positions Puritan legacy at the center of the nation's founding and overextends "Yankee society" from Connecticut to the nation, casting the Yankee as avatar of the state.¹¹ This model taps into the Whigs' efforts to assert New England supremacy over the less contoured South and the emerging West; as Nina Baym has argued, American identity becomes exclusive: "In a cruel paradox, non Anglo-Saxons could become American only insofar as they accepted the connection between Americanness and an Anglo-Saxon racial lineage" (Baym 1992a: 85).

According to Bushman, the ideology of New England's "puritan genetics" survived the implosion of the Whig Party in the 1850s, when their undecidedness about slavery became unacceptable. By the advent of the Civil War, sectional conflict was attributed to the culture clash among the English colonials:

> According to a theory in vogue [in the 1860s] the North had been settled by one party to the English Civil War, the Roundheads, and the South by the other, the royal party or the Cavaliers. The Yankee was a direct descendant of the Puritan Roundhead and the Southern gentleman of the English Cavalier, and the difference between the two was at least partly a matter of blood. (Taylor 1961: 15)¹²

The prominence of Puritan culture in the American national narrative was cemented further by American Studies. The Whigs created a national image of Americanness as white and Anglo-Saxon that has been perpetuated and critiqued in American Studies, most notably in the idea of an "American Renaissance" emanating from a group of New England writers. Renaissance discourse encoded "English heritage [. . .] which later scholars used to define Anglo-American men's cultural superiority to ethnic others" (Avallone 1997: 1103).¹³ The writers of the myth and symbol school endowed "American literature" with foundational myths from New England. Under the systemic threat of communism in the 1920s and 1930s, scholars of the emerging American Studies defended a U.S. national character imagined as democratic, individualistic, and economically progressive. This American character, the myth critics argued, sprang from New England. A deconstructed ideologeme, New England continues to incite criticism in American Studies due to its exceptionalist and masculinist core.¹⁴

As the following section shows, the Yankee undercuts Whig historiography and the formation of the American literary canon. His "going ahead" jars with Whiggish masculine self-restraint and with the learnedness attributed to some of the American Renaissance writers. His exaggerated performance renders absurd the narrative of a Puritan seed slowly germinating through adolescence into a mature American imperial masculinity. As homespun body, he articulates a vernacular version of the New England home.

The Yankee Schoolmaster as American Educator

> A sturdy lad from New Hampshire or Vermont who in turn tries all the professions, who teams it, farms it, peddles, keeps a school, preaches, edits a newspaper, goes to Congress, buys a township, and so forth in successive years, and always, like a cat, falls on his feet, is worth a hundred of these city dolls. (Ralph Waldo Emerson)

Emerson's praise of the New Englander in "Self-Reliance" (1841; qtd. in Conforti 2001: 162) capitalizes on the activity and survival skills ascribed to the "sturdy lads" from the New England states. To the Concord minister, who has been described as a "peddler of intellectual notions" (Buell 1987: 343), the rural New England men are more authentic than the affected city "dolls."

One of the stations in this typical life is "keep[ing] school," an occupation for which Yankee schoolmasters, like the peddlers, took to the road. Where the peddler was cast as a perpetrator interested only in selling, however, the schoolmaster is a missionary of New England culture. He displays the push and pull between institutionalized learning and innate Yankee shrewdness, impersonating at the same time Whig policy and Yankee character. Back home, he is placed conspicuously at the center of the New England village, both physically and ideologically, as the educator of the community's children. The wildly popular postbellum poetry collection *Rhymes of Yankee Land* (Greene 1872)[15] sketches the pastoralized New England white village in the section "The Smithville Worthies," with a spectrum of village figures including the "Yankee School-Master." In the short poem, the teacher William Wilson is portrayed as a retired community member admired for his professional "patience and kindly care" (ibid. 23) and his lasting influence ("Since Wilson gave up teaching school // ten years and five have passed // But through a century to come // His influence shall last," ibid. 24). The schoolmaster embodies communal effort. His simple schoolhouse next to the "Center Church [. . .] cost six hundred dollars, just // as records would appear," but it was dear to the students, not least because they were disciplined not with "birch" but with intellectual "checks" in the great books (ibid. 22, 23). At the age of eighty-five, Wilson is cast as a factotum of village life. He earns his keep by contributing to prosperity and growth.

In Greene's postbellum view of the village community, progress hinges on education; the children now go off to larger district schools and later to one of New England's universities. The schoolmaster stays behind as a living reminder of the community's effort to help their offspring get a good start in life. Narratives about the Yankee schoolmaster far from his New England home reverse the power play between the Yankee peddler and his customers. As a spokesperson of Yankeedom, the schoolmaster is ridiculed for his bookishness and hypocrisy. Where the peddler coerces villagers into buying famously dysfunctional or useless wares, the schoolmaster is inferior to the communities he tries (and often fails) to join. He is a restless traveler who inspires the villagers to affirm their own identity and distance themselves from Yankeedom.

The Yankee schoolmaster's strategy is captured in the short piece "The Schoolmaster" from the first issue of *New England Magazine*, published in July 1831 in the section "original papers." "The Schoolmaster" is the musing of a first-person narrator about his life and experience. He introduces himself as "a son of New England [. . .] educated in all her feelings and prejudices" who is urged by "a restless spirit" to travel (Schoolmaster 1831: 27). The story contrasts the traveler's understanding of the "world" (read as corruption of the mind, with a touch that "blights, and withers, and consumes us") with the notion of an unspoiled New England "home." The schoolchildren's minds are a *tabula rasa*; their hearts know "no desires beyond the circle of the paternal fireside" (ibid. 27, 28). He himself looks back at this state of ignorant bliss across space and time, from his vantage point as experienced European traveler (who has conspicuously left out England). Far away from home, he turns back the pages "in the [book] of the world" to his memory of New England: "The beauty of its rural scenes rose up before me; and when I called to mind the moral feeling which pervades the land, and the healthy virtues of its national character and institutions, I felt proud that it was my Native Land" (ibid. 28).

Narrated memory structures the story; in remembering New England, he relives his childhood as a site of "rural scenes," "moral feeling," and "healthy virtue." He paints the New England landscape with synesthetic metaphors of light and warmth; his thoughts of beloved friends and kin are "golden threads," "scattered rays of affection" that may be weakened by distance, but "glow, and burn, and brighten, around the peaceful threshold of home" (ibid. 8). Remembering makes the thinker feel the unbroken chords in a state of "fancy sickness" (ibid.), or nostalgia. The schoolmaster pits the pastoral of New England village childhood against a mundane knowledge of the world, cosmopolitanism, and institutionalized learning at universities. He promotes the children's commitment to "home," arguing that it is the teacher rather than the politician who forms republican citizens and ensures the community's survival (see ibid. 29).

How, then, does the schoolmaster teach? He indulges in an oxymoronic "busy idleness," a cognitive interplay of memory and discovery of the world: "when I strike upon a vein of thought, which has for me the charm of novelty, or is rich in the material or reflection, I pursue it in my evening rambles or in the solitude of the fireside, and note it down at leisure in simple prose, or unpretending verse" (ibid. 30). The schoolmaster travels in his imagination, following his whims. From his New England readers, he expects the same sense-searching, with his story in their hands.

The narrator tries to educate the readers, with the image of the rural fireplace and the sentiment of nostalgia, to develop a regional identity. But the story reveals a twist at second glance: the schoolmaster's "busy idleness" blends inward reflection with the typically restless Yankee mind. His silent contemplation cloaks the schoolmaster's assertion of Yankee superiority, which is given away by the epigraph:

> My character indeed, I would favor you with, but that I am cautious of praising myself, lest I should be told my trumpeter's dead; and I cannot find it in my heart at present to say anything to my own disadvantage. FRANKLIN. (Ibid. 27)

In this typically concocted quotation, the Yankee Benjamin Franklin basically asks his addressee to admire him for his greatness, but not to think that he, Franklin, asked her to do it. The epigraph exposes the narrator's blatant self-advertisement. Beneath the sentiment resides Yankee cunning and missionary zeal. The schoolmaster calls on his readers from the faraway shore to celebrate village life, as well as typical Yankee ingenuity.

In "The Schoolmaster," the narrator's travels enable him to sing New England's praises to the compatriots back home. As first-person narrator, he speaks directly to the readers in an unusual narrative situation; conventionally, the schoolmaster remains marginal, a New England presence in a community in turmoil. His presence helps affirm a communal identity, specifically in the stories of Washington Irving and James Fenimore Cooper. Their most widely known Yankee pedagogues, Ichabod Crane from "The Legend of Sleepy Hollow" (Irving 1820) and Jason Newcome from *Satanstoe* (Cooper 1845), are ethnic and classist Others in colonial settler communities. Yet both writers hint at the rise of the Yankee and of New England to national authority in the nineteenth century, criticize typical Yankee characteristics, such as restlessness and money-grabbing, and prefer a New York identity (Ringe 1988: 458–9).[16] To the teacher outsiders—or "newcomers," as Jason Newcome's surname suggests—Yankeedom is a source of pride. To the Dutch colonial settlers of Sleepy Hollow and the Dutch-English New York landowners, the Yankee schoolmasters are intolerant fanatics and snobbish country bumpkins.

In both stories, the Yankee schoolmaster fails to find inroads into the settler community; he is relegated to a powerlessness or leaves the community altogether. Ichabod Crane is famously haunted by his own imagination; his rival Brom Bones masquerades as the legendary headless Hessian and drives Ichabod out of town. The schoolmaster's professional ambition fails drastically in Sleepy Hollow, since learning does not occupy a central spot in the community, as Irving's description of the schoolhouse shows. It is located in a remote, "rather lonely situation" and is "rudely constructed of logs, the windows partly glazed, and partly patched with leaves of old copy books" (Irving 1983c: 1061; all subsequent references to this edition). The ragged building is a trap: "a thief might get in with perfect ease, [yet] he would find some embarrassment in getting out" (ibid.). Irving's Dutch colonial schoolhouse is a negative of the pristine New England school. Of course, after Ichabod's hasty departure, the Dutch farmers resolve not to send their children to school, because they "never knew any good came of this same reading and writing" (1086).

The conflict between Yankee bookishness and colonial complacency also discerns types of white masculinity. Ichabod's effeminate learning is vanquished by Brom Bones's frontier smartness, his Yankee deformity inferior to the Dutchman's "Herculean frame" (1069). Ichabod's description takes the Yankee's typically lank figure to the grotesque; his overall composition lacks cohesion ("his frame most loosely hung together," 1061), and his arrival is compared to catastrophe:

> long arms and legs, hands that dangled a mile out of his sleeves, feet that might have served as shovels [. . .] His head was small, and flat on top, with huge ears, large green glassy eyes, and a long snipe nose,

so that it looked like a weathercock perched upon his spindle neck, to tell which way the wind blew. To see him striding along the profile of a hill on a windy day, one might have mistaken him for the genius of famine descending upon the earth, or some scarecrow eloped from a cornfield. (Ibid.)

The teacher's walking silhouette resembles a supernatural figure, a plague sent from heaven. His consumption of tales is equally gargantuan ("no tale was too gross or monstrous for his capacious swallow," 1064), and his riding abilities recall the self-assertion of Don Quixote on his poor Rosinante (see 1073).

Ichabod's agenda is tied to his home state Connecticut, "a state which supplies the Union with pioneers for the mind and forest alike and sends forth its legion of frontier woodmen and country schoolmasters" (1060). Whereas all things Dutch are remnants of European folkways in the New World, he embodies New England cultural and political expansionism.[17] He also displays the typical Yankee faults, religious fanaticism and material greed. His superstition is linked to piety and Puritan texts like Cotton Mather's *History of New England Witchcraft* (1063). The prospect of taking over Van Tassel's farm makes "his mouth water" (1067) with ambition and greed. Finally, his failure at Sleepy Hollow initiates a steep career; he keeps school, studies law, "turn[s] politician, electioneer[s], writ[es] for the newspapers, and finally [is made] a Justice of the Ten Pound Court" (1086). Ichabod may well be the butt of Brom's jokes, but his progress in life distinguishes the Yankee from the sleepy Dutch colony. Irving's doubling of narrative perspective through Diedrich Knickerbocker's eyes also enables a critical reading of the colonial Dutch community, tucked away in "reverie" in the "still water" far away from the world (1059, 1060).

Irving's (or Diedrich's) preoccupation with the New Englanders also percolates elsewhere. In "The History of New York," the Dutch chronicler decries the "obnoxious" "horde of strange barbarians, bordering upon the eastern frontier," who "indulge their own opinions" and "presumptuously dare to think for themselves" (Irving 1983a: 498, 493). Diedrich argues that Yankee talkativeness is a threat to politics and to the "grand palladium of our country, the *liberty of speech*" (494). Yankee talk shows lack of education (in the American wilderness, the Yankees "enjoy[ed] unmolested, the inestimable luxury of talking") and, at best, it is void "without ideas and without information [. . .] misrepresenting public affairs [. . .] decrying public measures [. . .] aspersing great characters, and destroying little ones" (ibid.). Knickerbocker captures Yankee restlessness in a scenic description of a settlement in which the Yankee acts as peddler and farmer, repeating the same actions over and over.

> Having thus provided himself, like a true pedlar [*sic*], with a heavy knapsack, wherewith to regale his shoulders through the journey of life, he literally sets out on the peregrination. His whole family, household furniture and farming utensils are hoisted into a covered cart; [. . .] which done, he shoulders his axe, takes staff in hand, whistles "yankee doodle" and trudges off to the woods as confident of the protection of providence, and relying as cheerfully upon his resources as did ever a patriarch of yore [. . .] He soon grows tired of a spot, where there is no longer any room for improvement—sells his farm, [. . .] reloads his cart, shoulders his axe, puts himself at the head of his family, and wanders away in search of new lands—again to fell trees—again to clear cornfields—again to build a shingle palace, and again to sell off, and wander. (Ibid. 498–500)

The Yankee described here represents the doings of an entire "race" (494); he carelessly follows his urges and slowly conquers the continent, always looking for his own profit. This image highlights the real failure of Ichabod Crane in "Sleepy Hollow"; the Yankee can survive by himself but he does not play well with others. Irving's "worthy pedagogue" (1983c: 1063) cannot convert the Dutch to his New England mores. The same is true for Jason Newcome in Cooper's historical novel *Satanstoe*.

The Yankee schoolmaster Jason Newcome serves as an antidote to the protagonist narrator Corny Littlepage. *Satanstoe* is the first part of a trilogy that follows the fate of the Littlepage family through the colonial, revolutionary and republican eras. With the sequels *The Chainbearer* (1845) and *The Redskins* (1846), the trilogy "dramatize[s] the progress of the nation" (Dryden 1971: 51). The Littlepage family history reads much like Cooper's own (see House 1966: xvii–xx), and he takes the proprietor's side in the "anti-rent wars" of New York state in the 1840s. In the trilogy, the Newcomes gradually become the Littlepages' enemies, first scheming covertly and later trying to take over their land. The poor but ambitious Yankee schoolmaster initiates the conflict between landed gentry and Yankee expansionism. The relation between the naïve, loyal Corny and his awkward friend Jason establishes the contrast of civilizations in the U.S. throughout the entire trilogy; for brevity's sake, I limit my analysis to the Yankee teacher in the first part.[18]

In *Satanstoe*, Cooper's hero Corny Littlepage is the steward of the Littlepage estate in colonial times. Corny secures the 40,000 acre estate of Mooseridge in Albany, which his father bought from a Native chief; he wins a Dutch girl's heart, thus intermingling the English and Dutch heritages. The conflict between these two groups and the Yankees is irreconcilable. Throughout the novel, the narrator Corny compares Dutch and "liberal" English society with the Puritan New England of the Yankee schoolmaster who accompanies him. Corny is a meticulous observer not easily given to prejudice (Cooper 1990: 21; all subsequent references to this edition):

> Morality, as I understand the matter, has a good deal of convention about it. There is town-morality and country-morality, all over the world, as they tell me. But, in America, our morals were and long have been, separated into three great and very distinct classes; viz.— New England, or puritan-morals; Middle Colonies', or liberal morals; and Southern Colonies', or latitudinarian morals. (254)

In Corny's typology of American morals, the Yankee Jason remains a "moral enigma" (287). Unlike Corny, who keeps puzzling, Jason simply "turns up his nose," in typical Yankee manner, at the old Dutch colony of New York (14). He says:

> "There are comparisons that should never be made, on account of circumstances that overrule all common efforts. Now, York is a great colony—a very great colony, Miss—but it was once Dutch, as everybody knows, [. . .] and it must be confessed Connecticut has, from the first, enjoyed almost unheard of advantages, in the moral and religious character of her people, the excellence of her laws and the purity [. . .] of her people and church." (127)

In Jason's view, the Dutch is inferior to the Anglo-Saxon heritage. Yet, the novel shows the contrary in many instances: Jason is lost in the big city and scandalized by urban manners (e.g. 63); he lacks tact (287), insists on knowing everyone's habits (277, 278), and obnoxiously sneers at everything with "hypercriticism" (144). Even the "editor" adds to this image of New England arrogance and self-confidence in a footnote that compares the manners of Parisians and Italians with the unformed American "jumble of [. . .] senseless contradictions in [. . .] social habits." Against this nondescript American "being *in transitu*" (61) stands New England provincialism:

> The only American who is temporarily independent in such things is the unfledged provincial, fresh from his village conceit and village

practices, who, until corrected by communion with the world, fancies the south-east corner of the north-west parish in the town of Hebron, in the county of Jericho, in the State of Connecticut, to be the only portion of this globe that is perfection. If he should happen to keep a school, or conduct a newspaper, the community becomes, in a small degree, the participant of his rare advantage and vast experience! (Ibid.)

To the Yankee, the world revolves around the New England village; from there, print products and missionaries issue forth. In Jason's own worldview, he "form[s] a species of aristocracy," since keeping school is much better than inheriting land and a King's commission (44, 45). Like the schoolmaster from *New England Magazine*, Jason considers his ideological impact as teacher tantamount to Corny's gentlemanly task of building the colony, and, in the long run, the nation. Cooper's novel prefers Dutch traditions over puffery and performance.

The conflict between the gentleman and the Yankee is abysmal. Corny is struck by their different language use (a topic of ridicule and estrangement) and by their different training, which almost prevents mutual understanding (44). Jason was schooled at Yale and has built on this educational "hamlet foundation [. . .] a superstructure of New Haven finish and proportions"; yet, Corny finds that Jason makes "grossest possible mistakes, that were directly in opposition to his own theory" (42). Corny himself was sent to Princeton, not to Yale, because of his father's fear that "'the poy wilt be sp'ilt by ter ministers. He will go away an honest lat, and come pack a rogue. He will l'arn how to bray and to cheat'" (24). "Praying and cheating" profess the Yankee's hypocrisy. Jason is embarrassed when he is caught playing cards (292); he "bow[s] down to the golden calf, in spite of his puritanism, his love of liberty, his pretension to equality and the general strut of his disposition and manner" (43). And yet Jason "gets ahead." Corny describes him as a "happy man" who strikes a bargain for a mill seat; at the stroke of a Dutch owner's pen, Jason becomes a "sort of a land-holder [. . .] who had nothing to pay for ten years to come" (311).

Ultimately, *Satanstoe* uses the schoolmaster to mix regionalist with classist critique. Newcome remains an outsider to the Dutch-English minor landed gentry, a variation of the Jacksonian self-made man whose breeding can never "elevate him to that [gentleman] character" (430).[19] The Yankee is doubly "new": as a recent product of the Puritan seed on American soil, and as new addition to the older echelons of the European colonists. The schoolmaster creates a class for himself in the colony's proto-national society. Jason secures a piece of land and therefore articulates his claim to power in the new nation. In the sequel novels, he and his kin become greedier and greedier. In *The Chainbearer*, Jason works as agent of the mill seat for the Littlepages, but barters the proprietor's trust away by allowing a squatter to cut lumber. His focus remains on cutting bargains and making money. In *The Redskins*, his grandson Seneca Newcome joins the "anti-rent" partisans against the Littlepage family. He masquerades as an "Injin" and attacks the landowners at Ravensnest. Seneca Newcome is finally saved by his sister Opportunity, who also helps the Littlepages because she hopes to marry into the family. Ultimately, however, there is no way in for the Yankees, and the Newcomes and the Littlepages go their separate ways.

Like many of Cooper's historical figures (see e.g. Dryden 1971: 50), the Yankee schoolmaster reverberated with well-established types, in this case the stage Yankee and the Yankee peddler. Newcome is a colonial sample of the Yankees ridiculed at the beginning of the nineteenth century; he is exaggerated as a hypocritical schemer who in the long run endangers the communities he travels to. Cooper's view of New England's role in the union seems to have turned sour by the time he penned the Littlepage trilogy. Yet earlier in his career, in *Notions of the Americans* (1828), he paraded them as "least sophisticated [but] [. . .] truest specimen of the national character" (Cooper 1963: I, 53). Like Irving in "The History of New York," Cooper penned an assessment of American men and manners in response to British misrepresentation. *Notions* comments extensively on the Yankees from the point of view of an impartial European count.[20] The traveler contrasts the rural Yankee folk with the urban Dutch and English elites; he praises the Yankees for their "enterprise, frugality, order, and intelligence," even though they have poor manners (ibid. 91, 100). Cooper's positive assessment of New England and its inhabitants reads very differently from his portrayal of the Newcome clan.

Both Cooper and Irving employ the Yankee schoolmaster in historical narratives of colonial times to debate the role of New England in the nation; both are skeptical, if not dismissive, of New England expansionism and prefer the European stock over the Yankee influence; finally, both dismiss the schoolmaster's missionary zeal. However, the negotiation of New England's role was not limited to the North. Like the peddler, the Yankee schoolmaster incited sectional conflict well before the Civil War. Fictional representations of Yankee schoolmasters reproduce Southern communities' anxieties about their influence (see e.g. Groen 2012). When it comes to discussing sectional conflict, the Yankee schoolmaster changes drastically. In the texts examined here, the Yankee schoolmaster is the spearhead of Northern influence, a teacher and lover of Southern belles. He is elevated from an obnoxious marginal figure to potential romance hero, or at least to specimen of Yankeedom. In this setup, other Northern regional identities, including the Dutch or New Yorkers, as well as Southerners, cannot compete with the New England villager.

Sarah Hale's regionalist romance *Northwood* (1827/1852) features an episode which pits Northern and Southern identities against each other. The novel focuses on the identity quest of protagonist Sidney Romilly from Northwood, NH, who is raised in the South as heir to a plantation fortune and struggles to find his way back to Yankee simplicity and virtues. In Charleston, Sidney falls in love with a young woman who is already secretly married. Sidney proves himself "a hero," according to the chapter heading, after he hears her pitiable story. Zemira Atkinson was schooled in French and Latin by Charles Stuart, a "Yankee schoolmaster" from Massachusetts, "liberally educated, of fine talents, and whose prospects had once been brilliant" (Hale 1852: 194).[21] Stuart has little hope of winning over her father, a Southern businessman who values "wealth and success" over "genius and learning" (195). At this point of the narrative, the narrator inserts a moralistic reflection about the moneyed classes' complacency: "Those who are rich can conceive of no happiness without riches; for they are ignorant of the satisfaction the exertion to obtain eminence or fortune excites" (ibid.). The narrator deems the teacher worthy of Zemira, but her father has to be convinced first. Atkinson senior cites the greed of all Yankees who come to the South like "'locusts to devour whatever they can find'" (204); his daughter becomes an easy prey for that "'hypocritical race who are forever declaiming against slavery, and yet wish to reduce all the world to a dependence on themselves'" (ibid.). Stuart calmly listens to the Southerner's curses (199) and resolves to acquire wealth in the North so he can venerate his secret marriage to Zemira.

In *Northwood*, Charles Stuart the Yankee schoolmaster emerges as a mirror for the protagonist Sidney. When they meet for the first time, Sidney Romilly stands opposite Charles and examines his own image in a mirror placed next to the teacher, "and the view of his own face as compared with that of his rival did not afford him much pleasure" (221); Charles is more handsome than he is, and his beauty is expressed in intelligence and learning, both of which Sidney himself neglected in his spoiled youth.[22]

Charles's shining example makes Sidney realize his own loss of Yankee identity; with his move South, he has "wretchedly misimproved my opportunities" (218). Yet Charles has a positive effect on Sidney. In return, Charles becomes a spiritual friend and eventually retrieves Sidney's lost fortune. Even old Atkinson, on his deathbed, acknowledges the Yankee and gives the couple his blessing (219). For Hale, the Yankee schoolmaster's learning represents the pinnacle of Yankeedom. Stuart is endowed with the thrift to bring his talents to flourish. He teaches Sidney by showing him the right path to Yankee virtue:

> Stuart led back the heart and mind of [Sidney] from frivolous and pernicious pleasure to the love of study, of quiet scenes, and calm amusements. [...] Stuart was loosening the chains which fashion had twined around our hero, and restoring him to the freedom of that rational enjoyment which his soul was formed to appreciate, but for which the Circean cup of luxury had nearly destroyed his relish. (237)

In Hale's novel, the Yankee schoolteacher is an agent of civilization and friendly educator for the protagonist Sidney, and a shining example of New England's moral superiority over the South. In the novella *A Yankee Among the Nullifiers* (1833) by Asa Greene, the schoolmaster has the same fate. The Yankee schoolmaster Elnathan Elmwood goes South and marries a plantation heiress against all odds—and, most importantly, despite her father's resistance. The New York newspaperman Greene views the Yankee critically, but as still superior to the Southern temper. In his humoristic take on the schoolmaster as narrator/protagonist of a fictional autobiography, the Yankee's ambiguity percolates in his storytelling style and puffy self-presentation. Published as a response to the Nullification Crisis of the early 1830s, *A Yankee Among the Nullifiers* satirizes Southern efforts to do away with tariffs on British imports by nullifying federal laws.[23] The largely forgotten novella has been described as "A satire on Southern political ideas and manners, a contemporary romance, and perhaps a burlesque of the current romantic novels of adventure and their heroes" (Reed 1953: 103).

Greene pits the fictional autobiographer Elmwood against "hot nullifiers" such as his rival Harebrain Harrington, and against the South as a whole. In the manner of a memoir, the autobiographic narrative chronicles Elmwood's childhood and Northern education, including a short stint in college, after which he finds his "mind stored with Latin and Greek, but my pocket [. . .] destitute of pence" (Greene 1833: 11; all subsequent references to this edition). Elmwood works as a private teacher to the plantation belle Henrietta Harrington, founds a factory with a Yankee business partner, fights a duel against his rival for Henrietta, and saves her father's life during a slave revolt. In the end, he marries his love interest and establishes himself as self-made entrepreneur and future plantation owner.

Greene's novella experienced modest success and ran through two editions in 1833. Like most of Greene's writings, it is tinged with social and political satire; the South is depicted from the self-confident perspective of the Yankee parvenu. Greene's take on the Nullification Crisis was to beat the South with its own weapons: he has the enslaved decide to nullify slavery. Elmwood acts as a mediator and asserts in the preface that the North always comes out on top:

> In the numberless edifying stories related at the South, of the encounter of Northern and Southern wits, in the way of trade, one thing is constantly to be observed—namely, that the Southern is caught by the artifices of the Northern one; he is the dupe. It follows, of course, that the Yankee is the better man of the two; or at least, here is an acknowledgement of the efficiency of his head, whatever may be alleged of the obliquity for his heart. (Ibid. n.p.)

In the following, the narrator points out that the (Southern) anecdotes about "Yankee tricks" are "not particularly complimentary to Yankee honesty" (ibid.). The preface announces that the following story, told by a Yankee himself, is interspersed with little vignettes about Yankee fraudulence. The preface positions the story between auto- and hetero-stereotype in a deliberately confusing way, undermining expectations about reliability up front. Instead, the audience may expect exaggeration and grotesqueness—in short, entertainment.

Elnathan's story is enriched with a jumble of voices and positions that condemn Southern secessionist tendencies, nullification, or economics.[24] Embedded among many voices, Elnathan's own story cites the difficulty of Yankee heritage. For instance, he talks about his New England heritage from "the first people in the world" (7); unfortunately, though, all the "dignity" and "fame or fortune" are lost to following generations. Instead, Elnathan starts from scratch in making a name for himself. As a young boy, he looks to the village lawyer and to the minister for inspiration, and goes to college to study Latin, but, he states in retrospect, "the cocked hat and the bob wigs," the "oracular tongues" and his veneration for "the clerical character"

(9) were a passing whim. Elnathan finds no models in the colonial authority figures, the reverend and the lawyer, whose colonial status symbols (the "silver-gray wig and three cornered hat," ibid.) are outdated; his belief in classical learning falls prey to modernization. Elnathan positions himself at the helm of an anti-institutional, progressivist Yankeedom, in which Puritanism and learnedness are replaced by *savoir faire*. As in the texts discussed above, the Yankee schoolmaster uses this expertise to "improv[e] the minds and morals of the rising generation, and if one nation exceeds another in true greatness and substantial glory, it is that where the schoolmaster is most abroad in the land" (11).

Like the Franklinesque impetus of the "Yankee Schoolmaster," Elmwood's unreliability as narrator illustrates the weakness of this version of Yankeedom. He eavesdrops on conversations but later admits to other characters that he "accidentally overheard" a rabble-rousing speech by a slave leader (114–15); he code-switches between experiencing and observing modes, such as when he is accused by Henrietta's father of trying to steal her away:

> I went the next day to Mr. Harrington and boldly, but respectfully, asked him for the hand of his daughter. Heaven and earth! What a passion he flew into! [. . .] Besides other hard names, which I do not think it necessary to repeat, he called me a poor, peddling, penniless pedagogue. At the word peddling, I felt my ire beginning to rise; and had he not been the father of Henrietta, and had I not long ago resolved that passion should never get the best of me, I know not what might have been the consequence. As it was, I replied, coolly, that I was not aware of ever having been a pedlar; that I could not at present be called a pedagogue; and that, however poor I might once have been, so far from being now penniless, my practice was amply sufficient, not only for my own support, but also for the maintenance of a family. (62–3)

In this section, Elnathan uses indirect speech to describe the action (asking for his beloved's hand in marriage) but includes his own reaction to Harrington's outrage verbatim ("Heaven and earth!"). Harrington's alliterative insult ("a poor, peddling, penniless pedagogue") characterizes the Yankee schoolmaster type. The narrator admits that he was angered by the word "peddler," but that he stayed "cool" despite this, reiterating his own response in reported speech well, a composed riposte which undermines every single one of the accusations. As this quotation shows, Elnathan employs narrative technique to make his own light shine.

Like in Hale's *Northwood*, the schoolmaster's standing up against the wrath of his Southern prospective father-in-law is a key scene in which the allegedly hot Southern temper clashes with Yankee "calculation." Unlike in *Northwood*, however, Elnathan is not a virtuous romance hero but an awkward courter and involuntary word artist in the vein of rural Jonathan. He sends Henrietta secret letters or what he calls "bills of exchange," bragging that "never did any billet do me so much pleasure as a *billet-doux* from my adored mistress" (87); a little later, Henrietta sends him a material message, a cantaloupe engraved with an "I," signifying "I can't elope" (88). After some musing about Henrietta's propriety, he decides it must mean "I can't *consent to* elope" (89, emphasis added). The passage parodies English romance, which literally cannot be "translated" into an American setting; after all, by eloping with Henrietta, the Yankee would lose his prospects.[25]

For his critique of the Southern Nullifiers, Greene employs the satirical grotesque.[26] The Southerners consistently describe themselves as "high-minded" and "chivalrous" (see e.g. 17, 18, 20, 92, 122). They are shown as ready for a (fist)fight, as well as gossipy. For instance, when talking about Elnathan's new factory, they fall prey to the Southern myth of the peddler: "Some said [the factory] was to turn out wooden nutmegs; others, bass-wood pumpkin seeds; others, tin side-saddles; and others again, wooden clocks; while a fifth class swore roundly that it was to be a tariff manufactory" (93). In another instance, the Southerners fail to grasp the reason for the slave rebellion, which they ultimately blame on the Union Party (122).[27] They are hapless and helpless, with their "hot heads and generous hearts" and their "republican theory and aristocratic practice" (11). Elnathan distorts Nullification with puns and language games.[28] Building on the Southern threat of secession, the enslaved devise a scheme of "pertection" and "fleesession" (129), meaning to run away if they are not in agreement with their masters.

Elnathan brings many Yankee improvements to the South. He frees the slaves and sends them back to Liberia, a nod to the agenda of the Whigs' Colonization Society; he employs white Yankee workers (142) and, with the help of some Yankee inventions, modernizes field labor. What is more, Elnathan reconciles sectional conflict:

> For my part, I have long since toted all my prejudices to the moon, where I intend to let them rest, as well [. . .] with the wooden nutmegs, the pork and molasses, and all such things as never had a being, except in the store house of sectional fancy, or among the

tibbets of local scandal. I love New England with all its Yankee notions, for it is the land of my birth, my childhood, my education; I love the hospitable South, in spite of its Nullification, for it is the birthplace of my wife, the home of my adoption. (143)

The novella replays racist stereotypes and distortions and shows no abolitionist tinge.[29] The happy ending is Elnathan's and Henrietta's only, in a marital union that symbolizes the solution to the Nullification Crisis and that anticipates the postbellum "romance of reunion" (Silber 1993; see also Thomas 2017), in which cross-sectional marriage, much in the way of transatlantic matchmaking, reunites the war parties. Elmwood's career as schoolmaster, attorney at law, onetime political candidate, plantation owner, and self-made entrepreneur shows how the Yankee "goes ahead" to take over the South.[30]

In antebellum narratives, the Yankee schoolmaster becomes a vehicle for debating sectional conflict and Northern capitalism that is tied to a masculinist understanding of Yankeedom. This norm persists well into the Progressive Era, as the sectionalist play *Penn Hapgood, or The Yankee Schoolmaster* (Chase 1890) shows; it features a Yankee schoolmaster in Tennessee presented unequivocally as "Yankee abolitionist." The gendered version of aggressive schooling is highlighted further by a variation in which the schoolmaster is female, such as Lydia Baldwin's postbellum novel *A Yankee School-teacher in Virginia: A Tale of the Old Dominion in the Transition State* (1884). Baldwin's reflector figure is Maryan Stone, a Northern schoolmarm who experiences the beginnings of Virginian post-slavery society. The novel combines features of sentimental literature, the abolitionist novel, and the postbellum reconciliation narrative. For its greater part, it depicts the emancipation of the former slaves in a segregated community. They learn their ABCs, develop a political consciousness, and reject the influence of the conservative ex-Confederate soldier Percy Darnell (Baldwin 1884: 140–7). Loosely interspersed in this plot line are Ms. Stone's reflections. She struggles with the Southern "hostility toward the free slaves acquiring knowledge, and toward myself as connected with the [abolitionist] movement" (ibid. 93). In comparison to the Southerners, Maryan has better manners; she is a model specimen of republican womanhood, both in housekeeping and in character.[31] She is also a typical Yankee: when faced with a dilemma, she "weigh[s]" her options "in her mental balance, Yankee-like" (ibid. 227). Like her male colleagues, the Yankee teacher finally gains an inroad into Southern society by marriage. Maryan, who lost a fiancé Union soldier in the war, has a second chance at love with

Darnell, who vows to "'restore this pleasant old inheritance'" of his father's house and to make "'no more mistakes!'" (ibid. 238).

In Baldwin's novel, the female Yankee schoolteacher echoes the sentimental heroine and the woman civilizer of the Western narrative. The novel uses a simplistic display of poetic justice: the villains fall sick, the heroine's virtue is rewarded, the former slaves make their first steps towards responsibility and independence. In this setup, the Yankee schoolteacher fills the cultural void of the culturally decaying South with Northern virtues. She educates both black and white. While she is a true Yankee, her gender identity mitigates the schoolmaster's ambiguousness; Maryan is a positive character with little drive to expansionism.

"The Season of Youth for Nations and Individuals": New England Villages and Yankee Character

Fictional texts of the first half of the nineteenth century describing New England contribute to political and cultural debates about "Yankeedom." The examples discussed in this chapter couple two plot lines: the depiction of New England communities and the hero-centered romance or *Bildungsroman* plot. In portraying New England men and manners, the texts position the region between the (pejorative) transatlantic gaze and increasing sectional conflict, between a utopian and backwater image of the village, and they conservatively draw on earlier literary models (Buell 1987: 318, 299). Their topic is community resilience in liminal moments of crisis, created by black sheep fallen prey to the typical Yankee predicament for business. The suspense pertains to the resolution: will the New England community be preserved? Will it succumb to modernization, to hypocrisy and business schemes?[32]

The site of the New England home described in these stories is the backdrop for the romance story of a New England hero, whose family ties and legacy have to be reconciled with his plans for the future. The Yankee protagonist's story links the region to national mythography. It cites the coming-of-age narrative prevalent in visual culture in the same period, with the allegory of Brother Jonathan growing out of his clothes and into imperial size.

Sarah Hale's *Northwood* mixes the picturesque portrayal of the New England village novel with the *Bildungsroman* to cast a positive light on New England and its people.[33] The Yankees (a term Hale generally avoids) are viewed from various perspectives: the narrator's, an English traveler's, and a returning New Englander's, a gaze that attests to Hale's interest in American character, as her later publication *Sketches of American Character* (1843) shows. In the first part of *Northwood*, the narrator adopts a detached perspective but uses an Englishman as focalizer; in the second part, she[34] focuses on the individualist hero's story. In the opening chapters, the narrator describes the Romilly family to her readers, their worldview and lifestyle. She provides the story of Lydia Romilly's preference for the Southern gentleman Brainard over the upright Yankee Rueben Porter. After Lydia and her Southern husband have taken her brother's son Sidney down South, the narrative changes perspective in chapter 5 with a long description of the New England fall and foliage. The special "softness of the atmosphere" brought in by November is the story's beginning, when the light "throws over the faded earth a veil that, mirage-like, gives a charm beyond the brightness of summer noon. This is most perfect in November. It was perfect when our story opens" (Hale 1852: 42).

This exposition prepares the ground for the portrait of two well-to-do travelers who approach the town of Northwood, Sidney Romilly and his English friend Mr. Frankford. Their conversation views New England through an outsider's eyes. Sidney, who feels nostalgia upon returning to the place of his childhood ("'I have climbed that mountain many a time, and it looks like a friend!'", 47), is contrasted to the Englishman Frankford, who possesses an English "national contempt for everything American" (ibid.). A reviewer in the *Boston Spectator and Ladies' Album* critiqued this character constellation, claiming that they "must have grown morbid by feasting too much on foreign relations" (qtd. in Gossett and Bardes 1985: 13).

Hale couples the traveling Englishman with a Yankee returning to his childhood abode, thus contrasting a truly foreign view with a perspective estranged by a Southern education. Sidney's idealizing of New England is an urge rather than an expertise; he hardly knows the land he feels compelled to defend. A little later, in a key conversation, Frankford, young Sidney, and his father Squire Romilly discuss the success of the national "experiment," and the three characters become stand-ins for the American Revolutionary (Squire Romilly), the skeptical British imperialist (Frankford), and the young, ambitious American (Sidney). While Squire Romilly projects a prosperous future, Frankford speculates:

> "The season of youth for nations, as well as individuals, will soon pass; what character your country will finally attain I am not qualified

to decide. But I think there is reason to fear that what it gains in glory will be lost in purity."

"Ours is an experiment," said Sidney, "yet with our advantages there is not much fear but the result will be favorable to human nature." (163)

Frankford's inquiry about the fate of the U.S. predicts Sidney's own path; just as the young man, the nation is subjected to trials and crises. The nation's "purity," just as Sidney's own, will be corrupted in a rise to empire.

As visitors to "the old Granite State" of New Hampshire, Frankford and Sidney encounter Yankee ways together; they explore the regional culture in the landscape and in the characters, such as young Zeb, their coach driver. Sidney calls him "'a true slip from Puritan stock [. . .] determined to have his own way—that was their liberty of conscience'" (48). A little further down the road, they ask a "genuine Yankee" for directions. Again, Sidney acts the part of the guide to the foreigner Frankford: "'I know by his whistle [of *Yankee Doodle*] he is a true one. You have often enough heard him described and beheld him caricatured, now look at the original'" (50). The Yankee's description exhibits typical physical features. He is very tall and "rather spare," but has an athletic body, "bone and muscle of the land" (ibid.).

In the next chapters, the Englishman Frankford becomes the focalizer. His response to New England is shared freely with the reader through free direct thought and his dialogue and discussions with the Yankees. It allows the reader to witness his conversion from skeptic to fan of New England (see e.g. 80, 81, 103, 133).[35] Educated by storytelling and anecdotes offered by the Romilly family, Frankford experiences the history of the young nation (83–6). He is won over emotionally *and* rationally. Participation is as important as debate; in chapters 6–14, Frankford partakes in community rituals like a country wedding, a ball, and the Thanksgiving dinner.[36] For instance, Sidney's father maintains that there are no villains in New England, because of the Yankees' fear of God, education, and "free institutions" (70, 71). After Frankford describes democracy as rabble rule (48), he is charmed by the democratic virtue of hearing everyone out (148). The subjects of these conversations cover the topic of the day, including America's manifest destiny "to instruct the world [. . .] and Africa" (166–7);[37] slavery, and Squire Romilly's assurance that it will soon be abolished (127); the prejudiced views of Europeans;[38] democracy and meritocracy; and censorship (132). Similarly, the discussion with the Yankee Dr. Perkins illustrates the New England political mind in a list that unfolds its own dramaturgy:

> The conversation turned on the beauties of Latin and Greek poetry—the site of Troy—which Frankford had visited—Alexander and Bonaparte—Roman eloquence—aborigines of America—British manufactures—culture of turnips—American literature—Shakespeare—Milton—British Navy—Irish patriots—Emmet—character of Washington—and the study of physics in Europe. (158)

The conversation proceeds from comparing ancient and modern empires and empire building to turnip farming, from high-brow literature to literary canon formation. The U.S. is discussed in one breath with ancient Greece and Rome (the model republics), nineteenth-century France and England; its republican leader General Washington is put on a par with the emperors Alexander and Napoleon.

In the first part of *Northwood*, the reflector figure Frankford becomes enchanted with New England. In the second part of the novel, Hale foregrounds the fate of Sidney Romilly, whose return to his New England identity requires a return to truth and simplicity: "Sidney had never forgotten he was Yankee born, although half raised on a Southern plantation. The green hills of New Hampshire still rose in his 'mind's eye'" (285). After Frankford's return to England, the novel switches from a didactic debate over New England life to the psychological development of a Yankee spoiled by Southern luxury.

Sidney's story serves as an example of virtue recovered. His decision to help the unhappy lovers Zemira and Charles Stuart proves right when Charles, in return, helps Sidney regain his fortune; Sidney's assistance of the poor farmer Merrill earns him a loyal admirer who uncovers a scandal and unites him with his love interest Annie. The reversal of fortunes Annie and Sidney experience demonstrates the value of true love uninterested in wealth. In the ending, they are paraded as the pride of the Northern/Northwood community going South to educate, Christianize, and then free their slaves, who are replaced, just like in Greene's *Yankee Among the Nullifiers*, by Yankee machines. As specimen of the morally sound and virtuous Yankee race, Sidney resists Southern temptations. He works as a schoolmaster before taking over the family farm, and, with the help of Charles Stuart, comes into his own. He writes to Frankford,

> I am metamorphosed from a gay man to a grave one;—not sad, only considerate—and instead of strutting the gentleman with a score of servants waiting my commands, I am plain farmer [. . .] I am more respected and less feared; better, far better, beloved, yet less flattered [. . .] far happier and more useful in my humble retirement, than when parading in the streets of Charleston, the reputed heir of two hundred thousand dollars. (341)

Sidney's new sense of belonging is hard-won. When he cannot face the Northern winter like his little brothers can, he feels spoilt to effeminacy by the Southern lifestyle and unattractive for his crush Zemira (281). The reason for his crisis is not so much his loss of fortune but his inability to work: "I am nothing, for I can do nothing; I am neither educated for a profession, nor have I habits of industry to gain a subsistence by labor" (311). His deceased father's words guide him out of depression, and the knowledge of home finally allows him to combine the best of both worlds, the North and the South: "he thought [. . .] he should enjoy independence, and the advantages and pleasure of elegant society, combined with that dear domestic bliss which makes the heart's best, truest felicity" (369).

Hale positions Yankee manhood against sectional and transatlantic models, the Southern planter class, and the upper class of England. This contrast includes a critical look at the Yankee's compulsion to enter business. To Sidney, Englishmen appear more dignified than the Americans because they are not forced to compete for recognition in the public sphere. He writes in a letter to Frankford:

> I do think the real English gentleman has more of dignity, and less of arrogance, than our purse-proud citizens. The Englishman is more proud, perhaps, but is free from that puffing consequence which is the most offensive part of the folly in our own countrymen. This may arise from the superiority of the former being established and acknowledged, where our own gentlemen are continually striving to maintain their precarious honors, and seem determined, by making the most of what they happen to possess, to indemnify themselves for the transientness of its continuance. (245)

Much as the novel glorifies New England, Sidney's reflection paints an agrarian and pastoral community ideal. Hale's Yankee men are yeomen farmer-philosophers, not entrepreneurs. She defends the community narrative against the onslaught of individualist "going ahead." For Hale, the Yankee's rise from peddler or schoolmaster to factory owner is an act of self-inflation or puffery. Yankee greed produces a drive to wealth and puts the New England community and village ideals at risk. In Hale's vision, as in the bulk of New England writing, the commercial and intellectual centers of New York, Philadelphia, or Boston are nonexistent; "technology and the city exist mostly in parentheses" (Buell 1987: 301).[39]

In *Northwood*, character enters a symbiosis with the village, since the New Englanders have created the land they live in and shaped the settlement to bear their own character traits:

> The green hills of New Hampshire [. . .] those eminences swelling into an endless variety of forms, yet still retaining a character of softened grandeur, loft but not inaccessible, and severe without being savage, [they] might personify the stern, steadfast, yet generous race their cultivation had helped to form. (285)

With their "endless variety of forms," yet recognizable because of their "character," the hills symbolize the people. In this landscape, the white birch stand "like pillars" (52) of mountains that are "God's temples" (236). Another vista shows the New England village bathed in the last rays of the day:

> The tall steeple, whose spire was ornamented with a fish (doing duty as a weathercock), that still reflected the brightness of the western sky, looked like a sentinel guarding the humble abodes beneath and around it, and by the associations its sacred purposes inspired, served as a memento to lift the gazer's thought to heaven. (54)

Hale's New England tableau evokes what John Evelev (2007: 148) has called a "picturesque sensibility" that mixes historic realities with motifs of community and coherence. Northwood is grouped around the material and spiritual protective center of the village church, with a sprinkle of New England individualism in the choice of a fish for a weathervane.[40] The family farm has been cultivated in "unremitting industry" from the "wilderness"; now it includes a "garden," "orchard," and "comfortable house" (8). The chapter "Home as Found" (58) chronicles Sidney's return to his birthplace, the landscaped Romilly estate. Imported "Lombardy poplars" grow in the front yard, but this "error" has been compensated for with "native" plants, such as young elms and maples, as well as the "pride of the parterre," the mountain ash, "throwing up their heads as though proud of their coral clusters" (58, 59). The family has returned to "native" plants after following foreign horticultural fashions.

Hale contrasts the harmonious composition of the Romilly residence to the misshaped house of Deacon Jones, an ambiguous character. He adds an unshapely room to his house, which is already ridiculed (99). Jones dedicates it as a community and religious meeting room and, on this basis, proclaims himself town deacon. He gains authority by literally building a room, an act of self-inflation no one else had thought of (100). By contrast, the Romillys are a "good and happy pair" who live in "peace, sufficiency, and content" (89) and are avid readers. Book culture in the widest sense prevents the New Englanders from falling prey to business schemes. The novel emphasizes book culture's nation-building function, for instance in depicting the smart Romilly children (114), or when Merrill loses everything and his son implores him to keep the "dixionary," the most cherished object (289). The epistolary art is also a topic; the letters included speak for themselves, and Squire Romilly comments on his son's letters from the South, which are endowed with "many flourishes": "'It is utility, not show, we should encourage'" (40). With his diaries, Squire Romilly guides Sidney back to Yankeedom even after his death. Writing thus becomes an identity technology and ensures community survival that affirms Northern supremacy. Sidney stays home after he learns about his father's death from a letter; he finds a happy ending with Annie as landowner in the South, but is immune to the intellectual paralysis or "ennui" idle Southerners develop (see e.g. 30, 323, 342).

Hale called *Northwood* "conservative throughout, calm and considerate in its tone and reflections" (qtd. in Peterson 1998: 36). On the plot level, Hale shows rural New England as an orderly country, putting into effect Squire Romilly's reliance on the virtuous majority. The petty crimes that imperil Sidney's marriage are uncovered; the villain, Elnathan Skinner, who intercepted Sidney's correspondence with his mother and cashed his money orders, is put in prison (378). The other greedy and hypocritical Yankee character is Deacon Jones, whom everybody knows to be selfish (292, 322). His wordy sermons and fortune hunting are frowned upon by the villagers. His hope that Annie might die and her inheritance fall to him (362) is as morally deplorable as his opportunism when he "transfers his favor and his conscience from the falling to the rising fortune" (384).

On the discourse level, Hale addresses a female readership well versed in the literary conventions of the day and sensible enough to understand both the village novel and the romance plot she entangles. Amy Kaplan has described the politics of *Northwood* as "manifest domesticity," heralding the separate sphere model in which the housewife acts as the republican mother who educates and molds its citizens (Kaplan 2002; see also Gossett and Bardes 1985). Hale's focus on the material and symbolic meaning of the home can hardly be overstated and forms the kernel of almost every chapter's epigraph. Her narrative commentary asks the reader to do her own thinking, aiming to "leave none save agreeable or useful impressions on the mind" (384) and stating that "It is useless to attempt a description [. . .] Those who have souls will understand [. . .] To the dull, all books will be dull" (76). The relation between the narrator and the imagined reader builds on mutual understanding between similarly learned, no-nonsense women familiar with the conflicts in the novel.[41]

While Hale's narrator deliberately leaves some details to the reader's imagination, she puts extreme emphasis on describing the Thanksgiving dinner, despite the fact that "I never much relished" the "literary treat [represented] in the description of a feast" (87). In doing so, she maintains the bond with the republican housewife acquainted with the literary conventions.[42] With Sidney's development, she also provides a double edge. In the beginning, he waxes poetic when returning to his beloved New England and poses as a romance hero ("'I have often been told I had many traits of a novel hero in my character, and an old sibyl once predicted I would die for love,'" 53). Later, she regrets his very uselessness as hero material: "How I wish I had a perfect hero. One of the patent made creatures who either by nature or intuition are possessed of every virtue, art and accomplishment" (179). Due to his Southern (lack of) education, however, Sidney is an imperfect specimen. Finally, she submits him to the "crisis which by the universal consent of authors, rounds the period of a novel hero's historical existence; and the sage reader, no doubt, anticipates his exemption from further trials, and that he is soon to be consigned to marriage and obscurity" (328). The narrator thus links Sidney's story to the literary fashions of her day, announcing the reform of the spoilt Yankee and a retreat to "normal" life. As an epitome of the nation, Sidney's flawed heroism shows the same loss of "purity" Frankford prophesied for the U.S.; as Sidney brings his Northern predicament into the South, so should the nation deal with its defect of slavery. The New England village community as well as the individual hero can be preserved when they hold on to their New England ways and ideals and resist the rise of business and entrepreneurship.

Hale's novel is instrumental for reading Yankeedom and New England culture not least because of the time of its publication. The first edition in 1827 attempts to preserve the waning authority of New England after the crisis of the Hartford Convention. The second edition was published with only a few additions, such as Squire Romilly's diary, which provides moral guidance for Sidney as he sets out to become a plantation owner in the South. Hale's new foreword to the second edition, under the impression of increasing sectional conflict, states that she intended to write no "partisan book" (407)—even though the analysis of New England men and manners has shown otherwise. In 1852, Hale's rural Yankee communities contributed to the ongoing pastoralization of New England as a region and of its inhabitants as high-minded country noblemen. In the meantime, this image had long been parodied, such as in the truncated 1844 novella *The Hypocrite, or Sketches of American Society from a Residence of Forty Years*, which I discuss below.

Published anonymously, *The Hypocrite* is a didactic piece of roughly 100 pages aiming at "the correction of vice, by holding up vicious men and vicious actions" (Aesop 1844, n.p.; all subsequent references to this edition). It portrays the downfall of New England through hypocrisy and sexual libertinism among lewd clergymen and takes the opposite stance to Hale's glorification of New England tradition, showing how defects are passed down through generations. Where Hale blends the modes of social commentary with the romance plot, *The Hypocrite* jumbles both together in an incomplete narrative that does not follow a singular narrative progression. The identity of the self-named author Aesop remains unknown; the subtitle of the story, "From a Residence of Forty Years," projects the fictional author as an Englishman views the "Yankee," in different facets. The preface maps the agenda; like the classical fables, the text is to be read as an "algebraic equation" (n.p.), but this soberness is subjected in the same section to trenchant irony:

> The scene of this story [. . .] is laid in rural life, among the farmers of New England, and would, in any other country, be called *low*; but among republican farmers we acknowledge no such term; as the *hero* of the piece [. . .] might, from mere circumstance, fill the highest official station in the United States. The farmers in America are the lords of the soil, and the source of all political power [. . .] descriptions, therefore, of rural life in this free and happy country are, in Aesop's opinion, on an equality with descriptions of the nobility and gentry of Europe. We have no *low* in American society but the ignorant and vicious. (n.p.)

By calling the farmers the "lords of the soil," the narrator reiterates the egalitarian tropes of the Revolution. Ironically, he argues that the social class of this protagonist should be ignored, since the American farmer equals the English lord in nobility and virtue, yet the New Englanders shown are anything but noble, but "low" hypocrites. The text continues this inversion in the style of Augustan satire with quotes from the flawed figures. They have telling or literary names, such as the smart Yankee mother Amelia, whose advice to her son is to get ahead by making money. Their physiognomy gives away their character. Deacon Calvin Longface, for instance, is "tall and thin, with a long, grave, snarling countenance, on every feature of which you could read miser and bigot"; he has a "nasal twang and drawl" when reading the Bible, a well-known type: "No doubt the reader has seen many like him" (24). The villain Reverend Saint Bullneck is a brute, "about five feet eight inches high, thick set, with a large, wide forehead, projecting occiput, and thick neck. His general aspect was austere, with a canting hypocritical face, voluptuous mouth and vulgar features [. . .] his motions were slow but energetic" (38).[43]

The Hypocrite's satire reads crudely and lacks coherence. Yet its aesthetic failures render visible the different sources employed for constructing Yankeedom: English literature of the eighteenth century, American vernacular, and Puritan myth. The narrator Tristram Slyman, for instance, only enters the story after a general typology of the alleged "true Yankee" (10; see below). Much like his English namesake Tristram Shandy, Slyman's self-indulgent telling is entirely diverted. His voice veers so far off course that it dissolves altogether from page 32 onwards, when it is replaced by the voice of his maternal grandfather David Jones, who tells of his youth and courtship. Like Lawrence Sterne's social satire, *The Hypocrite* presents a few life stories of corrupted individuals and prioritizes narrative undulation over coherence.

Tristram's education is framed by opposing models of "church and world" (20), Puritanism and Enlightenment philosophy, passed down from England to his parents. His boorish Puritan father thinks his son's Yankee tricks are expressions of God's wrath and gets so hysterical about this that he goes insane (26, 27). His mother was educated by "the writings of Milton, Thomson, Dryden, Pope, Johnson, and Addison; and, notwithstanding the puritanical cast of the place and times in which she lived, Shakespeare could be found among her books" (20). Taken aback by his father's madness, young Tristram follows the maternal lineage and emulates his grandfather Jones, the Yankee schoolteacher, "in learning, libertinism, and hypocrisy" (15). The doctrine of "hypocrisy" is explicated twice in the story, as a suspicion of female virtue and of clergymen as "wolves in sheep's clothing" (97), who follow a "rule for pleasure, under the cloak of a smooth exterior" (44) and a "daring [soul] concealed under a smooth, condescending exterior" (53).

Hypocrisy gains a double meaning as religious blasphemy on the one hand and as masquerade on the other. It is demonstrated by Saint Bullneck, the reverend of David's hometown, whose crimes include adultery with David's mother, murder of the town doctor and the teacher, rape, and starving to death his own wife and daughter. Bullneck's crimes committed against David's family are a "thorn" in the boy's heart and prevent him from finding happiness, faith, and marital bliss with his first love Henrietta (56, 68, 102). Scandalized by Bullneck's crimes, David runs away. He returns home in disguise as "Marc Antony, a cosmopolite, a citizen of the world" (78), mimicking Yankeeisms and worldliness (70–1). David brings Bullneck to a confession, and then to justice by castration, after which the reverend takes his own life. With justice served and closure of David's story in sight, the ending of *The Hypocrite* changes the scene to Boston for an indictment of the New England practice of "bundling" in courtship.[44] During his stay in Boston, David boards with a Mrs. Easyman. The married landlady has an affair with Mr. Bushwhacker that carries on because the couple bundled in their youth. The final commentary thus blames rural libertinism and Puritan practices for the downfall of society in both village and city (117).

Much like Hale does in *Northwood*, *The Hypocrite* relates the fate of the (pseudo-) heroic Yankees Slyman and Jones to New England customs. The failure of the double English heritage of Puritanism and Enlightenment culture is linked to the fate of the narrators Tristram and David. Even before their story, though, the author provides a thirty-page general discourse about Yankee manners and tricks. In this first part, Aesop draws heavily from the Yankee myth and stereotypes of the day, enriching his moralism with an informative part about "Yankeedom" to "set the Europeans right on that subject" (3). The Yankee is defined by behavior, not by ethnicity; his "God is the dollar, whether he be an English Yankee, an Irish Yankee, a Scotch Yankee, a Jew Yankee, a Quaker Yankee, an American Yankee, or the highest, and only true blood, a *Yankee* Yankee" (3). While the "blood" Yankee resides in the New England states and sends out peddlers and schoolmasters (4), all those who abide by capitalism are part of the U.S. nation. Aesop distinguishes between a positively tinged "Yankee talent, ambition, and enterprise" which sweep Yankee schoolmasters such as Daniel Webster or John Quincy Adams into political office, and an idiomatic Yankee "shave":

> When it is said that "*He came the Yankee over him,*" it is meant that the person was most elegantly and cleanly shaved in the transaction alluded to, so that the *shaver* can again meet the *shavee* with a fine, full, bold, quizzical look, that says, "I stuck it into you that time, didn't I?" and which gives the shaver no kind of pain, but, on the contrary, a good deal of self-gratulation. (5)

In Aesop's view, "Yankeedom" can be imitated and performed, and its valuable feature is Yankee thrift. When reading his portrayal of Slyman and Jones together with his typology of Yankee shavers and achievers, Aesop's portrait of New England Yankeedom is a negative and misogynist one, causing the downfall of North American civilization through lewdness and capitalist desires; Saint Bullneck seduces Amelia to get the family farm, and he dies of his own shame, yet the blame goes to the New England women and republican mothers who pass on their deficiency to the following generations.

Aesop's narrator gestures towards the virtues they should aspire to. If Aesop's satire fails to fully live up to the genre convention he so avidly canvasses, this can be attributed to the Yankee typology of the beginning of *The Hypocrite*. His failure or unwillingness to fully denounce the Yankee concoction of sexual libertinage and economic greed makes the entire satire go awry.

John Neal's Down-Easters: Whittling, Storytelling Yankees

Regardless of their view of the Whig enterprise of New Englandizing America, the texts examined here grapple with the Yankee figure's turn to business, pleading the preservation of pre-capitalist, rural, and unintellectual Yankeedom. Particularly, the life and writings of New England writer John Neal (1793–1876) distinguish different types and shades of Yankeedom. Ultimately, Neal's many Yankee types are dissolved in his particular way of storytelling that posits a cunning American voice.

John Neal's New England novels *Brother Jonathan, or The New Englanders* (1825) and *The Down-Easters* (1833), which comprises a novel and two additional novellas, were commercial failures and have gained little scholarly attention.[45] To recent critics like David S. Reynolds in *Beneath the American Renaissance*, Neal "subverts" the poetics of the American Renaissance. In Neal's "likeable criminals" and "reverend rake figures," Reynolds traces a new "irrational style" (Reynolds 2001: 183).[46] Watts and Carlson argue that Neal's potpourri of literary fashions explodes the English models; punning on Reynolds's title, they claim that "rather than beneath American Renaissance, Neal is scattered all over it" (Watts and Carlson 2012: iv).

Commentators have speculated that in comparison to Cooper's plot-driven stories, Neal's conversationalist style was too heterogeneous for the era's literary taste; English writer William Hazlitt, for instance, accused Neal of "running riot" on details: "In the absence of subjects of real interest, men make themselves an interest out of nothing, and magnify mole-hills into mountains. This is not the fault of Mr. Cooper: He is always true, though sometimes tedious; and [. . .] has great unity of purpose and feeling" ("American Literature," *Edinburgh Review* 50 (1829): 142; qtd. in Pethers 2012: 29).

Neal himself indulged in his unconventional style, stating that "I shall write as others drink, for exhilaration" (qtd. in Daggett 1920: 3). Neal's career shows a deep involvement with national and regional culture. He worked as an editor, art critic, and historiographer, co-writing the *History of the American Revolution* (1822, 3 vols., with Paul Allen and Tobias Watkins), and negotiated between New England regionalism and nationalism, sketching them as "performative space[s], where identities cannot be taken at face value" (Holt 2012: 187). Neal's impact on the writers of the American Renaissance is undisputed. Nathaniel Hawthorne admits "that wild fellow John Neal" nearly "turned [his] boyish brains" (qtd. in Reynolds 2001: 203). Neal was also the first reviewer of Edgar Allen Poe's writings ("Poems by Edgar Allen Poe," *Morning Courier and New York Enquirer*, July 8, 1831) and boosted Poe's early career (see also Neal, "Edgar Allen Poe," *Portland Advertiser Weekly*, April 26, 1850).

As an editor and literary man, Neal articulated a pluralistic view of New England, distinguishing the intellectual and economic centers of Concord and Boston from northern New England, particularly with the breaking away of his home in Maine from New Hampshire in 1820. He took up residence in Newport, RI, and from there issued his acerbic commentary on all things literary. Despite this regionalism, Neal was businessman enough to transform his magazine *The Yankee and Boston Literary Gazette* (1828–9) into the co-edited *Boston Literary Gazette* to ensure its survival.

Neal impersonates a literary activist version of Yankeedom. His decision, in the 1820s, to go to England was prompted by English poet Sydney Smith's famous quip "Who in the four corners of the globe reads an American book?" (see Meyerlob 2012). Neal abandoned his law practice and became a cultural mediator between England and the newly independent U.S. During his stay in London (1824–7) Neal published criticism, first anonymously as "A.B." in the prestigious *New England Magazine*, then masquerading as an Englishman and travel writer, "Carter Holmes." About his role as American critic in England, Neal wrote:

> My chief object from the first was to bring together—not to segregate, alienate, or embitter—two great nations, with a common literature, a common purpose, and a common interest. To do this effectually, I must write as an Englishman, or at least not as an American; being always careful to say the truth, and always to acknowledge the faults of *others*, especially of my countrymen. (Qtd. in Daggett 1920: 10)

Neal negotiated transatlantic kinship and rapprochement between New England and Britain. In his signature evasive style, he also explained "American character" to the English in the essays "Yankee Notions" and "Character of the Real Yankees" (both 1826). Both feature pompous opening claims and then peter off; in the former, he records his own travels from America to England, building a degree of suspense about the meaning of "Yankee Notions" that he deliberately refuses to bring to closure. In his essay "Sketches of American Character" (1825), he writes: "The New England Character bears the stamp not only of *nationality* but of *individuality*. You may know a Yankee anywhere. Their language, dress, habits, laws, usages, and manners, alike distinguish them from all their brethren, east, west, north, and south" (qtd. in Holt 2012: 206). His essays emulated a consciousness of national stereotypes and myths that also percolates in his fictional writings.

In his New England stories *Brother Jonathan* and *The Down-Easters*, Neal mingles patriotic discourse, Yankee types, and complicated storylines to critique Whiggish literary nationalism. His oeuvre simultaneously paints and erases a New England or American type; he holds up the typified character as a signifier, only to then remove it in the undulations of the plot. He shows that Yankeedom is imaginary, rendered exclusively in a white, male body which only looks hegemonic at first view but is afflicted by interior troubles. Neal's Yankees grapple with a mixed ancestry and the haunting presence of Others, such as abandoned women, Native Americans, and Southerners. Neal thus adapts the Yankee as a figment of a national character which is much more pluralistic on the inside, a nationalist project who pretends to be white and male at the cost of internal troubles and nervous breakdowns. Similarly, he was skeptical of historiography's treatment of Native Americans. In a chapter in *Brother Jonathan* about "the original North American [. . .] and legitimate proprietor of the Western World" (Neal 1825: II, 1; all subsequent references to this edition), Neal critiques the denomination "Savage," painting "the Wild man of North America" as brave and virtuous. To present-day readers, this may sound like another rendition of the noble savage, but Neal warns against visual typing: "The pictures of him are only pictures. They are not portraits—they are imaginary faces. History itself [. . .] is full of exaggeration, full of heroic enlargement concerning the Red man of North America" (II, 2).

Brother Jonathan was written in England to present the true character of Americans to English and American readers alike. It consists of two sections, about small-town life in Gingertown, CN, at the onset of the Revolution, disturbed by a rabble-rousing Yankee, and, in the second part, the story of "our young hero" Walter Harwood. In a nutshell, the story chronicles the life of Harwood, who leaves his Gingertown home to fight in the Revolutionary War and win over his Southern love interest Edith Cummin. Walter is haunted by a murder mystery surrounding his biological parentage involving one Warwick Savage, who visits the Gingertown community in the guise of the Yankee schoolmaster Jonathan Peters and becomes Walter's mentor. Walter's mother was a Native American woman; his father, Squire Harwood, is a village authority who turns out to be a liar. As a young man, he destroyed the relationship between Warwick and Walter's mother and fought Warwick to the death. The presumed murder victim returns to Gingertown as Jonathan Peters, provoking scandal in the community and breaking the family harmony of the Harwood household. His son Walter is torn between his impulses to live in the wild and his revolutionary fervor. He frequently faints, has fever dreams, and is generally a troubled protagonist.

The title *Brother Jonathan* uses the national allegory and the narrative of masculine growth I discussed in Chapter 1 to frame Walter's story as allegorical coming-of-age of the U.S. Like the young nation, Walter is a youth not only conflicted by his unknown mother's Native American legacy, but also torn between two father figures: the colonial hypocrite Squire Harwood, firmly anchored in his community, and the shapeshifter Warwick Savage/Jonathan Peters, a man without an ancestry who acts as Yankee schoolteacher but really disturbs the peace. Walter's split filiation reiterates the debates over Puritan roots and Yankee uniqueness; in the course of the novel, both become inadequate and Walter casts his own path into the future. The two parts of *Brother Jonathan* represent different phases of Walter's life. At first, he is a child, a marginal, immature figure in the Harwood household who is mostly outdoors. At the end of volume 1, his physique and comportment change radically. In a pivotal scene, he raises his voice and speaks of himself as "a man," emerging as the hero of the second, romance part (I, 380).

The dilemma the Gingertowners face is thus an innate one. Compared to Irving's and Cooper's complacent colonial Dutch/English communities, Neal's Gingertowners cannot cast out the Yankee interloper Jonathan Peters but have to decide on their role in the Revolution. The Yankee shapeshifter is therefore the center of the action, equipped with the traits of the Yankee peddler and the educational zeal of the Yankee schoolmaster. He improves Walter's accent, helping him to find a sophisticated language, and he lays bare the little lies and complacencies of the Gingertown personnel. Peters exposes the self-styled "Brigadier" Ephraim Johnson as town drunk, using not only "arguments" as weapons of choice but also board games; he beats Johnson "at fox and geese, then, at morris, then at checkers, or draughts" (I, 7). This mixture of braggadocio and performance shows the characteristic competitiveness of the New Englanders and the Yankee's mission; Peters makes the Gingertowners "uncomfortable, by making them wiser" (I, 9). Even after he is expelled from the village, he haunts the surrounding hills as squatter, a "sort of he-witch" (II, 4).

Neal's combination, in *Brother Jonathan*, of the New England village novel and the romance in three volumes is tethered to the historical romance, a genre which offered self-location to his present-day audience in the 1820s. Neal's narrator enacts this function on the story level, by depicting events in an undecided way and asking the reader to judge for herself. The novel is set "about one year before the 'Battle of Lexington,' a sharp skirmish between the New England or Yankee bushfighters, and his majesty's troops, who were sent over to keep the peace in the revolutionary war of North America" (I, 1). Neal here creates an ambiguity about the war; the reverent mention of "his majesty's troops who keep the peace" stands against the Yankees. The face of Jonathan Peters, the Yankee stranger, is ambivalent, depending on the light: "A shadow more, or less—a slight fluctuation of color—and [his face] would have been that of a rebel, or a patriot; a regicide, or a martyr" (I, 6). Neal thus responds to the fashionable pro-American depictions of the war with a complicated dialectic which leaves the interpretation of Peters as "rebel or patriot" to the reader.

Brother Jonathan articulates Neal's poetics of an American voice. Walter's troubles growing into manhood and discovering his secret heritage are represented in a distinct narrative strategy. In the pivotal scene when Walter almost dies in a spring freshet, Neal intermingles the narrator's observant commentary and Walter's emotional outrage, contrasting free indirect speech, direct speech, and stream-of-consciousness with the voice of reason offered by the narrator. As a child, Walter writes his name onto the rocks at this favorite dwelling space, claiming the wilderness for himself (I, 321). In the freshet, the rocks fall, and as Walter faints, he sees the stars falling (I, 329–33) in a total collapse of subjectivity: "Walter began to lose himself. At last in the tremendous tumult about him [. . .] he had no voice, no breath [. . .] his bodily power was gone—his hearing—his eye-sight—he had no hope" (I, 337). On the plot level, Walter is saved by his dog Panther's baying, which shatters his rapture; regarding the discourse level, the collapse of Walter's voice in the sublime of the freshet enacts a typical rite of passage, after which Walter emerges as revolutionary fighter and American man: "A new character came out on his forehead [. . .] a new light from his eyes [. . .] fuller of serious manhood" (I, 391; see also Schäfer 2017).

Neal's *Down-Easters* also offers a mixed bag of hero narrative cum community tableau, but the latter is more condensed than the Gingertowners' fate in *Brother Jonathan*. In the first half, *The Down-Easters* parades Yankee types aboard a ship going up North (a rendition of the transatlantic ship); the second abandons the Yankee travelers for a complicated gothic romance plot about womanizer George Middleton. The story begins on a steamship from Philadelphia to Baltimore in 1814, where the narrator Peter meets Middleton, a young plantation owner of Northern descent, the beautiful Quaker Elizabeth, and Atherton Gage, an obscure Yankee. Middleton has a conflicted heritage. Like Hale's Sidney Romilly, he grapples with reconciling his Southern childhood with his Northern education and values, but whereas Sidney is a born Yankee, Middleton inherits the identities of both sections from his parents. As his name indicates, he struggles for a middle ground between Northern self-restraint and Southern temper: "I discovered that he was born of a New-England mother [. . .] and that his father, a Georgia planter, [. . .] died in a duel, [. . .] and that after travelling in the south of Europe, he had been educated in the North for the very purpose of counteracting his fiery temper, and fortifying his brave lineage by other and better principles than he had imbibed in the South" (Neal 1833: I, 11–12; all subsequent references to this edition).

George's complicated past also includes a marriage to a Native American whom he left; this legacy renders impossible his relation with Elizabeth. In the course of the novel, George changes from dashing cavalier to haunted lunatic, due in equal parts to his Southern arrogance and to leaving his first wife. On the ship, not only Middleton but also Peter the narrator and the Yankee Gage compete for Elizabeth's favor. Peter wavers (he admires her, then refrains, then admires her again; see I, 10, 28). In the course of the story, both Peter and Gage tell stories about Middleton, meeting him time and again in New York ballrooms or the salon of Martha P—, Peter's love interest who eventually abandons him for Middleton. Amidst the jumble of love triangles, the narrator Peter remains opaque. The final part is told in epistolary form by Gage, who saves the traumatized Middleton after Elizabeth dies in his arms.

The Down-Easters is noteworthy not so much for its plot as for its commentary on the literary industry and its depiction of Yankee types. The Preface (I, iii–vii) and the metanarrative addition of the chapter "Catastrophe" (II, 110–11) at the end explicate Neal's literary agenda; he seeks to preserve "authentic" Yankeedom by embracing its absurdities. The Preface bemoans that, fifty years hence, the knowledge about the "business of life," the "speech, dress and general deportment," the "fire-side feelings, the every-day habits" will be lost to following generations (I, iii). The author proposes to record the "dialogue of the[ir] day" verbatim from the talker, a "rough sketch if you will, but trustworthy and characteristic, and all alive with individuality" (I, iii). His preference for linguistic and cultural authenticity opposes imagined and fictionalized renditions of North Americans in "quiet, sleepy, good-for-nothing book[s]" such as "British Classics hashed over" (I, iv).[47] In the same breath he lashes out at critics of vernacular literature:

> Tell me not that faithful representations of native character, which are neither intended for example nor offered for imitation, are of no use. They *are* of use. They bring strangers acquainted with what we are most anxious to conceal—the *truth*, and what is more, they bring us acquainted with ourselves, with our own peculiarities and our own faults. (I, iv)

Neal discards exemplum narratives alongside critically revered works of the American literati Cooper, Irving, and Charles Brockden Brown:

"their books are not American, though *they* are" (I, vi, emphasis added). Conversely, his own representation of "peculiar and [. . .] absurd" language and manners is useful: "the more absurd and the more peculiar, [. . .] they deserve to be portrayed," making New Englanders see their own faults and facilitating their "improvement" (I, vi, vii). Finally, to Neal, "truth" (read: authenticity) is more important than patriotic elevation. He closes the Preface by declaring that he will stick to "truth," even at the cost of "betraying" his country (I, vii).

In the chapter "Catastrophe," which follows the ending of *The Down-Easters*, Neal responds to his publisher's criticism "that I have left out the catastrophe" by bemoaning that "if I do not account for every man, woman and child I have brought upon the stage [. . .] nobody will ever give me credit for a *plot*" (II, 110). While the Preface expressed his ethnologic interest, the chapter "Catastrophe" deals with fictional conventions and reader expectation. He argues that "incidents *of themselves* are interesting in *real* life, unconnected though they are, with a story before and a story after them" (II, 110). He tells readers hoping for closure that "every mother's son, herein before mentioned, is alive now, in good health and spirits, save some three or four, who have either married outright or died a natural death" (II, 111)—except for the hero Middleton and the marginal Yankee figure Obadiah:

> Middleton is believed to be a Methodist preacher who shall be nameless; and as for Obadiah, from all that I can gather, I am half inclined to think, though I do not know of a certainty, that he is now figuring away at Washington under the name of Major Jack Downing. [. . .] New York, October 1st, 1833. (II, 111)

In the end, Neal snubs both his readers and his publisher. In one stroke, he turns the morally decrepit Middleton into a clergyman and the New Englander Obadiah into the fictional celebrity Major Jack Downing.[48] Read together, the Preface and "Catastrophe" articulate a Yankee twist to his high-flying agenda. On the one hand, he lists authenticity and expertise as the desiderata for a yet-to-be-fathomed "American" literature. On the other hand, he admits to treading the thin line between fact and fiction himself when he creates such fabulous afterlives for his characters.

This is spelled out in the gallery of Yankee figures exhibited in the opening of *The Down-Easters*. Aboard the steamship, the narrator meets an uncanny (and nameless) Yankee peddler, the swappers and country bumpkins Amos and Obadiah, and two educated Bostonian literati. The first Yankee Peter meets is the mysterious "stiff, straight, bony-looking Down Easter, with a straw hat, high cheek-bones, a nose like a sun-dial, and the sharpest mouth you ever saw in a domesticated Yankee" (I, 3). This Yankee scares the narrator with threats and riddles he cannot solve (I, 12);[49] he paces back and forth on the deck, swiping his coat tails across the passengers' faces (I, 7) and raving in unintelligible dialect monologues of which "I couldn't make out one word in forty" (I, 13), and finally he starts selling quack medicine (I, 16, 17). The narrator compares the man to a train:

> O that you could see him! His newly paved boots falling on the deck at every step like a *machine* driving piles, or a beetle shod with sole-leather; and his pockets *rattling as he drove*, hitting first one person and then another, like a *newly-freighted waggon* finding its way downhill backwards without a driver. (I, 18, emphasis added)

A creation of the literature of the age, the man-machine Down Easter literally makes a stir of print products, "till every thing was in motion about him—leaves, pamphlets, dust, ribbons, and newspapers" (I, 4), To this jumble of the literary imaginary, the narrator adds his own spectacular Yankee sketch. He makes him look grotesque, especially his disfigured nose, "like a sword-fish" (I, 11), commenting: "I never did see such a nose!—it was about the color and very much the size of a long-necked winter-squash—the more I saw of it the more I was troubled, and I saw more of it every time I looked that way—no, no, I never did see such a nose!" (I, 21). In one scene, the uncanny Yankee is challenged to a humbugging game by another Down Easter, but the narrator refrains from description, explaining that

> [t]here is no describing his look or manners; both must be left to the reader's imagination after all, if he has never happened to see a live Yankee about to engage another at a game of poke-fun, as they call it where it flourishes most. Didn't you never hear tell o'them air creuked sticks they cut away down-east—so creuked they wun't lay still—hey? (I, 8)

The question remains how the reader should imagine something she is not familiar with ("Didn't you never hear tell [. . .]?"). However, the fantasy part is filled in at the end of the quotation, when the narrator refers to the Yankee's whittling down the "creuked" (crooked) sticks while storytelling. As a leisure activity, "cutting" or "whittling away" at little sticks symbolizes Yankee storytelling. The teller whittles while talking, adding action to his words.

Yet both the storytelling and the whittling are idle; they lead to nothing—in the end, the stick is gone and the story comes to no closure. The crooked sticks that don't lie still stand for the two Yankees who are word-haggling each other. They typically answer each question with a question in return (see e.g. I, 3, 8, 47). Neal repeats the motif several times; later, a Yankee uses a knife, a "ninepenny *whittler*, as he called [it]" (I, 73; see also Cooper 2003 on the whittling boy).

Whittling is a central motif of Yankee mannerisms in the novel. A little later, the Yankee swapper Obadiah asks another Down Easter "if he could whittle against the wind," trying to get him to hand over his knife and trade with him. The whittler will not be tricked into parting with his knife, however. His artistry in storytelling equals his whittling expertise, even though the product seems fantastically delicate. He has been transforming a piece of soft pine wood "into forty successive shapes," finally into a "miniature snuff-box with a moveable cover and a perfect hinge, cut out of the solid wood" (I, 80).

The panoply of Yankee types onboard the ship also includes a Bostonian and an "educated and travelled Yankee." The narrator ridicules both. The Bostonian's hyperbolic language feigns superiority ("[in Boston], every shop is a *store*, every stick a *pole*, every stone a *rock*, every stall a *factory*, and every goose a *swan*," I, 26). The Bostonian is a Whig literary critic, who "dabbled in literature, puffed poetry for the *North American Review*, and the *North American Review* for the newspapers" (ibid.). He lets on that he "makes poetry" (I, 27) and fills in his own writings with words from a volume captioned "Lines *beneath* a Nosegay" (I, 28), a pun on the English poet John Carter Allen's ode "Lines in Return for a Nosegay" (1822). "Nosegay" denotes the gift of a small flower bouquet; where the English poem offers a "return" for this gift, the Bostonian's "lines *beneath* a nosegay" indicates exchanging whispers or more savory gestures. Neal's Boston literati deflate the literary industry and the critical impact of the *North American Review*.

The Bostonian's companion, an "educated Yankee," is "cold, supercilious, and stiff, [. . .] standing like [a] statue and [. . .] talking like a book" (I, 26). The two represent "a fair specimen of [. . .] the talented and gifted of their several classes" (ibid.), their distinction tied to behavior and speech. The narrator describes the Bostonian's avoidance of "typical" New England words, such as "I guess." This is replaced by ten other verbs, among which the economic expression of Yankee thrift, "I calculate," ranges last. Try as they might, however, the Boston literati are easily detected, by

> talking through the nose in jets, by whimpering at the end of a long sentence, and by saying [. . .] Yankeeism[s], while counterfeiting the manners and speech of the South, and affecting to pity his New England brethren for their strongly-marked and hopeless barbarism of language and behavior—there! That'll do for the present! (I, 27)

The narrator's diatribe accuses urban and educated Yankees of contorting New England identity: "the rudest Yankee will employ the word guess after the manner of the best old English authors; while the educated Yankee and the Southerner, will resort to [. . .] bastard and absurd phraseology" (I, 27). Neal attributes "truth" and "individuality" to the country bumpkins Amos and Obadiah. During a dinner conversation, they sketch out their home in Yankeeland with fantastical tall tale humor, as the place "'where a cow an' a caff an' a calico gown is a gal's portion [. . .]; where a potater patch with cracks in't so wide, that the grass-hoppers are picked up at the bottom by handfuls—all their necks broke trying to jump over—is a portion for the eldest son'" (I, 103).[50]

Neal depicts the "true Yankees" as rural shrewd types. Obadiah and Amos are scheming swappers who try to get the narrator's watch in a con game (I, 82–4). The narrator resolves the swapping conversation by calling on an umpire and tricking both the swapper Obadiah and the umpire Amos (I, 86). Finally, he agrees to buy the two rascals dinner. They are shocked when he claims he is a native New Englander, and feel sorry for "having preyed upon their own kith and kin" (I, 109–10). Later, they heroically save a drowning girl, while Middleton and the narrator look on cowardly. Amos and Obadiah are a comic hero version of the chorus who incessantly comment on every little action ("'Obadiah! Obadiah! I've gut her, by jingo!'", I, 118).

Neal's gallery of Down Easters is completed by Atherton Gage. Gage is described enthusiastically as "a New Englander of the right sort; a full-blooded, old-fashioned Yankee"; he is "self-assured," "easy," and "natural" (I, 29). He plays tricks on others but no one bears a grudge because of his charming manner. Gage's humor is unspoiled by "professional wit" pretense, or education. The narrator shows Gage's capacity for "reasoning" in two debates among the travelers, on Quaker religion (ending in Gage's cleverly veiled admiration for Elizabeth) and about the pronunciation of the word "tzar," which grows into a discussion of republican superiority over monarchy (see I, 33–50). In both instances, Gage proves himself a smart but not aloof discussant who defends a nationalist stance. The debates are presented like a boxing match which ends in a knock-out ("Time! Time! And the adversary not being able to come up, Gage untied his handkerchief and jumped over the ropes," I, 55).

According to Obediah, Gage is a "rayal Yankee," the son of "Jerry P. R. Gage of Quamphegan, best wrastler [sic] in New England" (I, 62), and thus a match for Davy Crockett.[51] In the tableau of Yankees, Gage serves as a kind of alter ego to the narrator. Despite his legendary heritage, he remains largely nondescript, like the Yankee narrator Peter himself. Gage is smart and strong and respected by the narrator. The relationship between the two is strangely undeveloped, yet Gage and Peter, these two obscure and larger-than-life Down Easters,[52] are posited against Middleton, who fails to reconcile his split heritage.

In *The Down-Easters*, Neal offers fractions of Yankeedom, ranging from the heroic "rayal Yankee" Gage and the struggling romance hero Middleton to the nondescript Yankee narrator with authorial contours, whose Yankee storytelling whittles the romance plot down to trifles. Like many other commentators of his day, Neal attributes sectional conflict to the clash between the Southern "hot temper" and Northern coolness. At the same time, however, Neal pluralizes this monolithic image of the Yankees. His preference for an unspoiled country schemer like Obadiah over the learned and "statue-like" urban Yankee attacks the Whig elites, and pins "authentic" Yankeedom onto a live body. Neal's "rayal Yankee" is alive and kicking, a rendition of the stage Yankee with his dialect and odd behavior (as in Obadiah and Amos), his legendary superhero powers (as in Gage's wrestler father), and his uncanny peddler persona (as in the Down Easter). Neal also dabbles in the reactions these Yankee figures inspire. The narrator is scared by the Down Easter and awed by Gage's discussion skills ("Fifty to one for Gage—all to nothing!", I, 54). In the opening chapters, he often smiles or even laughs "till my sides ached" (see e.g. I, 9, 79). His Yankees portray the truth of absurdities unspoiled by learning and affectation. Only the "real" ones evoke "real" feeling, like terror, laughter, and awe. Neal's American character is ultimately relational. Whittling and storytelling, pacing the deck and talking, swapping, and republican debates all happen in the public sphere aboard the ship. They engage the other travelers and the readers alike and discourage a neutral observer's position. Neal's Americans only come alive through interaction with an audience; when put in the museum of anthropological interest, they are "dead as a door knob."

Compared with *Brother Jonathan*, *The Down-Easters* toys deliberately with concepts of national and Yankee character. The novels also differ regarding coherence; *The Down-Easters*' Yankee gallery is far more removed from the narrator's love turmoils than the depiction of the Gingertown community from Walter Harwood's growing into adulthood. When read together, the two novels articulate Neal's poetics of Yankee storytelling. Both address a recent phase in the U.S. past and shatter a simplistic reading of regional identity, uttering a critique of colonial complacency, Whiggish learning, and the postcolonial dialectic between an urban and political center (New York and Boston) and a periphery. Instead, Neal proposes a logic of Yankee performance on the road (or on the boat), in which American revolutionary fighters and Yankee storytellers are formed through travel and interaction. Set in 1814, the year of the Hartford Convention, Neal's gallery of fictional Yankees draws from the types of the stage Yankee, the Yankee peddler, and the country bumpkin. He therefore discards European literary models and argues that, while everyone knows the Yankee to be a fantastical creature, he embodies New England influence.

The concluding part of this chapter brings the whittling, storytelling Yankees back home. The New England hearth, as origin of Yankee types, schoolteachers, and peddlers, fabricates the Yankee homespun. In this setup, the hearth in the New England household symbolizes the family as smallest unit of community organization. Gossett and Bardes maintain that the home is the basis of nation-building: "Virtue is seen as developing sequentially through the three levels of community organization—family, village, country" (1985: 19). The polysemous concept of the Yankee homespun uses female virtue as a platform for the male Yankee in the public sphere, catering to an image of U.S. masculine citizenry rendered in storytelling. I explore the linkage between the republican home with Yankee yarnspinning in the fabrication of stories and the weaving and wearing of homespun cloth.

Yankee Homespun

The success of Sarah Hale's *Northwood* and its publication history in two editions thirty years apart illustrates the positioning of New England in nineteenth-century cultural politics. In the second edition, Hale spelled out her anti-abolitionist agenda and changed the epigraphs.[53] The first edition featured two: the first, "He who loves not his country, can love nothing," was maintained in the 1852 edition; the second one was dropped: "Home is the resort of love, of joy, of peace and plenty, where supporting and supported, polished friends and dear relations mingle into bliss." The concept of "home" is a central motif throughout the novel in both editions, but the 1852 edition shifts this towards resolving sectional conflict, foreshadowing Abraham Lincoln's 1858 dictum that "A house divided against itself cannot stand." Hale also changed the subtitle, from "A Tale of New England" to "Life North and South, Showing the True Character of Both." The coupling of hearth and *patria* in the first edition illustrates the imaginary construction of a New England home in the 1820s; the second edition's focus on a unified homeland defends the embattled Union against the centrifugal force of Northern abolitionism.

In *Northwood*, Hale describes "home" as intellectual and sentimental harbor. Sidney's spiritual struggle for his Northern heritage is echoed in the feelings of warmth and comfort, which Hale evokes repeatedly with the central motif of the Romilly fireplace ablaze. The fire of his home is the first thing Sidney sees when returning to Northwood; a "strong gleam, as a blaze from a fire, illuminated the windows" (59). The Romilly home is described from the outside, with its landscaped garden and domestic trees, but its inside is also laid out as the model home of the American family, centering on the mantelpiece, ornamented with an American bald eagle,

> his head powdered with stars, his body streaked with white and red alternately, his crooked talons grasping an olive branch and a bundle of arrows; this significantly declaring, that although he loved peace, he was prepared for war; and in his beak he held a scroll, inscribed with the talisman of American liberty and power—*E pluribus unum*. (60)

Around this altar of American national symbols, the family is grouped on many occasions, offering to Sidney a sense of belonging: "pleasure has been the idol of my pursuit; and I have [. . .] sought it in every place except where alone it is to be found—in a virtuous home" (73).

The light of the fire also comforts visitors like Frankford. When he approaches the doctor's house, he is struck by its downbeat looks, but "when the door opened, the gentleman found that the cheerlessness was all without. The doctor ushered them into his parlor, where a rousing fire, carpeted floor, and cushioned chairs, promised them all of comfort an Englishman could desire" (153). Frankford's look around the parlor starts with the "rousing fire," sweeping from the light to the floor and chairs upon which the visitor is invited to rest. The fire's welcoming atmosphere is frequently contrasted against the cold New England winter. When Sidney struggles through the snow to get to the schoolhouse, he is first embarrassingly overtaken by his students. But upon his arrival, he finds in the schoolhouse a "comfortable room, warm fire, and smiling faces to welcome him; and a sensation of pleasure, hitherto unknown, swelled in his bosom when he saw them all waiting his nod" (281). Yet even the fire's welcoming atmosphere can be comically overdone—as in the fire which farmer Merrill makes to welcome his benefactor Sidney at his half-finished farmhouse:

> A right fire shone through the small windows and open door as they drove up [. . .] [Merrill] ushered them into the only finished room [. . .] They formed a circle around a fire that literally blazed like a furnace. Mr. Merrill, thinking one essential rite of hospitality in such a cold night was to provide a good fire for his guests, had contrived [. . .] to have on their arrival what might very well represent a bonfire. The strong light displayed the neat room and furniture, bought for use not show, to the best advantage, every article looking as clean as if it were under the superintendence of those fairies who of yore presided over the department of the tidy housewife. [. . .] Over the mantelpiece, suspended on a wire hook, hung a file of newspapers, and beside them an almanac. (286–7)

Merrill's is a home in the making. It has all the important features, starting with the fireplace, but he has to curb his enthusiasm. Again, the light of the fire welcomes the visitors from the outside before the host himself does, but it resembles an industrial "furnace" (too hot) and an outdoor "bonfire" (too bright). Hale's ideal fire is the heartwarming ideological and physical core of the New England home.[54]

In *Northwood*, the Romillys gather for family rituals, including a wedding, a funeral, and a Thanksgiving dinner. Squire Romilly explains the ritual to Frankford as a cultural practice, stressing its sentimental, family-strengthening value, and recommends that it become a national practice.[55] During these family rituals, Hale also addresses the family dress codes and attire. For the wedding, Squire Romilly "was arrayed in a suit of black, *home made* merino, and Silas in one of deep blue—*bran* [sic] new for the wedding. Mrs. Romilly wore a black satin dress, Lucy a changeable silk, and the children looked not only neat, but handsomely attired" (81). At the Thanksgiving dinner table, they "were all arrayed in their best; the young ladies in white, the married in silks or crapes [sic], and the men mostly in suits of dark-colored cloth, which, although *homespun*, would not, in some instances, have suffered much by comparison with foreign manufacture" (104, emphasis in original). The clothes are part and parcel of the Romillys' presentation of home, as the graphic emphasis of "home made" and "homespun" underlines. The family is recognizable by their homespun dress. It is exquisite in quality and fit for international comparison (see below), and bears witness to their economic and spiritual wealth. Mrs. Romilly produces the homespun in diligent fulfillment of her housewife duties. Hale uses the family to parade the ideological meaning of the "homespun," but she goes to greater detail when the travelers Sidney and Frankford meet their first "genuine Yankee" on their way to Northwood. Sidney recognizes him because of his dress:

> He was habited in a dark colored suit, made of what is termed "home manufactured," for the celebrated Lucretia herself could not spin with a more becoming grace than *did*, at that time, the fair wives and daughters of New England farmers; and not to keep their families comfortably clothed, would have reflected great discredit on their industry, and consequently on their characters. His clothes were fitted nearly in the London fashion, [. . .] the "fashions" are [. . .] more universally followed throughout the United States, than by any other nation of the world. [. . .] his array [. . .] appeared to unite comfort and economy with a tolerable degree of taste, and showed the wearer was one who thought something of himself and meant to appear in such a manner as to claim attention and respect from others. (50, emphasis in original)

The narrator compares the New England wives and daughters to the virtuous housewife in the narrative of "The Rape of Lucretia,"[56] who commits suicide after she is raped. Lucretia weaves her virtue and chastity into her fine linens, an ideal Hale extends to the New England women and republican mothers, who would risk "discredit on their industry, and consequently on their characters" if they failed to keep their family clothed. To the virtue of American homespun, Hale adds its fashionableness and its formative potential: homespun distinguishes its wearer and supports his self-image. The "genuine Yankee" thinks highly of himself and hopes to make an impression with his dress; he represents a version of the eponymous self-fashioned American. Hale's homespun commands "attention" and "respect"; its sincerity clashes with the "puffing consequence" of Americans Sidney complains about (245). While she acknowledges the importance of self-presentation to others, Hale prefers dress over talk and materiality over words.

The concept of the homespun is instrumental in the making of U.S. national myths. Laurel Thatcher Ulrich's *The Age of Homespun* (2001) unfolds a textile history of the U.S. between the 1670s and the 1840s, focusing on everyday domestic and working-class culture, along the lines of orator Horace Bushnell's 1851 eulogy on the end of "The Age of the Homespun" (Bushnell 1864). In colonial times, homespun clothes symbolized American political and economic independence. As Michael Zakim has shown, the homespun evolved from a colonial coarse "dress of honesty" (2001: 1559) to evidence of industrial progress. Drawing on the linkage of a domestic textile production with a national economy, Zakim traces the homespun's transition from manufactured production to the industrial nation state. For instance, George Washington's choice of a homespun coat from the Hartford Wool Company at his inauguration was applauded and ushered in a new phase for the homespun as readymade cloth. The *Gazette of the United States* raved about it because it "was so fine a Fabric, and so Handsomely finished, that it was universally mistaken for a foreign manufactured superfine cloth" (qtd. in Zakim 2001: 1567). Whereas before, the homespun's simplicity had projected a frugal self-image, this changed in the Early Republic, when the importation of Merino wool improved the quality (see also Hale's luxurious Merino wool attire, 81).

By the 1830s, textiles were no longer produced at home, but while "[t]he homespun era was officially over" (Zakim 2001: 1573), its association with the nation's hearth remained in place, as I argue below. Building on Zakim's and Ulrich's historical studies, I explore the polysemous meaning of the term in relation to storytelling in the texts examined here. The homespun was used for the "invention of tradition" (Hobsbawm and Granger 1983) in Bushnell's "The Age of the Homespun," a speech held at Litchfield at the state centennial celebration of Connecticut in 1851. Bushnell's speech creates a "usable past" (Matthews 1978) in Whiggish manner, using metaphors of organic growth instead of incendiary discourse when discussing the American Revolution. Its narrative of New England progress, from the nostalgic "age of the homespun" to the industrial present, is built around the biblical story of King Lemuel's wife (Proverbs 31; see Bushnell 1864: 370–1).[57] It professedly honors the unsung (because unrecorded) memory of the "humble" Litchfield forbears (373), described as

> the sturdy kings of Homespun, who climbed among these hills, with their axes, to cut away room for their cabins and for family prayers, and so for the good future to come. [. . .] their sons, who foddered

their cattle on the snows, and built stone-fences while the corn was sprouting in the hills, getting ready, in that way, to send a boy or two to college. [. . .] the good housewives that made coats, every year, [. . .] for their children's body, and lined their memory with catechism. [. . .] Who they are by name we cannot tell [. . .] enough that they are the king Lemuels and their queens, of the good old time gone by—kings and queens of Homespun, out of whom we draw our royal lineage. (Ibid. 374–5)

Bushnell ennobles the offspring of the unknown dead, calling on the Litchfielders to preserve a tradition they hardly know, transforming from female carework to industry, "from mother and daughter power to water and steam-power" (376). The community is shown in three tableaux: the family grouped around a blazing fire; the village school; and, finally, the meeting house. Bushnell's version of the family "winter's fire" fuelled by conviviality echoes Hale's: "Not the stove, but the fire, the brightly blazing, hospitable fire. In the early dusk, the home circle is drawn more closely and quietly around it"; as more friendly neighbors are welcomed into the circle, "a new stick [is] added for every guest. There is no restraint, no affectation of style. They tell stories, they laugh, they sing" (381). The homespun community is "back of the world," geographically, economically, and intellectually:

> [T]he society of the homespun age [. . .] was not that society that puts one in connection with the great world of letters, or fashion, or power, raising as much the level of his consciousness and the scale and style of his action; but it was society back of the world, in the sacred retreats of natural feeling, truth and piety. (Ibid. 382)

Bushnell's age of homespun sowed "small seeds" (ibid. 396) that invisibly germinated and have a residual effect in the present. From this invisible thread originate the traits that unite the Litchfield community in common toil: thrift and the "habit of economy [. . .] [H]arnessed [all] together, into the producing process, young and old, male and female, from the boy [. . .] to the grandmother [. . .] they had no conception of squandering lightly what they all had been at work, thread by thread, and grain by grain, to produce" (ibid. 394–5).

Bushnell's kings and queens of the homespun channel Hale's lords of the soil; they are ennobled by their work, and the riches they pass down to their heirs are "merit and patience, [and] integrity before God and men" (ibid. 397). By 1850, the homespun defines a regional identity and chimes in with national myths. Before an audience that included people returning from settlements out West (Ulrich 2001: 12), Bushnell rehearses the tropes of exceptionalism and manifest destiny. His jeremiad cautions his Litchfield listeners to keep calm and continue sowing the "small seeds," even though first signs of industrial expansion after a dire period might seduce them to do otherwise.

Since the growing New England textile industry brought women to the spinning wheel and into the professional workplace (Ulrich 2001: 7–8), the imageries of republican motherhood and domestic labor done by women had to be reconciled. After all, the production of a homespun linen shirt required a sixteen-month work cycle and a broad range of skills, technologies, and resources (Zakim 2003: 15). Bushnell obscures the role of women in the industrial present of the Litchfield textile industry and establishes his "kings and queens" of old in the spheres model, with the men breaking the ground and taming the wilderness, and the women lining their children's clothes "with the catechism" (Bushnell 1864: 375). Bushnell's sources from Livius and Proverbs 31 affirm male superiority and control of the female reproductive organs. Similarly, Sarah Hale uses the homespun to plead the housewife's competence. She obscures the labor part and shows only the results of the Romilly women's toiling, the neatly dressed family celebrating holidays.[58]

Produced by the republican mother and the New England home, the homespun adorned the male citizens' bodies and the national economy and symbolized transatlantic power play and trade conflicts. With the Jacksonian government's bolstering of the domestic industry with tariffs on foreign exports and imports, the homespun expressed partisanship of Northern protective policies. Consequently, the Southerners in Greene's *A Yankee Among the Nullifiers* pride themselves on sporting imported attire. In a vignette, a "hot nullifier" brags to a Yankee: "'I would go bareheaded and barebacked till the end of time, sooner than I would wear a coat made of American cloth, or a hat manufactured in an American shop.'" In response, the Yankee claims that he himself produced the Southerner's coat and hat in a Northern manufacture, and that he also printed the fake coat label "Bond Street London" (Greene 1833: 39–41). The poor Southerner realizes he has been doubly tricked, since the Yankee homespun is indistinguishable from London fashion, and he paid an outrageous price. The homespun here condenses sectional conflict between fancy Southerners and entrepreneurial Yankees.[59]

John Neal's *Brother Jonathan, or The New Englanders* uses the homespun to devise a sentimental nostalgic framework for staging an unsentimental masculinist founding character. The temper of the New Englanders shows "little or no heart," since "[e]verything is a matter of serious calculation [. . .] They abound in virtues [. . .] and a provokingly sober business-like way of doing matters, which would be 'sentimental,' or affecting, if they were done by any other people, under heaven; or, in any other way, under heaven" (154–6). Conversely, the homespun becomes the metaphor for inspiring patriotic sentiment and historical self-positioning for Neal's readers in the 1820s.

As I argued above, in *Brother Jonathan*, Neal argues that the Revolution changes the face of individuals and communities. Therefore, events that are historically significant and ones that appear mundane or absurd are to be read together (notwithstanding Hazlitt's criticism of Neal "running riot" on narrative detail, qtd. in Pethers 2012: 29). Two such interlinked events are the scandal around Squire Winslow's coat and the Gingertown town meeting about the Boston Tea Party, linked through the homespun.

The narrator opens the chapter about the scandal surrounding Winslow's coat with an elaborate reflection on the farmers' "behavior, dress and appearance," contrasting the resilience of a colonial "go-to meeting coat" of "fifty years ago" with the short-lived fashions of country youths on the brink of becoming revolutionary "Yankee bushfighters" (147, 148). In colonial days, he says, the coat would have been passed on, recycled in the family dye-pot, "outlast[ing] several generations of substantial American farmers." After serving as a coat (in "long and short—breeches and waistcoat—double and single breasted, with and without flaps," 149), it would go through a series of "transmigrations" as "pin cushions, coverlets, or carpets." Nowadays, however, the narrator sighs, "The country people are quite as extravagant, fashionable and foolish as they can be" (ibid.). Against this coat of the colonial days, Winslow's new and fancy calico waistcoat provokes a scandal, and he is called to trial "for having appeared with certain outlandish finery on the Lord's day, contrary to the articles of association" (151). The outrageous ensemble is described thus:

> The corporal wore, beside [the coat], in all weathers [. . .] a heavy spotted swandown jacket, which had also been the property of one or two progenitors—under another of chintz, flowered all over, and a pair of nankeen pantaloons, rather tighter than his own skin—of a burning flesh color; which altogether—being a good deal too tight, and a little too short for him—were quite an abomination to the maiden lady [. . .] who, whenever she spoke to him, always turned away her head. (149)

The many jackets opposite the skin-tight pants contort Winslow's body shape. He is foppishly overdressed in flowered cloth and quasi-naked from the waist down. The narrator fears that the revealing tightness may corrupt the lady's virtue; however, the frivolous fashion does not render it less manly. In the same breath, the narrator corrects himself:

> Yet—yet—corporal Winslow, awkward as he was, and stupid as he appeared, in these absurd habiliments, [. . .] was one of the very men who did the heavy business of the American Revolution. Would it have been as well done, think you—you, his countrymen of this age, if he had been brought up, as you are, in ruffles and gloves, purple and fine linen? After a little time, this very man was remarkable for his bold, free, military carriage; so easy is it, for a *man*, to be made any thing of, and of so little substantial disadvantage is that rude, awkward manner, which the country people are so anxious to throw off—to their destruction, always. (150, emphasis in original)

Winslow's "awkward" and "stupid" dress pales in comparison to his heroic contribution to the Revolution; the dress does not make the man. Neal's nostalgic view of the colonial period employs settler colonial fantasies of spontaneous nation-building in the threshold phase. The New Englanders "come out of the woods" to fight in the war and to become "instantaneously—as it were, by inspiration—soldiers, orators and statesmen" (15). Like in *The Down-Easters*, the "real" Yankees are the backwoods people, whose "cyphering temper" enables them to play any given role (154). In the coat scandal, awkwardness and poor taste indicate backwoods demeanor and the Yankee's ability to transform "by inspiration" into a community servant. The narrator emphasizes Winslow's manliness to his readers of the 1820s, whose rearing in "ruffles and gloves, purple and fine linen" has softened them in comparison.

This chapter of the novel mingles various fashion stories. First, the narrator tells his readers about the olden days; then Winslow, in self-defense, tells the coat's homespun story in a long, winding monologue; and finally, Jonathan Peters, the stranger, appeals to the Gingertowners to join the rebellion, using Winslow and his coat as a shining example:

> "[B]ehold this man! A giant; a Goliath—able to make head, alone, [. . .] against a great multitude of ordinary men. Behold him—a strong man; a mighty man—casing his broadchest, not with a harness of iron—but with a breast-plate of painted cotton; wearing a badge of servitude—

openly—bravely—before the people—into the house of the Lord—I would rather see a sister of mine [. . .] swathed in her burial sheet, a son of mine [. . .] dead upon the scaffold [. . .] than clothed in a material spun by the fingers of them that have become to us, and our little ones, even what the Egyptians were to the people of God, in their bondage [. . .] Hewers of wood, and drawers of water—slaves and bondmen—have we been all our lives long." (162–3)

Even though the virtuous spinning housewife gets no mention here, Peters's mention of "the Egyptians" casts the English as biblical oppressors of God's chosen people. He claims that freedom from oppression entails freedom from English clothes; the revolutionary sacrifice demands not only heroic death, but also wearing homespun habiliments.

Peters uses the outrage over Winslow's coat to brand him a Yankee hero whose fancy dress exceeds any military uniform. The coat may only be a cotton breast-plate, but as a product of the colonies, it constitutes and ornaments the revolutionary body and casts the citizen-soldier of the republic: an American in American dress. To emphasize the scenario of heroism and historical perspective, Neal combines two telling scenarios, diegetic and extradiegetic, as well as two rhetoric modes, the comic and the epic. With this concoction, Neal advertises the concept of the "homespun," designating both U.S.-fabricated cloth and the "down east" country folk as original homespun characters.

Neal's layering of meanings onto the homespun articulates the material experience of living in America: Winslow's story of how he got the coat not only tells the coat's history, it also performs Yankee homespun character through storytelling and reiterates Yankee trickery in action. Before the community court, Winslow provokes the jury by answering their questions with questions in return; when he is pressed to testify about his coat, he insists on "'tell[ing] my story arter my own way'" (153). Like the scary Yankee peddler in *The Down-Easters*, Winslow gets into a specific storytelling posture, "dropping his head; leaning over on one side with his right foot forward; and swaying his ponderous body, like a schoolboy, repeating his lesson" (156). Winslow's long, winding story (156–60) boils down to a grotesque face-off between him and the salesman, in which Winslow pretends to keep his cool by whistling *Yankee Doodle* (158). The two Yankees duel each other with the weapons of Yankee business conduct, first by verbal insults ("you don't know a pitch-pine hay-mow from a sugar maple tree," 156) and by showing off the money they carry in their pockets. In the end, Winslow's telling is interrupted by Peters's call to revolutionary action, and it remains unclear how he finally obtained the scandalous homespun jacket. We are left to wonder if Winslow, the country bumpkin, has been tricked by the salesman or vice versa in a typical instance of Yankee ambiguity. As the story peters off, the trial also falls apart; Winslow's voice is drowned out as the audience gets interested in something else, due to his poor performance as storyteller and yarn-spinner, which saves him from trial.

As my readings show, storytelling is the cultural practice of Yankeedom; it doubles the narrative scenario of literary texts and draws attention to narrative construction and progression, and to reader expectations. Neal's story about the scandalous coat takes a characteristic turn; after talking elaborately about old coats and new coats, and about Winslow's many jackets and his barely-there pants, he never provides further detail about the coat itself, but only remarks: "We have alluded once to the calico waistcoat in which he appeared before the preacher" (150). Just as the Gingertowners who put Winslow to trial are tricked by his Yankee shrewdness, the reader of Neal's novel is duped by the narrator, and the coat itself becomes a red herring, all the rage in Gingertown, but really to no avail for the story the narrator wants to tell.

In the course of the nineteenth century, the homespun advanced from family enterprise to "male prerogative" (Zakim 2003: 2), an articulation of a nationalist politics in the public sphere. By 1850, when the homespun had been replaced by the ready-made, the term transitioned into the realm of New England character and storytelling. The homespun links fashion and storytelling as tools for performing citizenship and national character. Both are subjected to an economy of performance and recognition; both appear coarse at first sight but cloak a second message, about producing one's own clothes independently and about "shaving" an audience who expect this deceit. Finally, by 1830, the usage of "homespun" for domestic textiles became anachronistic. The homespun-as-dress was pastoralized just like New England as a whole, and the homespun-as-storytelling travelled from the domestic space to the national entertainment industry. The homespun transitions from the family circle into the arena of national character performance and the American spinner of Yankee yarns, who is venerated by an audience expecting to be "shaved" for their money's worth.

This economy of storytelling is illustrated, for instance, in *The Hypocrite*, which includes a vignette about the Yankee schoolteacher David returning home to "one of those quiet, delightful villages in

Massachusetts" (Aesop 1844: 36). David poses as a downeaster by (over) using typical expressions italicized in the text ("I guess," "I calculate," 70). The first person he meets is the nosy innkeeper Boniface, who inquires about news from "down east" (ibid.). Since the innkeeper is a downeaster himself, he hardly needs to ask for news from the neighborhood. His question expresses the imaginary quality of "downeast" as a region where stories are told in a particular way. David, who poses as a travelling peddler "in the bookworm business" (70), complies happily. He tells the innkeeper that "'The bridge at Bellows Falls has tumbled over into the Connecticut river [. . .] It went off with a crash, one night last week, just as a tin peddler and his wagon had—,' 'Do tell!'" (70–1). The innkeeper is impatient to hear the story at the first mention of the "tin peddler." David's story is a typical Yankee yarn, and thus the narrative focus rests on the listener's indulgence rather than the content:

> "Why, you see," said I; "the pedler's wagon had one horse in it, and the night being extremely dark when he arrived at the bridge, the peddler did not see its condition; but the horse did; and this horse, being an old traveler, took the middle plank, which brought the wheels of the wagon on the two other planks, for the bridge had no floor, and in this manner, without the pedler's knowing anything of his danger, he went over safe."
>
> During this sentence, Boniface had gradually raised his arms, and opened his mouth and eyes, just like a man expecting every instant to tumble into the gulf below; but when I concluded with "went over safe," he fell back on the bench, with a long breath, exclaiming, "Wasn't that a darnation escape, I tell you? But what made the bridge fall?"
>
> "Why, they had just put up the skeleton of the bridge, and had not time to stay it, when the freshet caused by the great shower of the same afternoon carried the whole away."
>
> The news told, there was some little pause, when Boniface observed, "Beaint you somewhat hungry, traveler?" (Aesop 1844: 71)

The suspense shows in Boniface's physical reactions. The innkeeper lifts his arms, rises out of his seat, and opens his mouth and eyes wide; his disappointment at the punchline inverts this movement: He "fell back on the bench" and, after being breathless before, now asks about the solution "with a long breath." To the underwhelming ending to the story (the bridge was swept away), he does not react at all. The telling and deadpan ending show the Yankee "in action."

In *A Yankee Among the Nullifiers*, the plot of Elnathan's toils in the South is nearly lost in a host of stories inserted into each other like *matryoshka* dolls. The Southern narrator of the episode about the homespun coat from Bond Street, London, introduces his story as follows:

> "This reminds me," he said, "of a story, which I have before related, and which I understand by some means or other found its way into the *New York Citizen*. How it got there I will not pretend to say; unless it was by some speculator in Yankee notions, who chanced to hear me relate it. But because my story has been unluckily filched and peddled off, it is no reason why I should not tell it to the present company." (Greene 1833: 42–3)

Stories are traded as commodities, as "Yankee notions," "stolen" from the Southern teller's lips and "peddled off" to a magazine by a smart "speculator," maybe even a Yankee peddler. The cultural value of these vignettes is measured by their dissemination; the teller is proud to read his anecdote in the *New York Citizen*, despite the "unlucky" breach of copyright by the Yankee peddler who sold it (and given the Nullifiers' general stupidity in Greene's text, the suggestion here is that the story is not the Southerner's and he is falsely taking all the credit). After this exposition, the story's actual content about the homespun coat reverberates on the metanarrative level: "homespun" is not only the perfectly manufactured coat the Southerner mistakes for London quality, but also the story itself, which gets pirated by yet another smart Yankee.

The short anecdote "Yankee Homespun" from Thomas Chandler Haliburton's collection *Traits of American Humor* (1852) projects the meaning of the homespun onto the storytelling scenario:

> Yankee Homespun
> "When I lived in Maine," said Uncle Ezra, "I helped to break up a new piece of ground; we got the wood off in the winter, and early in the spring we begun ploughing on't. It was so consarned rocky that we had to get forty yoke of oxen to one plough—we did faith—and I held that plough more'n a week; I thought I should die. It e'en a most killed me, I vow. Why one day I was hold'n, and the plough hit a stump which measured just nine feet and a half through it—hard and sound white oak. The plough split it, and I was going straight through the stump when I happened to think it might snap together again, so I threw my feet out and had no sooner done this, than it snapped together, taking a smart hold of the seat of my pantaloons. Of course

I was tight, but I held on to the plough-handles, and though the teamsters did all they could, that team of eighty oxen could not tear my pantaloons, nor cause me to let go my grip. At last though, after letting the cattle breathe, they gave another strong pull altogether, and the old stump came out about the quickest; it had monstrous long roots, too, let me tell you. My wife made the cloth for them pantaloons, and I haven't worn any other kind since."

The reply made to this was: "I should have thought it would have come hard on your suspenders."

"Powerful hard." (Haliburton 1852: 273–4)

Uncle Ezra's tall tale parades rural work and hardships in the American wilderness. The gigantic stump ("nine feet and a half") is matched by an equally exaggerated physical power of forty yokes of oxen. Smack in the middle of this is the narrator Uncle Ezra, who will let go neither of the plough nor of the stump, and who finally manages to pull it out, somewhat involuntarily, with the bottom part of his pantaloons. The telling is done in typical fashion, with details that are repeated ("forty yoke of oxen," "that team of eighty oxen") and also made ridiculous ("I thought I should die. It e'en a most killed me"). The suspense builds to the climax, from holding "that plough more'n a week" to "one day," when the stump splits, snaps back together, and catches the farmer's pants. The resolution comes when "the old stump came out about the quickest," including a gap the listeners fill in their imagination: the stump must have hit Ezra's buttocks with full force. Additionally, the typical deadpan telling style subverts the ending; after proclaiming that the stump had gigantic roots, the teller adds as a non sequitur: "My wife made the cloth for them pantaloons, and I haven't worn any other kind since." The farmer's heroism is diverted to his homespun pants, and, as the anonymous audience adds, to his suspenders as well. This ending alters the entire story, from a masculinist braggadocio about mastering the wilderness to an appraisal of his wife's spinning skills and the quality of the homespun. The ending also contains a note of self-deprecation: the pants are too tough for him ("I haven't worn any other kind since") and he has been ridiculously going without, and presumably staying home. This final twist encapsulates the cultural work of the text: Uncle Ezra's pantaloons are fit for cultivating the wilderness and a tool of civilization. Yet this is not even surprising to the (American) listeners to the story, who only wonder about the pull on the suspenders (and Ezra's behind). The humor of "Yankee Homespun" is based on the audience's knowledge about the conflation between the material and mannerism, the fabric and the telling practice. The story lumps together the physical experience (in clothes that are "made in America") with the yarnspinning ways of the people.

Portrayals of storytelling in narrative texts blend oral and print culture; the telling permeates and transcends the written text, with a double addressee within and without the story: the listeners are the innkeepers or village people, but also the readers and listeners themselves. The Yankee texts examined in this chapter feature storytelling vignettes that broker a shortcut to an expanding archive of Yankee anecdotes. As this chapter has shown, antebellum literary texts dealing with New England struggle with the Yankee's interruption of the region's pastoral and remote image. They use the homespun to incorporate the Yankee as ambiguous character and let him debate the region's role in the Union. The homespun functions as a chronotope that relates the imagined pasts and projected futures of region and nation. On the one hand, it accommodates the conflicted narratives of a Puritan English legacy and the originality of this "new man," the Yankee. On the other hand, it projects Yankeedom as progressive narrative for the national future, linking the already past coarseness of the manufactured cloth to the growth of a national textile industry and a mature Yankee manhood.

By the end of the Civil War, the New England home had become a nostalgic flashcard for reflecting the American present. Besides the popular *Rhymes of Yankee Land* (1872) cited at the beginning of this chapter, James Russell Lowell's *Biglow Papers* (1885), about the "down east community," the satirical writings of "Orpheus C. Kerr," as well as the humor collections of George Augustus Sala (1866) and Thomas Chandler Haliburton (1852) anthologized the comic downeasters.

The Yankee's ambiguity did not jar with his popularity in the remainder of the nineteenth century. The text that illustrates best the inherited mechanisms of Yankee mythmaking might be John Greenleaf Whittier's 1866 "Snow-Bound: A Winter Idyll" (Whittier 1904). It cites the figure of the Yankee schoolmaster as missionary, the homely hearth, the display of Yankee storytelling, and the invention of history in an argument about Yankeedom's illuminating effect on an allegedly dark North American continent. Dedicated to the memory of Whittier's antebellum childhood home in Haverhill, Massachusetts, "Snow-Bound" was immensely popular, second in sales numbers only to Longfellow's "Song of Hiawatha" (Rocks 1993).

The narrative long poem chronicles a winter storm that gathers the family around the fire for games and storytelling. The poem is presented as memory of a lyrical I who mediates the scene and synthesizes the scenario of Yankee storytelling. Among the family's guests is the "master of the district school," a young schoolteacher educated at Dartmouth. He translates the classic fables for the children and invents a literary tradition on American soil in

> [. . .] mirth-provoking versions [. . .] of classic legends rare and old,
> Wherein the scene of Greece and Rome
> Had all the commonplace of home,
> And little seemed at best the odds
> 'Twixt Yankee peddlers and old gods;
> Where Pindus-born Arachthus took
> The guise of any grist-mill brook,
> And dread Olympus at his will
> Became a huckleberry hill. (Whittier 1904: 495)

Of all the storytellers around the family hearth, the schoolmaster is tasked with forging a national literary tradition. His success becomes obvious in the narrator's description of the transformation of mundane grist-mill brooks and huckleberry hills into sites of epic struggle. Among these metamorphoses is also the transformation of a Yankee peddler into a god from antiquity. Zooming out from the storytelling, the narrator projects the Yankee schoolmaster's future—after the Civil War, the "careless boy" becomes an ideological torch carrier:

> At his desk he had the look
> And air of one who wisely schemed [. . .]
> Large-brained and clear-eyed, of such as he
> Shall Freedom's young apostles be,
> Who, following War's bloody trail
> Shall [. . .] uplift black and white alike;
> [Shall plant] [. . .] a schoolhouse on every hill,
> Stretching in radiate nerve-lines thence
> The quick wires of intelligence;
> Till North and South together brought,
> Shall own the same electric thought,
> In peace a common flag salute (Whittier 1904: 495)

In a display of Northern superiority, the Yankee schoolhouses on the hills are beacons of a luminous network. Radiating light and electricity across the South, these "nerve-lines" are a modern version of Tocqueville's New England fires lit across the hills. For his epigraph to "Snow-Bound," Whittier takes a quotation from Agrippa's *Occult Philosophy* that equates the "wood fires" of the homestead to the

"Celestial Fires [that] drive away dark spirits" (Whittier 1904: 487). While Tocqueville, Hale, and others went to great lengths to describe the New England hearth, Whittier's postbellum narrative puts his nostalgic childhood memory in the service of building a national future. Whittier's network metaphor installs the industrial present of his home state Massachusetts on the pedestal of an imagined pastoral past; the virtuous queens of the homespun have been replaced by the electricity-run textile industry. "Snow-Bound" also embraces the construction of a literary past; by interlacing a double scenario of narration (the lyrical I tells the reader about the schoolmaster telling the children), he reiterates the fantasy of New England in the long poem as a whole. He shows a Yankee yarn in the making, told by the schoolmaster and by the lyrical I. The audience willingly and knowingly let themselves be lured into this winter idyll in the guise of a classical myth that unravels, somewhat unexpectedly, amongst America's huckleberry hills.

Notes

1. On New England's "mythic" status, see e.g. the overview article in the *Encyclopedia of American Studies* (O'Keefe 2018). On its pictorial quality, see Evelev 2007; Truettner and Stein 1999.
2. Buell addresses the Yankee in the chapter on "Comic Grotesque," which serves, with the subsequent part on "Provincial Gothic," as illustration of the specifics of New England's literary regionalist "spirit of place" (Buell 1987: 335–70). He discusses the features of the Yankee (338–49), contrasting his shrewdness with his stolidity and sublimation, but leaves this ambiguity unresolved, to argue that this depiction can only "throw out hints of ulterior depths" (350).
3. I take the concept of critical regionalism from Heike Paul (2014), who maintains that critical regionalist study lays bare the discursive formation of regions, critiquing their essentialist and romanticized image, debating their relation to the nation as geopolitical structure, inventing alternative geographies, and devising new connections among regions.
4. Conforti's cultural history in *Imagining New England* (2001) examines "regional identity as the cultural terrain where the imagined and the historic New England 'interpenetrate'" (6); Nissenbaum's essay "New England as Region and Nation" (1996) dismantles cultural myths. Ironically, New England's industrialization contributes to its definition; while the rural image remained alive in people's minds, the region received its boost from the textile industry's immigrant workforce (see Van Dusen 1975). After the Civil War, many "downeasters" moved out west, much in the sense of Tocqueville's spreading fires.

5. See Sheidley 1998 and Onuf 1996. The Webster/Hayne debate is available at <http://jmisc.net/hwoutlin.htm#webstr2d/> (accessed November 3, 2020); see [53]. Webster's famed Yankee cunning was fictionalized in the 1936 short story by Stephen Vincent Benet, "The Devil and Dan Webster," in which a jury of U.S. historical figures sits on trial over a Yankee farmer defended by Webster. By the 1820s, sectionalism was perceived as commitment to heritage, while Unionists were accused of calculation and compromise (Onuf 1996: 35).
6. The Hartford Convention was a hot topic in the Webster/Hayne debate of 1830; Webster rejected Hayne's reproach that the Convention, in typical Yankee manner, tried to "calculat[e] the value of the Union," a trope that resurfaces, e.g. in Greene's *A Yankee Among the Nullifiers*, discussed below.
7. Wood (1991) discusses Concord (MA) and Litchfield (CT) as inventions of American Romanticist thought. Kermes (2008, esp. 15–56) makes the same argument, but limits her time frame up to 1825. She discusses foreign visitors, such as General Lafayette and Frederick the Great, making only passing mention of the Yankee's "notorious reputation" (ibid. 50). On New England's visual composition, see e.g. Truettner and Stein 1999, or Abrams's imagologist analysis of landscape in American Renaissance writing (2004).
8. For a discussion of the myth of the New England white village in visual culture, see e.g. Conforti's analysis of the engravings by John Barber. Conforti argues that Barber's idealized white village vanquishes both "industrialism and romantic sublime nature as the reigning visual image of the regional landscape" (Conforti 2001: 144). On the architectural composition of the New England farm, see Hubka 2004.
9. Matthews 1978: 198; see Choate's "The Colonial Age of New England" and "The Importance of Illustrating New England History by a Series of Romances like the Waverly Novels" (1849). He claims that "Poems and romances which shall be read in every parlor, by every fireside, in every school-house, behind every counter, in every printing office, in every lawyer's office, at every weekly evening club, in all the States of the Confederacy must do something, along with more palpable if not more powerful agents, toward moulding and fixing that final, grand, complete result—the national character" (qtd. in Laird 1993: 83). Choate followed Webster in office as senator of Massachusetts.
10. Baym (1992a) discusses the competition between the Northern and Southern models; Den Ouden (2005) maps the struggle for history and territory Native populations fought against Puritan superiority in New England; Conforti (2001) lists two instructive examples: the autobiographical New England stories of Pequot William Apess (1798–1839) and African American Harriet Wilson (1808–c. 1870). Apess's criticism of cultural memory formation was completely erased in the nineteenth century, and his work, like Wilson's, has only been recently discovered. Apess's autobiography *A Son of the Forest* (1829)

records the slow distortion of his people into the treacherous Indian stereotype; he mythologizes King Philipp as a "Native American George Washington" in his *Eulogy on King Philipp* (1836), held twice in Boston. Harriet Wilson's *Our Nig, or Sketches from the Life of a Free Black* (1859) offers similar revisionist criticism of white New England as an exclusionist and racist society, despite the absence of slavery, during a time when the Northern abolitionists claimed the moral high ground (see Conforti 2001: 198–200).

11. This rhetoric strategy has been debated widely and will not be reiterated here; see e.g. Kermes 2008: 15–56. The 1975 "History of Connecticut" series adapts Bushman's argument about Connecticut's evolution from "the small, primitive Bible State of the 1630s" to a part of "the new, rational western world which was bursting with new energies and new visions. Connecticut's people stood poised for their advance into an exciting future" (Andersen 1975: 126–7).

12. Refining this narrative, Christopher Hanlon (2013) has shown that New Englanders saw themselves as descending from sturdy Saxons while Southerners proclaimed heritage from conquering aristocratic Normans.

13. For an overview of the most recent postnationalist turn in American Studies, see Fluck and Pease 2014. Buell (1992) has linked New England to transatlanticism, revising the monolithic image of the region. In American literary historiography, New England has become a focal point primarily as home of the writers of the "American Renaissance"; F. O. Matthiessen's 1941 book proclaims that the works published in a mere five-year period between 1850 and 1855 by New England writers Emerson, Melville, Thoreau, Whitman, and Hawthorne mark the first literary movement on American ground. An explanation for this mushrooming of literary greatness was offered in Van Wyck Brooks's Pulitzer Prize-winning historical work on New England literary culture, *The Flowering of New England Literary Culture, 1815–1865* (1936); Brooks offers an assessment of cultural growth and cross-pollination that has been contested but hardly undone. A third strand is Perry Miller's work on the Puritans and their spiritual transformations, which emphasizes their "adversarial relationship [to] [. . .] a commercial class that spawned an optimistic materialism" (Fuller 2006: 107). For a history of the idea of renaissance in the U.S. and a critique of its gendered genealogy, see Avallone 1997.

14. See, for instance, the research overview in Avallone 1997. Feminist literary critic Nina Baym provides an example: she argues that even though this has been contested, if teachers "hope to produce better Americans, a better America, or even just a better understanding of the *real* America, then the supposedly suppressed and overturned Whig project continues in full force" (Baym 1992a: 101).

15. By 1876, *Rhymes of Yankee Land* had gone through seven editions. The collection consists of simple iambic poems. The first part, with its folkloristic "Smithville Worthies," is followed by Civil War poetry from a

Northern perspective ("Light from Dark") and a third, "Miscellaneous," which features commemorative pieces for the 46th Massachusetts Regiment or the battle of Williamsburg. *Rhymes of Yankee Land* made it from the remote country to the urban publishing industry. The first edition, printed in Springfield, MA, was soon taken over by a major publishing house located in Boston and New York.

16. Ringe discusses Irving and Cooper as conservative New York writers who view New England expansionism skeptically. The difference between "Yankees and Yorkers" is discussed in the eponymous historical study by Fox (1940), which calls "New Englandism" a "phenomenon of transplantation" (26). Chronicling the relation between English "Yankee" and Dutch settlers from colonial times to the middle of the nineteenth century, Fox argues that the former usually "win [. . .] by aggressive speculation and quick-rooting settlement" (150). New York "resist[s] New England at the borders for over two centuries, but is still infiltrated by Yankee culture" (ibid.).

17. Hoffman shows that in "Sleepy Hollow" Irving used a more realistic depiction of the Dutch than in his other tales; he also compares Brom Bones to the equally authentic Dutchman Guert Ten Eyck in Cooper's *Satanstoe* (Hoffman 1953: 427). Daigrepont (1984) points out that Ichabod is driven out of town by a myth about a Hessian trooper losing his head while fighting *against* a revolution (77); he reads the schoolmaster's effeminacy and popularity with women as a weakening of the figure (70). But while Ichabod's effeminacy makes him pale in comparison to Brom, it also pinpoints, first, the conventional role of the housewife and republican mother as educator of future citizens, which will be discussed further below, and second, the Yankee peddler's culling of frontier housewives shown in the previous chapter.

18. Ringe's (1960) comprehensive reading of the trilogy argues that, while critics have linked it to Cooper's disenchantment with democracy, the Littlepage trilogy debates the potential of social change. In the conflict between the Littlepages and the Newcomes, hereditary affluence and moral piety is pitted against the lack of the parvenu's "civilizing graces" (ibid. 289). Hence, in the course of the trilogy, the contrast between the two is not so much about ethnic differences between Dutch-English and New England manners, but veers towards a more democratic, meritocratic distinction. In another contribution, Ringe (1988) discusses Irving's critical view of the Yankees in "Rip Van Winkle."

19. Dryden (1971: 53, 55) argues that the Littlepage trilogy traces the "evolution of the American gentleman"; see also House 1966. The full quotation is interesting because Corny compares the dead Dutchman Guert Ten Eyck and the bookish Yankee, stressing that local origins, breeding, as well as nature itself make them differ: "Poor Guert! [. . .] A finer physical man I never beheld, or one who better satisfied the eye, in all respects. That the noble tenement was not more intellectually occupied,

was purely the consequence of a want of education. Notwithstanding, all the books in the world could not have converted Guert Ten Eyck into a Jason Newcome, or Jason Newcome into a Guert Ten Eyck. Each owed many of his peculiarities, doubtless, to the *province* on which he was bred and born, and to the *training* consequent on these accidents, but *nature* had also drawn broad distinctions between them. All the wildness of Guert's impulses could not altogether destroy his feelings, tone and tact as a gentlemen; while all the soaring, extravagant pretensions of Jason never could have ended in elevating him to that character" (430, emphasis added).

20. Cooper's *Notions of the Americans* marks the beginning of his decade-long comparison of Europe and America. His response to allegedly unjust British travelogues is penned by a European observer traveling with an international group of bachelors, including one American, Cooper's alter ego, "John Cadwaller, of Cadwaller, N.Y.," who has "destroyed the coat of arms of [his] European ancestors" (Cooper 1963: I, xiii). He is invited to join the noble club in the "task of peregrination" (ibid. xiv) and serves as an interpreter of America for the traveling Europeans (see e.g. ibid. 53).

21. All subsequent quotations from Hale's *Northwood* refer to the second edition: *Northwood, or Life North and South, Showing the True Character of Both* (New York: Long & Brother, 1852). Reference to the first, 1827 edition, entitled *Northwood: A Tale of New England* (Boston: Bowles & Dearborn), will be indicated as "Hale 1827."

22. Hale's concept of male beauty focuses on intelligence: Charles does not conform to the "rules of art" because of his "irregular" features, yet "[h]is was the beauty of deep thought, the lofty expression of superior intelligence, giving to his countenance an irresistible fascination [. . .] his eyes literally flashed forth the feelings and meaning of his soul [. . .] and few could meet their keen, searching, expressive glance, without feeling a sense of inferiority" (221).

23. In 1832, South Carolina issued an "Ordinance of Nullification" on federal tariffs. Since the War of 1812, the American government had been trying to bolster American industry by imposing tariffs on goods imported from Great Britain. The South was doubly affected, having to pay higher prices on imported goods and facing difficulties in cotton trade relations with the British. South Carolina politician John C. Calhoun proposed nullification, based on his theory of the states' right to nullify, or invalidate, any federal law which that state has deemed unconstitutional. The theory of nullification was ultimately rejected by the Supreme Court.

24. Greene includes stump speeches and political oratory, such as a lecture about "The Value of the Union" (51–6), which reacts to the 1830 Webster/Hayne debate. In his first response to Hayne, Webster criticized the Southern argument viewing the union as a commodity: "They

declare that it is time to calculate the value of the union, and their aim seems to be to enumerate and magnify all the evils, real and imaginary, which the government under the union produces." Hayne's responses recalled the Hartford Convention: "At this dark period of our national affairs [after the War of 1812] where was the senator of Massachusetts? How were his political associates employed? 'Calculating the value of the union'" (from <http://jmisc.net/hwoutlin.htm#webstr2d/> [53]). In Greene's text, the attempt of a Southern orator to "calculate" the value of the union for the South fails, because only Yankees can do "calculation." The Southern orator contradicts himself several times (see 56). Later on, Harebrain is ridiculed for "calculat[ing]" and then "miscalculat[ing] the effects of Southern logic upon a Northern man" (86); in the end, the Yankee outsmarts the Southern Harebrain.

25. The elopement plot is one example of his disposition; in another instance, a friend tells him he is refused Henrietta's hand because, apart from being a Yankee and on the wrong side politically, "'you do not drive a carriage and four, or engage in a fox-hunt, or a horse race'" (59).

26. Greene imitates English satire. The figures in *A Yankee Among the Nullifiers* are a continuation of Greene's pieces in magazines, which also featured telling names like the "Huckabuck, Ballywhack, Touchwoods and Timbertoes contemporaries he sketched in the native idiom in his journalistic writing" (Reed 1953: 125).

27. Among the suspects are the adversaries to the Southern economic system, the Yankees, the Quakers, and the Colonization Society led by Henry Clay (122). That the blame for the slave revolt is (falsely) attributed to the Union Party highlights the political threat nullification posed to the Union; Greene's irony here, of course, is the fact that the Nullifiers themselves provoked the rebellion.

28. See, for instance, Harebrain's duel challenge to Elnathan: "To Elnathan Elmwood, Esquire. SIR—the insult you offered me last evening must be washed out with the blood of one of us. Either you or I must be *nullified*. The case admits of no protection. The *Union* of soul and body, on one part or the other, must be dissolved. The chivalry of the South demands it. Therefore meet me, at eight o'clock tomorrow morning, on the spot where the outrage was offered, that the scene of your insolence may also be the place of your punishment. Yours &c. HAREBRAIN HARRINGTON" (143, emphasis in original).

29. Elnathan makes sure to keep his enslaved butler Tom in check to prevent "insubordination" (117); his Yankee business partner Treadwell makes a fortune with the invention of the "Anti-African-Odor-Gas-Generator" (92). During the rebellion, the enslaved are shown in a more gruesome and racist depiction than the Southern fighters.

30. Elnathan's career from Yankee schoolmaster to plantation owner also reverberates with Hale's *Northwood*, as will be discussed below. Even

Simon Legree, the evil plantation owner from Harriet Beecher Stowe's *Uncle Tom's Cabin* (1851), is described as a Yankee who runs his plantation "like a factory, for maximum short-term profit" (Nissenbaum 1996: 55). Despite its setting in the South and West, *Uncle Tom's Cabin* "can be read as a parable of the social history of New England during the first half of the nineteenth century" (ibid.).

31. Maryan has a superior sense of morality, manners, and propriety. Percy observes that her house looks cleaner than the Southern houses (Baldwin 1884: 148); he admires her hospitality (150), and accepts her criticism of an overpriced doctor's bill (153). Her view of Southern avarice and negligence of table manners is illustrated in her disappointment at the sight of the Sunday breakfast table: she "survey[s] [. . .] the dingy square of oilcloth, the smoking cornpone [*sic*], the cracked, blue-rimmed dish of bacon swimming in liquid fat, the dried elderberry pie, of a juiceless consistency, of which one taste sufficed; and vaguely wonder[ed] why a pat of fresh butter could not be coaxed from the supplies in the pantry, destined for the nearest market town" (ibid. 90).

32. I take the concept of the liminal society from anthropologist Victor Turner's description of the "social drama" of community development (1988). He identifies a "dramatic" movement of communities through crisis that unfolds in successive stages: breach (of the order by an individual or group), crisis, redressive action, and as a result reversion or schism (ibid. 63). Turner finds in the redressive phase an instance of "public reflexivity" (ibid. 64) that relates to the texts examined here; the narrative about New England communities in crisis is framed by an inquiry, skeptical or affirmative, into the national project of the U.S.

33. Women writers dominated the formation of the New England village novel; see e.g. Gossett and Bardes 1985, or Evelev 2007. Ulrich (1998) examines self-sufficiency and female trade relations in the novel; Kaplan (2002) reads it as domestic fiction. Zagarell (1987: 225) argues that the female authors "demonstrate that [. . .] some women liberally extended official definitions of the nation to imagine an America grounded in inclusiveness and communitarianism." Catharine Maria Sedgwick's novella *A New England Tale* (1822) and her novel *Redwood* (1824) are earlier examples of New England village writing.

34. As I will show, the narrator addresses a female readership as allies and thus can be read as female herself.

35. After a conversation with Squire Romilly, Frankford digests the things he saw: "to the Englishman, [the day] was unique at least. It displayed human nature in a light which he had never beheld nor considered probable. Here was the father of a family living in all the simplicity and retirement, inuring his children to habits of prudence and industry" (133).

36. After the Thanksgiving dinner, Frankford states: "'my armor is fast dissolving. A few days spent in your hospitable society have taught me how to appreciate your character better than would an age of study;

and I shall certainly regret to leave your country, although to visit my own'" (138). The warm welcome is both *observed* by him from an outsider's view and *felt*, when he is nursed by Mrs. Romilly and falls in love with Sophia Romilly. In observing Sidney's return to his family home, he "*learned a lesson* from the exhibition of natural feelings, which made him ever after disgusted with the heartlessness and frivolity of the fashionable world" (63, emphasis added).

37. Hale's support of the Colonization Society's returning the enslaved to their homeland is also spelled out in Squire Romilly's diary in chapter 24. Hale added this chapter to the second edition of her novel in 1852 as a response to the 1851 success of Harriet Beecher Stowe's abolitionist *Uncle Tom's Cabin*. Hale not only reissued *Northwood* with a new chapter and subtitle ("Life North and South, Showing the True Character of Both"); as editor of the immensely successful *Godey's Lady's Book* she also argued against abolitionism, with "silence" on the slavery question and the Civil War, and with praise for "Anti-Tom" publications (Peterson 1998: 30; see also Kaplan 2002).

38. Hale acknowledges comic depictions of the Yankee (50), but has Squire Romilly dismiss the British criticism: "'It is true we have citizens who [. . .] deserve to be ridiculed by Europeans; but they are not those who possess the esteem and confidence of their own countrymen. [. . .] Neither must you decide, because you find among us those who are egotists in conversation and bigots in religion, that egotism and bigotry are therefore characteristics of Americans'" (113). Similarly, Dr. Perkins singles out the Connecticut villain Skinner as a "bad apple": "'Connecticut is an excellent State, and has given birth to excellent men, [. . .] and one restless, intriguing fellow shall go forth and do more mischief than a dozen good ones can repair'" (156).

39. Nina Baym argues that in *Northwood* North and South are "unifie[d] to contrast the United States with England" (1992b: 170), but the absence of Northern cityscapes tells a different story. Likewise, Sidney's sojourns in the urban South of Charleston and at the Brainard plantation get no narrative attention; they happen off-screen, so to speak. The Southern cityscape remains opaque; the plantation is shown only very selectively in Lydia Romilly's hysterical letters. When the Yankee farmer Merrill travels down South, Northern prejudices about the Southern alleged backwardness are implied, with Merrill's naïve exclamations in dialect: "Merrill said he should *raly* like to stay a few days and look about the country; he thought the place and the people too looked pretty smart, much better, and more civil than he expected, and he *raly* liked them both very well" (377, emphasis in original).

40. On the forms and functions of inventive New England weathercocks, see Kaye 1975.

41. In a metanarrative commentary about the beauty of the Romilly sisters, Hale chastises the readers for their vanity: "every fair reader who

honors these pages with perusal, and doesn't think [the Romilly girls] at least as handsome as herself, may be certain she possesses either a vain head or an envious heart" (65). Another example for female interest is Lydia Romilly's unhappy marriage. Spoiled and self-centered, she wants to impress a suitor with the courtship of the Southern gentleman Brainard; from this misunderstanding results a childless marriage to Brainard. In her letters, Lydia reveals herself to be overwhelmed with her new life (see 19–26). In Nina Baym's terms of "woman's fiction" of the Early Republic, Lydia is a "modern belle" who falls prey to her shallowness (140). Annie and Zemira represent opposites to this type as women who assert themselves and win their true love, despite poverty or parental disapproval (see Baym 1993: 28 *et passim*).

42. Hale's backlash on literary conventions and expectations is best illustrated in Mrs. Watson, the "Yankee sibyl" (342) and antidote to the Shakespearean witch type: "She was a very unclassical priestess of futurity; very unlike also the witches of Macbeth, or the more modern Nornas and Megs of popular romance. Those remarkable women are represented as enormously tall [. . .] with long, skinny arms to match; sunken features; weather-beaten; [. . .] and then their hair, such a frightfully grizzled, disheveled, matted mass! How I have wished the ingenious authors, rich as they are in invention, could have afforded them a comb!" (347).

43. Other telling names imply professional commentary on the skills of Dr. Cureall and Dr. Squash (who nearly kills David's father; see 22), and Mr. Quibble, the ignorant schoolteacher who tries to cover his ignorance of Latin (108–9).

44. "Bundled" adolescents could spend the night together in a bed, sewn into body bags. The narrator rants: "Sometimes the girl partly stripped, and sometimes both were stripped. No harm in *the thing* you know! [. . .] the same thing is carried on among the Dutch settlers of New York, Pennsylvania, and New Jersey as well as in New England" (31). Bundling corrupts true love. David recalls bundling with the country girl Sally Dwight. He talked poetically about the stars until she told him to kiss her (34), but he is not sure a marriage to Sally would last (36). Irving's Diedrich Knickerbocker also comments on Yankee bundling in "The History of New York": "a superstitious rite observed by the young people of both sexes [. . .] their courtships commencing, where ours usually finish. [. . .] [It generates] an amazing number of sturdy brats annually born unto the state" (Irving 1983a: 496, 497).

45. Literary scholars have focused on his depiction of Native Americans, most prominently in *Logan* (1822), and his historiographic view of the Revolution in *Seventy-Six* (1823); his focus on women's rights in *Randolph* (1823) and his most famous novel *Rachel Dyer* (1828) is equally interesting. On Neal's "Indians," see also Pethers 2012.

46. In *Beneath the American Renaissance*, Reynolds discusses writers like Neal, George Lippard, and George Thompson, whose fiction enacts "fully the wild cultural forces" of the Early Republic. He mentions Neal's "sensational novels and literary manifestoes" of the 1820s, briefly acknowledging "the remarkable use of narrative ellipsis and directionless dialogue in the first half of *The Down Easters*" (Reynolds 2001: 203). However, Reynolds makes no connection to oral storytelling and to Neal's attempts to express a national character, which will be discussed in detail here.
47. Neal's language politics are quite elaborate and oppose Noah Webster's influential proposition of a unified national language untinged by regional varieties.
48. Jack Downing is an invention by humor writer Seba Smith, a figure from "Down East" who would go to Congress and ultimately accompany President Jackson. Downing's commentaries and tall tales are published in the *Letters of Jack Downing* from 1829 onwards, with sequels in 1833 (2 vols.), 1834, and 1859. Smith also published the collection *Way Down East* (1854). See Schroeder 1977 for a discussion of Smith's politics in the Downing letters.
49. The Yankee leans over him in the first chapter and utters a weird threat in Yankee dialect: "'If he [the narrator] is a stranger in these parts, I can tell him he'd better have his eye teeth cut afore he's much older; if he don't (lowering his voice to a sort of whistle, and puckering up his mouth into the oddest of all shapes for a mouth, stooping over, turning up one foot sideways, and beginning to count the stitches in the shoe), if he don't shave putty nigh the grinstun, somebody't he's ben so ter'rble thick with'll show him what's what, afore he done with him—ketch a weazle asleep, hey? (clocking his eye at me), wish his cake dough; if he don't there's none o' me, that's all'" (I, 3).
50. The tall tale humor of this description reverberates in the photomontage of tall tale postcards in the late nineteenth and early twentieth centuries. Photographers would cut out close-ups of potatoes, pumpkins, or corn and put them onto photographed wagons. The tall tale postcard is a predominantly rural phenomenon, bragging about "the kind of corn we grow" in the Midwestern and New England states. The humor of the postcard lies in the gargantuan produce and the dapper commentary. See, for instance, the Michigan State University Museum's tall tale postcard collection (<http://traditionalarts.msu.edu/resources/collections/collection/?kid=A2-33F-47>; last accessed November 16, 2020) or Cynthia Elyce Rubin and Morgan Williams (eds.), Larger Than Life: The American Tall Tale Postcard, 1905–1915 (New York: Abbeville Press, 1990).
51. In his gossipy description of Jerry Gage, the Yankee remarks that Gage went "'right away inter Kentucky, jess to have a try there with some o'them air fellers that's brought up to Ingeen hug among the

bears, [. . .] Old rough an' tough they used to call his dad, famous wrestler he was too, warped with hoop-poles an' filled with oven-wood'" (62).

52. The narrator reveals himself as a Yankee when he describes things "in the fashion of my country" (I, 2), but his last name and origin remain unclear. The nosy Obadiah tries to find out where Peter lives and lists all the New England small towns, in vain. Peter only concedes: "'[I live] here and there and every where, in other words, nowhere'" (I, 64). When he is suspected to be European, the narrator "laughed aloud, and long and heartily" (ibid.). The Yankee also quizzes him about allegedly typical, if not all meaningful, New England games and behavior, all of which he denies: "'D'you play checkers? Or fox an' geese? Or morris? [. . .] Draw cuts? Or open a book for the nighest letter? Or chalk the floor? Hey! Or jump up and kick?'" (I, 70–1).
53. Hale stresses the role of women as civilizing figures and symbols for national unity in the last chapter of the 1852 version: "[This is] no partisan book, but intended to show selfishness her own ugly image, where it appears—north or south; and also to show how the good may overcome the evil. 'Constitutions' and 'compromises' are the appropriate work of men: women are conservators of moral power, which, eventually as it is directed, preserves or destroys the work of the warrior, statesman, and the patriot. Let us trust that the pen and not the sword will decide the controversy now going on in our land" (Hale 1852: 407). The founding texts mentioned here are attributed to male strategies of nation-building. About Hale's agenda and her view of men and women as vessels for the national projects, Nina Baym writes: "[Hale] was shaped intellectually, ideologically, and politically by the agitations and values of New England during the early republican era. From first to last she wrote on behalf of a vision of the United States as a Christian republic destined to lead the world into the millennium. She was not an individualist; she defined women and men in relation to each other, to the nation, and to the nation's goals" (Baym 1992b: 168; see also 174–6).
54. The "rude hearth stone" is also the opening image of the temperance narrative *The Life and Adventures of William Harvard Stinchfield* (Robinson 1851: 11). The young peddler departs from his parents' New England home reluctantly.
55. Hale's depiction of Thanksgiving in *Northwood* famously gave rise to the status of the celebration as the most important family holiday in the U.S., even though the mythical origins exclude the mention of Native Americans helping the first settlers through a rough winter that is tied to the celebration today. In Squire Romilly's version, it relates to the gratitude felt by the settlers when a ship from England arrived with goods that helped them survive (68). Already in 1852, *Harper's Magazine* published a short nostalgic piece about the Thanksgiving dinner, in which a "down

east Yankee" bemoans that the tradition is falling apart (Anon. 1852). Apart from making a name for herself as the "inventor" of Thanksgiving, Hale also contributed another "classic" to U.S. culture, the nursery song "Mary Had a Little Lamb."

56. The story of the wife who killed herself after being raped by the enemy around 390 BC is recounted by Roman historian Livius in the *History of Rome* as instrumental in the founding of the Roman Republic. The scandal caused anti-monarchist rebellion and was framed by discourses of republican virtue and female chastity; it echoes with the story of King Lemuel and his wives cited below and persisted in the visual and literary cultural archive, most notably in Shakespeare's "Rape of Lucrece" (published 1594). British composer Benjamin Britten transformed the theme into an opera libretto (prem. 1946).

57. Proverbs 31 as quoted by Bushnell reverberates with Roman Lucretia's virtuous weaving: "She layeth her hands to the spindle and her hands hold the distaff. She is not afraid of the snow for her household; for all her household are covered with scarlet. Her husband is known in the gates, when he sitteth among the elders of the land. She openeth her mouth in wisdom and her tongue is the law of kindness. She looketh well to the ways of her household, and eateth not the bread of idleness" (qtd. in Bushnell 1864: 369). Bushnell adds: "Overlooking other points of the picture, she is a frugal, faithful, pious housewife; clothing her family in garments prepared by her industry, and the more beautiful honors of a well-kept, well-mannered house" (ibid.).

58. Hale's depiction of the inferior housewife in the Romilly household reiterates an all-too-familiar patriarchal image of New England communities and families, as Gossett and Bardes (1985) have shown in their comparison between *Northwood* and Catharine Maria Sedgwick's *Hope Leslie*. The spheres were a mythical construct that does not bear historical study. Ulrich has argued that "18th century [housewife] diaries [. . .] describe a world in which wives as well as husbands traded with their neighbors, where young women felt themselves responsible for their own support, where matches were made in the tumult of neighborhood frolics, and where outsiders as well as family members were involved in the most intimate events of life. The New England we have explored was a world neither of free-floating individuals nor of self-contained households" (1998: 248).

59. As Zakim has shown, on the eve of the Civil War, the homespun is worn by Southerners to articulate a critique of Northern fashions, thus bringing its political uses full circle, a "patriotic symbol of virtuous sacrifice in the face of a political and military threat posed by a corrupt economic giant" (2001: 1586).

Chapter 5

Yankee Politics: A Coda

> I never care to do a thing in a quiet way; it's got to be theatrical or I don't take any interest in it.
>
> I reckon we are fools. Born so, no doubt. (Hank Morgan, *A Connecticut Yankee in King Arthur's Court* Twain 1982: 178, 201)

In the nineteenth century, American national identity is played out in a farce orchestrated by and starring the Yankee. His yarnspinning and whittling typically lead nowhere, to a dead end in the story and a pile of shards left by the storyteller. Likewise, his fabulous growth from early national allegory into mature governmental figure is deflated by his ambiguities. At the core, the Yankee is a cunning nihilist who sells his audience a chance at self-deception and self-edification. He plays his theatrics for a readership who build a national literary marketplace and a political arena for the Yankee's fantastic body politic. The peddler's "going ahead" transforms his body, like Brother Jonathan's body politic, into the civilization machine for the settler nation state.

The Yankee's fusion of literary confabulation and nation-building works through time; he invents a colonial past and promises an industrial future, framing the contemporary moment in a grand narrative of national purpose and fantastic unity. In Mark Twain's *Connecticut Yankee in King Arthur's Court,* this purposeful layering percolates in the motif of the palimpsest: the narrator reads Hank's own story from a parchment, "yellow with age [. . .] Under the old dim writing of the Yankee historian appeared traces of a penmanship which was older and dimmer still—Latin words and sentences, fragments from old monkish legends, evidently" (Twain 1982: 10). Twain's novel itself also functions as a palimpsestic retelling of the Arthurian legend, as Hank rises to power at Camelot thanks to his storytelling and business skills. He works as a newspaperman, prophet, boss of an arms factory, and insurance agent, thus upending sixteenth-century English court culture in a toxic leap forward that Hank calls "the march of civilization" (Twain 1982: 227). But Hank's Promethean impulse depends on repetition. In a scene Hank compares to Geoffrey Chaucer's *Canterbury Tales*, he conquers his British audience of "pilgrims" (107) through storytelling:

> the fifth time I told it, they began to crack in places, the eighth time I told it, they began to crumble, at the twelfth repetition they fell apart in chunks, and at the fifteenth time they disintegrated, and I got a broom and swept them up. This language is figurative. Those islanders—well, they are slow pay, at first, in the matter of return for your investment of effort, but in the end they make the pay of all other nations poor and small by contrast. (Twain 1982: 115–16)

Twain's economy of storytelling thrives on repetition and palimpsestic layering. Hank's story on the ancient parchment as well as Twain's novel update different pasts into a present-moment experience, a succession of excitements akin to the newspaper Hank introduces to Arthur's Court, the "Camelot Weekly Hosanna and Literary Volcano" (Twain 1982: 148).

The Yankee figures examined in *Yankee Yarns* update colonial and national pasts for a nineteenth-century national audience deeply vested in its imperial future. Yankee Doodle, Brother Jonathan, the stage Yankee, the Yankee peddler, and Uncle Sam repeat their stories and enact their braggadocio to create a routine of patriotic huzza akin to a volcanic eruption of white nationalist fervor. The Yankee of the U.S. cultural imaginary is very much a creature of nineteenth-century ideology; apparently, you can take the Yankee out of the nineteenth century, but you can't take the nineteenth century out of the Yankee. By the 1880s, Mark Twain had become not only a practitioner and theorist of American humor but also a cultural representative and commentator. Twain's commentary on the U.S., through his Yankee Hank Morgan, is marked by misanthropy and distrust in the promises of American democracy. A homespun embodiment of the white settler nation, Twain's Yankee shows a destructive force that has to be contained, and his rhetoric and entrepreneurship need to be curbed lest they divide communities and explode the institutions of democracy.

Today, we can only speculate about what futures nineteenth-century audiences of Yankee performances had in mind. Yet revisiting the Yankee may yield some perspectives on contemporary top-level politics.

Populist rhetoric, daily social media eruptions, and the business skill to "shave" opponents were phenomena of the Trump presidency that remain to be historicized and contextualized in American Studies. Yet it also seems as if people living in America have heard enough of Yankee storytelling.

Appendices

Appendix I: "Yankee Phrases"

As sound as a nut o'er the plain,
I of late whistled chuck full of glee;
A stranger to sorrow and pain
As happy as happy could be.
As plum as a partridge I grew,
My heart being lighter than cork
My slumbers were calmer than dew!
My body was fatter than pork!
Thus happy I hop'd I should pass,
Sleak as grease down the current of time
But pleasures are brittle as glass,
Although as a fiddle they're fine.
Jemima, the pride of the vale,
Like a top nimbly danced o'er our plains:
With envy the lasses were pale—
With wonder stood gaping the swains.
She smil'd like a basket of chips—
As tall as a hay pole her size—
As sweet as molasses her lips—
As bright as a button her eyes.
Admiring I gaz'd on each charm,
My peace that would trouble so soon,
And thought not of danger nor harm,
Any more than the man in the moon.
But now to my sorrow I find,
Her heart is as hard as a brick:
To my passion forever unkind,
Though of love I am full as a tick.
I sought her affection to win,
In hope of obtaining relief,

Till I, like a hatchet, grew thin,
And she, like a haddock, grew deaf.
I late was as fat as a doe
And playful and spry as a cat:
But now I am dull like a hoe,
And as lean and weak as a rat.
Unless the unpitying fates
With passion as ardent shall cram her,
As certain as death or as fates,
I soon shall be dead as a hammer.
("Yankee Phrases," 1803)

Appendix II: "The Yankee in New York, or the Mistake of a Clown" (*Boston Weekly Magazine*, August 5, 1817)

Custom makes every thing palatable, as the Dutchman said when he ate the fried stockage.

A Yankee late from Boston came,
To view this wond'rous city;
And none may sure the Yankee blame,
'Tis all so clean and pretty.
This Yankee—be it understood,
Was both polite and civil,
And though, in some things not so *good*,
He always fear'd the *Devil*.
But Boston folks, as buckskins say,
Are very full of notions;
In fact they prove it ev'ry day
By taking ***'s potions.
Our Yankee too a notion had,
That *Swine* were *Satan's* cousins,
Which, for to plague the good and bad,
Were sent on earth by dozens.
Down Pearl-street Isaac shap'd his course,
(Mouth gaping wide with wonder)
Thinking which was the *greatest curse*,
A city could fall under.
While busied with such thoughts as these,
Thoughts dear to Yankee rover,
A *Hog*, just feasting on some pease,
He tumbled headlong over.

Recovering from the shock, he rose,
"Chock full" of *trepidation*,
Rubb'd down his shins and brush'd his clothes,
Then swore "*retaliation.*"
"Help! help!" full loud the Yankee crie'd,
(A Yankee's "up to" bawling)
"A hog! A hog! I'll tan his hide"
For help he still kept calling.
At length appear'd a man in blue,
With cudgel like Hercules,
Demanding what the Yankee meant
By such d—d cries as these.
"What mean" said Isaac, with a grin
"I mean this hog to slay, or
Quick to the 'pound' to put him in,
Then go and tell the '*Mayor*.'"
"Curse on thy Yankee wooden head,"
Cry'd out the man quite witty,
"Did'st thou not know that hogs have, here,
The *freedom* of the *city*."
Quoth Isaac, "then if that's the case
And you're the city's *master*,
Father, I think, will *buy* the place,
And send his *Hogs* to *pasture*."

Appendix III: Joshua Silsbee as Jonathan Ploughboy

Figure i Engraving: Joshua Silsbee as Jonathan Ploughboy in *The Forest Rose*. Courtesy of University of Illinois Library, Theatrical Print Collection.

Bibliography

Primary Sources

Addison, Joseph (1712). In *The Spectator* 357 (April 13): 435.
Aesop (1844). *The Hypocrite, or Sketches of American Society from a Residence of Forty Years.* New York: Thomas Fox.
Anonymous (1845). "Sam Slick in England." *The Living Age* 4.36 (January 18): 155–61.
Anonymous (1852). "[Thanksgiving is at Hand]." *Harper's New Monthly Magazine*. 848.
Arbuthnot, John [1712] (1766). *Law is a Bottomless Pit [. . .]: Or, The History of John Bull. In Two Parts.* Glasgow: Printed for Robert Urie.
Baldwin, Joseph G. [1853] (1987). *The Flush Times of Alabama and Mississippi.* Ed. James H. Justus. Baton Rouge and London: Louisiana State University Press.
Baldwin, Lydia Wood (1884). *A Yankee School-teacher in Virginia: A Tale of the Old Dominion in the Transition State.* New York: Funk and Wagnalls.
Barker, James Nelson (1807). *Tears and Smiles.* New York.
Beach, Lazarus (1807). *Jonathan Postfree, or the Honest Yankee.* New York: David Longworth.
Bernard, John (1887). *Retrospections of America, 1797–1811.* Ed. Laurence Hutton and Brander Matthews. Bowie, MD: Heritage Books.
Blackington, Alton H. (1954). *Yankee Yarns.* New York: Dodd, Mead & Company.
Brooks, Van Wyck (1918). "On Creating a Useable Past." *The Dial* 64 (April 11): 337–41.
Brydges, Harrold (1888). *Uncle Sam at Home.* New York: Henry Holt.
Burnett, J. G. (1858). *Blanche of Brandywine: An American Patriotic Spectacle.* New York: Samuel French.
Bushnell, Horace (1864). "The Age of the Homespun." In *Work and Play, or Literary Varieties.* New York: Scribner's. 368–402.
Chase, George B. (1890). *Penn Hapgood, or The Yankee Schoolmaster.* Clyde, OH: Ames.
Colman, George (1828). *Jonathan in England: A Comedy in Three Acts.* Boston: William V. Spencer.

Colton, Calvin (1833). *The Americans, or An American in London*. London: Fredrick Westley.

Cooper, James Fenimore [1828] (1963). *Notions of the Americans: Picked up by a Travelling Bachelor*. Ed. Robert E. Spiller. 2 vols. New York: Frederick Ungar.

— [1845] (1990). *Satanstoe, or the Littlepage Manuscripts: A Tale of the Colony*. Ed. Jay Seymour House. Albany: State University of New York Press.

— [1821] (2006). *The Spy: A Tale of the Neutral Ground*. London: Nonsuch Classics.

Coxe, Arthur Cleveland (1838). *St. Jonathan: The Lay of a Scald*. New York: Thomas J. Crowen.

Crockett, Davy (1833). *Sketches and Eccentricities of Col. David Crockett of West Tennessee*. London: O. Rich.

Daggett, Windsor (1920). *A Down East Yankee from the District of Maine*. Portland: A. J. Huston.

Dunlap, William (1832). *History of the American Theater from its Origins to 1832*. New York: J. & J. Harper.

— [1828] (1966). "A Trip to Niagara, or Travels in America." In *Dramas from the American Theater 1762–1909*. Ed. Richard Moody. Boston: Houghton Mifflin. 178–97.

Durivage, Oliver E. (1847). *The Stage-Struck Yankee: A Farce in One Act*. New York and London: Samuel French.

Felton, Cornelius (1844). "Sam Slick in England: Change of American Notes." *North American Review* 58.122: 211–27.

Fessenden, Thomas Green (1795). *The Country Lovers*. New Haven.

— [1806] (1925). "Jonathan's Courtship." In *The Life and Works of Thomas Green Fessenden*. Ed. Porter Gale Perrin. Orono: Maine University Press. 186–92 (appendix b).

Fidfaddy, Frederik Augustus [1816] (1970). *The Adventures of Uncle Sam, in Search after his Lost Honor*. Reprint. Upper Saddle River, NJ: Literature House/Gregg Press.

Field, A. Newton (1883). *The Yankee Duelist: An Original Farce*. Clyde, OH: A. D. Ames.

Gay, E. Jane (1868). *The New Yankee Doodle, Being an Account of the Little Difficulty in the Family of Uncle Sam by Truman Trumbull*. New York: Oland Bourne.

Greene, Aella (1872). *Rhymes of Yankee Land*. Springfield, MA: Whitney & Adams.

Greene, Asa (1833). *A Yankee Among the Nullifiers*. New York: William Pearson.

Hale, Sarah J. (1827). *Northwood: A Tale of New England*. 2 vols. Boston: Bowles & Dearborn.

— (1843). *Sketches of American Character*. Philadelphia: Perkins and Purves.

— (1852). *Northwood, or Life North and South, Showing the True Character of Both*. New York: Long & Brother.

Haliburton, Thomas Chandler (1852). "Yankee Homespun." In *Traits of American Humor*. Ed. Thomas Chandler Haliburton. Vol. 1. London: Colburn and Co. 273–4.

— [1887] (1995). *Sam Slick, the Clockmaker: Series One, Two, and Three*. Ed. George L. Parker. Ottawa: Carleton University Press.

Harris, George Washington [1867] (1966). *Sut Lovingood's Yarns*. Ed. M. Thomas Inge. New Haven: College & University Press.

Herne, James A. [first perf. 1892] (1966). "Shore Acres." In *Dramas from the American Theater 1762–1909*. Ed. Richard Moody. Boston: Houghton Mifflin. 671–720.

Hooper, Johnson Jones [1845] (1993). *Adventures of Captain Simon Suggs*. Ed. M. E. Bradford. Nashville: J. S. Sanders & Company.

Irving, Washington (1983a). *History, Tales, and Sketches*. Ed. James Tuttleton. New York: Library of America.

— [1819–20] (1983b). "John Bull." In *Washington Irving: History, Tales, and Sketches*. Ed. James Tuttleton. New York: Library of America. 1029–39.

— [1819–20] (1983c). "The Legend of Sleepy Hollow." In *Washington Irving: History, Tales, and Sketches*. Ed. James Tuttleton. New York: Library of America. 1058–88.

Jefferson, Joseph (1890). *The Autobiography of Joseph Jefferson*. New York: Century Publishing Company.

Jefferson, Thomas [1785] (1975). "To Chastellux: Paris Sep 2, 1785." In *The Portable Jefferson*. Ed. Merrill D. Peterson. New York: Penguin. 386–8.

Jones, J. S. (1833). *The Green Mountain Boy*. New York and London: Samuel French.

— [1839] (1890). *Solon Shingles, or The People's Lawyer*. New York: Harold Roorbach.

Kettell, Samuel (1837). *Yankee Notions: A Medley by Timo. Titterwell, Esq.* 4th edn. Illus. D. C. Johnston. Boston: Otis, Broaders and Company.

LaBree, Ernest (1841). *Ebenezer Venture*. New York and London: Samuel French.

Lindsley, Abraham B. (1809). *Love and Friendship, or Yankee Notions: A Comedy in Three Acts*. New York: D. Longworth.

Logan, Cornelius A. (1844). *The Vermont Wool-Dealer: A Farce in One Act*. New York and London: Samuel French.

Lowell, James Russell (1885). *The Biglow Papers*. Boston: Houghton Mifflin.

Moncrieff, William Thomas (1825). *Tarnation Strange, or More Jonathans!* London: Dramatic Repository.

Mowatt, Anna Cora [1845] (1997). "Fashion, or Life in New York." In *Early American Drama*. Ed. Jeffrey H. Richards. London and New York: Penguin. 304–67.

N.N. (1817). "The Yankee in New York. Or the Mistake of a Clown." *Boston Weekly Magazine*. 5 August. 172.

— (1841). "The History of Uncle Sam's Patriarchal System of Government." *The United States Magazine and Democratic Review* 9.42: 585.

— (1843). *Brother Jonathan Magazine*. New York: Wilson and Company.

— (1852a). *Brother Jonathan's Epistle*. Boston: White and Potter.

— (1852b). "Portrait of Uncle Sam." *German Reformed Messenger* 18.2 (15 September).

— (1853). "Playbill Broadway Theatre." 19 August. 17: 24.

— (1964). "Noted for Wooden Nutmegs But Started a Great System." *Hartford Courant*. 18 October. 22F.

Neal, John (1825). *Brother Jonathan, or The New Englanders*. 3 vols. Edinburgh: Blackwood.

— (1826). "Character of the Real Yankees; What They Are Supposed to Be, and What They Are." *New Monthly Magazine and Literary Journal* 2: 247–56.

— (1833). *The Down-Easters*. 2 vols. New York: Harper.

— (1835). "Story-Telling." *The New England Magazine* 8.1: 1–12.

Newton, Henry G. (1928). "Wooden Nutmegs: Explanation of How State Got Its Nickname." *Hartford Courant*. 13 November. 8.

O'Leary, Jeremiah (1916). *The Fable of John Bull and Uncle Sam: A History in Prose and Picture of the Real Relations between John Bull and Uncle Sam*. New York: The American Truth Society.

Pairpoint, Alfred (1857). *Uncle Sam and His Country, or Sketches of America, in 1854–55–56*. London: Simpkin, Marshall & Co.

Paul, Howard (1860). *The Courtship and Adventures of Jonathan Homebred, or The Scrapes and Escapes of a Live Yankee*. New York: Dick & Fitzgerald.

Paulding, James Kirke (1812). *The Diverting History of John Bull and Brother Jonathan / by Hector Bull-us*. New York: D. & G. Bruce.

— (1825). *John Bull in America, or The New Munchhausen*. New York: Charles Wiley.

— (1851). "Uncle Sam and his B'Hoys." *The United States Magazine and Democratic Review*. 299.

— (1853). "Brother Jonathan." *U.S. Democratic Review* 32.5: 433–9.

— (1855). "Saint Jonathan." *The United States Review* 35.2: 99–106.

— (1867). *The Bulls and the Jonathans*. Ed. William Paulding. New York: Scribner.

— [1812] (1993). "The Bucktails." In *The Lion of the West and The Bucktails*. Ed. Frank Gado. Lanham: Rowman & Littlefield. 1–86.

Plummer, Jonathan (1795). *A Sketch of the History of the Life and Adventures of Jonathan Plummer, Written by Himself*. Newburyport: Blunt & March.

Q.Q. (1834). "Yankee Notions." *The New Monthly Magazine and Literary Journal* 42.166: 160–7.

Robinson, John Hovey (1851). *The Life and Adventures of William Harvard Stinchfield, or The Wanderings of a Traveling Merchant*. Portland: Thurston and Co.
Savary, John (1899). *Uncle Sam, the Real and the Ideal: A Dissertation*. Washington, DC.
"The Schoolmaster" (1831). *New England Magazine* 1.1: 27–30.
Steele, Silas Sexton (1846). *The Brazen Drum, or The Yankee in Poland*. Philadelphia and New York: Turner & Fisher.
Taylor, Tom (1858). *Our American Cousin*. Project Gutenberg etexts.
Thompson, Denman (1889). *Denman Thompson's The Old Homestead, Written from the Celebrated Play of 'The Old Homestead'*. New York: Street & Smith Publishers.
Twain, Mark [1897] (1962a). "How to Tell a Story." In *Selected Shorter Writings of Mark Twain*. Ed. Walter Blair. Boston: Houghton Mifflin. 239–45.
— [1865] (1962b). "The Celebrated Jumping Frog." In *Selected Shorter Writings of Mark Twain*. Ed. Walter Blair. Boston: Houghton Mifflin. 13–18.
— [1889] (1982). *A Connecticut Yankee in King Arthur's Court*. Ed. Allison R. Ensor. New York and London: W. W. Norton Company.
Tyler, Royall [1787] (1997). "The Contrast." In *Early American Drama*. Ed. Jeffrey H. Richards. New York: Penguin. 1–57.
Whittier, John Greenleaf [1866] (1904). "Snow-Bound: A Winter Idyl." In *The Complete Poetical Works of John Greenleaf Whittier*. Boston and New York: Houghton Mifflin. 487–99.
Woodworth, Samuel [1825] (1966). "The Forest Rose or American Farmers: A Pastoral Opera." In *Dramas from the American Theater 1762–1909*. Ed. Richard Moody. Boston: Houghton Mifflin. 155–74.
Wordsworth, William (1985). *The Pedlar, Tintern Abbey, The Two-Part Prelude (Poems)*. Ed. Jonathan Wordsworth. Cambridge: Cambridge University Press.
"Yankee Clock Pedlars in the West" (1846). *Hartford Daily Courant*. 31 October. 2.
"A Yankee Notion" (1895). *San Francisco Call*. 17 November.
"Yankeeisms" (1832). *The New England Magazine* 3.5: 377–82.

Secondary Sources

Abrams, Robert E. (2004). *Landscape and Ideology in American Renaissance Literature: Topographies of Skepticism*. Cambridge: Cambridge University Press.
Adams, Charles H. (1985). "'The Guardian of the Law': George Washington's Role in *The Spy*." In *James Fenimore Cooper: His Country and His Art*. Ed. George A. Test. Oneonta and Cooperstown: State University of New York Press. 47–59.

Aderman, Ralph M. (1993). "Paulding's Anonymous Writings: New Attributions and Speculations." *Studies in Bibliography*. 370–81.
Aderman, Ralph M. and Wayne R. Kime (2003). *Advocate for America: The Life of James Kirke Paulding*. Selinsgrove and London: Associated University Press.
Andersen, Ruth O. M. (1975). *From Yankee to American: Connecticut 1865–1914*. Chester: Pequot Press.
Anderson, Donald (2006). "Grounded Perceptions: Land and Value in Two Plays of the New England Decline." *American Drama* 15.2: 1–29.
Appleby, Joyce (2000). *Inheriting the Revolution: The First Generation of Americans*. Cambridge and London: Harvard Belknap Press.
Atherton, Lewis E. (1945). "Itinerant Merchandising in the Antebellum South." *Bulletin of the Business Historical Society* 19.2: 35–59.
Augst, Thomas (2003). *The Clerk's Tale: Young Men and Moral Life in Nineteenth-Century America*. Chicago: University of Chicago Press.
Avallone, Charlene (1997). "What American Renaissance? The Gendered Genealogy of a Critical Discourse." *PMLA* 5: 1102–20.
Bailey, Brigitte (2019). *American Travel Literature, Gendered Aesthetics and the American Tour, 1824–1862*. Edinburgh: Edinburgh University Press.
Bank, Rosemarie K. [1997] (2010). *Theater Culture in America, 1825–1860*. Reprint. Cambridge: Cambridge University Press.
Banta, Martha (2003). *Barbaric Intercourse: Caricature and the Culture of Conduct, 1841–1936*. Chicago and London: University of Chicago Press.
Baym, Nina (1992a). "Early Histories of American Literature: A Chapter in the Institution of New England." In *Feminism and American Literary History: Essays*. New Brunswick: Rutgers University Press. 81–103.
— (1992b). "Sarah Hale, Political Writer." In *Feminism and American Literary History: Essays*. New Brunswick: Rutgers University Press. 167–82.
— (1993). *Woman's Fiction: A Guide to Novels by and about Women in America, 1820–70*. Champaign: University of Illinois Press.
Bentley, Eric (1991). *The Life of the Drama*. Rev. edn. London: Applause Theater Books.
Bergmann, Joahnnes Dietrich (1969). "The Original Confidence Man." *American Quarterly* 21.3: 560–77.
Berlant, Lauren (1991). *The Anatomy of National Fantasy: Hawthorne, Utopia, and Everyday Life*. Chicago and London: University of Chicago Press.
— (1997). "Introduction: The Intimate Public Sphere." In *The Queen of America Goes to Washington City: Essays on Sex and Citizenship*. Durham, NC: University of North Carolina Press. 1–24.
Bermel, Albert (1990). *Farce: A History from Aristophanes to Woody Allen*. Carbondale: Southern Illinois University Press.
Bivins, Thomas H. (1987). "The Body Politic: The Changing Shape of Uncle Sam." *Journalism Quarterly* 64.1: 13–20.

Blackburn, Alexander (1988). "The Pícaro in American Literature." In *Dictionary of Literary Themes and Motifs*. Ed. Jean-Charles Seigneuret. Vol. 2. Westport: Greenwood Press. 983–91.
Blair, Walter (1937). *Native American Humor (1800–1900)*. New York: American Book Company.
— [1944] (1987). *Tall Tale America: The Legendary History of Our Humorous Heroes*. Chicago and London: University of Chicago Press.
Bluestone, Daniel (1992). "The Pushcart Evil." In *The Landscape of Modernity: New York City, 1900–1940*. Ed. David Ward and Oliver Zunz. New York: Russell Sage. 287–308.
Böger, Astrid (2010). *Envisioning the Nation: The Early American World's Fairs and the Formation of Culture*. Frankfurt: Campus.
Böger, Astrid and Christof Decker (2007). "Transatlantic Perspectives on American Visual Culture." *Amerikastudien/American Studies* 52.1: 5–13.
Botkin, B. A. [1947] (1989). *A Treasury of New England Folklore: Ballads, and Traditions of Yankee Folk*. Rev. edn. New York: American Legacy Press.
Brake, Laurel (2006). "Maga, the Shilling Monthlies, and the New Journalism." In *Print Culture and the Blackwood Tradition, 1805–1930*. Ed. David Finkelstein. Toronto, Buffalo and London: Toronto University Press. 184–211.
Bramen, Carrie Tirado (2017). *American Niceness: A Cultural History*. Cambridge, MA: Harvard University Press.
Brand, Peter and Lino Pertile (eds.) (2001). *The Cambridge History of Italian Literature*. Rev. edn. Cambridge: Cambridge University Press.
Brown, Carolyn S. (1989). *The Tall Tale in American Folklore and Literature*. Nashville: University of Tennessee Press.
Brown, Dona and Stephen Nissenbaum (1999). "Changing New England: 1865–1945." In *Picturing Old New England: Image and Memory*. Ed. William H. Truettner and Roger B. Stein. New Haven and London: Yale University Press/Smithsonian Institution. 1–14.
Buchenau, Barbara (2002). *Der frühe amerikanische historische Roman im transatlantischen Vergleich*. Frankfurt: Peter Lang.
Buell, Lawrence (1987). *New England Literary Culture: From Revolution through Renaissance*. Cambridge: Cambridge University Press.
— (1992). "American Literary Emergence as a Postcolonial Phenomenon." *American Literary History* 4.3: 411–42.
— (2003). "Green Disputes: Nature, Culture, American(ist) Theory." In *Nature's Nation Revisited: American Concepts of Nature from Wonder to Ecological Crisis*. Ed. Hans Bak and Walter H. Höbling. Amsterdam: VU University Press. 43–50.
Buhle, Paul (2007). "Popular Culture." In *The Cambridge Companion to Modern American Culture*. Ed. Christopher Bigsby. Cambridge: Cambridge University Press. 392–410.

Bushman, Richard L. (1967). *From Puritan to Yankee: Character and the Social Order in Connecticut, 1690–1765*. Cambridge, MA: Harvard University Press.

Carlyle, Thomas (2010). *Past and Present: The Works of Thomas Carlyle*. Ed. Henry Duff Traill. Cambridge and New York: Cambridge University Press.

Chielens, Edward E. (1986). *American Literary Magazines: The Eighteenth and Nineteenth Centuries*. Westport: Greenwood Press.

Choate, Rufus (1849a). "The Colonial Age of New England." In *Addresses and Orations of Rufus Choate*. Ed. Samuel Gilman Brown. Boston: Little Brown. 347–93.

— (1849b). "The Importance of Illustrating New England History by a Series of Romances like the Waverly Novels. Delivered at Salem, 1833." In *Addresses and Orations of Rufus Choate*. Ed. Samuel Gilman Brown. Boston: Little Brown. 321–46.

Clark, Jennifer (1990). "John Bull's American Connection: The Allegorical Interpretation of England and the Anglo-American Relation." *Huntington Library Quarterly* 53.1: 15–39.

— (2013). *The American Idea of England, 1776–1840: Transatlantic Writing*. Burlington: Ashgate.

Cohen, Joanna (2017). *Luxurious Citizens: The Politics of Consumption in Nineteenth-Century America*. Philadelphia: University of Pennsylvania Press.

Cohen, Lara Langer (2012). *The Fabrication of American Literature: Fraudulence and Antebellum Print Culture*. Philadelphia: University of Pennsylvania Press.

Cohen, Michael (2008). "Peddlers, Poems, and Local Culture: The Case of Jonathan Plummer, a 'Balladmonger' in Nineteenth-Century New England." *ESQ: A Journal of the American Renaissance* 51.1–4: 9–32.

Conforti, Joseph A. (2001). *Imagining New England: Explorations of Regional Identity from the Pilgrims to the Mid-Twentieth Century*. Chapel Hill and London: University of North Carolina Press.

— (2006). *Saints and Strangers: New England in British North America*. Baltimore: Johns Hopkins University Press.

Connell, R. W. (1996). *Masculinities*. Cambridge: Polity Press.

Cooper, Carolyn C. (2003). "Myth, Rumor, and History: The Yankee Whittling Boy as Hero and Villain." *Technology and Culture* 4.1: 82–96.

Crowley, John W. (ed.) (1999). *Drunkard's Progress: Narratives of Addiction, Despair and Recovery*. Baltimore and London: Johns Hopkins University Press.

Cubitt, Geoffrey (1998). "Introduction." In *Imagining Nations*. Ed. Geoffrey Cubitt. Manchester and New York: Manchester University Press. 1–21.

Cunliffe, Marcus (1951). "America at the Great Exhibition of 1851." *American Quarterly* 3.2: 115–26.

Daigrepont, Lloyd M. (1984). "Ichabod Crane: Inglorious Man of Letters." *Early American Literature* 19.1: 68–81.

Daly, Peter M. (2003). "Sixteenth-Century Emblems and Imprese as Indicators of Cultural Change." In *Interpretation and Allegory: Antiquity to the Modern Period*. Ed. John Whitman. Boston and Leiden: Brill. 383–420.

Danbom, David B. (2015). "Americanism Distilled: The Place of the Countryside in American Thought." In *Rural America*. Ed. Antje Kley and Heike Paul. Heidelberg: Winter. 13–34.

Davies, Richard A. (2005). *Inventing Sam Slick: A Biography of Thomas Chandler Haliburton*. Toronto, Buffalo and London: University of Toronto Press.

Davis, Jessica Milner [1978] (2003). *Farce*. New Brunswick and London: Transaction Publishers.

Dekker, George (1993). "James Fenimore Cooper and the American Romance." In Wilhelm Verhoeven. *James Fenimore Cooper: New Historical and Literary Contexts*. Amsterdam: Rodopi. 19–29.

Dekker, George and John P. Williams (1997). *James Fenimore Cooper: The Critical Heritage*. London and New York: Routledge.

Delogu, Daisy (2015). *Allegorical Bodies: Power and Gender in Late Medieval France*. Toronto, Buffalo and London: University of Toronto Press.

Den Ouden, Amy E. (2005). *Beyond Conquest: Native Peoples and the Struggle for History in New England*. Lincoln: University of Nebraska Press.

Denison, Patricia D. (1996). "The Legacy of James A. Herne." In *Realism and the American Dramatic Tradition*. Ed. William A. Damastes. Tuscaloosa and London: University of Alabama Press. 18–36.

Ditz, Toby L. (2011). "Afterword: Contending Masculinities in Early America." In *New Men: Manliness in Early America*. Ed. Thomas A. Foster. New York: New York University Press. 256–68.

Dolan, J. R. (1964). *The Yankee Peddlers of Early America: An Affectionate History of Life and Commerce in the Developing Colonies and the Young Republic*. New York: Bramhall House.

Dorson, Richard M. (1940). "The Yankee on the Stage: A Folk-Hero of American Drama." *New England Quarterly* 13.3: 467–93.

— (1941). "America's Comic Demigods." *The American Scholar* 10.4: 389–401.

— (1943). "Jonathan Draws the Long Bow." *New England Quarterly* 16.2: 244–79.

— (2002). "Life Styles and Legends (1971)." In Simon J. Bronner. *Folk Nation: Folklore in the Creation of American Tradition*. Wilmington, DE: Scholarly Resources. 215–23.

Doyle, Laura (2009). "Liberty's Empire." In *American Studies: An Anthology*. Ed. Janice Radway, Barry Shank, Penny von Eschen and Kevin Gaines. Malden: Blackwell. 59–68.

Dryden, Edgar A. (1971). "History and Progress Some Implications of: Form in Cooper's *Littlepage* Novels." *Nineteenth-Century Fiction* 26.1: 49–64.
Eggs, Ekkehard (2015). "Metaphorizität und Uneigentlichkeit." In *Handbuch Literarische Rhetorik*. Ed. Rüdiger Zymner. Berlin: De Gruyter. 243–80.
Epp, Michael (2010). "The Imprint of Affect: Humor, Character and National Identity in American Studies." *Journal of American Studies* 1: 47–65.
Erbacher, Eric, Nicole Maruo-Schröder, and Florian Sedlmeier (eds.) (2014). *Rereading the Machine in the Garden: Nature and Technology in American Culture*. Frankfurt: Campus Verlag.
Evelev, John (2007). "Picturesque Reform in the New England Village Novel, 1845–1867." *ESQ: A Journal of the American Renaissance* 53.2: 148–83.
Fink, Robert A. (1974). "Harvey Birch: The Yankee Peddler as American Hero." *New York Folklore Quarterly* 30: 137–52.
Fisher Fishkin, Shelley (2005). "Crossroads of Cultures: The Transnational Turn in American Studies." *American Quarterly* 57: 17–57.
Fischer-Lichte, Erika [1983] (1994). *Semiotik des Theaters Band I: Das System der theatralischen Zeichen*. Tübingen: Narr.
Fitz, Karsten (2010). *The American Revolution Remembered, 1830s to 1850s: Competing Images and Conflicting Narratives*. Heidelberg: Winter.
Fliegelman, Jay (1982). *Prodigals and Pilgrims: The American Revolution against Patriarchal Authority, 1750–1800*. Cambridge: Cambridge University Press.
Fluck, Winfried (2000). "From Aesthetics to Political Criticism: Theories of the Early American Novel." In *Early America Re-Explored: New Readings in Colonial, Early National, and Antebellum Culture*. Ed. Klaus H. Schmidt and Fritz Fleischmann. New York: Peter Lang. 225–68.
Fluck, Winfried and Donald E. Pease (eds.) (2014). *Towards a Post-Exceptionalist American Studies*. REAL – Yearbook of Research in English and American Literature. Vol. 30. Tübingen: Narr.
Fotis, Matt (2011). "Jonathan Goes to Washington: The Stage Yankee, George W. Bush, and the American Presidency." *Journal of American Drama and Theatre* 23.3: 57–75.
Fox, Dixon Ryan (1940). *Yankees and Yorkers*. New York and London: Oxford University Press.
Franke-Ruta, Garance (2013). "When America Was Female." *The Atlantic.com*. 5 March. <https://www.theatlantic.com/politics/archive/2013/03/when-america-was-female/273672/> (accessed May 19, 2016).
Freytag, Wiebke (1992). "Allegorie, Allegorese." In *Historisches Wörterbuch der Rhetorik*. Ed. Gert Ueding. Vol. 1: A-Bib. Tübingen: Max Niemeyer. 330–93.
Friedman, Walter A. (2005). "Hawkers and Walkers." In *Birth of a Salesman: The Transformation of Selling in America*. Cambridge, MA: Harvard University Press. 14–33.

Fuller, Randall (2006). "Errand into the Wilderness: Perry Miller as American Scholar." *American Literary History* 18.1: 102–28.

Gannon, Mark (2001). "Escaping 'Mr. Jefferson's Plan of Destruction': New England Federalists and the Idea of a Northern Confederacy, 1803–1804." *Journal of the Early Republic* 21.3: 413–34.

Gardiner, W. H. (1822). "The Spy: A Tale of the Neutral Ground (review)." *North American Review* 11.36: 250–82.

Gibbons, William (2008). "'Yankee Doodle' and Nationalism, 1780–1920." *American Music*. Summer. 243–74.

Gifford, Terry (1999). *Pastoral*. London: Routledge.

Giles, Paul (2001). *Transatlantic Insurrections: British Culture and the Formation of American Literature, 1730–1860*. Philadelphia: University of Pennsylvania Press.

Gilmore, William J. (1989). *Reading Becomes a Necessity of Life: Material and Cultural Life in Rural New England, 1780–1835*. Knoxville: University of Tennessee Press.

Godeanu-Kenworthy, Oana (2009). "The Political Other in Nineteenth-Century British North America: The Satire of Thomas Chandler Haliburton." *Early American Studies: An Interdisciplinary Journal* 7.1: 205–35.

Gossett, Suzanne and Barbara Ann Bardes (1985). "Women and Political Power in the Republic: Two Early American Novels." *Legacy* 2.2: 13–30.

Greenberg, Amy (2005). *Manifest Manhood and the Antebellum American Empire*. Cambridge: Cambridge University Press.

Greenblatt, Stephen (2009). "A Mobility Studies Manifesto." In *Cultural Mobility: A Manifesto*. Ed. Stephen Greenblatt et al. 250–3.

Greteman, Blaine (2010). "Stock Characters: The Literary Lives of American Businessmen." In *Merchants, Barons, Sellers and Suits: The Changing Images of the Businessman through Literature*. Ed. Christa Mahalik. Newcastle upon Tyne: Cambridge Scholars Press. 176–203.

Griggs, Harry (1952). "Drought Will Not Affect Wooden Nutmeg Harvest." *Hartford Courant*. 22 August. 3.

Grimsted, David [1968] (1987). *Melodrama Unveiled: American Theater and Culture, 1800–1850*. Berkeley and Los Angeles: University of California Press.

Groen, Mark (2012). "Teaching, Learning, and Emerging National Identity in the American South." *American Educational History Jounal* 40.1/2: 21–36.

Hanlon, Christopher (2013). *America's England: Antebellum Literature and Atlantic Sectionalism*. Oxford: Oxford University Press.

Harkins, Anthony (2004). *Hillbilly: A Cultural History of an American Icon*. Oxford and New York: Oxford University Press.

Harrison, Henry (1917). *The Origin of "Yankee"*. London: The Morland Press.

Hastings, Adrian (1997). *The Construction of Nationhood: Ethnicity, Religion and Nationalism*. Cambridge: Cambridge University Press.

Hastings, George E. (1929). "John Bull and his American Descendants." *American Literature* 1.1: 40–68.
Herzogenrath, Bernd (2010). *An American Body Politic: A Deleuzian Approach*. Lebanon, NH: Dartmouth College Press.
Hobsbawm, Eric and Terence Granger (eds.) (1983). *The Invention of Tradition*. Cambridge and New York: Cambridge University Press.
Hodge, Francis (1964). *Yankee Theater: The Image of America on the Stage, 1825–1850*. Austin: University of Texas Press.
Hoffman, Daniel G. (1953). "Irving's Use of American Folklore in 'The Legend of Sleepy Hollow.'" *Publications of the Modern Language Association of America*. 425–35.
Hokenson, Jan Walsh (2006). *The Idea of Comedy: History, Theory, Critique*. Madison: Fairleigh Dickinson University Press.
Holt, Kerin (2012). "Here, There and Everywhere: The Elusive Regionalism of John Neal." In *John Neal and Nineteenth-Century American Literature and Culture*. Ed. Edward Watts and David J. Carlson. Lewisburg: Bucknell University Press. 185–208.
House, Kay Seymour (1966). *Cooper's Americans*. Columbus: Ohio State University Press.
Hubka, Thomas C. (2004). *Big House, Little House, Back House, Barn: The Connected Farm Buildings of New England*. Lebanon, NH: University Press of New England.
Hunt, Tamara L. (2003). *Defining John Bull: Political Caricature and National Identity in Late Georgian England*. London: Ashgate.
Inge, Thomas M. (ed.) (1969). *Agrarianism in American Literature*. New York: Odyssey Press.
Jaffee, David (1991). "Peddlers of Progress and the Transformation of the Rural North, 1760–1860." *The Journal of American History* 78.2: 511–35.
— (2011). *A New Nation of Goods: The Material Culture of Early America*. Philadelphia: University of Pennsylvania Press.
Jones, Eric (2011). *New Hampshire Curiosities: Quirky Characters, Roadside Oddities and Other Offbeat Stuff*. Lanham: Rowman & Littlefield.
Jones, LuAnn (2000). "Gender, Race, and Itinerant Commerce in the Rural New South." *The Journal of Southern History* 66.2: 297–320.
Jordan, Cynthia S. (1989). *Second Stories: The Politics of Language, Form, and Gender in Early American Fictions*. Chapel Hill: University of North Carolina Press.
Jortner, Maura (2013). "Nineteenth-Century Travel Accounts of America and Bayle Bernard's 'The Yankee Pedlar'." *Nineteenth-Century Theater and Film* 40.1: 74–97.
Josephson, Matthew [1934] (1962). *Robber Barons: The Great American Capitalists, 1861–1901*. Boston: Houghton Mifflin/Mariner Books.
Kaplan, Amy (1998). "Manifest Domesticity." *American Literature* 70.3: 581–606.

— (2002). *The Anarchy of Empire in the Making of U.S. Culture*. Cambridge, MA: Harvard University Press.

Kaye, Myrna (1975). *Yankee Weathervanes*. Illus. Corinne Pascoe. New York: E. P. Dutton.

Kelley, Theresa M. (1997). *Reinventing Allegory*. Cambridge: Cambridge University Press.

Kelly, Darlene (1985). "Haliburton's International Yankee." In *The Thomas Chandler Haliburton Symposium*. Ed. Frank M. Tierney. Ottawa: University of Ottawa Press. 124–35.

Kermes, Stephanie (2008). *Creating an American Identity: New England, 1789–1825*. Basingstoke: Palgrave Macmillan.

Ketchum, Alton (1959). *Uncle Sam: The Man and the Legend*. New York: Hill & Wang.

Killheffer, Marie (1928). "A Comparison of the Dialect of 'The Biglow Papers' with the Dialect of Four Yankee Plays." *American Speech* 3.3: 222–36.

Kimmel, Michael (2012). *Manhood in America: A Cultural History*. New York: Oxford University Press.

Kimmel, Michael and Abby L. Ferber (2006). "'White Men Are This Nation': Right-Wing Militias and the Restoration of Rural American Masculinity." In *Country Boys: Masculinity and Rural Life*. Ed. Hugh Campbell, Michael Bell and Margaret Finney. University Park: Pennsylvania State University Press. 121–37.

Kippola, Karl (2012). *Acts of Manhood: The Performance of Masculinity on the American Stage, 1829–1865*. New York: Palgrave Macmillan.

Klarer, Mario (1999). "Cannibalism and Carnivalesque: Incorporation as Utopia in the Early Image of America." *New Literary History* 30.2: 389–410.

Kley, Antje and Heike Paul (eds.) (2015). *Rural America*. Heidelberg: Winter.

Kline, Priscilla Carrington (1939). "New Light on the Yankee Peddler." *New England Quarterly* 12.1: 80–98.

Knight, Charles A. (1989). "The Images of Nations in Eighteenth-Century Satire." *Eighteenth-Century Studies* 22.4: 489–511.

Kolodny, Annette (1975). *The Lay of the Land: Metaphor as Experience and History in American Life and Letters*. Chapel Hill: University of North Carolina Press.

Kramer, Lloyd (2011). *Nationalism in Europe and America: Politics, Culture, and Identities since 1775*. Chapel Hill: University of North Carolina Press.

Kroetsch, Robert (1989). *The Lovely Treachery of Words*. Toronto, New York, and Oxford: Oxford University Press.

Laird, Matthew R. (1993). "Nativist American Humor: Sam Slick and the Defense of New England Whig Culture." *Canadian Review of American Studies* 23.4: 71–88.

Lanzendörfer, Tim (2016). "Periodicals and Journalism in Nineteenth-Century America." In *Handbook of Transatlantic North American Studies*. Ed. Julia Straub. Berlin: De Gruyter. 316–33.
Lease, Benjamin (1953). "Yankee Poetics: John Neal's Theory of Poetry and Fiction." *American Literature* 24.4: 505–19.
Lee, Robert A. (1993). "Making History, Making Fiction: Cooper's *The Spy*." In *James Fenimore Cooper: New Historical and Literary Contexts*. Ed. W. M. Verhoeven. Amsterdam and Atlanta: Rodopi. 31–46.
Leeming, David and Jake Page (1999). *Myths, Legends and Folktales of America: An Anthology*. Oxford and New York: Oxford University Press.
Lehuu, Isabelle (2000). *Carnival on the Page: Popular Print Media in Antebellum America*. Chapel Hill: University of North Carolina Press.
Lemelle, Jr., Anthony J. (2010). *Black Masculinity and Sexual Politics*. London: Routledge.
Leverenz, David (1989). *Manhood and the American Renaissance*. Ithaca: Cornell University Press.
Levine, Lawrence W. (1988). *Highbrow/Lowbrow: The Emergence of Cultural Hierarchy in America*. Cambridge, MA: Harvard University Press.
Levine, Robert (1998). "Section and Nation: The Missouri Compromise and the Rise of 'American Literature'." In Brook Thomas. *Literature and the Nation*. REAL – The Yearbook of Reserach in English and American Literature. Vol. 14. Tübingen: Narr. 223–40.
Lofaro, Michael A. (1978). *The Tall Tales of Davy Crockett: The Second Nashville Series of Crockett Almanacs, 1839–1841*. Knoxville: University of Tennessee Press.
— (2001). *Davy Crockett's Riproarious Shemales and Sentimental Sisters: Women's Tall Tales from the Crockett Almanacs, 1835–1856*. Mechanicsburg, PA: Stackpole Books.
McCloskey, John C. (1935). "The Campaign of Periodicals after the War of 1812 for National American Literature." *PMLA* 50.1: 262–73.
McConachie, Bruce (1998). "American Theatre in Context, from the Beginnings to 1870." In *The Cambridge History of American Theatre*. Ed. Don B. Wilmeth and Christopher Bigsby. Vol. 1. Cambridge: Cambridge University Press. 111–81.
McDermott, Douglas (1998). "Structure and Management in the American Theater from the Beginning to 1870." In *The Cambridge History of American Theatre*. Ed. Don B. Wilmeth and Christopher Bigsby. Vol. 1. Cambridge: Cambridge University Press. 182–215.
McGirr, Elaine (2007). *Eighteenth-Century Characters: A Guide to the Literature of the Age*. Basingstoke: Palgrave Macmillan.
Machosky, Brenda (2013). *Structures of Appearing: Allegory and the Work of Literature*. New York: Fordham.
McLamore, Richard V. (2000). "The Dutchman in the Attic: Claiming an Inheritance in *The Sketch Book of Geoffrey Crayon*." *American Literature* 72.1: 31–57.

McNeil, Peter (1999). "'That Doubtful Gender': Macaroni Dress and Male Sexualities." *Fashion Theory: The Journal of Dress, Body, and Culture* 3.2: 411–47.
Madsen, Deborah L. (1996). *Allegory in America: From Puritanism to Postmodernism*. Basingstoke: Palgrave Macmillan.
Major, Emma (2012). *Madam Britannia: Women, Church and Nation, 1712–1812*. Oxford and New York: Oxford University Press.
Manning, Susan and Andrew Taylor (eds.) (2007). *Transatlantic Literary Studies: A Reader*. Edinburgh: Edinburgh University Press.
Marsh, Clayton (2005). "Stealing Time: Poe's Confidence Men and 'The Rush of the Age'." *American Literature* 77.2: 259–89.
Marshall, Tom (1976). "Haliburton's Canada." *Canadian Literature* 68/69: 134–8.
Martin, Roger (2005). "Yankee." *Empire Du Mal? Dictionnaire Iconoclaste des Etats Unis*. Paris: Le Cherche Midi. 308–10.
Martin, Scott C. (2014). "The Politics of Antebellum Melodrama." In *The Oxford Handbook of American Drama*. Ed. Jeffrey H. Richards and Heather S. Nathans. Oxford: Oxford University Press. 67–80.
Marx, Leo [1967] (2000). *The Machine in the Garden: Technology and the Pastoral Ideal in America*. Oxford and New York: Oxford University Press.
— (2003). "The Pandering Landscape: On American Nature as Illusion." In *Nature's Nation Revisited: American Concepts of Nature from Wonder to Ecological Crisis*. Ed. Hans Bak and Walter W. Hölbling. Amsterdam: VU University Press. 30–42.
Matthews, Albert (1908). *Uncle Sam*. Worcester: Davis Press.
Matthews, Brander (1879). "The American on the Stage." *Scribner's Monthly* 18: 321–33.
Matthews, J. V. (1978). "'Whig History': The New England Whigs and a Usable Past." *New England Quarterly* 51.2: 192–208.
Matthews, Roy T. (2007). "Britannia and John Bull: From Birth to Maturity." *The Historian* 62.4: 799–820.
Mellini, Peter (2012). "John Bull." <http://www.britishempire.co.uk/biography/johnbull.htm> (accessed April 8, 2016).
Meserve, Walter J. (1986). *Heralds of Promise: The Drama of the American People in the Age of Jackson, 1829–1849*. Westport: Greenwood Press.
— (2000). "Introduction: Neighbor Jackwood." In Walter J. Meserve and Mollie Ann Meserve. *Fateful Lightning: America's Civil War Plays*. New York: Feedback Theaterbooks and Prospero Press.
— and Mollie Ann Meserve (2000). "An Introduction." In *Fateful Lightning: America's Civil War Plays*. New York: Feedback Theaterbooks and Prospero Press. xiii–xxii.
Meyerlob, Maya (2012). "Celebrated Rubbish: John Neal and the Commercialization of Early American Romanticism." In *John Neal and Nineteenth-Century American Literature and Culture*. Ed. Edward Watts and David J. Carlson. Lewisburg: Bucknell University Press. 99–122.

Miller, Lewis H. (1980). "The Supernaturalism of *Snow-Bound*." *New England Quarterly* 53.5: 291–307.

Miller, Tice L. (2007). *Entertaining the Nation: American Drama in the Eighteenth and Nineteenth Centuries*. Carbondale: Southern Illinois University Press.

Mirzoeff, Nicholas (1995). *Bodyscape: Art, Modernity, and the Ideal Figure*. London and New York: Routledge.

Moody, Richard (1966a). "Introduction: The Forest Rose." In *Dramas from the American Theater 1762–1909*. Ed. Richard Moody. Boston: Houghton Mifflin. 143–54.

— (1966b). "Introduction: Shore Acres." In *Dramas from the American Theater 1762–1909*. Ed. Richard Moody. Boston: Houghton Mifflin. 659–71.

Morgan, Winifred (1989). *An American Icon: Brother Jonathan and American Identity*. Newark: University of Delaware Press.

Morgensen, Scott Lauria (2012). "Theorising Gender, Sexuality and Settler Colonialism: An Introduction." *Settler Colonial Studies* 2.2: 2–22.

Morrison, Toni (1992). *Playing in the Dark: Whiteness and the Literary Imagination*. Reprint. London: Vintage.

Mussey, Barrows (ed.) (1937). *We Were New England: Yankee Life by Those Who Lived It*. New York: Stackpole Books.

Nathans, Heather (2003). *Early American Theatre from the Revolution to Thomas Jefferson*. Cambridge: Cambridge University Press.

— (2014). "Representing Ethnic Identity on the Antebellum Stage, 1826–1861." In *The Oxford Handbook of American Drama*. Ed. Jeffrey H. Richards and Heather S. Nathans. Oxford: Oxford University Press. 97–113.

Nelson, Dana (1998). *National Manhood: Capitalist Citizenship and the Imagined Fraternity of White Men*. Durham, NC, and London: Duke University Press.

Nevins, Allen (1975). *A Century of Political Cartoons: Caricature in the United States from 1800 to 1900*. New York: Octagon.

Newman, Gerald (1997). *The Rise of English Nationalism: A Cultural History 1740–1830*. New York: St. Martin's Press.

Nissenbaum, Stephen (1996). "New England as Region and Nation." In *All Over the Map: Rethinking American Regions*. Ed. Edward L. Ayers, Patricia Nelson Limerick, Stephen Nissenbaum, and Peter S. Onuf. Baltimore and London: Johns Hopkins University Press. 38–61.

Nuquist, Reidun (2003). "s.v. Green Mountain Boys." In *The Vermont Encyclopedia*. Ed. John J. Duffy, Samuel B. Hand, and Ralph I. Orth. Lebanon, NH: University Press of New England. 143–4.

O'Keefe, John T. (2018). "New England." In *Encyclopedia of American Studies*. Ed. Simon J. Bronner. <http://eas-ref.press.jhu.edu/view?aid=307> (accessed November 16, 2020).

O'Malley, Michael (1990). *Keeping Watch: A History of American Time*. New York: Viking Penguin.

Onuf, Peter S. (1996). "Federalism, Republicanism, and the Origins of American Sectionalism." In *All Over the Map: Rethinking American Regions*. Ed. Edward L. Ayers, Patricia Nelson Limerick, Stephen Nissenbaum, and Peter S. Onuf. Baltimore and London: Johns Hopkins University Press. 11–37.

Painter, Nell Irvin (2010). *The History of White People*. New York: W. W. Norton.

Panofsky, Ruth (1992). "The Publication of Thomas Chandler Haliburton's *The Clockmaker*, 2nd Series." *Papers of the Bibliographical Society of Canada* 30.2: 21–37.

— (1993a). "The Publication of Thomas Chandler Haliburton's *The Clockmaker*, 1st Series." *Canadian Literature* 138–9: 5–20.

— (1993b). "The Publication of Thomas Chandler Haliburton's *The Clockmaker*, 3rd Series." *Papers of the Bibliographical Society of Canada* 31.2: 7–20.

Parkins, Wendy (2002). *Fashioning the Body Politic: Dress, Gender, Citizenship*. London: Bloomsbury.

Paul, Heike (2013). "Agrarianism, Expansionism, and the Myth of the American West." In *The Myths that Made America*. Bielefeld: transcript. 311–66.

— (2014). "Critical Regionalism and Post-Exceptionalist American Studies." *Towards a Post-Exceptionalist American Studies*. REAL – Yearbook of Research in English and American Literature. Vol. 30. Ed. Winfried Fluck and Donald E. Pease. Tübingen: Narr. 397–424.

Paul, Heike, Alexandra Ganser, and Katharina Gerund (2012). "Introduction." In *Pirates, Drifters, Fugitives: Figures of Mobility in the US and Beyond*. Ed. Heike Paul, Alexandra Ganser, and Katharina Gerund. Heidelberg: Winter. 11–27.

Pavis, Patrice (1988). *Semiotik der Theaterrezeption*. Tübingen: Narr.

— (2002). "Reception." In *Dictionnaire du Théâtre*. Paris: Armand Colin. 290–2.

Pease, Donald E. (1994). *National Identities and Post Americanist Narratives*. Durham, NC, and London: Duke University Press.

— (1998). "Commentary: Imperial Discourse." *Diplomatic History* 22.4: 605–15.

Peck, Daniel H. (1977). *A World by Itself: The Pastoral Moment in Cooper's Fiction*. New Haven and London: Yale University Press.

Peterson, Beverly (1998). "Mrs. Hale on Mrs. Stowe and Slavery." *American Periodicals* 8: 30–44.

Pethers, Matthew (2012). "'I Must Resemble Nobody': John Neal, Genre, and the Making of American Literary Nationalism." In *John Neal and Nineteenth-Century American Literature and Culture*. Ed. Edward Watts and David J. Carlson. Lewisburg: Bucknell University Press. 1–38.

— (2013). "That Eternal Ghost of Trade: Anglo-American Market Culture and the Antebellum Stage Yankee." In *The Materials of Exchange* between Britain and North East America, 1750–1900. Ed. Daniel Maudlin and Robin Peel. London: Routledge. 87–116.

Pfister, Joel (1991). "A Garden in the Machine: Reading a Mid-19th-Century, Two-Cylinder Parlor Stove as Cultural Text." *Technology in Society* 13: 327–43.

Pickering, James H. (1966). "Enoch Crosby, Secret Agent of the Neutral Ground: His Own Story." *New York History* 47.1: 61–73.

Plett, Heinrich (1979). "Konzepte des Allegorischen in der englischen Renaissance." In *Formen und Funktionen der Allegorie*. Ed. Walter Haug. Stuttgart: Metzler. 310–35.

Postlewait, Thomas (1999). "From Melodrama to Realism: The Suspect History of American Drama." In *Melodrama: The Cultural Emergence of a Genre*. Ed. Michael Hays and Anastasia Nikolopoulou. Basingstoke and London: Macmillan. 39–60.

Ragussis, Michael (2000). "Jews and Other 'Outlandish Englishmen': Ethnic Performance and the Invention of British Identity under the Georges." *Critical Inquiry* 26.4: 773–97.

Reed, Arthur Lachlan (1953). "Asa Greene, New England Publisher, New York Editor and Humorist, 1789–1838." Dissertation, University of Minnesota.

Reid, Margaret K. (2004). *Cultural Secrets as Narrative Form: Storytelling in Nineteenth-Century America*. Columbus: Ohio State University Press.

Reynolds, David S. [1998] (2001). *Beneath the American Renaissance: The Subversive Imagination in the Age of Emerson and Melville*. Foreword by Sean Wilentz. Oxford: Oxford University Press.

Rezek, Joseph (2015). *London and the Making of Provincial Literature: Aesthetics and the Transatlantic Book Trade, 1800–1850*. Philadelphia: University of Pennsylvania Press.

Richards, Jeffrey H. (1991). *Theater Enough: American Theater and the Metaphor of the World Stage, 1607–1789*. Durham, NC, and London: Duke University Press.

— (2000). "Race and the Yankee: Woodworth's *Forest Rose*." *Comparative Drama* 34.1: 33–52.

— (2005). *Drama, Theatre, and Identity in the American New Republic*. Cambridge: Cambridge University Press.

— (2014). "Early Republican Drama." In *The Oxford Handbook of American Drama*. Ed. Jeffrey H. Richards and Heather S. Nathans. Oxford: Oxford University Press. 50–66.

Richardson, Riché (2007). *Black Masculinity and the U.S. South: From Uncle Tom to Gangsta*. Athens: University of Georgia Press.

Ringe, Donald A. (1960). "Cooper's Littlepage Novels: Change and Stability in American Society." *American Literature* 32.3: 280–90.

— (1988). *James Fenimore Cooper*. Updated edn. Boston: Twayne.

Roach, Joseph (1998). "The Emergence of the American Actor." In *The Cambridge History of American Theater*. Ed. Don B. Wilmeth and

Christopher Bigsby. Vol. 1. Cambridge: Cambridge University Press. 338–72.
Rocks, James E. (1993). "Whittier's *Snow-Bound*: 'The Circle of our Hearth' and the Discourse of Domesticity." *Studies in the American Renaissance.* 339–53.
Roehm, A. I. (1943). "That Awful Word 'Yankee'." *Peabody Journal of Education* 21.3: 150–1.
Rose, Anne C. (1995). *Voices of the Marketplace: American Thought and Culture, 1830–1860.* New York: Twayne.
Rosenthal, Caroline (2011). *New York and Toronto Novels after Postmodernism.* Rochester: Camden House.
Rosenthal, Caroline and Stefanie Schäfer (2014). "Introduction." In *Fake Identity? The Impostor Narrative in North American Culture.* Ed. Caroline Rosenthal and Stefanie Schäfer. Frankfurt: Campus. 1–11.
Rourke, Constance [1931] (2004). *American Humor: A Study of the National Character.* New York: New York Review of Books.
Royot, Daniel (1985). "Sam Slick and American Popular Humor." In *The Thomas Chandler Haliburton Symposium.* Ed. Frank M. Tierney. Ottawa: University of Ottawa Press. 123–34.
Rubin, Joan Shelley (1980). *Constance Rourke and American Culture.* Chapel Hill: University of North Carolina Press.
St. Armand, Barton Levi (1978). "Harvey Birch as the Wandering Jew: Literary Calvinism in James Fenimore Cooper's *The Spy.*" *American Literature* 50.3: 348–68.
Schäfer, Stefanie (2012). "Towards a National Drama: James K. Paulding's *The Lion of the West.*" In *Transnational American Studies.* Ed. Udo Hebel. Heidelberg: Winter. 183–206.
— (2015). "'Forever friends': Der stage yankee als Reflexionsfigur für das junge Amerika." In *Empathie, Sympathie und Narration: Strategien der Rezeptionslenkung in Prosa, Drama und Film.* Ed. Caroline Lusin. Heidelberg: Winter. 105–20.
— (2016). "(Un)Settling North America: The Yankee in the Writings of John Neal and Thomas Chandler Haliburton." In *Traveling Traditions: Nineteenth-Century Cultural Concepts and Transatlantic Intellectual Networks.* Ed. Erik Redling. Berlin: De Gruyter. 231–46.
— (2017). "John Neal and the Problem of American Romanticism." In *Reading the Canon: Literary History in the 21st Century.* Ed. Philipp Löffler. Heidelberg: Winter. 309–26.
Scheiding, Oliver (2003). *Geschichte und Fiktion. Zum Funktionswandel des frühen amerikanischen Romans.* Paderborn: Ferdinand Schöningh.
Schilling, Michael (1979). "Allegorie und Satire auf illustrierten Flugblättern des Barock." In *Formen und Funktionen der Allegorie.* Ed. Walter Haug. Stuttgart: Metzler. 405–18.
Schlereth, Thomas J. (1992). "Columbia, Columbus, and Columbianism." *Journal of American History* 79.3: 937–68.

Schlueter, Jennifer (2008). "'A Theatrical Race': American Identity and Popular Performance in the Writings of Constance M. Rourke." *Theater Journal* 60: 529–43.
Schmitz, Neil (1977). "Tall Tale, Tall Talk: Pursuing the Lie in Jacksonian Literature." *American Literature* 48.4: 471–91.
Schneck, Peter (2003). "Double Vision: (Not) A Definition of Visual Culture." In *Visual Culture in the American Studies Classroom*. Ed. Udo Hebel and Martina Kohl. Vienna: U.S. Embassy/Teacher Academy. 1–24.
Scholz, Susanne (2000). *Body Narratives: Writing the Nation and Fashioning the Subject in Early Modern England*. Basingstoke: Macmillan.
Schroeder, John H. (1977). "Major Jack Downing and American Expansionism: Seba Smith's Political Satire, 1847–1856." *New England Quarterly* 50.2: 214–33.
Schweighauser, Philipp (2016a). *Beautiful Deceptions: European Aesthetics, the Early American Novel and Illusionist Art*. Charlottesville: University of Virginia Press.
— (2016b). "The Early American Novel and Sentimentalism." In *Handbook of Transatlantic North American Studies*. Ed. Julia Straub. Berlin: De Gruyter. 213–33.
Seyhan, Azade (2003). "Allegory as the Trope of Memory: Registers of Cultural Time in Schlegel and Novalis." In *Interpretation and Allegory: Antiquity to the Modern Period*. Ed. John Whitman. Boston and Leiden: Brill. 437–50.
Shaffer, Jason (2007). *Performing Patriotism: National Identity in the Colonial and Revolutionary American Theater*. Philadelphia: University of Pennsylvania Press.
Shalhope, Robert E. (2002). "Bennington and the Green Mountain Boys: The Emergence of Liberal Democracy in Vermont, 1760–1850." In *Republicanism and Liberalism in America and the German States, 1750–1850*. Ed. Jürgen Heideking and James A. Henretta. Washington, DC, and Cambridge: Publications of the German Historical Institute/Cambridge University Press. 147–64.
Sheidley, Harlow W. (1998). *Sectional Nationalism: Massachusetts Conservative Leaders and the Transformation of America, 1815–1836*. Boston: Northeastern University Press.
Shoaff, Robert E. (1964a). "Swiss Press Gives Big Play of Yankee Peddler's Exhibit." *Hartford Courant*. 4 October. 22A.
— (1964b). "Yankee Peddler Creates Airport Problem." *Hartford Courant*. 21 September. 23.
— (1964c). "Yankee Peddler a Hit in Rome." *Hartford Courant*. 27 September. 1B.
— (1964d). "Yankee Peddler Makes Good Copy in Berlin." *Hartford Courant*. 11 October. 17A.
— (1964e). "Yankee Peddler Reaches Munich During Festival." *Hartford Courant*. 10 October. 8.

Silber, Nina (1993). *The Romance of Reunion: Northerners and the South, 1865–1900*. Chapel Hill: University of North Carolina Press.

Smith-Rosenberg, Carroll (1992). "Dis-Covering the Subject of the 'Great Constitutional Discussion', 1786–1789." *Journal of American History* 79.3: 841–73.

— (2014). "Modernity Clothing: Birthing the Modern Atlantic/Birthing the Modern Republic." In *Fashioning the Nineteenth Century: Habits of Being 3*. Ed. Cristina Giorcelli and Paula Rabinovitz. Minneapolis: University of Minnesota Press. 29–51.

Smurthwaite, Cynthia (1997). "Slouching Towards Slickville: Sam Slick's Chilly Reception." *Studies in Canadian Literature* 2.2: 39–55.

Spingarn, Lawrence P. (1958). "The Yankee in Early American Fiction." *New England Quarterly* 31.4: 484–95.

Stephenson, Robert C. (1960). "Farce as Method." *Tulane Review of Drama* 51.2: 85–93.

Stiegler, Bernd (2014). "Visual Culture." In *De Gruyter Handbuch Literatur und Visuelle Kultur*. Ed. Claudia Benthien and Brigitte Weingart. Berlin: De Gruyter. 159–72.

Straub, Julia (2017). *The Rise of New Media 1750–1850: Transatlantic Discourse and American Memory*. London: Palgrave Macmillan.

Tamarkin, Elisa (2008). *Anglophilia: Deference, Devotion, and Antebellum America*. Chicago: University of Chicago Press.

Tambling, Jeremy (2010). *Allegory*. London: Routledge.

Taylor, Miles (1992). "John Bull and the Iconography of Public Opinion in England c. 1712–1929." *Past & Present* 134: 93–128.

Taylor, William R. (1961). *Cavalier and Yankee: The Old South and American National Character*. New York: Harper & Row.

Tenneriello, Susan (2013). *Spectacle Culture and American Identity, 1815–1940*. Basingstoke: Palgrave Macmillan.

Thomas, Brook (2017). *The Literature of Reconstruction: Not in Plain Black and White*. Baltimore: Johns Hopkins University Press.

Tocqueville, Alexis de [1831] (2000). *Democracy in America*. Trans. Harvey C. Mansfield and Delba Winthrop. Chicago: University of Chicago Press.

Traister, Bryce (2010). "The Object of Study: Are We Being Transnational Yet?" *Journal of Transnational American Studies* 2.1: 1–29.

Trees, Andy. (2000). "Benedict Arnold, John André and his Three Yeoman Captors: A Sentimental Journey or American Virtue Defined." *Early American Literature* 35.3: 246–78.

Truettner, William H. and Roger B. Stein (1999). *Picturing Old New England: Image and Memory*. New Haven and London: Yale University Press/Smithsonian Institution.

Turner, Victor (1988). *The Anthropology of Performance*. New York: PAJ Publications.

Ubersfeld, Anne (1991). "Der lückenhafte Text und die imaginäre Bühne." In *Texte zur Theorie des Theaters*. Ed. Klaus Lazarowicz and Christopher Balme. Stuttgart: Reclam. 394–400.

Ulrich, Laurel Thatcher (1998). "Housewife and Gadder: Themes of Self-Sufficiency and Community in Eighteenth-Century New England." In *Families in the U.S.: Kinship and Domestic Politics*. Ed. Karen V. Iansen and Anita Ilta Garey. Philadelphia: Temple University Press. 241–50.
— (2001). *The Age of Homespun: Objects and Stories in the Creation of an American Myth*. New York: Knopf.
Uselding, Paul J. (1975). "Peddling in the Antebellum Economy: Precursor of Mass-Marketing or a Start in Life?" *American Journal of Economics and Sociology* 34.1: 55–66.
Van Dusen, Albert E. (1975). "The Puritan Becomes a Yankee." In *Puritans Against the Wilderness: Connecticut History to 1763*. Vol. 1. Chester: The Pequot Press. 110–28.
Vanderbeck, Robert M. (2006). "Vermont and the Imaginative Geographies of American Whiteness." *Annals of the Association of American Geographers* 96.3: 641–59.
Veracini, Lorenzo (2013). "'Settler Colonialism': Career of a Concept." *Journal of Imperial and Commonwealth History* 41.2: 313–33.
Verheul, Jaap (2012). "'A Peculiar National Character': Transatlantic Realignment and the Birth of American Cultural Nationalism after 1815." *European Journal of American Studies* 7.2 (online).
Verhoeven, W. M. (1993). "Neutralizing the Land: The Myth of Authority and the Authority of Myth in Fenimore Cooper's *The Spy*." In *James Fenimore Cooper: New Historical and Literary Contexts*. Ed. W. M. Verhoeven. Amsterdam and Atlanta: Rodopi. 71–87.
— (2002). *Revolutionary Histories: Transatlantic Cultural Nationalism, 1775–1815*. Basingstoke: Palgrave Macmillan.
Vincent, Thomas (1985). "Stratagems of Satire in North American Literature before Haliburton: A Background Paper." In *The Thomas Chandler Haliburton Symposium*. Ed. Frank Tierney. Ottawa: University of Ottawa Press. 53–64.
Vinson, J. Chal. (1957). "Thomas Nast and the American Political Scene." *American Quarterly* 9.3: 337–44.
Wald, Priscilla (1998). *Constituting Americans: Cultural Anxiety and Narrative Form*. Durham, NC, and London: Duke University Press.
Waldstreicher, David (1997). *In the Midst of Perpetual Fetes: The Making of American Nationalism, 1776–1820*. Chapel Hill and London: University of North Carolina Press.
Walker, Warren S. (1956). "The Prototype of Harvey Birch." *New York History* 27.3: 399–413.
Wallace, James D. (1985). "Cultivating an Audience: From *Precaution* to *The Spy*." In *James Fenimore Cooper: New Critical Essays*. Ed. Robert Clark. London: Vision Press. 38–54.
— (1986). *Early Cooper and His Audience*. New York: Columbia University Press.

Ward, A. W. and W. P. Trent [1921] (2000). "The Yankee Plays." In *The Cambridge History of English and American Literature. Vol. XV: Colonial and Revolutionary Literature; Early National Literature, Part I.* New York: Bartleby.com.

Warner, Marina [1985] (2000). *Monuments and Maidens: The Allegory of the Female Form.* Berkeley: University of California Press.

Watts, Edward (1998). *Writing and Postcolonialism in the Early Republic.* Charlottesville: University of Virginia Press.

Watts, Edward and David J. Carlson (eds.) (2012). *John Neal and Nineteenth-Century American Literature and Culture.* Lewisburg: Bucknell University Press.

Whitman, John (2003). *Interpretation and Allegory: Antiquity to the Modern Period.* Boston and Leiden: Brill.

Wiegman, Robyn (1999). "Whiteness Studies and the Paradox of Particularity." *Boundary 2* 26.3: 115–50.

Williams, Raymond (1975). *The Country and the City.* St. Albans: Paladin.

Wilmer, S. E. (2002). *Theatre, Society and the Nation: Staging American Identities.* Cambridge: Cambridge University Press.

Winterer, Caroline (2005). "From Royal to Republican: The Classical Image in Early America." *Journal of American History* 91.4: 1264–90.

Witkowski, Terence H. (1996). "Farmers Bargaining: Buying and Selling as a Subject in American Genre Painting." *Journal of Macromarketing* 16: 84–101.

Wolter, Jürgen (1979). "Die Helden der Nation: Yankee, Pionier und Indianer als nationale Stereotypen im amerikanischen Drama vor dem Bürgerkrieg." *Amerikastudien/American Studies* 24.2: 246–63.

Wonham, Henry B. (1993). *Mark Twain and the Art of the Tall Tale.* New York and Oxford: Oxford University Press.

Wood, Joseph S. (1991). "'Build, Therefore, Your Own World': The New England Village as Settlement Ideal." *Annals of the Association of American Geographers* 81.1: 32–50.

Wright, Richardson [1927] (1965). *Hawkers and Walkers in Early America: Strolling Peddlers, Preachers, Lawyers, Doctors, Players and Others, from the Beginning to the Civil War.* New York: Frederick Ungar.

Yokota, Kariann Akemi (2011). *Unbecoming British: How Revolutionary America Became a Postcolonial Nation.* New York and Oxford: Oxford University Press.

Zagarell, Sandra A. (1987). "Expanding 'America': Lydia Segourney's 'Sketch of Connecticut' and Catherine Sedgwick's 'Hope Leslie'." *Tulsa Studies in Women's Literature* 6.2: 225–45.

Zakim, Michael (2001). "Sartorial Ideologies: From Homespun to Ready-Made." *The American Historical Review* 106.5: 1553–86.

— (2003). *Ready-Made Democracy: A History of Men's Dress in the American Republic, 1760–1860.* Chicago and London: University of Chicago Press.

Ziter, Edward (2010). "Charles Matthews, Low Comedian, and the Intersections of Romantic Ideology." In *The Performing Century: Nineteenth-Century Theatre's History*. Ed. Tracy C. Davis and Peter Holland. Basingstoke: Palgrave Macmillan. 199–214.

Index

"Aesop," *The Hypocrite*, 198, 227–30, 252–3, 266n
allegory, 16, 33, 35, 45, 49, 51, 52, 55, 62, 68, 75n, 136, 182, 186, 219
  allegoresis, 26–8, 43, 111
  female, 23–33, 39, 43, 57, 66, 69, 74n, 111, 199
  history of, 23–30, 59–61
  national, 15, 23–32, 36, 38–44, 48, 57–8, 59, 61, 69–70, 73, 74n, 91, 135n, 183, 233, 270
  vs. symbol, 28–9
American humor, 7, 13–14, 70, 187n, 192n, 271
Arbuthnot, John, *Law is a Bottomless Pit*, 24–8, 29, 32, 36, 64, 74n
Astor Place Riot, 37, 84, 133n

Baldwin, Lydia, *A Yankee School-teacher in Virginia*, 218–19, 264n
Battle of Bunker Hill, 46, 88, 106–7
Baym, Nina, 203, 259–60n, 265–6n, 268n
Benjamin, Walter, 28
Bernard, John, 86
  Retrospections of America, 87, 140–7, 156, 158, 174, 184, 185–6, 187n, 191n
Bernard, William Bayle, 86–7, 122, 144
Blair, Walter, 7
Brother Jonathan's Epistle, 15, 51–5
Buell, Lawrence, 198, 201, 204, 219, 224, 258n, 260n
Bushnell, Horace, "The Age of the Homespun," 246–8, 269n

Carlyle, Thomas, 26–7
Choate, Rufus, 201, 259n

Civil War, 7, 23, 40, 45–6, 51, 60, 66, 71, 75n, 112, 114, 126, 140, 147, 180, 182, 184, 188n, 199, 203, 212, 256–7, 258n, 260–1n, 265n, 269n
Columbia, 22–3, 31, 32, 44, 66–8
con man/con game, 11, 14, 17, 152, 168, 174, 188n, 240
Connell, Raewyn W., 9
Cooper, James Fenimore, 6, 19–20n, 35, 192n, 231, 236–7, 261n
  Littlepage trilogy, 209, 212, 261n:
    Satanstoe, or the Littlepage Manuscripts, 207, 209–11, 234, 261–2n
  Notions of the Americans, 212, 262n
  The Spy, 16, 102, 140, 153–62, 174, 176–8, 188–90n
Coxe, Arthur Cleveland, *St. Jonathan: The Lay of a Scald*, 15, 45, 47–51, 75–6n
Crockett, Davy, 11–12, 20n, 80, 119, 146, 187n, 241
  Sketches and Eccentricities of Col. David Crockett of West Tennessee, 151–3, 162, 176, 178, 180, 183, 191n, 195n
Cruikshank, Edward, 86
Crystal Palace Exhibition, 41, 51–2, 55–6, 58

Democratic Review, 37, 39, 40, 75n
Dolan, J. R., *The Yankee Peddlers of Early America*, 147, 149–50, 151, 187–9n, 195n
Dunlap, William
  André, 133n
  A History of American Theater, 89
  A Trip to Niagara, 90, 121

Durivage, Oliver E., *The Stage-Struck Yankee*, 78, 91

Emerson, Ralph Waldo, 145, 172, 204, 260n

farce, 14, 49, 87, 91–2, 106, 131, 132n, 134n, 270
Fessenden, Thomas Green, *The Country Lovers/Jonathan's Courtship*, 16, 94–7
Fidfaddy, Frederik Augustus, *The Adventures of Uncle Sam, in Search after his Lost Honor*, 45, 75n

Gay, Elizabeth Jane, 75n
  The New Yankee Doodle, 45–7
Giles, Paul, 23, 33, 47
Goethe, Johann Wolfgang von, 28–9
Green Mountain Boys, 129
Greene, Aella, *Rhymes of Yankee Land*, 204–5, 256, 260–1n
Greene, Asa, *A Yankee Among the Nullifiers*, 16, 198, 214–17, 222, 248, 254, 259n, 262–3n
guying, 94

Hale, Sarah, 6
  Northwood, 10, 16, 198, 213–14, 217, 219–27, 229, 235, 242–8, 258, 262n, 263n, 264–6n, 268–9n
Haliburton, Thomas Chandler, 7, 256
  Sam Slick, the Clockmaker, 16, 20n, 59, 140, 162–70, 173, 174–5, 184–5, 190–3n
  "Yankee Homespun," 254–5
Harper's Weekly magazine, 23, 60–3, 65, 67, 68, 69, 268–9n
Hartford Convention, 200, 227, 242, 259n, 263n
Hawthorne, Nathanael, 19n, 231, 260n
Herne, James A., *Shore Acres*, 16, 94, 108, 112–18, 131, 135n
hillbilly, 18n, 20n
Hobsbawm, Eric, 17, 18n, 197, 199, 246
homespun, 15, 16–17, 41, 86, 108, 198–9, 204, 242, 245–52, 254–6, 258, 269n, 271

Irving, Washington, 6, 15, 31, 33, 212, 234, 236, 261n
  "The History of New York," 208–9, 212, 266n
  "John Bull," 33–5, 36–7
  "The Legend of Sleepy Hollow," 207–9, 261n
  "Rip van Winkle," 261n

Jefferson, Thomas, 3, 90, 140, 200
John Bull, 15, 46, 50, 51, 52, 62–4, 69, 74n, 132, 182
  development of, 24–8, 31, 32–4, 36, 54–5, 59, 70, 73
  in Irving, 31, 33–5, 36
  as national character, 2, 24–8, 29–31, 34, 53–5, 58, 73, 121, 163
  origin of, 24–6, 28, 29, 31
  in Paulding, 31, 33, 35–9, 41
  physical features of, 31, 34, 54–5, 58, 62
Jones, J. S.
  The Green Mountain Boy, 78, 87, 129, 133n
  Solon Shingles, or The People's Lawyer, 80, 96

Knickerbocker School, 15, 33, 35, 69, 120

LaBree, Ernest, *Ebenezer Venture*, 91–3, 96, 107–8
Lady Liberty, 22, 27, 31, 32, 66–7
Lincoln, Abraham, 45–7, 59, 60, 66, 75n, 126, 182, 243
Lindsley, Abraham B., *Love and Friendship, or Yankee Notions*, 87, 94, 105–7
Lowell, James Russell, *The Biglow Papers*, 108, 256

mammoth newspapers, 71
Marx, Leo, *The Machine in the Garden*, 98, 99, 114
Mathews, Charles, 85–6
Matthews, Brander, "The American on the Stage," 80, 81, 131n
mock epic, 15, 25, 44, 45, 47–8

Moncrieff, William Thomas, *Tarnation Strange, or More Jonathans!*, 91, 118–20

Nast, Thomas, 23, 59–68, 76n
Neal, John, 6, 231–3, 266–7n
  Brother Jonathan, or The New-Englanders, 16, 198, 230, 232–5, 242, 248–52
  "Character of the Real Yankees," 232
  The Down-Easters, 16, 198, 230, 232, 235–42, 250–1, 267–8n
  "Sketches of American Character," 232
  "Story-Telling," 13
  "Yankee Notions," 232
Nelson, Dana N., 8–9, 18n, 153
New England, 3, 7, 16, 17n, 47, 82, 116, 140–2, 146–7, 157, 171–2, 179, 186, 195n, 197–215, 218, 219–32, 234, 241, 242–6, 252, 256–8, 258–62n, 264–9n
  historiography, 138–51, 179, 188n, 195n, 197–203, 246, 258–61n, 269n
  homestead, 16, 99, 105, 108, 111–15, 117–18, 124–5, 134–5n, 171–2, 198, 204–6, 208, 219, 222–4, 230, 242–4, 248, 256–8, 268n
  schoolmarm, 218–19
  schoolmaster, 2, 16, 198, 204–19, 222–3, 229–30, 233–4, 242, 256–8, 263n
  white village, 201, 204, 259n
Nullification Crisis, 42, 214–15, 217–18, 248, 254, 262–3n

Paul, Heike, 139, 258n
Paulding, James Kirk, 15, 20n, 31, 33, 35, 75n, 120–1, 187n
  "Brother Jonathan," 37, 38–40, 44, 47
  The Bulls and the Jonathans, 35
  The Diverting History of John Bull and Brother Jonathan, 35, 36–7
  John Bull in America, or The New Munchhausen, 35
  "Saint Jonathan," 37, 40–4, 47
  A Sketch of Old England, by a New England Man, 35
  "Uncle Sam and his B'Hoys," 37–8, 40, 44

Pilgrims, 17n, 44, 146, 190n, 195n, 198, 200–1
Poe, Edgar Allen, 19n, 35, 231
Pope, Alexander, 25, 47, 228
Puck magazine, 58, 59
puffery, 10, 211, 223
Punch magazine, 26, 51–2, 58, 59
Puritans, 9, 54, 88, 106, 141, 198, 200–3, 208, 210–11, 216, 221, 228–9, 234, 256, 259–60n

Revolutionary War, 1, 31, 38, 68, 85, 88, 96, 102, 112, 120, 121, 127–31, 153–61, 177, 189n, 202, 228, 233–5, 246, 249–50, 266n
Reynolds, David S., 231, 267n
Robinson, John Hovey, *The Life and Adventures of William Harvard Stinchfield*, 140, 170–5, 178, 184, 193–4n, 268n
Romanticism, 29
  American, 19n, 259n
  German, 28
Rourke, Constance M., 187n
  American Humor: A Study of the National Character, 7, 12, 144–7, 187n

settler colonial, 32, 38, 54, 139, 148, 200, 202, 207, 250, 261n, 270, 271
Smith-Rosenberg, Carroll, 8–9, 22–3
The Spectator, 29
star system (theater), 78, 81
Steele, Silas, *The Brazen Drum*, 16, 126–31

tall tale/tall talk 10, 11–14, 17, 19–21n, 81–2, 89, 93, 125, 127, 128, 152, 240, 255, 267n
Taylor, Tom, *Our American Cousin*, 16, 121–6, 131
Thompson, Denman, *The Old Homestead*, 94, 96, 108–12, 116, 134n
Thoreau, Henry David, 260n
Twain, Mark
  A Connecticut Yankee in King Arthur's Court, 17, 270–1
  "How to Tell a Story," 13–14, 20n
Tyler, Royall, *The Contrast*, 2, 16, 78, 80, 85, 87–9, 105, 132n

Ulrich, Laurel Thatcher, 246, 248, 264n, 269n

Waldstreicher, David L., 12
Washington, George, 8, 30, 64–6, 123, 128, 135n, 140, 153, 155–61, 177, 188–90n, 222, 246, 260n
Webster, Daniel, 75n, 199–201, 230, 259n
Webster/Hayne debate, 199, 259n, 262–3n
Whig Party/politics, 24, 31, 166, 192n, 200–3, 204, 217, 230, 260n
whiteness, 5, 7, 8–9, 18n, 31, 83, 101–2
   Anglo-Saxon, 7, 31
   Vermont, 129
Whittier, John Greenleaf, "Snow-Bound," 16, 256–8
Williams, Raymond, 90
wooden nutmegs, 16, 53, 81, 140, 166, 175, 178, 180, 184–6, 196n, 217
Woodworth, Samuel, *Forest Rose, or American Farmers*, 16, 94, 97–105, 109, 110, 114, 131, 134n, 183, 276
Wordsworth, William, "The Pedlar," 186–7n
Wright, Richardson, *Hawkers and Walkers in Early America*, 147–50, 151, 184, 187–8n, 195n, 202

Yankee actors, 78, 81–2, 89, 94
   Hackett, James Henry, 2, 78, 80, 82, 121
   Hill, George Handel, 78, 80, 82, 86–7, 97, 121, 133n
   Jefferson, Joseph, 80, 85, 93–4, 102, 112, 122
   Locke, G. E. "Yankee," 78–80, 121
   Marble, Danforth, 78, 92, 121, 144
   Silsbee, Joshua, 78, 87, 97, 104, 121, 144, 276
   Wignell, Thomas, 85, 88

Yankee behaviors and expressions
   calculation/cyphering, 43, 146, 168, 217, 249, 250, 259n, 263n
   "going ahead," 5, 12, 82, 138, 164, 167–9, 174–5, 183, 198, 199, 203, 218, 223, 270
   soft sawder and human nature, 167–8, 174, 175, 177–8, 186
   whittling, 41, 66, 71–3, 180, 230, 238–9, 241–2, 270
   Yankeeisms (speech), 106, 132n, 229, 240
   yarnspinning, 2, 5–6, 10–15, 17, 146, 170, 179, 199, 214, 230, 238–9, 241–2, 246, 251–2, 254, 256–7, 270–2
Yankee Doodle (song and character), 1, 2, 18n, 20n, 44–6, 51–2, 55, 58, 96, 106, 128–9, 209, 221, 251, 271
Yankee figures
   clockmaker, 162, 165, 167
   vs. European others, 6, 7, 120, 128–30, 136–7, 141–2, 146, 185–6, 205, 212, 219–23, 229, 262n, 264–5n
   Hank Morgan, 17, 270–1
   schoolmarm, 218–19
   schoolmaster, 2, 16, 198, 204–19, 222–3, 229–30, 233–4, 242, 256–8, 263n
   vs. the Southener, 3–4, 46, 82, 106–7, 142–3, 145, 147–8, 150–1, 166–7, 180–2, 184–5, 203, 210, 212–23, 225–6, 232–3, 235–6, 240–1, 248, 254, 260n, 263–5n, 269n
   Yankee girl, 3, 80, 82, 95, 132n
   vs. the Yorkshireman, 85, 121, 146, 187n
Yankee notions, 52–3, 71, 106–7, 136, 140, 175, 180, 183, 195n, 204, 218, 254, 274
Yankee Notions magazine, 71–3, 180–2
Yankee peddler genre paintings, 175–6, 194n

EU representative:
Easy Access System Europe
Mustamäe tee 50, 10621 Tallinn, Estonia
Gpsr.requests@easproject.com